Scott Foresman

First Dictionary

Hi! Let's learn some new words!

Scott Foresman

Editorial Offices: Glenview, Illinois • Parsippany, New Jersey • New York, New York
Sales Offices: Parsippany, New Jersey • Duluth, Georgia • Glenview, Illinois
Carrollton, Texas • Ontario, California

ISBN 0-673-64500-2

This picture dictionary includes a few entries that are registered trademarks in the United States at the time of this book's copyright. No judgment should be made or understood, however, as to the actual legal status of any word in the dictionary.

8 9 10 - V052 - 09 08 07 06 05 04 03

Table of Contents

It's easy to use this book!

Welcome!

The Scott Foresman *First Dictionary* is a colorful, readable book of words, meanings, and sentences, illustrated with helpful and engaging pictures. This book is intended for children who need more than a simple "picture dictionary" but are not yet ready for a large school dictionary. The Scott Foresman *First Dictionary* helps children make a successful transition to a larger dictionary by familiarizing them in a friendly way with the skills necessary for good dictionary use.

This *First Dictionary* is written for children who know the alphabet and can alphabetize letters and words. The entries in this book are listed in alphabetical order. Each entry word is in large, bright type. Following the entry word is a simple guide to pronouncing it. Entries have easy-to-read, full-sentence definitions, example sentences that show the word in context, or both. Function words are given example sentences that show how they are used. Most single-definition entries and nearly all multi-definition entries also have example sentences. Finally, we show the part of speech and additional inflected forms, such as noun plurals (where they exist), verb forms, and adjective forms. Each irregular inflected form is given as a separate entry. Guide words appear at the top of every page in the dictionary and correspond to the first and last entry words on the page.

All illustrations are next to the words they picture. The more than 800 illustrations were carefully selected to be both appealing and informative. Every illustration has a caption to further connect it to the entry word. We show a variety of original art and photographs to help the child visualize the word being defined. When necessary, speech balloons or additional caption words are included to help explain the connection between the picture and the entry word.

The opening illustrations for each letter of the alphabet feature the Dictionary Pals, who illustrate words beginning with that letter. The Pals appear as friendly faces throughout the book.

The nearly 4000 entries in the *First Dictionary* were selected from words that young readers and writers encounter in their reading and at home. In addition, all Dolch words are included, along with other frequently used words in English.

At the back of the book is a student reference section of useful information, including maps, spelling and punctuation tips, the food pyramid, bones of the body, and weights and measures.

Scott Foresman has been making the best children's dictionaries for more than sixty years. This book prepares children to go on to use our larger dictionaries and thesauruses, including the Thorndike Barnhart *School Dictionary* and the *Beginning Writer's Thesaurus.* Our books teach children the dictionary skills that they will need and use all their lives.

A...B...C...

How to Read an Entry

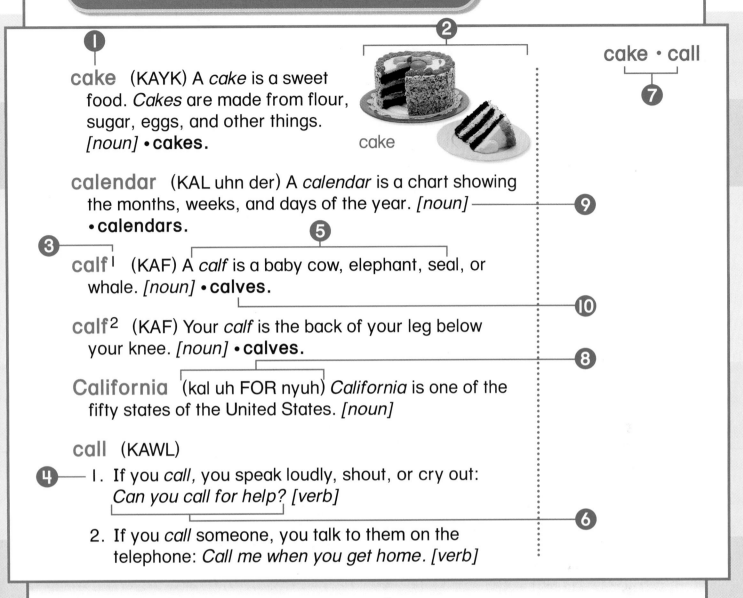

①

cake (KAYK) A *cake* is a sweet food. *Cakes* are made from flour, sugar, eggs, and other things. *[noun]* •**cakes.**

cake

②

⑦

calendar (KAL uhn der) A *calendar* is a chart showing the months, weeks, and days of the year. *[noun]* •**calendars.**

⑨

③

⑤

calf¹ (KAF) A *calf* is a baby cow, elephant, seal, or whale. *[noun]* •**calves.**

⑩

calf² (KAF) Your *calf* is the back of your leg below your knee. *[noun]* •**calves.**

⑧

California (kal uh FOR nyuh) *California* is one of the fifty states of the United States. *[noun]*

call (KAWL)

④ 1. If you *call,* you speak loudly, shout, or cry out: *Can you call for help? [verb]*

⑥

2. If you *call* someone, you talk to them on the telephone: *Call me when you get home. [verb]*

---

① The entry word is printed in bright red so that it is easy to find. It shows you how the word is spelled.

② A picture helps show the meaning of the word. Each picture has a caption that is the same as the entry word or a form of the entry word. Sometimes the caption is a sentence.

③ The small raised number tells you that two different entry words with the same spelling have different meanings.

④ A number is printed before each meaning for a word when more than one meaning is given.

⑤ A definition tells you the meaning of the word.

⑥ A sentence shows you how the word is used.

⑦ The guide words tell you what words you will find on this page.

⑧ The pronunciation tells you how to say the word.

⑨ The part of speech tells you how words can be used.

⑩ Extra forms come at the end of the entry. These include noun plurals, forms of the verb, and forms of adjectives. They are printed in heavy black type.

A5

ABCDEFG
HIJKLMN
OPQRSTU
VWXYZ

What Is a Dictionary?

A dictionary is a book that lists words in alphabetical order. It gives the meanings of words, and it is filled with all kinds of other information about words, including these things:

- How a word is spelled
- How a word is pronounced
- How a word is used in a sentence
- The forms of a word
- The part of speech of a word

These are just some of the important kinds of information you will find in a dictionary. You will learn in the following pages that a dictionary is a very useful tool.

A dictionary tells you how to spell a word!

It also shows you how to use that word in a sentence!

When Should You Use Your Dictionary?

You should use your dictionary whenever you have a question about a word. If you want to know what a word means, how to say it, or what part of speech it is, look it up in your dictionary.

This dictionary is very easy to use, so that you can learn how to use a dictionary well. Being able to use a dictionary is a skill that you will need all your life. As you become a better reader, you can use bigger and bigger dictionaries that have more words and more information about every word.

Pete uses the dictionary when he needs spelling help.

Mikayla uses the dictionary to look up a word's meaning.

Keiko uses the dictionary to learn how to say a word.

Practice

Make a list of all the reasons why you might want to use a dictionary. Can you write a short story about a person who needs to use a dictionary? Use a reason from the list in your story.

Entry Words

The **entry word** is printed in bright red type to make it easy to find. It shows you how the word is spelled.

Some entry words begin with a small letter.

> **cart** (KART) A *cart* is a kind of wagon used for carrying things from place to place. A grocery *cart* is a metal basket on four wheels. Other *carts* are wooden and can be pulled by animals. *[noun]* •**carts**.

Look for the red type. These are entry words!

Some entry words begin with a capital letter.

> **Chiapas** (chee AH pahss) *Chiapas* is a state in the east part of Mexico. *[noun]*

Some entry words are made up of more than one word.

> **compact disc** (KOM pakt DISK) A *compact disc* is a small, thin plastic disk that contains music, computer programs, and other kinds of information. The abbreviation for *compact disc* is *CD*. •**compact disks**.

Practice

Look at the following words.

ice cream	**Guerrero**
Alabama	**car seat**
square	**Canada**

1. Write the entry word that begins with a small letter *s*.

2. Write the entry word that is made up of two words and begins with the letter *c*.

3. Write the entry word that begins with a capital letter *A*.

4. Write the entry word that is made up of two words and begins with an *i*.

5. Write the entry word that begins with a capital *G*.

Alphabetical Order

How do you find a word in a dictionary? Most dictionaries put the words in alphabetical order to make them easy to find.

Alphabetical order is the order of the letters in the alphabet. These letters are in alphabetical order:

a b c d e f g h i j k l m n o p q r s t u v w x y z

In a dictionary, the words that begin with the letter *a* will come first. These words will be followed by words that begin with the letter *b,* and so on all the way through the alphabet. The last words in the dictionary will begin with the letter *z.*

These things are in alphabetical order!

berries

fan

panda

Practice

Look at the following groups of words.
Put each group of words in alphabetical order.

1. frog, toad, alligator

2. eyes, teeth, nose

3. farmer, artist, judge

4. Delaware, Alabama, Washington

5. brother, sister, mother

celery

More About Alphabetizing

Suppose you are looking up the word *celery.* You would find it in the group of words beginning with the letter *c,* but would it come before or after the word *camera?*

Sometimes you need to look at the second letter of a word. The word *celery* would come after the word *camera.* That is because the second letter of *celery* is *e,* and the second letter of *camera* is *a.* The letter *e* comes after the letter *a* in the alphabet.

Would the word *celery* come before or after the word *cracker?* You would find the word *celery* before the word *cracker* in a dictionary because the letter *e* comes before the letter *r* in the alphabet.

camera ⋯⋯⋯

Practice

Put the words in each group in alphabetical order. You will need to look at the second letter of each word.

1. crab, clam, chipmunk

2. leopard, lizard, lamb

3. dentist, doctor, driver

4. tomato, tea, taco

5. apple, asparagus, acorn

Using the Yellow Bars

This dictionary has yellow bars to help you find words. Close the book and look at the side with the three yellow bars.

The top bar shows the beginning part of the dictionary. Look here for words beginning with A, B, C, D, E, F, G, H, and I.

The middle bar shows the middle part of the dictionary. Look here for words beginning with J, K, L, M, N, O, P, Q, and R.

The bottom bar shows the last part of the dictionary. Look here for words beginning with S, T, U, V, W, X, Y, and Z.

Where would you find the word *maracas?* Would it be in the beginning, middle, or end pages? Should you use the top bar, the middle bar, or the bottom bar?

maracas

mirror

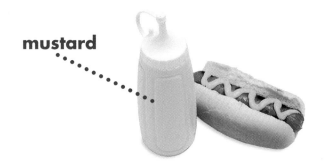

mustard

Practice

Number your paper 1–10. Write the following words. Then write *top bar, middle bar,* or *bottom bar* after the word to show where it can be found in this dictionary.

1. raccoon
2. antelope
3. zebra
4. tiger
5. buffalo
6. giraffe
7. iguana
8. sheep
9. panda
10. otter

Guide Words

Guide words help you find your way around a dictionary. They are at the top of every page, and they show you what words will be on the page.

Guide words look like this:

ache · act

The first guide word, *ache,* is the same as the first entry word on the page. The second guide word, *act,* is the same as the last entry word on the page.

Suppose you want to find the meaning of the word *acorn.* In alphabetical order, *acorn* comes between *ache* and *act.* You would find the meaning of *acorn* on the page with these guide words.

ache

act

Practice

Number your paper 1–10. Find the page in your dictionary for each entry word in this list. Write the guide words you found on that page.

1. copy	6. rice
2. bed	7. Idaho
3. family	8. poem
4. awake	9. customer
5. mitten	10. ear

Word-Finding Strategies

Suppose you come across a word you do not know. How do you find the meaning or pronunciation of that word in a dictionary? Here are some steps to follow.

1. Begin by using the yellow bars to find the part of the dictionary that has words beginning with the letter of the word you want to look up.

2. Remember to use the guide words to find the page that has the word you need to know.

3. In a dictionary, a whole group of words will begin with the same letter, so you will need to look past the first letter of the word. First try using the second letter. If this does not work, you will need to look at the third letter or keep going until you find letters that are different. For example, in the words *accept* and *accident,* you need to look at the letter that comes after *acc-*.

4. Once you have found the page, you don't need to read all of the words. You can look quickly at the list of words in bright red type to find the one you want. Always read all the definitions, not just the first one, to make sure you understand the word.

Steps 1-2

a (uh *or* ay) *There's a book for you on the is a pen. Your birthday comes once a year*

abbreviation (uh bree vee AY shuhn) An *abbreviation* is a short form of a word. *St.* is the *abbreviation* for *Street. AL* is an *abbreviation* for *Alabama.* [noun] •**abbrev**

able (AY buhl) If you are *able* to do somet can do it: *She is able to tie her shoes.* [adj •**abler, ablest.**

Steps 3-4

Finding words is easy!

Practice

Divide your paper into 3 columns. In the first column, write each of the following words. In the second column, write whether you used the top, middle, or bottom yellow bar. In the third column, write the guide words on the page.

1. egg

2. spaghetti

3. macaroni

4. jam

5. raspberry

More Word-Finding Strategies

What should I do?

Suppose you are looking at the page where you expect to find a word, but the word isn't there. What can you do next?

- Remember that some words in the dictionary are forms of entry words. They are listed at the end of an entry. Check to see if your word is listed under a different entry word. For example, you might look for *trees* under *tree,* since *trees* is the plural of *tree.*

- Some words are not spelled the way you expect. If you hear a word pronounced NEEL, you might look for it with the *n* words, but you would not find it there. Remember that the sound of the letter *n* can be spelled with a *kn.* The word pronounced NEEL is spelled *kneel.* Use the *Spellings of English Sounds* chart on pages A24-A25.

- Not every word in our language is included in all dictionaries. You may need to look in a larger dictionary for some words not in this dictionary.

- Sometimes you will want to look in a special dictionary. Some special dictionaries list words in other languages. Other special dictionaries list the names of places in the world or names of important people in history.

Practice

Find each of the following words in your dictionary. Write the number of the page where you found the word. If you decide you will have to go to another dictionary, write *other dictionary.*

1. audiences
2. asking
3. phone
4. who
5. knot

6. Chicago
7. Edison
8. bueno
9. stuck
10. brightest

Definitions

Suppose a friend says to you, "My aunt works in a skyscraper." Do you know what *skyscraper* means? Does your friend's aunt work on a spaceship or in a tall building? If you do not know the meaning of *skyscraper,* you can look up the definition in a dictionary. A definition tells what a word means.

skyscraper

Here is the definition of *skyscraper* from this dictionary:

skyscraper (SKY skray per) A *skyscraper* is a very tall building. *[noun]* •**skyscrapers.**

In the entry for *skyscraper,* the meaning comes after the pronunciation. The definition tells that a *skyscraper* is a building. The words *very tall* help you understand that a *skyscraper* is not just any building. It is a building that is much taller than average.

Look up the words below. On your paper, write each definition with a word from the list in place of the blank.

harbor

firehouse

school

restaurant

backyard

1. A _____ is a place to buy and eat a meal.

2. A _____ is an area of water where ships are safe.

3. A _____ is a place where you learn things.

4. A _____ is a building where fire engines are kept.

5. A _____ is a yard behind a house or building.

Example Sentences

Sentences help you understand what a word means. They show how a word is used. You will find example sentences in many of the entries in this dictionary.

I am able to tie my shoes!

> **able** (AY buhl) If you are *able* to do something, you can do it: *She is able to tie her shoes.* [*adjective*] •**abler, ablest.**

Notice the slanted type for the sentence, "She is able to tie her shoes." It shows that this sentence is an example sentence.

Some words are difficult to explain. In this dictionary, the meanings of some words are shown only with example sentences.

> **along** (uh LAWNG) *Trees are planted along the street. We took our dog along.* [*preposition* or *adverb*]

Practice

Look up each word in this list. Copy one or more of the example sentences. Underline the word that is being explained.

1. hall
2. rain
3. age
4. am
5. dangerous

6. grab
7. carry
8. easily
9. lain
10. beside

Using Definitions

That is the definition!

Often you can guess what a word you hear or read means. You probably learn the meanings of many words in this way, but sometimes you do not want to guess.

Suppose your cousin writes a letter saying that he has gotten a saxophone for his birthday. To answer his letter you need to know what a *saxophone* is. Is it a kind of telephone, an unusual pet, or a musical instrument? If you are wondering, read the entry below. Notice that the meaning comes right after the pronunciation.

> **saxophone** (SAK suh fohn) A *saxophone* is a musical instrument that is played by blowing into it. *[noun]* •**saxophones.**

Practice

Look up the words listed at the left. Match each one with its meaning.

alert	1. a soft shirt
fare	2. a bundle
jersey	3. awake and watching
package	4. a label
sticker	5. money paid to ride in a bus, taxi, plane, or subway

conductor

Definition Numbers

Do you know what a *conductor* does? You may think that a conductor collects tickets on trains, but your friend says a conductor leads a group of musicians. Both of you are right. The numbers **1** and **2** before the meanings in the entry below show that there are two meanings of the word.

> **conductor** (kuhn DUHK ter)
>
> 1. A *conductor* is a person who helps the people who ride trains: *The conductor collects tickets and fares.* [noun]
> 2. A *conductor* is also someone who leads a group of musicians: *The conductor started the concert.* [noun]
> • **conductors.**

Some words have more than two meanings. In this dictionary, each meaning is numbered. When you use a dictionary, it is a good idea to read all of the meanings. The second or third meaning may better match the way the word is being used than the first one does.

Practice

Read each sentence and look up the word in bold. Then number your paper from 1–5. Write the number of the definition that makes the best sense for the way the word is used in the sentence.

1. When you finish, put the crayons **back** in your desk.

2. My brother sits too close to the television **screen.**

3. Use a **nail** to hang your picture.

4. It is important to be **patient** when you are training a pet.

5. The screen on the computer froze, and the **mouse** would not work.

Different Words with the Same Spelling

bank

What does the word *bank* mean? Your parents may keep their money in a *bank*, but your sister may enjoy sitting on a *bank*.

A *bank* where you keep money is very different from the *bank* of a river or stream. That is because there are two different words that are spelled **bank.** Each one has a separate entry. The words are followed by small numbers: *bank¹* and *bank².* When you see these kinds of numbers, you know that there is at least one other word with the same spelling. Such words are called *homographs.*

Remember to look for another entry word if the first one you find is not the word you need.

Practice

Number your paper 1–5. In your dictionary, look up each word in bold. Write the number (1, 2, or 3) of the entry word that makes sense in the sentence.

1. There is a **bat** living in that cave.

2. The bird was carrying a worm in its **bill.**

3. She lost the **bow** for playing her violin.

4. The cow and her **calf** are in the meadow.

5. It was so dark we turned on a **light.**

Symbols That Stand for Sounds

In this dictionary, letters that show how to pronounce the words come in parentheses right after the entry word. These letters are symbols that stand for sounds.

My painting is beautiful!

desk (DESK) A *desk* is a piece of furniture with a flat or slanting top. People write, read, and use computers at *desks*. [noun] •**desks.**

The letters D, E, S, and K all stand for sounds these letters usually spell. In some words the letters in the pronunciation do not match the spelling of the word. To use the pronunciations, say the letters with their usual sounds. Use the *Spellings of English Sounds* chart on pages A24–A25.

beautiful (BYOO ti fuhl) If something is *beautiful*, it is very pretty to see or hear: *After the rain stopped, it became a beautiful, sunny day.* [adjective]

Practice

Match each word below with its pronunciation.

1. bear	6. dinner	a. (FOHN)	f. (di LISH uhss)
2. cereal	7. pilot	b. (KWEEN)	g. (PY luht)
3. many	8. above	c. (SEER ee uhl)	h. (MEN ee)
4. queen	9. phone	d. (uh BUHV)	i. (DIN er)
5. careful	10. delicious	e. (KAIR fuhl)	j. (BAIR)

Syllables and Stress

Some words have just one syllable:

act (AKT)   bus (BUHSS)   quite (KWYT)

bus

Other words have two or more syllables. In this dictionary, there is a space between syllables in the pronunciation of the word:

balloon (buh LOON)   activity (ak TIV uh tee)

balloons

Notice that the word *balloon* in the list above has a space between *buh* and *LOON*. This means that the word has two syllables. The word *activity* has four syllables.

In this dictionary, the syllables are written in small letters or in capital letters. The syllable written in all capital letters is the one you say in the stronger tone of voice. In the word *balloon,* the second syllable is said with more force. It gets the stress.

Practice

Number your paper 1–5 and fold it to make three columns. Write the words below in the first column. In the second column, write the number of syllables in each word. In the third column, write the letters that show how to pronounce the syllable that gets the stress.

1. airport   4. queen

2. beginning   5. caterpillar

3. October

Different Pronunciations

orange

How do you pronounce the word *orange?* Do you say (AR inj) or (OR inj)? Whichever way you say the word, you are correct. The dictionary shows that *orange* can be pronounced both ways.

---

orange (AR inj *or* OR inj)

1. An *orange* is a round fruit that grows on trees. *Oranges* are full of juice. [noun]
2. O*range* is the color of an orange or a pumpkin. [adjective or noun]
•**oranges.**

Here are some other words that are pronounced in two ways. Try saying each word both ways. Which one is the way you usually say the word?

acorn (AY kern *or* AY korn)   **our** (AR *or* OWR)

Sometimes a word has different pronunciations for different meanings. What are the two ways to say *estimate?*

---

estimate (ESS tuh mit *or* ESS tuh mayt *for definition 2*)

1. An *estimate* is a guess about how much or how many. An *estimate* is made from what you already know: *The painter gave an estimate of how much it would cost to paint the house.* [noun]
2. To *estimate* is to guess about how much or how many, using what you already know: *He asked her to estimate the answer to the addition problem.* [verb]
•**estimates.** •**estimates, estimated, estimating.**

Practice

Number your paper 1–5. These words have two correct pronunciations. Write the one you use.

1. family (FAM lee *or* FAM uh lee)

2. hello (huh LOH *or* he LOH)
3. inside (in SYD *or* IN syd)
4. aunt (ANT *or* AHNT)
5. quarrel (KWOR uhl *or* KWAH ruhl)

Your dictionary can help you spell almost any word, but sometimes it may be hard to decide where to look. Here are some hints:

fireman

- Say the word slowly and carefully. Listen for the sounds. What are the sounds in the first syllable?

- If you can't find the word by looking up the letters that usually spell the first few sounds, think about other ways the sounds could be spelled. For example, the *f* sound you hear in the word *fireman* is the same sound that is spelled with the letters *ph* in *phone*.

- Look at the chart on the next two pages. It shows different ways to spell sounds in the English language. Suppose you want to spell the word for the number 8. Say the word to yourself: AYT. Under the sound *ay* in the chart, you see examples of words with that sound spelled all sorts of ways. The spellings are shown by letters in orange type. One of the ways that *ay* can be spelled is *eigh,* as in the word *eight.*

Practice

Number your paper 1–10. Write the word that matches each pronunciation. Remember to use the chart and your dictionary to check the spelling.

1. RAWNG
2. BREE<u>TH</u>
3. SPESH uhl
4. GOHST
5. KOHT
6. BANGZ
7. EYESS berg
8. KWIT
9. SOH
10. FOH tuh graf

Spellings of English Sounds

This chart shows all the sounds of the English language, and it lists the ways in which each sound may be spelled. It can help you find words you can say but do not know how to spell.

The pronunciation symbols used in this dictionary are shown in blue. Each symbol represents a different sound.

Following each symbol are words showing different ways the sound may be spelled. The letters used to spell the sound are printed in orange type. Common spellings are listed first.

Sound	Spelling and Examples
a	at, cat, half, laugh
ah	father, calm, iguana
air	chair, berry, there, care, library, their, pear
ar	arm, park, heart, guard
aw	awful, all, walk, sauce, thought, cough, broad, moth
ay	say, rain, age, made, eight, reindeer, straight, they, break, ballet

b	bad, rabbit
ch	child, future, watch, question, cello
d	did, add, curved
e	ten, end, bread, again, any, adventure, friend, leopard
ee	bee, meet, each, seat, equal, happy, ski, key, believe, people, Hawaii
eer	fear, beard
er	herd, earth, first, turn, work, worry, courage, purr
eye	ice, iron, island, aisle, eye
f	fat, buffalo, laugh, phone
g	go, egg, ghost, guest
h	he, Guanajuato, who, Oaxaca
i	pin, bandage, enough, been, build, busy, handkerchief, symbol
j	jam, gentle, large, bridge, digit, soldier, adjective
k	kind, coat, back, character, ache, quit, broccoli, excited, antique, liquid
l	land, sale, pedal, tell, swallow

m	me, calm, climb, plumbing, common, autumn
n	no, manners, knife, gnat
ng	long, ink, banquet, tongue, handkerchief
o	dot, odd, honest
oh	oh, oak, old, bone, toe, folks, doughnut, own, owe, sew, Quintana Roo
oi	oil, boy
oo	food, move, shoe, soup, through, rule, blue, fruit, threw, jewel, who, two
or	order, floor, course, quart, war, dinosaur, board, toward
ow	out, owl, hour, Tamaulipas
p	pay, happy
r	run, carry, rhythm, wrong
s	say, sword, cent, pretzel
sh	she, sugar, special, machine, ocean, nation, tissue
ss	perhaps, disappear, actress, ambulance, else, muscle, listen

t	tell, button, stop, two, doubt, pterodactyl
th	thin
th	then, breathe
u	full, wolf, good, should Missouri
uh	under, about, certain, alien, asteroid, April, other, flood, does, trouble
v	very, have, of
w	will, wheat, quick, Chihuahua
y consonant	your, onion, figure
y vowel	mile, my, light, fried
yoo	you, beauty, few, use, curious, argue, vacuum cleaner
z	zero, buzz, has, amuse, scissors, xylophone, clothes, raspberry
zh	television, pleasure

judge

astronaut

Some doctors use medical dictionaries!

What if you look up a word and can't find it? Words that first and second graders need the most are listed in this dictionary, but not every word in our language is listed.

There are other dictionaries that are written for older students. Those dictionaries have more words. There are also many kinds of special dictionaries.

- A large reference dictionary is not shortened at all. You may have seen one in a public library. These dictionaries are often really big! They are great for looking up unusual words, but they are so large that it can take a long time to find the word you need.

- Biographical dictionaries are special dictionaries that have information about people. Geographical dictionaries are useful when you want to know about places. Some maps may show place names that are not in our dictionary. You can look up these place names in a geographical dictionary. Biographical and geographical dictionaries are helpful when you are writing a report.

- There are also special dictionaries for people who have certain jobs, such as doctors and chemists.

- Bilingual dictionaries are dictionaries in two or more languages. They help people use or learn another language.

Sometimes a dictionary is not the book you need. For some information, such as annual rainfall in a place or batting averages, you can use an almanac. If you need a lot of information about one subject, such as fish or stars, you should use an encyclopedia. Sometimes, you can find the information you need on the Internet.

The important thing to remember is that there are many different kinds of dictionaries and reference books. Ask your teacher or librarian to help you find the right one.

Parts of Speech

Remember that some words name persons, places, and things. These words are called *nouns*. When the word *backpack* names a bag that is worn on the back, it is a noun.

Besides the meaning and the pronunciation of a word, you will also find a part of speech label in this dictionary. It tells you the way the word can be used. Look for the word *noun* in the entry below.

Nouns

book

> **backpack** (BAK pak) A *backpack* is a bag worn on the back by people walking or going to school. In *backpacks* you carry things such as clothes, books, and food: *Can you fit your books in your backpack?* [noun] •**backpacks.**

Some words can be used in more than one way. The word *buzz* is a noun when it names a sound. It is a verb when it means making a humming sound. Look for the part of speech labels in the entry below.

paint

> **buzz** (BUHZ)
> 1. A *buzz* is the humming sound made by flies, mosquitoes, or bees: *The loud buzz of a fly woke me up.* [noun]
> 2. To *buzz* means to make a steady humming sound: *Mosquitoes buzz outside the screen.* [verb]
> •**buzzes.** •**buzzes, buzzed, buzzing.**

Practice

Number your paper 1–10. Write the entry words in this list and then write *noun* or *verb* to show the part of speech given in this dictionary. If a word can be both a noun and a verb, write both words.

1. bake
2. cactus
3. dance
4. example
5. find
6. gasoline
7. insult
8. kiss
9. pineapple
10. submarine

More Parts of Speech

Nouns and verbs are just two of the part of speech labels you will find in the entries in this dictionary. *Adjectives* are another part of speech. Remember that an *adjective* is a word that describes a noun. Find the label for *adjective* in the entry below.

> **ripe** (RYP) When something is *ripe*, it is grown and ready to be picked and eaten: *We bought ripe apples at the store.* [adjective] • **riper, ripest.**

An *adverb* is a word that tells how, when, or where something happens. Find the label *adverb* in the entry below.

> **quickly** (KWIK lee) *Quickly* means in a short time: *When I asked him a question, he answered quickly.* [adverb]

A *pronoun* is a word that takes the place of a noun.

> **he** (HEE) *He is my friend. My dog is so old he can't see.* [pronoun]

In this dictionary, you will also find parts of speech labels for *conjunctions* and *prepositions*.

A word that is formed when two words are put together is called a *contraction*. Words such as *hadn't* and *I'll* are contractions.

ripe

He is my friend!

Practice

Number your paper 1–10. Write the entry words in this list and the part of speech or contraction label given in this dictionary.

1. hairbrush
2. she
3. Nebraska
4. if
5. just
6. oh
7. lazy
8. make-believe
9. don't
10. know

Forms of the Word

Plurals

When you talk about more than one person, place, or thing, you use a *plural noun*. Remember that an *-s* or an *-es* is added to most nouns to form the plural. Sometimes the letter *y* is changed to an *i* before adding *-es*. This dictionary shows plural forms. The plural is printed in small, dark type at the end of the main entry.

alligator

> **alligator** (AL uh gay ter) An *alligator* is a large animal with thick skin, a large mouth, and a long tail. *Alligators* live in lakes and rivers in warm states, such as Florida. *[noun]* • **alligators.**

Some singular nouns change to a different word to name more than one. This dictionary will help you find the plurals of these words. Look for them at the end of the main entries.

> **leaf** (LEEF) A *leaf* is one of the thin, flat, green parts of a tree or plant. *[noun]* • **leaves.**

leaves

Practice

Number your paper 1–10. Write the entry words listed at the right. Then write the plural for each entry word.

1. berry
2. cafeteria
3. dish
4. factory
5. girl scout
6. half
7. mouse
8. ostrich
9. policewoman
10. ranch

Verbs

The forms of a verb change with the way you use the word. The verb *admit* tells that something is true. If you are talking about more than one person, you say, "They admit their mistake." If you are talking about just one person, you say, "He admits his mistake."

> **admit** (uhd MIT) When you *admit* something, you say that it is true: *She admitted that I was right.* [verb] • **admits, admitted, admitting.**

Notice the words printed in small, dark type at the end of the main entry. The form with *-ed* tells what happened in the past. The form with *-ing* is used when the verb is used with another verb.

Sometimes the letter *e* is dropped when *-ed* or *-ing* is added to a verb. Other times one word changes. Find the verb forms of the word *drive* in the entry below.

> **drive** (DRYV)
>
> 1. When you *drive* a car, bus, or truck, you make it go: *My sister is learning to drive a car.* [verb]
> 2. To *drive* also means to go somewhere or carry people in a car or bus: *Please drive us to school. I drove to the hospital.* [verb]
> • **drives, drove, driven, driving.**

I admit I was wrong!

Practice

Number your paper 1–10. Write these entry words and then write all of the verb forms that are at the end of each entry.

1. argue
2. beg
3. carry
4. disappoint
5. find
6. grow
7. keep
8. learn
9. own
10. rise

Adjectives

The forms of an adjective change with the way you use the word. The adjective *small* tells the size of something. If you are talking about two things, you say "Our classroom is smaller than theirs." If you are talking about three or more things, you say "We have the smallest classroom in the whole school."

small (SMAWL) If something is *small*, it is not big, tall, large, or many: *We own a small house.* [*adjective*] • **smaller, smallest.**

Notice the words printed in small, dark type at the end of the main entry. The form with *-er* is used to compare two things. The form with *-est* is used to compare three or more things.

Sometimes the forms for comparing things are completely different words.

bad (BAD) If something is *bad*, it is not good, not right, or not as it should be: *Teasing animals is a bad thing to do. That bad dog ate my lunch. I feel bad about being late for the parade.* [*adjective*] • **worse, worst.**

Small things

I am small!

Practice

Number your paper 1–10. Write these entry words and then write all of the adjective forms that are at the end of each entry.

1. smart
2. jolly
3. calm
4. happy
5. fair
6. good
7. kind
8. large
9. old
10. rainy

Practice Answers

Page A7
Answers will vary.

Page A8
1. square
2. car seat
3. Alabama
4. ice cream
5. Guerrero

Page A9
1. alligator, frog, toad
2. eyes, nose, teeth
3. artist, farmer, judge
4. Alabama, Delaware, Washington
5. brother, mother, sister

Page A10
1. chipmunk, clam, crab
2. lamb, leopard, lizard
3. dentist, doctor, driver
4. taco, tea, tomato
5. acorn, apple, asparagus

Page A11
1. raccoon-middle
2. antelope-top
3. zebra-bottom
4. tiger-bottom
5. buffalo-top
6. giraffe-top
7. iguana-top
8. sheep-bottom
9. panda-middle
10. otter-middle

Page A12
1. cooperate-cork
2. beaver-beet
3. fall-fan
4. avenue-ax
5. miss-mitten
6. Rhode Island-ridden
7. icicle-I'll
8. pocket-point
9. curtain-cut
10. each-early

Page A13
1. egg, top, eat-eighteen
2. spaghetti, bottom, southeast-speak
3. macaroni, middle, macaroni-made
4. jam, middle, jam-jellyfish
5. raspberry, middle, ramp-rather

Page A14
1. audiences 23
2. asking 22
3. phone 288
4. who 436
5. knot 220
6. Chicago, other dictionary
7. Edison, other dictionary
8. bueno, other dictionary
9. stuck 388
10. brightest 51

Page A15
1. restaurant
2. harbor
3. school
4. firehouse
5. backyard

Page A16
1. The <u>hall</u> leads to the auditorium.
2. The <u>rain</u> got us all wet as we walked home from school. Will it <u>rain</u> today?
3. She entered school at the <u>age</u> of five.
4. I <u>am</u> eight years old. I <u>am</u> in the school play.
5. Skating on thin ice is <u>dangerous</u>.
6. I saw the dog <u>grab</u> the bone and run.
7. We <u>carried</u> the groceries into the house.
8. The boy was strong enough to lift the table <u>easily</u>.
9. She has <u>lain</u> down to take a nap.
10. His dog sat <u>beside</u> him.

Page A17
1. jersey
2. package
3. alert
4. sticker
5. fare

Page A18
1. back: 4
2. screen: 2
3. nail: 1
4. patient: 1
5. mouse: 2

Page A19
1. 2
2. 2
3. 2
4. 1
5. 1

Page A20
1. j
2. c
3. h
4. b
5. e
6. i
7. g
8. d
9. a
10. f

Page A21
1. airport 2 AIR
2. beginning 3 GIN
3. October 3 TOH
4. queen 1 KWEEN
5. caterpillar 4 KAT

Page A22
Answers will vary.

Page A23
1. wrong
2. breathe
3. special
4. ghost
5. coat
6. bangs
7. iceberg
8. quit
9. so
10. photograph

Page A27
1. bake-verb
2. cactus-noun
3. dance-noun or verb
4. example-noun
5. find-verb
6. gasoline-noun
7. insult-noun or verb
8. kiss-noun or verb
9. pineapple-noun
10. submarine-noun

Page A28
1. hairbrush-noun
2. she-pronoun
3. Nebraska-noun
4. if-conjunction
5. just-adverb
6. oh-interjection
7. lazy-adjective
8. make-believe-adjective
9. don't-contraction
10. know-verb

Page A29
1. berry-berries
2. cafeteria-cafeterias
3. dish-dishes
4. factory-factories
5. girl scout-girl scouts
6. half-halves
7. mouse-mice
8. ostrich-ostriches
9. policewoman-policewomen
10. ranch-ranches

Page A30
1. argue-argues, argued, arguing
2. beg-begs, begged, begging
3. carry-carries, carried, carrying
4. disappoint-disappoints, disappointed, disappointing
5. find-finds, found, finding
6. grow-grows, grew, grown, growing
7. keep-keeps, kept, keeping
8. learn-learns, learned, learning
9. own-owns, owned, owning
10. rise-rises, rose, risen, rising

Page A31
1. smart-smarter, smartest
2. jolly-jollier, jolliest
3. calm-calmer, calmest
4. happy-happier, happiest
5. fair-fairer, fairest
6. good-better, best
7. kind-kinder, kindest
8. large-larger, largest
9. old-older, oldest
10. rainy-rainier, rainiest

a (uh *or* ay) *There's a book for you on the table. Here is a pen. Your birthday comes once a year.*

abbreviation (uh bree vee AY shuhn) An *abbreviation* is a short form of a word. *St.* is the *abbreviation* for *Street. AL* is an *abbreviation* for *Alabama.* [noun] •**abbreviations.**

able (AY buhl) If you are *able* to do something, you can do it: *She is able to tie her shoes.* [adjective] •**abler, ablest.**

about (uh BOWT) *This book is about trains. It is about ten o'clock. About a dozen cars were in the parking lot.* [adverb *or* preposition]

above (uh BUHV) *The sun is above the trees. Read the line above the picture. The temperature was above freezing.* [preposition]

I am able to tie my own shoes.

able

1

absent (AB suhnt) If someone is *absent,* he or she is not here or not where he or she is supposed to be: *Two pupils were absent today.* [adjective]

accept (AK sept)

1. If you *accept* something that is offered to you, you take it: *The teacher accepted our gift.* [verb]

2. If you *accept* an invitation, you say yes to it: *I accepted the invitation to his birthday party.* [verb]

3. *Accept* can also mean believe: *The teacher accepted our excuse.* [verb]

•**accepts, accepted, accepting.**

accept

accident (AK suh duhnt)

1. An *accident* is something bad that happens when it isn't supposed to: *Slipping and falling on the ice was an accident.* [noun]

2. An *accident* can also be anything that happens when you don't expect it: *Meeting her yesterday was an accident.* [noun]

•**accidents.**

accuse (uh KYOOZ) When you *accuse* someone of something, you say that the person did something bad: *Dad accused us of breaking the window.* [verb]
•**accuses, accused, accusing.**

ache (AYK)

1. An *ache* is a steady pain: *I had a stomach ache after eating too much.* [noun]

ache

2. If you *ache*, you have a steady pain:
My muscles ached after exercising. [verb]
•**aches.** •**aches, ached, aching.**

acorn (AY kern *or* AY korn)
An *acorn* is the nut of
an oak tree: *Did you
see the squirrel eat the
acorn?* [noun]
•**acorns.**

acorns

acrobat (AK ruh bat) An *acrobat* is a person who can
do interesting tricks on the ground or in the air.
Acrobats usually work in the circus: *We saw acrobats
in the parade.* [noun] •**acrobats.**

across (uh KRAWSS) *The cat walked across
the yard. My friend lives across the street.*
[preposition]

act (AKT)

1. An *act* is something you do: *Sharing treats
is a kind act.* [noun]

2. To *act* is to behave in a certain way: *They act
like babies.* [verb]

3. To *act* is also to pretend to be someone else.
People *act* in movies, on television, in plays,
or on the radio: *She likes to act in plays.* [verb]
•**acts.** •**acts, acted, acting.**

action (AK shuhn)

1. *Action* is doing something for a reason: *The quick
action of the firefighters kept the house from
burning down.* [noun]

2. *Action* is also the events in a story or play: *We
enjoyed the movie because it had a lot of exciting
action.* [noun]
•**actions.**

act

activity (ak TIV uh tee) An *activity* is something you do for fun or to learn: *We enjoyed games, races, and other activities at the picnic. We did a spelling activity before recess.* [noun] •**activities.**

actor (AK ter) An *actor* is a person who acts in movies, on TV, on the stage, or on the radio: *He wants to be an actor when he grows up.* [noun] •**actors.**

activity

actress (AK truhss) An *actress* is a woman or girl who acts on stage, in movies, on TV, or on radio. Many people also use the word *actor* to mean a woman who acts: *His sister is a good actress.* [noun] •**actresses.**

actual (AK choo uhl) If something is *actual,* it is real: *He told us about an actual event.* [adjective]

actually (AK choo uh lee) When you say *actually* you mean that something is really true: *We are actually going to the play!* [adverb]

add (AD) To *add* is to put numbers or things together: *Add 5 and 3 to make 8. The cook added two more eggs to the batter.* [verb] •**adds, added, adding.**

addition (uh DISH uhn) *Addition* is adding one number to another: *The addition of 3 to 5 gives the sum of 8.* [noun]

address (uh DRESS)

1. Your *address* is the place where your mail is sent: *Write the address on the envelope.* [noun]

address

2. When you *address* a letter or package, you write on it the place where you want it to be sent: *Address the letter with a pen.* [verb]

•addresses. •addresses, addressed, addressing.

adjective (AJ ik tiv) An *adjective* is a word that tells more about a person, place, animal, or thing. *Adjectives* can tell how many, what color something is, what size it is, or what shape it is. "He lives in a yellow house." *Yellow* is the *adjective* that tells what color the house is. "Two bears swim." *Two* is the *adjective* that tells how many bears swim. "A big lion roars." *Big* is the *adjective* that tells the size of the lion. [noun] •**adjectives.**

yellow

two

big

adjectives

admit

admire (ad MYR)

1. When you *admire* something, you look at it with pleasure: *We all admire your painting.* [verb]

2. If you *admire* someone, you respect that person and think well of him or her: *I admire you.* [verb]

•**admires, admired, admiring.**

admit (uhd MIT) When you *admit* something, you say that it is true: *She admitted that I was right.* [verb]

•**admits, admitted, admitting.**

adopt (uh DOPT)

1. If you *adopt* a child, you bring it up as your own:

I admit I was wrong.

adults

They want to adopt six children. [verb]

2. If you *adopt* something, you accept it as your own or as your own choice: *I liked your idea and adopted it. The club voted to adopt the new rules.* [verb]
•**adopts, adopted, adopting.**

adorable (uh DOR uh buhl) Someone or something that is *adorable* is cute and nice to look at: *What an adorable kitten!* [adjective]

adult (uh DUHLT *or* AD uhlt) An *adult* is a grown-up person: *An adult went along with our group on our trip to the zoo.* [noun] •**adults.**

adventure (uhd VEN cher) An *adventure* is an exciting or unusual thing to do: *Riding a raft down the swift river was a great adventure.* [noun]
•**adventures.**

adverb (AD verb) An *adverb* is a word that tells about a verb. An *adverb* may tell when an action takes place. It may tell where or how an action takes place. "We will run today." *Today* is an *adverb*. It tells when we will run. "We ran quickly." *Quickly* tells how we ran. [noun]
•**adverbs.**

advertise (AD ver tyz) When you *advertise,* you tell people about something you want them to buy. You can *advertise* in newspapers, magazines, on radio, and on TV: *We decided to advertise our school play in the newspaper.* [verb]
•**advertises, advertised, advertising.**

advertise

advice (uhd VYSS) When you give *advice,* you tell someone what you think should be done: *The teacher's advice to us was to read the story again.* [noun]

afraid (uh FRAYD) When you are *afraid,* you feel scared or worried about something: *What are you afraid of? I was afraid that you wouldn't come.* [adjective]

afraid

after (AF ter) *After school we'll go to the park. Wednesday comes after Tuesday. The dog ran after the cat.* [conjunction or preposition or adverb]

afternoon (af ter NOON) The *afternoon* is the part of the day between morning and evening: *On Saturday we played all afternoon.* [noun] •**afternoons.**

again (uh GEN) When you do something *again,* you do it one more time: *Please say that again.* [adverb]

against (uh GENST) *The two teams played against each other. The rain beat against the house.* [preposition]

against

age (AYJ) Your *age* is the number of years you have lived: *She entered school at the age of five.* [noun]

ago (uh GOH) *Ago* means in the past: *I saw him two weeks ago. Long ago people lived in caves.* [adjective or adverb]

agree (uh GREE) When you *agree* with someone, you have the same idea about something: *We all agree that it is a good story.* [verb] •**agrees, agreed, agreeing.**

Aa

Aguascalientes · aisle

Aguascalientes (ah gwahss ka LYEN tes)
Aguascalientes is a state in central Mexico. [noun]

ahead (uh HED) *Please go ahead of me. Go ahead with your work. She is ahead of everybody in reading. [adverb]*

aim (AYM)

1. When you *aim* at something, you are trying to hit it: *I aim carefully at the basket before I shoot. [verb]*
2. *Aim* is also the act of aiming at something: *His aim was so bad that he missed the tree. [noun]*

   • **aims, aimed, aiming.**

aim

air (AIR) *Air is what we breathe. Air is all around us. It has no smell, taste, or color: Fresh air is good for us. Birds fly through the air. [noun]*

aircraft (AIR kraft) An *aircraft* is a machine that flies. Airplanes, helicopters, and balloons are *aircraft. [noun]* •The plural of *aircraft* is *aircraft.*

airplane (AIR playn) An *airplane* is a machine with wings that flies through the air. *Airplanes* have engines that make them go. *[noun]* •**airplanes.**

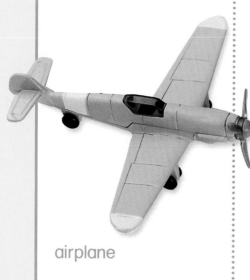

airplane

airport (AIR port) An *airport* is a place where airplanes land and take off. *[noun]* •**airports.**

aisle (EYE uhl) An *aisle* is a space between rows of seats: *We walked down the aisle at the movies, looking for empty seats. [noun]* •**aisles.**

Alabama (al uh BAM uh) *Alabama* is one of the fifty states of the United States. *[noun]*

alarm (uh LARM)

1. An *alarm* is something that makes a loud noise to tell people of danger: *When the fire alarm went off, we all went outside.* *[noun]*

2. When you *alarm* someone, you frighten them or make them afraid: *We alarm the deer with our noise.* *[verb]*

•**alarms.** •**alarms, alarmed, alarming.**

Alaska (uh LASS kuh) *Alaska* is one of the fifty states of the United States. *[noun]*

Alberta (al BER tuh) *Alberta* is one of the ten provinces of Canada. *[noun]*

alert (uh LERT) When you are *alert,* you are awake and watching: *The dog was alert to every sound.* *[adjective]*

alien (AY lyuhn) An *alien* is a make-believe creature from outer space: *The movie was about an alien landing on Earth.* *[noun]* •**aliens.**

alike (uh LYK) When two things are *alike,* they are like one another: *Twins often look and dress alike.* *[adverb]*

alive (uh LYV) When something is *alive,* it has life and is living. It is not dead: *The bird was badly hurt, but it is still alive.* *[adjective]*

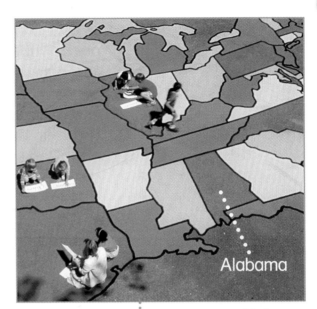

Alabama

alike

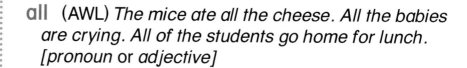

Aa all · aloud

alligator

all (AWL) *The mice ate all the cheese. All the babies are crying. All of the students go home for lunch.* [*pronoun* or *adjective*]

alley (AL ee) An *alley* is a narrow street behind or between buildings in a city or town. Garbage cans are often seen in an *alley: The big truck could not drive through the narrow alley.* [*noun*] •**alleys.**

alligator (AL uh gay ter) An *alligator* is a large animal with thick skin, a large mouth, and a long tail. *Alligators* live in lakes and rivers in warm states, such as Florida. [*noun*] •**alligators.**

allow (uh LOW) When you *allow* someone to do something, you let them do it: *My parents allow me to stay up until 8 o'clock. I allow him to ride my bike.* [*verb*] •**allows, allowed, allowing.**

almost (awl MOST) *I almost missed the bus. It is almost time for lunch.* [*adverb*]

alone (uh LOHN) If you are *alone,* you don't have anyone or anything with you: *He sat alone because he didn't know the others. One tree stood alone on the hill.* [*adjective* or *adverb*]

alone

along (uh LAWNG) *Trees are planted along the street. We took our dog along.* [*preposition* or *adverb*]

aloud (uh LOWD) When you talk or read *aloud,* you talk so that people can hear you. Talking *aloud* is the opposite of talking in a whisper: *She read the story aloud to the class.* [*adverb*]

alphabet (AL fuh bet) The *alphabet* is all the letters of a language. Our *alphabet* is a, b, c, d, e, f, g, h, i, j, k, l, m, n, o, p, q, r, s, t, u, v, w, x, y, z. Letters of the *alphabet* are put together to make words. *[noun]*
•**alphabets.**

alphabetical (al fuh BET uh kuhl)
If you put things in *alphabetical* order, you put them in the order of the letters of the alphabet: *The words in the dictionary are listed in alphabetical order. If you put the names in our class in alphabetical order, Anna is first and Ben second. [adjective]*

ABCDEFG
HIJKLMN
OPQRSTU
VWXYZ

alphabetical

always

I always brush my teeth.

already (awl RED ee) *She ran to the bus stop, but the bus had already gone. He has already read this book.* *[adverb]*

also (AWL soh) *He has a dog, but he likes cats also. She likes to ride her bike to school, but she also likes to walk. [adverb]*

although (awl THOH) *Although it rained all day, we still went on our walk. [conjunction]*

always (AWL wayz) If you do something *always*, you do it all the time or every time: *Always eat a good breakfast before you go to school. Always ride your bike in the same direction the cars are going. [adverb]*

am (AM) *I am eight years old. I am in the school play. [verb]*

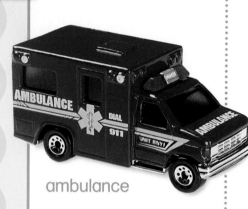

ambulance

amazing   (uh MAY zing) Something that is *amazing* is very surprising: *The hero made an amazing escape.* [*adjective*]

ambulance   (AM byuh luhnss) An *ambulance* is a special kind of car or van that takes sick or hurt people to the hospital very quickly. *Ambulances* have flashing lights and sirens. [*noun*] •**ambulances.**

America   (uh MAIR uh kuh)

1. *America* is a another name for North America. Some people use the name *America* to mean the United States. [*noun*]

2. *America* is also another name for North and South America together. The two continents are sometimes called *the Americas.* [*noun*]

American   (uh MAIR uh kuhn)

1. An *American* is a person born or living in the United States, or in North or South America. [*noun*]

2. An *American* thing belongs to or comes from the United States or North or South America: *The American flag is red, white, and blue.* [*adjective*]
•**Americans.**

We are Americans.

Americans

among   (uh MUHNG) *Divide the fruit among all of us. The house sits among the trees. The United States is among the largest countries in the world.* [*preposition*]

amount (uh MOWNT) The *amount* of something is how much there is or how many there are: *The amount of snow that fell yesterday was two inches. Five cents is a small amount of money.* [noun] •**amounts.**

amphibian (am FIB ee uhn)
An *amphibian* is an animal that lives both on land and in water. Most baby *amphibians* live in the water until they grow lungs for living on land. Frogs and toads are *amphibians.* [noun] •**amphibians.**

amphibian

amuse (uh MYOOZ) If you *amuse* someone, you make them laugh or smile: *The clown's jokes amuse everyone.* [verb] •**amuses, amused, amusing.**

an (UHN *or* AN) *Is there an apple in the box? She is an inch taller than I am. She earns five dollars an hour for baby-sitting.*

anchor (ANG ker) An *anchor* is a heavy piece of iron or steel that is dropped in the water to keep a ship or boat in place: *The anchor kept the boat in the harbor.* [noun] •**anchors.**

and (UHND *or* AND) *Yesterday we went to the beach and to the zoo. The boy asked if 4 and 2 make 6. She washed the dishes and her brother dried them.* [conjunction]

angry (ANG gree) If you are *angry,* you feel upset or mad: *Dad was angry when he saw the broken car window.* [adjective] •**angrier, angriest.**

angry

animal • annual

animal

animal (AN uh muhl) Any living thing that can move about is an *animal*. *Animals* cannot make their own food from sunlight as plants do. People, dogs, birds, fish, snakes, insects, and worms are *animals*. *[noun]* •**animals.**

ankle (ANG kuhl) Your *ankle* is the part of your body between your foot and your leg. *[noun]* •**ankles.**

ankylosaurus (ANG kuh loh sor uhss) The *ankylosaurus* was a dinosaur that had hard plates and spikes covering its body. It had short legs and ate plants. *[noun]* •**ankylosauruses.**

anniversary (an uh VER suh ree) An *anniversary* is a special date that you remember every year: *Your birthday is an anniversary you like to have remembered. [noun]* •**anniversaries.**

annoy (uh NOY) If you *annoy* someone, you bother them or make them angry: *The barking dog annoyed the neighbors. [verb]* •**annoys, annoyed, annoying.**

annual (AN yoo uhl)

1. Something that is *annual* comes once a year: *Your birthday is an annual event. [adjective]*
2. An *annual* is a plant that lives only one year or season. *[noun]*

•**annuals.**

annual

another (uh NUHTH er) *He asked for another glass of milk. I chose another book.* [*adjective* or *pronoun*]

answer (AN ser)

1. If you *answer*, you speak or write something when someone asks a question: *She answered three questions out of four.* [*verb*]

2. An *answer* is the words said or written when a question is asked: *I wrote the answer on a sheet of paper.* [*noun*]

3. To *answer* is also to do something when someone calls: *She answered the phone. I answered the door.* [*verb*]
•**answers, answered, answering.** •**answers.**

How old are you?

I am seven years old.

answer

ant (ANT) An *ant* is a small insect that lives in tunnels in the ground or in wood. *Ants* live together in large groups. [*noun*] •**ants.**

antelope (AN tuh lohp) An *antelope* is an animal that looks like a deer. *Antelope* can run as fast as deer. [*noun*] •**antelope** or **antelopes.**

antique (an TEEK) If something is an *antique*, it was made a long time ago: *This toy is a real antique.* [*noun*] •**antiques.**

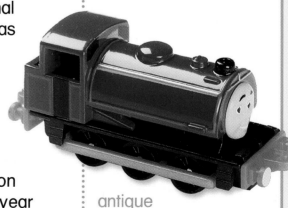

antique

antler (ANT ler) An *antler* is a horn that grows on the head of a male deer. *Antlers* fall off once a year and grow back again the next year. [*noun*] •**antlers.**

Aa anxious · anyway

Is anybody here?

anybody

anxious (ANGK shuhss)

1. If you are *anxious*, you are worried because you are afraid something bad may happen: *As it grew dark, the boy felt anxious when his dog did not come home.* [adjective]

anxious

2. *Anxious* can also mean that you really want to do something: *The baseball player was very anxious to get up to bat. They were anxious to start their vacation.* [adjective]

any (EN ee) *Choose any game you like. Are there any cookies left?* [adjective]

anybody (EN ee buh dee) *The boy yelled down the empty hall, "Is anybody here?"* [pronoun]

anymore (en ee MOR) If you don't do something *anymore,* you used to do it, but you don't do it now: *He used to jog every morning, but he doesn't anymore. I don't like that game anymore.* [adverb]

anyone (EN ee wuhn) *Can anyone go to this movie, or is it just for adults?* [pronoun]

anything (EN ee thing) *She asked if there was anything to eat in the refrigerator. My bike isn't anything like yours.* [pronoun or adverb]

anytime (EN ee tym) *You are welcome to visit us anytime.* [adverb]

anyway (EN ee way) *She was not invited to the party, but she went anyway.* [adverb]

anywhere (EN ee wair) *I'll meet you anywhere you say. He could not find his book anywhere.* [adverb]

apart (uh PART)

1. If you take something *apart,* you separate the thing's pieces or parts: *She took the watch apart to see how it runs.* [adverb]

2. *Apart* can also mean away from: *The twins felt very lonely when they sat apart from each other. Keep the dogs apart or they will fight.* [adverb]

apartment (uh PART muhnt) An *apartment* is a room or group of rooms to live in: *Our apartment is on the seventh floor.* [noun] •**apartments.**

apatosaurus (uh pat uh SOR us) The *apatosaurus* was a huge dinosaur with a very long neck and a tail. The *apatosaurus* ate plants. [noun] •**apatosauruses.**

ape (AYP) An *ape* is a large animal with long arms, a lot of hair, and no tail. *Apes* can stand almost straight and walk on two feet. A gorilla is an *ape.* [noun] •**apes.**

apiece (uh PEESS) *Apiece* means each: *The rooms have two beds apiece. These pencils are ten cents apiece.* [adverb]

apologize (uh POL uh jyz) When you *apologize,* you say that you are sorry for something you have done: *I apologize for being so late.* [verb] •**apologizes, apologized, apologizing.**

apostrophe (uh POS truh fee) An *apostrophe* is a mark (') of punctuation. An *apostrophe* shows that a letter has been left out of a word. "She isn't home." An *apostrophe* takes the place of the letter *o* in the word *not* when you write

ape

apologize

I apologize to you.

isn't. "We'll meet you at the party." An *apostrophe* takes the place of the letters *wi* in the word *will* when you write *we'll.* [noun] •**apostrophes.**

appear (uh PEER)

1. When something *appears,* it comes into sight: *Stars appear in the sky after the sun has gone down.* [verb]
2. *Appear* can also mean to seem: *The apple appeared to be good, but it was rotten inside.* [verb]

•**appears, appeared, appearing.**

apple (AP uhl)
An *apple* is a round fruit that grows on a tree. *Apples* have red, yellow, or green skin. They are eaten either raw or cooked. [noun] •**apples.**

apple

Apples have red, yellow, or green skin.

appliance

appliance (uh PLY uhnss) An *appliance* is a machine that helps make work around the house easier. Toasters and refrigerators are *appliances.* [noun] •**appliances.**

approach (uh PROHCH) If you *approach* something, you go near it or nearer it: *Be quiet as you approach the baby's crib. Winter is approaching.* [verb] •**approaches, approached, approaching.**

apricot (AY pruh kot *or* AP ruh kot) An *apricot* is a round, orange-colored fruit that grows on a tree. *Apricots* are smaller than peaches and have a smoother skin. [noun] •**apricots.**

April (AY pruhl) *April* is the fourth month of the year. It has 30 days. It comes after March and before May. *[noun]*

apron (AY pruhn) An *apron* is a cloth you tie around your waist or neck to protect your clothes: *Wear an apron when you cook. [noun]* •**aprons.**

aquarium (uh KWAIR ee uhm)

1. An *aquarium* is a glass container in which you keep fish or other water animals as pets. *[noun]*
2. An *aquarium* is also a building where you can see many fish and other water animals. *[noun]*

•**aquariums.**

are (AR) *You are right. We are ready. They are waiting for us. [verb]*

aquarium

area (AIR ee uh)

1. The *area* of something is the amount of space something covers: *A large area of the earth is covered by water. [noun]*
2. An *area* is also a place: *The playground area is right outside. [noun]*

•**areas.**

aren't *Aren't* is a shorter form of *are not*: *My friends aren't going to the game with me. [contraction]*

argue (AR gyoo) When you *argue*, you fight with words in an angry way: *He argued with his sister about who should wash the dishes. [verb]* •**argues, argued, arguing.**

argument • around

argument (AR gyoo muhnt) An *argument* is a talk between people who do not agree: *There was an argument over who was first.* [noun] •**arguments.**

Arizona (a ruh ZOH nuh) *Arizona* is one of the fifty states of the United States. [noun]

Arkansas (AR kuhn saw) *Arkansas* is one of the fifty states of the United States. [noun]

arm (ARM) Your *arm* is the part of your body between your shoulder and your hand. [noun] •**arms.**

armadillo (ar muh DILL oh) An *armadillo* is a small animal with a very hard shell. *Armadillos* are often found in Florida and Texas. [noun] •**armadillos.**

armor (AR mer) *Armor* is special metal clothing worn by knights. *Armor* protects you from being hurt. [noun]

army (AR mee) An *army* is a large group of soldiers. An *army* fights to protect its country in a war. [noun] •**armies.**

aroma (uh ROH muh) An *aroma* is a strong, pleasing smell: *Smell the aroma of the cake baking in the oven.* [noun] •**aromas.**

around (uh ROWND) *The top spun around. She planted flowers all around the house. The new students took a walk around the school.* [adverb or *preposition*]

armadillo

around

arrange (uh RAYNJ)
When you *arrange* something, you put it in some kind of order: *The books were arranged in alphabetical order.* [*verb*] •**arranges, arranged, arranging.**

arrange

arrive (uh RYV) If you *arrive* somewhere, you get there: *We arrived ten minutes early for the show, so we could find our seats. My grandmother arrived a week ago for a visit.* [*verb*]
•**arrives, arrived, arriving.**

arrow (A roh)
  1. An *arrow* is a pointed stick that is shot from a bow. *Arrows* are used as weapons. [*noun*]
  2. An *arrow* is also a sign (→) used to show a direction on maps and road signs. [*noun*]
  •**arrows.**

art (ART) Pictures and statues are kinds of *art*: *My class is studying art this month.* [*noun*]

artist (AR tist) An *artist* is a person who makes art. *Artists* can make pictures and statues. [*noun*]
•**artists.**

as (UHZ *or* AZ) *She ran as fast as she could. Mr. Smith will act as your teacher today. As they were walking, it began to rain.* [*adverb* or *preposition* or *conjunction*]

artist

art

ash (ASH) *Ash* is the gray powder that is left after something burns: *A little smoke still rose from the ash.* [noun] •**ashes.**

ashamed (uh SHAYMD) If you feel *ashamed,* you feel bad because you have done something wrong or silly: *I felt ashamed because I had not told the truth.* [adjective]

ask (ASK)

1. If you *ask* someone something, you want to find out the answer to a question: *We had to ask the way to the monkey house.* [verb]

2. *Ask* also means to invite: *I asked them to my party.* [verb]

•**asks, asked, asking.**

Can I borrow your markers?

ask

asleep (uh SLEEP) When you are *asleep,* you rest your body and your mind. When you are *asleep,* your eyes are closed. You are not awake: *The cat is asleep.* [adjective]

asparagus (uh SPA ruh guhs) *Asparagus* is a tender green vegetable. [noun]

asteroid (ASS tuh roid) An *asteroid* is a rock that orbits the sun. It is much smaller than a planet. There are thousands of rocky *asteroids* in our solar system. [noun] •**asteroids.**

astronaut (ASS truh nawt) An *astronaut* is a person who has been trained to fly in a spacecraft. While in space, *astronauts* repair space stations and do experiments. [noun] •**astronauts.**

at (AT) *There is someone at the front door. He goes to bed at nine o'clock. Look at me.* [preposition]

astronaut

ate (AYT) *Last night he ate dinner late. [verb]*

athlete (ATH leet) An *athlete* is a person who has trained to be very good at a sport. Baseball players and swimmers are *athletes. [noun]* •**athletes.**

athlete

attach (uh TACH) When you *attach* two things, you join them together: *I attached a rope to my sled. [verb]* •**attaches, attached, attaching.**

attack (uh TACK) If you *attack* someone or something, you start fighting: *The dog attacked the cat. [verb]* •**attacks, attacked, attacking.**

attention (uh TEN shuhn) If you give or pay *attention* to something, you think about it or care for it: *Pay attention while she explains this math problem. The boy gives his dog a lot of attention. [noun]*

attic (AT ik) An *attic* is the space in a house just below the roof. An *attic* is often used for storing things. *[noun]* •**attics.**

audience (AW dee uhnss) An *audience* is a group of people that is watching something or listening to something: *The audience liked the circus. The radio station received many phone calls from its audience. [noun]* •**audiences.**

audience

auditorium (aw duh TOR ee uhm) An *auditorium* is a large room with seats for many people: *The school play was held in the auditorium. [noun]* •**auditoriums.**

August (AW guhst) *August* is the eighth month of the year. It has 31 days. It comes after July and before September. *[noun]*

aunt (ANT *or* AHNT) Your *aunt* is your father's sister, your mother's sister, or your uncle's wife. *[noun]* •**aunts.**

author (AW ther) An *author* is a person who writes books, stories, poems, or plays. *[noun]* •**authors.**

auto (AW toh) *Auto* is a short form of the word *automobile*. *[noun]* •**autos.**

automobile (AW tuh muh beel) An *automobile* is a machine that people ride in. An *automobile* has an engine and four wheels. Another word for *automobile* is *car*. *[noun]* •**automobiles.**

autumn (AW tuhm) *Autumn* is one of the four seasons. It is the season of the year between summer and winter. *Autumn* is the season when the harvest takes place. *Autumn* is also called *fall*. *[noun]* •**autumns.**

autumn

avenue (AV uh noo) An *avenue* is a street: *We live on Maple Avenue.* [noun] •**avenues.**

avocado (av uh KAH doh) An *avocado* is a soft, green fruit. An *avocado* is about the size of a pear. It has thick green or black skin and a large, smooth seed. [noun] •**avocados.**

asleep

awake

awake (uh WAYK) If you are *awake*, you are not asleep. Your eyes are open: *She was still awake at midnight.* [adjective]

away (uh WAY) *Stay away from the street. The dog ran away from the bear. Go away. The neighbors will be away for a week.* [adjective or adverb]

awful (AW fuhl) If something is *awful,* it is very bad, terrible, or ugly: *An awful storm came up suddenly. My friend fell down and got an awful bump on her head.* [adjective]

awhile (uh WYL) If you do something for *awhile,* you do it for a short time: *I usually read awhile before going to bed.* [adverb]

ax or **axe** (AKS) An *ax* is a tool with a flat, sharp edge used for chopping wood. [noun] •**axes.**

baby · back

Bb

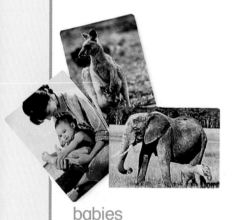

babies

baby (BAY bee)

1. A *baby* is a very young child. [noun]
2. *Baby* animals are young or small animals: *She went to the zoo to see the baby elephants.* [adjective]
•**babies.**

baby-sit (BAY bee sit) If you *baby-sit*, you take care of a child while the parents are away. [verb]
•**baby-sits, baby-sat, baby-sitting.**

baby-sitter (BAY bee sit er) A *baby-sitter* is a person who takes care of a child while the parents are away. [noun] •**baby-sitters.**

back (BAK)

1. Your *back* is the part of your body opposite your chest and stomach: *It's hard to scratch the middle of your back.* [noun]

2. The *back* is also the side of anything opposite the front side: *The back of our neighbor's house has four windows.* [noun]

3. If you come *back* from a place, you return to the place where you began: *We came back from the playground before it was dark.* [adverb]

back

4. When you put something *back,* you put it where you found it: *Did you put the book back on the shelf?* [adverb]

•**backs.**

backboard (BAK bord) The *backboard* is the flat board the basket is attached to for basketball. [noun] •**backboards.**

backpack (BAK pak) A *backpack* is a bag worn on the back by people walking or going to school. In *backpacks* you carry things such as clothes, books, and food: *Can you fit your books in your backpack?* [noun] •**backpacks.**

backward (BAK werd)

1. If you move *backward,* you go in the direction opposite to the front of something: *Be careful not to fall when you walk backward. He dived backward into the pool.* [adverb]

2. If something is *backward* it is the way opposite to how it usually is: *"Tim" spelled backward is "mit."* [adverb]

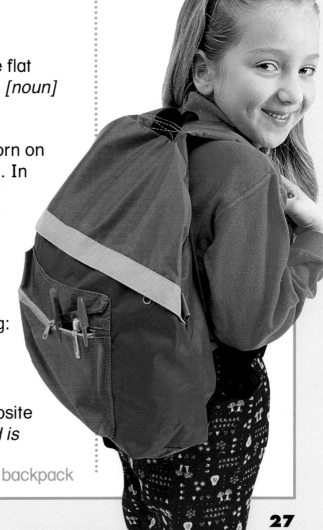

backpack

backyard • baker

bagpipes

backyard (BAK YARD) A *backyard* is a yard behind a house or building. *[noun]* •**backyards.**

bad (BAD) If something is *bad,* it is not good, not right, or not as it should be: *Teasing animals is a bad thing to do. That bad dog ate my lunch. I feel bad about being late for the parade.* *[adjective]* •**worse, worst.**

badly (BAD lee) If you do something *badly* you do it in a wrong or clumsy way: *She dances badly.* *[adverb]*

bag (BAG) A *bag* is something used to hold things. *Bags* are made of paper, cloth, plastic, or leather. *[noun]* •**bags.**

bagpipe (BAG pyp) A *bagpipe* is a musical instrument made of a tube to blow through, a leather bag for pumping air, and four pipes. •**bagpipes.**

Baja California Norte (BAH hah kal lee FOR nyah NOR tay) *Baja California Norte* is a state in the northwest part of Mexico. *[noun]*

Baja California Sur (BAH hah kal lee FOR nyah SUR) *Baja California Sur* is a state in the northwest part of Mexico. *[noun]*

bake (BAYK) If you *bake* something, you cook it in an oven: *The cook bakes bread every morning.* *[verb]* •**bakes, baked, baking.**

baker (BAY ker) A *baker* is a person who makes or sells bread, pies, and cakes. *[noun]* •**bakers.**

baker

Bb

bakery (BAY kree) A *bakery* is a place where bread and cakes are sold. *[noun]* •**bakeries.**

balance (BAL uhnss)

1. When you *balance,* you are steady and do not fall over: *He lost his balance and fell down. [noun]*
2. If you *balance* something, you keep or hold it so that it does not fall over: *She balanced the book on her head. [verb]*
•**balances, balanced, balancing.**

ball[1] (BAWL)

1. A *ball* is something round, often a toy used in games: *In baseball, you throw the ball and hit it. [noun]*
2. *Ball* is also any game in which a ball is used, usually baseball or basketball: *Let's play ball. [noun]*
•**balls** *for definition I.*

ball[1]

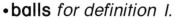
balloons

ball[2] (BAWL) A *ball* is a large party for dancing: *The princess went to the ball. [noun]* •**balls.**

ballet (BAL ay) *Ballet* is a special kind of dancing. A *ballet* usually tells a story through dancing and music. *[noun]* •**ballets.**

balloon (buh LOON)

1. A *balloon* is a toy made of thin rubber filled with air, or a gas lighter than air. *[noun]*
2. A *balloon* is also a large rubber or plastic bag filled with hot air, or a gas lighter than air. People can ride in baskets attached to *balloons. [noun]*
•**balloons.**

29

banana • banquet

Bb

banana (buh NAN uh) A *banana* is a curved, yellow fruit that grows in large bunches. *Bananas* grow in warm countries on a tall plant like a tree. *[noun]* •**bananas.**

band (BAND) A *band* is a group of musicians playing together: *The band played music for an hour.* *[noun]* •**bands.**

bandage (BAN dij) A *bandage* is a strip of cloth that covers a cut: *The nurse put a bandage on the cut.* *[noun]* •**bandages.**

bandage

bang (BANG) A *bang* is a sudden, loud noise: *We heard the bang of fireworks.* *[noun]* •**bangs.**

bangs (BANGZ) *Bangs* are hair cut short and worn over the forehead. *[noun plural]*

banjo (BAN jo) A *banjo* is a musical instrument with strings. It has a round body. You play it with your fingers. *[noun]* •**banjos.**

bank¹ (BANK) The *bank* of a river or lake is the ground beside it: *He sat on the river bank.* *[noun]* •**banks.**

bank² (BANK) A *bank* is a place where people keep their money: *Mom and Dad put money in the bank every week. My brother has a bank for nickels and pennies.* *[noun]* •**banks.**

bank

banquet (BANG kwit) A *banquet* is a large meal with many different kinds of food. People have *banquets* for special celebrations: *They had a banquet for their wedding.* *[noun]* •**banquets.**

bar (BAR)

1. A *bar* is a long piece of something solid: *I bought a candy bar.* [noun]

2. A *bar* is also a long, round piece of wood or metal, used to close an opening: *All the windows were protected by steel bars.* [noun]

• **bars.**

barbecue (BAR buh KYOO)

1. *Barbecue* is meat cooked over an open fire. *Barbecue* can be made with a hot or spicy sauce: *We ate barbecue last night.* [noun]

2. When you *barbecue* meat, you cook it over an open fire: *We barbecue meat on Saturday nights.* [verb]

• **barbecues, barbecued, barbecuing.**

barbecue

barber (BAR ber) A *barber* is a person who cuts hair. [noun] • **barbers.**

bare (BAIR) If something is *bare,* it is without covering or clothes: *The sun burned his bare shoulders.* [adjective] • **barer, barest.**

barefoot (BAIR fut) If you are *barefoot,* you are wearing nothing on your feet: *I ran barefoot in the yard.* [adjective or adverb]

bark¹ (BARK) *Bark* is the rough outside covering of the trunk and branches of a tree. [noun]

bark² (BARK)

1. A *bark* is the sharp sound that a dog makes: *She heard a loud bark in the middle of the night.* [noun]

barefoot

barn • basement

Bb

2. To *bark* means to make the sharp sound that a dog makes: *Why does that dog bark at me? [verb]*
•**barks.** •**barks, barked, barking.**

barn (BARN) A *barn* is a farm building. It is used to store food for animals. Cows and horses are kept in the *barn* at night. *[noun]*
•**barns.**

barrel (BA ruhl) A *barrel* is a large round container. *Barrels* have round, flat tops and bottoms and curved sides. *[noun]* •**barrels.**

barn

barrette (buh RET) A *barrette* is something you use to hold your hair in place. *[noun]* •**barrettes.**

base (BAYSS)

1. A *base* is the bottom of something: *The metal base of the floor lamp might scratch the floor. [noun]*
2. A *base* is also an object in some games: *The runner stopped at third base. [noun]*
•**bases.**

baseball (BAYSS bawl)

1. *Baseball* is a game played with a bat and ball by two teams. Each team has nine players. *Baseball* is played on a field with four bases. *[noun]*
2. A *baseball* is also the ball used in this game. *[noun]*
•**baseballs** *for definition 2.*

baseball

basement (BAYS muhnt) A *basement* is the underground rooms of a house or other building. *[noun]* •**basements.**

basket (BAS kuht)

1. A *basket* is something to carry or store things in. *Baskets* are made of straw, plastic, or strips of wood. *[noun]*
2. In basketball a *basket* is used as a goal. The *basket* is made of a metal ring with a net hanging from it. *[noun]*
   • **baskets.**

basketball (BAS kuht bawl)

1. *Basketball* is a game played with a large, round ball between two teams of five players each. *[noun]*
2. A *basketball* is the ball used in this game. *[noun]*
   • **basketballs** *for definition 2.*

bat¹ (BAT)

1. A *bat* is a thick stick or club, made of wood or aluminum, used to hit the ball in games. *[noun]*
2. To *bat* means to hit with a bat: *She will bat first in today's game. [verb]*
   • **bats.** • **bats, batted, batting.**

bat² (BAT) A *bat* is an animal that looks like a mouse with wings covered by thin skin. *Bats* fly at night. *[noun]* • **bats.**

bath (BATH) If you take a *bath,* you get into a large tub of water and wash yourself: *I took a bath last night. [noun]* • **baths.**

bathe (BAY<u>TH</u>) To *bathe* means to take a bath yourself or give someone a bath: *I bathe every day. Mother is bathing the baby. [verb]*
• **bathes, bathed, bathing.**

bathing suit (BAY <u>thing</u> SOOT) You wear a *bathing suit* when you go swimming.
• **bathing suits.**

basketball

bathing suits

bathroom (BATH room) A *bathroom* is a room where you can take a bath. *Bathrooms* often have a toilet, a sink, a mirror, and other things. *[noun]* •**bathrooms.**

bathtub (BATH tuhb) A *bathtub* is a large, open tub people use to take a bath in. *[noun]* •**bathtubs.**

batter[1] (BAT er) *Batter* is a mixture of flour, milk, and eggs that becomes solid when cooked. Cakes, cookies, and muffins are made from *batter. [noun]*

batter[2] (BAT er) In baseball, a player whose turn it is to bat is called a *batter. [noun]* •**batters.**

batter[2]

battery (BAT er ee) A *battery* is something that stores electricity. Flashlights and many toys run off small *batteries.* Large *batteries* make cars start. *[noun]* •**batteries.**

bay (BAY) A *bay* is a part of a sea or lake not completely surrounded by land: *We like to sail on the bay. [noun]* •**bays.**

be (BEE) *We will be there in an hour. He tried to be on time. Be good to animals. [verb]*

beach (BEECH) A *beach* is an area of land found next to a body of water. *Beaches* are covered with sand or stones. *[noun]* •**beaches.**

bead (BEED) A *bead* is a small bit of glass, metal, or plastic, with a hole so it can be put on a thread. *[noun]* •**beads.**

beaches

beak (BEEK) A *beak* is the hard part of the mouth of a bird. Another word for *beak* is *bill*. [noun] •**beaks.**

bean (BEEN) A *bean* is a smooth, flat seed eaten as a vegetable. *Beans* grow in pods. The *bean* pod is often eaten as a vegetable and also called a *bean*. [noun] •**beans.**

bear (BAIR) A *bear* is a large animal with thick hair and a very short tail. Many *bears* sleep through most of the winter. [noun] •**bears.**

bear

beard (BEERD) A *beard* is the hair that grows on a man's face. [noun] •**beards.**

beat (BEET)

beat

1. To *beat* means to hit again and again: *The baby beat the toy drum with a stick.* [verb]
2. To *beat* someone is to do better in a game or contest: *Our team beat yours.* [verb]
3. To *beat* can also mean to mix by stirring: *Beat three eggs to put in the cookie batter.* [verb]

•**beats, beat, beaten, beating.**

beaten (BEET uhn) *Have you beaten the eggs for the cake?* [verb]

beautiful (BYOO ti fuhl) If something is *beautiful* it is very pretty to see or hear: *After the rain stopped, it became a beautiful, sunny day.* [adjective]

beauty (BYOO tee) *Beauty* is the quality that makes something very pretty to see or listen to: *We enjoyed the beauty of the sunset.* [noun] •**beauties.**

beaver · beet

beaver

beaver (BEE ver) A *beaver* is an animal with soft fur, a wide, flat tail, and large front teeth. *Beavers* cut down trees with their teeth and build dams in streams. *[noun]* •**beavers.**

became (bi KAYM) *It became dark very early.* *[verb]*

because (bi KAWZ) *Because* is a word you use to show a reason for doing something or to show why something is a certain way: *Dad called us in because supper was ready. She is at home because she broke her leg.* *[conjunction]*

become (bi KUHM) *It is becoming warmer. He has become stronger as he has grown older.* *[verb]* •**becomes, became, becoming.**

bed (BED) A *bed* is something to sleep or rest on: *I sleep in a big bed.* *[noun]* •**beds.**

bedroom (BED room) A *bedroom* is a room to sleep in: *I share a bedroom with my sister.* *[noun]* •**bedrooms.**

bee (BEE) A *bee* is an insect that flies and makes honey. *Bees* sting. Some *bees* live in groups in a hive. *[noun]* •**bees.** bedroom

beef (BEEF) *Beef* is the meat from cattle, used for food. Hamburger and steak are *beef.* *[noun]*

been (BIN) *This boy has been here for hours. We have been friends for years. Have you been to Canada?* *[verb]*

beet (BEET) A *beet* is a thick, red root that grows underground. The root and its leaves are eaten as vegetables. *[noun]* •**beets.**

beetle (BEET uhl) A *beetle* is a small insect. Its shiny front wings cover its back wings when it is not flying. *[noun]* •**beetles.**

before (bi FOR) *Wash your hands before you eat. I have been here before. His turn comes before mine.* *[preposition* or *adverb* or *conjunction]*

beg (BEG) If you *beg,* you ask for something as a gift: *Some people have to beg for food. The dog begged for a treat.* *[verb]* •**begs, begged, begging.**

began (bi GAN) *She began to sing.* *[verb]*

begin (bi GIN) When you *begin* something, you start it: *When the music starts, we begin to dance. The party will begin soon.* *[verb]* •**begins, began, begun, beginning.**

beetle

beginning (bi GIN ing)
1. The *beginning* is the time when something starts: *The beginning of school is in September.* *[noun]*
2. The *beginning* is also the first part of something: *She liked the beginning of the story.* *[noun]*
•**beginnings.**

begun (bi GUHN) *It has begun to rain.* *[verb]*

behave (bi HAYV)
1. If you *behave,* you do what is right: *The little boy behaves in school.* *[verb]*
2. To *behave* also means to act in a certain way: *Some people behave badly.* *[verb]*
•**behaves, behaved, behaving.**

behind (bi HYND) *Who is behind me? Her class is behind in its work.* *[preposition* or *adverb]*

being · bench

being (BEE ing) *She is being difficult. Being angry is a waste of time.* [verb]

believe (buh LEEV)

1. If you *believe* something, you think that it is true: *We believed the weather report that promised rain.* [verb]

2. If you *believe* someone, you think that person tells the truth: *Did her friends believe her?* [verb]
•**believes, believed, believing.**

bell (BELL) A *bell* is a hollow piece of metal shaped like an upside-down cup. It makes a ringing sound when you hit it. [noun] •**bells.**

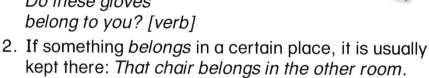

bells

belong (bi LAWNG)

1. If something *belongs* to you, you own it: *Do these gloves belong to you?* [verb]

2. If something *belongs* in a certain place, it is usually kept there: *That chair belongs in the other room.* [verb]
•**belongs, belonged, belonging.**

belt

below (bi LOH) *In our house, the kitchen is below my parents' room. The temperature is below freezing.* [preposition]

belt (BELT) A *belt* is a strip of cloth or leather worn around your waist. A *belt* helps to hold up your trousers. [noun] •**belts.**

bench (BENCH) A *bench* is a long wooden seat: *We sat on a bench and waited for the bus.* [noun] •**benches.**

bend (BEND)

1. Something that *bends* is not straight. If you *bend* something, you make it curve: *Try to bend this bar. The branch began to bend as I climbed it.* [verb]

bend

2. A *bend* is a part that is not straight: *There is a bend in the road here.* [noun]

3. When you *bend,* you move the top of your body toward the ground: *Try to bend over and touch your toes.* [verb]
•**bends, bent, bending.** •**bends.**

beneath (bi NEETH)
If something is *beneath* something else, it is below it, under it, or in a lower place: *His coat is beneath that pile of books. Your glasses are on the shelf beneath the clock.* [adverb or *preposition*]

bent (BENT)

1. *She bent the fork. I have bent over and touched the floor.* [verb]

2. Something that is *bent* is not straight: *I used a bent pin for a hook.* [adjective]

berries

berry (BAIR ee)
A *berry* is a small fruit with many seeds. Strawberries and raspberries are *berries.* [noun] •**berries.**

beside (bi SYD)
If something is *beside* you, it is by your side or near you: *His dog sat beside him.* [preposition]

besides (bi SYDZ)
He didn't want to hurry home; besides, he was having fun. Others came to the picnic besides our family. [adverb or *preposition*]

best · big

Bb

best (BEST) When someone or something is the *best,* that person or thing is better than anything or anyone else: *He's a good swimmer, but his brother is the best swimmer I've ever seen.* [*adjective* or *noun*]

bet (BET) When you *bet,* you say you will give something to someone if that person is right and you are wrong: *He bet that he could beat me to the corner.* [*verb*] •**bets, bet, betting.**

better (BET er) *Better* means more than good: *Her plan is good, but I think ours is better. She sang that song well, but she sang this one better.* [*adjective*]

between (bi TWEEN) *There is a rock between the two trees. We'll be home between two and three o'clock.* [*preposition* or *adverb*]

beyond (bi YOND) If something is *beyond* something else, it is on the other side of or farther away than that thing: *Look beyond the fence for your ball. Don't go beyond the corner.* [*preposition*]

I am between Jay and Mike.

between

bicycle (BY sik uhl) A *bicycle* is a thing to ride that has two wheels, one behind the other. You ride it by pushing down on two pedals with your legs and feet. [*noun*] •**bicycles.**

big (BIG) If something is *big,* it is more than the usual size: *They own a big dog. Is it bigger than ours? It's the biggest dog I've ever seen.* [*adjective*] •**bigger, biggest.**

bicycle

Bb

bike (BYK) *Bike* is a short word meaning *bicycle:
I rode my bike to school.* [noun] •**bikes.**

bill¹ (BILL) A *bill* is a piece of paper that tells how much
money you must pay for something: *The waiter
brought the bill for our dinner.* [noun] •**bills.**

bill² (BILL) A *bill* is the hard part of the mouth of a bird.
Another word for *bill* is *beak.* [noun] •**bills.**

biography (by OG ruh fee) A *biography* is the story
of a person's life written by another person. [noun]
•**biographies.**

bird (BERD) A *bird* is an animal that has wings,
feathers, and two legs. Most *birds* can fly. [noun]
•**birds.**

birds

birdbath (BERD bath) A *birdbath* is a place for birds
to bathe. [noun] •**birdbaths.**

birdhouse (BERD howss) A *birdhouse* is a box for
birds to make their nests in. [noun] •**birdhouses.**

birthday

birth (BERTH) A *birth* is the time that someone or
something is born: *We heard about the birth of the
baby.* [noun] •**births.**

birthday (BERTH day) Your *birthday* is the day that
you were born. Most people celebrate their *birthdays*
every year. [noun] •**birthdays.**

biscuit (BISS kit) A *biscuit* is a small cake that
is not sweet. [noun] •**biscuits.**

bit¹ (BIT) A *bit* is a small piece: *Would you
like a bit of this cake?* [noun] •**bits.**

bit² (BIT) *He bit into the candy bar.* [verb]

41

bite · bled

bite (BYT)

1. When you *bite* down on something, you cut it with your teeth. If something *bites* you, it hurts you with its teeth: *Did she bite her tongue? My dog won't bite.* [verb]

2. A *bite* is the amount you bite at one time: *I only ate a bite of my apple.* [noun]
•**bites, bit, bitten, biting.** •**bites.**

bite

bitten (BIT uhn) *She was bitten by the dog.* [verb]

bitter (BIT er) If something is *bitter,* it has a sharp, bad taste. The skin of an orange tastes *bitter.* [adjective]

black (BLAK)

1. *Black* is a very dark color. *Black* is the opposite of white: *The words in this book are printed in black.* [noun]

2. *Black* can also mean without light or very dark: *Without a moon the night was black.* [adjective]
•**blacker, blackest.**

blackboard (BLAK bord) A *blackboard* is a smooth, hard surface, used for writing or drawing on with chalk. Another word for *blackboard* is *chalkboard.* [noun] •**blackboards.**

blacksmiths

blacksmith (BLAK smith) A *blacksmith* is a person who makes things from iron. *Blacksmiths* also put horseshoes on horses. [noun] •**blacksmiths.**

blanket (BLANG kuht) A *blanket* is a soft, warm covering for a bed: *We bought a new, wool blanket.* [noun] •**blankets.**

bled (BLED) *My nose bled for a minute.* [verb]

bleed (BLEED) If you *bleed,* you lose blood from a cut: *When I cut my knee, it started to bleed.* [verb] •**bleeds, bled, bleeding.**

blew (BLOO) *The wind blew the tree down.* [verb]

blind (BLYND) If you are *blind,* you are not able to see: *The man with the guide dog is blind.* [adjective] •**blinder, blindest.**

blindfold (BLYND fohld)

1. If you *blindfold* someone, you cover that person's eyes: *We blindfolded her for the game.* [verb]
2. A *blindfold* is a piece of cloth that covers the eyes: *We need a blindfold for this game.* [noun] •**blindfolds, blindfolded, blindfolding.** •**blindfolds.**

blizzard (BLIZ erd) A *blizzard* is a big storm with snow and strong winds. [noun] •**blizzards.**

blindfold

block (BLOK)

1. A *block* is a thick piece of wood or plastic: *My little brother held one green block and two blue ones.* [noun]
2. If you *block* something, you fill it so that nothing can pass by: *I saw a large truck block traffic.* [verb]
3. A *block* is also an area of a city that has a street on each side: *I walked down the block to my friend's house.* [noun] •**blocks.** •**blocks, blocked, blocking.**

blood · blow

Bb

blood (BLUHD) *Blood* is the red liquid that flows from a cut in your skin. Your heart pumps *blood* to every part of your body. *Blood* carries food through your body. *[noun]*

bloom (BLOOM) To *bloom* means to have flowers: *Roses bloom every year.* *[verb]* •**blooms, bloomed, blooming.**

blossom (BLOSS uhm)

1. A *blossom* is a flower of a plant that produces fruit: *Can you smell the orange blossoms?* *[noun]*
2. To *blossom* means to have flowers: *The plum trees blossom in the spring.* *[verb]*

•**blossoms.** •**blossoms, blossomed, blossoming.**

blossom

blouse (BLOWSS) A *blouse* is a shirt worn by women and girls: *My favorite blouse is red with big buttons.* *[noun]* •**blouses.**

blow (BLOH)

1. To *blow* means to move air quickly: *A strong wind blew all night. She blew out all the candles on her birthday cake.* *[verb]*
2. To *blow* is also to make a sound by blowing air into something: *He heard the teacher blow the whistle to stop the game.* *[verb]*

•**blows, blew, blown, blowing.**

blouse

Bb

blown (BLOHN) *She has blown up the balloon.* [verb]

blue (BLOO)

1. *Blue* is the color of the clear sky during the day. [noun]
2. If something is *blue,* it has this color: *The water in the lake looks very blue.* [adjective]

•**blues.** •**bluer, bluest.**

blue

blueberry (BLOO bair ee) A *blueberry* is a small, blue fruit. *Blueberries* grow on bushes. [noun] • **blueberries.**

blue jay (BLOO JAY) A *blue jay* is a noisy blue bird.
•**blue jays.**

board (BORD)

1. A *board* is a long, thin, flat piece of wood: *One board on the garage needs painting.* [noun]
2. To *board* something up means to cover it with boards: *We had to board up the windows of the empty house.* [verb]

•**boards.** •**boards, boarded, boarding.**

boat (BOHT) A *boat* is something that carries people and things over the water. A *boat* can be moved by a motor, by sails, or by people rowing. [noun] •**boats.**

boats

body (BOD ee) A *body* is all of a person or animal: *Exercise helps keep your body healthy.* [noun] •**bodies.**

boil (BOIL)

1. To *boil* means to get very hot and give off steam: *Has the water begun to boil yet?* [verb]
2. When you *boil* something, you cook it in boiling water: *Boil the egg three minutes.* [verb]

•**boils, boiled, boiling.**

bone · boring

bone (BOHN) A *bone* is one of the hard parts of the body of a person or animal. *Bones* help hold up the body and protect soft parts inside. [noun] •**bones.**

book (BUK) A *book* is made of sheets of paper put together inside two covers. The pages in this *book* have writing and pictures on them. [noun] •**books.**

books

bookshelf (BUK shelf) A *bookshelf* is a piece of furniture with one or more shelves for holding books. A *bookshelf* can also be one or more shelves attached to a wall. [noun] •**bookshelves.**

boot (BOOT) A *boot* is a heavy covering for the foot and leg: *Where is my left boot?* [noun] •**boots.**

border (BOR der) A *border* is a strip on the edge of anything: *The napkin has a pink border.* [noun] •**borders.**

bore (BOR)

1. To *bore* means to make a hole in something by pushing a tool in it or through it: *The drill bored through the wall.* [verb]

2. If you *bore* people, you make them not want to listen to you: *He bored us by talking about his great new bike.* [verb]
•**bores, bored, boring.**

boring (BOR ing) If something is *boring,* it is dull. *Boring* things are not interesting or fun: *He thought the movie was very boring.* [adjective]

boots

born (BORN) When you're *born,* you're brought into life: *The baby was born yesterday.* [verb]

borrow (BAR oh *or* BOR oh) If you *borrow* something, you get it from a person just for a while: *I like to borrow books from the library.* [verb] •**borrows, borrowed, borrowing.**

borrow

boss (BOSS)
1. A *boss* is a person who gives people jobs or guides them. A *boss* is also a person who is in charge of a project or job: *I told my boss I would be late.* [noun]
2. If you *boss* someone, you try to control that person: *He complained that she was trying to boss him.* [verb] •**bosses.** •**bosses, bossed, bossing.**

both (BOHTH) *Both houses are pink. Both dogs are mine. Both belong to her.* [adjective *or* pronoun]

bother (BOTH er) If you *bother* someone, you make that person angry or annoyed: *Do not bother me while I work.* [verb] •**bothers, bothered, bothering.**

bottle (BOT uhl) A *bottle* is something used to hold liquids. A *bottle* can be made of glass or plastic and usually has a cap. [noun] •**bottles.**

bottom (BOT uhm) The *bottom* is the lowest part of anything: *There are cookies at the bottom of the jar.* [noun] •**bottoms.**

bought (BAWT) *She bought a coat. She has bought a pair of shoes.* [verb]

bottles

bounce • bowling

bounce (BOWNSS)
To *bounce* means to spring back after hitting something: *She made the ball bounce off the wall. She bounced the ball.* [verb] •**bounces, bounced, bouncing.**

bounce

bound (BOWND) To *bound* means to jump quickly: *We watched the deer bound through the woods.* [verb] •**bounds, bounded, bounding.**

bow[1] (BOW)

1. When you *bow,* you bend your head or body towards another person: *He bowed to us.* [verb]
2. A *bow* is a bending of your head or body: *The singer made a deep bow as we clapped.* [noun]

•**bows, bowed, bowing.** •**bows.**

bow[2] (BOH)

1. A *bow* is a strip of wood bent by a string. A *bow* shoots arrows. [noun]
2. A *bow* is also a knot with two small circles. You make a *bow* when you tie your shoe. [noun]
3. A *bow* is also a piece of wood used to play violins and other instruments like violins. [noun]

•**bows.**

bow[3] (BOW) A *bow* is the forward or front part of a ship or boat. [noun] •**bows.**

bowl (BOHL) A *bowl* is a hollow, deep dish: *He ate a bowl of cereal this morning.* [noun] •**bowls.**

bowling (BOH ling) *Bowling* is a game in which you roll a heavy ball at wooden pins to knock them down. [noun]

bowls

box (BOKS) A *box* is something with four sides, a bottom, and a top. *Boxes* are made of wood, metal, or paper: *We put our things in a box.* [noun] •**boxes.**

boxes

boy (BOI) A *boy* is a male child. A *boy* grows up to be a man. [noun] •**boys.**

boy scout (BOI SKOWT) A *boy scout* is someone who belongs to the Boy Scouts of America. This group helps boys grow into healthy, strong young men. •**boy scouts.**

bracelet (BRAY sluht) A *bracelet* is a piece of jewelry worn on the wrist. [noun] •**bracelets.**

braces (BRAY suhz) *Braces* are metal wires used to straighten crooked teeth: *The dentist put braces on my brother's teeth.* [noun plural]

brachiosaurus (brak ee uh SOR uhss) The *brachiosaurus* was a huge dinosaur with a very long neck and a tail. The *brachiosaurus* ate plants. [noun] •**brachiosauruses.**

braids

braid (BRAYD) A *braid* is a band of hair made by weaving hair together: *She liked to wear her hair in a braid.* [noun] •**braids.**

Braille (BRAYL) *Braille* is a way of writing and printing for people who cannot see. In *Braille,* letters and numbers are shown by different groups of raised dots and are read by touching them. [noun]

brain (BRAYN) The *brain* is the part of your body that is inside your head. You use your *brain* to learn, think, and remember. Your *brain* also makes it possible for you to talk and move around. [noun] •**brains.**

Bb

brake (BRAYK) A *brake* is used to stop something or slow it down. Bicycles and automobiles have *brakes.* *[noun]* •**brakes.**

branch (BRANCH) A *branch* is a part of a tree that grows out from the trunk: *A swing hung from the branch. [noun]* •**branches.**

branch

brave (BRAYV) If you are *brave*, you are not afraid: *The brave girl pulled her little brother away from the burning garage.* *[adjective]* •**braver, bravest.**

bread (BRED) *Bread* is food made from flour mixed with milk or water and baked. *[noun]* •**breads.**

break (BRAYK)

1. When you *break* something, you make it fall to pieces or stop working: *I saw the football hit the window and break it. Did he break the radio? [verb]*

2. To *break* also means to fail to keep: *I would never break a promise. [verb]*

3. A *break* is a short rest period: *We had a milk break before recess. [noun]*
•**breaks, broke, broken, breaking.** •**breaks.**

breakfast

breakfast (BREK fuhst) *Breakfast* is a meal eaten at the beginning of the day: *We ate cereal and fruit for breakfast. [noun]* •**breakfasts.**

breath (BRETH) *Breath* is air taken into and sent out of the lungs: *Take a deep breath.* [noun] •**breaths.**

breathe (BREE<u>TH</u>) When you *breathe,* you take air into your lungs and then send it out. [verb] •**breathes, breathed, breathing.**

brick (BRIK) A *brick* is a block of clay that is baked. *Bricks* are used to build walls and sidewalks. [noun] •**bricks.**

bridge (BRIJ) A *bridge* is a road built over water. People walk across *bridges.* Cars and trucks can drive over *bridges.* [noun] •**bridges.**

bridges

broccoli

bright (BRYT) If something is *bright,* it shines and gives a lot of light. *Shining* is another word for *bright: The moon is bright tonight.* [adjective] •**brighter, brightest.**

bring (BRING) When you *bring* something, you carry it from another place: *Please bring me a napkin.* [verb] •**brings, brought, bringing.**

British Columbia (BRIT ish kuh LUHM bee uh) *British Columbia* is one of the ten provinces of Canada. [noun]

broad (BRAWD) If something is *broad,* it is very wide across: *The wagons crossed a broad river.* [adjective] •**broader, broadest.**

broccoli (BROK uh lee) *Broccoli* is a vegetable with green stalks and flower buds. [noun]

broke (BROHK) *Who broke this dish?* [verb]

broken · brush

broken (BROH kuhn) *He has broken a window. [verb]*

brook (BRUK) A *brook* is a small stream of running water. Another word for *brook* is *creek. [noun]*
• **brooks.**

broom (BROOM) A *broom* is a brush with a long handle. A *broom* is used to sweep the floor. *[noun]*
• **brooms.**

brother (BRU<u>TH</u> er) Your *brother* is a boy or man that has the same parents as you do. *[noun]* • **brothers.**

brought (BRAWT) *He brought raisins in his lunch. [verb]*

brothers

brown (BROWN)

1. *Brown* is a dark color like that of chocolate. *[noun]*
2. If something is *brown,* it has a color like that of chocolate: *Many horses are brown. [adjective]*
• **browns.** • **browner, brownest.**

brownie (BROW nee)

1. A *brownie* is an elf or fairy in a story. *Brownies* like to help people. *[noun]*
2. A *Brownie* is someone who belongs to the Girl Scouts of America. *Brownies* are between eight and ten years old. *[noun]*
• **brownies** *for definition 1,* **Brownies** *for definition 2.*

brush (BRUHSH)

1. A *brush* is a tool made of stiff hairs, plastic, or wire. You use one kind of *brush* to paint a house and another kind to clean your teeth. *[noun]*
2. To *brush* means to clean, rub, or paint with a brush: *Brush your teeth. [verb]*
• **brushes.** • **brushes, brushed, brushing.**

Brownie

bubble (BUH buhl) A *bubble* is a round drop of liquid that is filled with air: *Bubbles rose up when she stirred the soap and water.* [noun] •**bubbles.**

bucket (BUHK uht) A *bucket* is something used to carry things in. You can carry water or sand in a *bucket.* Another word for *bucket* is *pail.* [noun] •**buckets.**

buckets

bud (BUHD) A *bud* is a small new growing part on a plant. A *bud* will grow into a flower, leaf, or branch. [noun] •**buds.**

buddy (BUD ee) A *buddy* is a close friend: *He has been my buddy since first grade.* [noun] •**buddies.**

buffalo (BUHF uh loh) A *buffalo* is a large animal with long hair on its head. [noun] •**buffaloes.**

bug (BUHG) A *bug* is anything that crawls or flies like an insect. Ants and flies are often called *bugs.* [noun] •**bugs.**

build (BILD) To *build* means to make something by putting things together: *It takes many people to build a bridge.* [verb] •**builds, built, building.**

bug

building (BIL ding) A *building* is something that has been built. A *building* has walls and a roof. Schools, houses, and barns are *buildings.* [noun] •**buildings.**

built (BILT) *They built a sand castle. They have built two castles today. We built a model car for our class project.* [verb]

bulb · bump

bulb (BUHLB)

1. A *bulb* is a hollow glass light that glows when electricity is turned on. *[noun]*
2. A *bulb* is also a round bud or stem that you plant in the ground: *I grew tulips from a bulb.* *[noun]*
•**bulbs.**

bulb

bull (BUL) A *bull* is a large male cow. A male elephant or buffalo is also called a *bull*. *[noun]* •**bulls.**

bulldozer (BUL doh zer) A *bulldozer* is a heavy machine with a large metal piece in front. *Bulldozers* are used to clear trees away. They can also make flat areas where roads or buildings are to be built. *[noun]* •**bulldozers.**

bullet (BUL it) A *bullet* is a small piece of metal that is shot from a gun. *[noun]* •**bullets.**

bulletin board

Summer!

bulletin board (BUL uh tuhn BORD) A *bulletin board* is a board that you put news, notes, or notices on. •**bulletin boards.**

bumblebee (BUHM buhl bee) A *bumblebee* is a large bee which makes a loud buzzing sound. *[noun]* •**bumblebees.**

bump (BUHMP)

1. When you *bump* something, you hit against it: *I was careful not to bump into her when I ran around the corner. She bumped her arm against the door.* *[verb]*
2. A *bump* is a place that swells up from being hit: *He got a bump on the head when he fell down.* *[noun]*
•**bumps, bumped, bumping.** •**bumps.**

bumpy (BUHM pee) If something is *bumpy*, it is rough or has a lot of bumps: *The plane ride was very bumpy. This street is too bumpy to skate on.* [adjective]
•**bumpier, bumpiest.**

bun (BUHN) A *bun* is a long or round piece of bread. Hamburgers or hot dogs are put on *buns.* [noun]
•**buns.**

bunch (BUHNCH) A *bunch* is a group of things that are alike: *He ate a bunch of grapes for lunch. She gathered a bunch of flowers after school.* [noun] •**bunches.**

bunch

bundle (BUHN duhl) A *bundle* is a number of things tied up together or wrapped together: *She carried a bundle of newspapers down to the basement.* [noun]
•**bundles.**

bunny (BUHN ee) *Bunny* is another word for *rabbit: A bunny ran across the yard.* [noun] •**bunnies.**

burn (BERN)

1. To *burn* means to be on fire or to set on fire: *The fire will burn all night. We burned several logs in the fireplace.* [verb]

2. A *burn* is a sore caused by too much heat: *He got a burn on his arm from the hot iron.* [noun]

•**burns, burned, burning.** •**burns.**

burrow (BER oh)

1. A *burrow* is a hole that an animal digs in the ground. Rabbits live in *burrows.* [noun]

bunny

2. To *burrow* means to dig a hole in the ground: *Did you see the rabbit burrow under the bush?* [verb]
•burrows. •burrows, burrowed, burrowing.

burst (BERST)

1. To *burst* means to fly apart suddenly: *That balloon burst as I was blowing it up.* [verb]

2. To *burst* can also mean to go into or come out of suddenly: *He burst into the room without knocking.* [verb]

•**bursts, burst, bursting.**

burst

bury (BAIR ee)

1. When you *bury* something, you put it in the ground: *The children wanted to bury their dead pet.* [verb]

2. To *bury* can also mean to hide something or cover it up: *It was so cold that she buried her head under the covers.* [verb]

•**buries, buried, burying.**

bus

bus (BUHSS) A *bus* is a large machine with a lot of seats for people to ride in. *Buses* carry people along certain streets or roads. [noun] •**buses.**

bush (BUSH) A *bush* is a plant that is smaller than a tree. A *bush* has branches that start near the ground. Some *bushes* are grown for their flowers, and some for their fruit. [noun] •**bushes.**

bushy (BUSH ee) If something is *bushy,* it spreads out like a bush: *Squirrels have bushy tails.* [adjective] •**bushier, bushiest.**

Bb

business (BIZ niss) *Business* is work done to make money: *What business is your father in?* [noun]
•**businesses.**

busy (BIZ ee) If you are *busy*, you have a lot to do: *The principal is a busy person. We were busy playing outside.* [adjective] •**busier, busiest.**

but (BUHT) *You may go, but you may not stay late. We wanted to go to the movie, but we couldn't. You can have any crayon but the red one.* [conjunction or preposition]

butcher (BUCH er) A *butcher* is a person who cuts and sells meat. [noun] •**butchers.**

butter (BUHT er)

1. *Butter* is a soft yellow food made from cream. [noun]
2. When you *butter* something, you put butter on it: *Please butter my toast for me.* [verb]
•**butters, buttered, buttering.**

butterfly (BUHT er fly) A *butterfly* is an insect with a small, narrow body. *Butterflies* have four large, bright-colored wings. [noun]
•**butterflies.**

button (BUHT uhn)

1. A *button* is a flat, round piece of plastic or metal. *Buttons* keep clothes together. A shirt has *buttons* down the front. [noun]
2. To *button* means to put buttons into holes: *It was hard for him to button his shirt.* [verb]
3. A *button* is also a part you push to make something work: *When she pushed the button, the bell rang.* [noun]
•**buttons.** •**buttons, buttoned, buttoning.**

business

butterfly

buy • by

Bb

buzz

buy (BY) When you *buy* something, you get it by paying money for it: *Can you buy me a pencil for school?* [verb] •**buys, bought, buying.**

buzz (BUHZ)

1. A *buzz* is the humming sound made by flies, mosquitoes, or bees: *The loud buzz of a fly woke me up.* [noun]

2. To *buzz* means to make a steady humming sound: *Mosquitoes buzz outside the screen.* [verb]
•**buzzes.** •**buzzes, buzzed, buzzing.**

by (BY) *Stand by the door. She went by the river road. She travels by bus. Be here by twelve o'clock.* [preposition]

She travels *by* bus.

cab (KAB) A *cab* is a car with a driver that you pay to take you somewhere. *[noun]* •**cabs.**

cabin (KAB in) A *cabin* is a small house: *They have a log cabin in the woods.* *[noun]* •**cabins.**

caboose (kuh BOOSS) A *caboose* is a small railroad car. The *caboose* is often the last car of a train. Some of the train crew ride in the *caboose.* *[noun]* •**cabooses.**

cactus (KAK tuhss) A *cactus* is a plant with sharp parts but no leaves. Most *cactuses* grow in very hot, dry areas of North and South America. Many have bright flowers. *[noun]* •**cactuses.**

cafeteria (kaf uh TEER ee uh) A *cafeteria* is a place to eat in a school, office building, or factory. You choose your food and carry it to a table. *[noun]* •**cafeterias.**

caboose

cage · call

Cc

cage (KAYJ) A *cage* is a box or place closed in with wires or bars. Birds and wild animals are kept in *cages*. *[noun]* •**cages.**

cake (KAYK) A *cake* is a sweet food. *Cakes* are made from flour, sugar, eggs, and other things. *[noun]* •**cakes.**

cake

calculator (KAL kyuh lay ter) A *calculator* is a machine that is used to find the answers to number problems. When numbers and symbols on a *calculator* are pressed, answers appear on a screen. *[noun]* •**calculators.**

calendar (KAL uhn der) A *calendar* is a chart showing the months, weeks, and days of the year. *[noun]* •**calendars.**

calf[1] (KAF) A *calf* is a baby cow, elephant, seal, or whale. *[noun]* •**calves.**

calf[2] (KAF) Your *calf* is the back of your leg below your knee. *[noun]* •**calves.**

California (kal uh FOR nyuh) *California* is one of the fifty states of the United States. *[noun]*

call (KAWL)

1. If you *call,* you speak loudly, shout, or cry out: *Can you call for help?* *[verb]*

2. If you *call* someone, you talk to them on the telephone: *Call me when you get home.* *[verb]*

3. To *call* someone can also mean to ask or order them to come: *Please call your brother to dinner.* *[verb]*

call

Can I speak to Julie?

4. *Shout* is another word for *call*: *I don't think they heard my call.* [noun]

5. *Call* can also mean to give something a name: *We call our dog Brownie.* [verb]

6. A *call* can also be the special sound that a bird or animal makes: *We sat in the yard and listened for the bird call.* [noun]
•**calls, called, calling.** •**calls.**

calm (KAHM) If you are *calm,* you are quiet and still. People and things can both be called *calm*: *The lake is calm today. She was frightened, but she answered with a calm voice.* [adjective] •**calmer, calmest.**

calves (KAVZ) *Calves* is the plural of the word *calf*: *We saw several calves in the field with the cows. My calves hurt from running.* [noun plural]

calves

camcorder (KAM kor der) A *camcorder* is a TV camera and video recorder together. [noun] •**camcorders.**

came (KAYM) *They came to our house for dinner.* [verb]

camel (KAM uhl) A *camel* is a large animal that can go a long time without water. *Camels* are used to carry people and things in the desert. [noun] •**camels.**

camera (KAM uh ruh) A *camera* is a machine for taking pictures or making movies. [noun] •**cameras.**

camera

camp (KAMP)

1. A *camp* is a group of tents or cabins where people live for a while: *I spent a week at summer camp. We set up camp near the river.* [noun]

Campeche · candle

2. To *camp* means to live outdoors or in a tent for a while: *We will camp in the woods for five days.* [verb]
•**camps.** •**camps, camped, camping.**

Campeche (kahm PAY chay) *Campeche* is a state in southeast Mexico. [noun]

campground
(KAMP grownd) A *campground* is a place for camping, especially one with fireplaces for cooking. [noun]
•**campgrounds.**

campground

can¹ (KUHN *or* KAN) *She can run fast. Can we go to the circus next week?* [verb] •**could.**

can² (KAN) A *can* is a round, metal thing used to hold other things: *I opened a can of soup. He bought a can of red paint.* [noun] •**cans.**

Canada (KAN uh duh) *Canada* is the country north of the United States. [noun]

Canadian (kuh NAY dee uhn)

1. A *Canadian* is a person born or living in Canada. [noun]

2. Something that is *Canadian* is from Canada or belongs to Canada: *The Canadian flag has a maple leaf on it.* [adjective]
•**Canadians.**

candles

candle (KAN duhl) A *candle* is a stick of wax with a string inside it. As the string burns, the *candle* gives light. [noun] •**candles.**

candy (KAN dee)
Candy is a sweet food made of sugar or syrup. It often has chocolate, fruit, or nuts mixed in. *[noun]* •**candies.**

candy

cane (KAYN) A *cane* is a stick used to help a person walk. *[noun]* •**canes.**

cannot (ka NOT *or* kuh NOT) *He cannot come to the party.* *[verb]*

canoe (kuh NOO) A *canoe* is a small boat that a person moves with a paddle. *[noun]* •**canoes.**

can't *Can't* is a shorter form of *cannot: I can't go with you tomorrow.* *[contraction]*

cantaloupe (KAN tuh lohp) A *cantaloupe* is a large fruit that is hard and rough on the outside and soft and orange inside. *Cantaloupes* are melons and grow on vines. *[noun]* •**cantaloupes.**

canyon (KAN yuhn) A *canyon* is a narrow valley with high, steep sides. A *canyon* usually has a stream at the bottom. *[noun]* •**canyons.**

cap (KAP)

1. A *cap* is a soft covering for your head: *I can't find my baseball cap.* *[noun]*
2. A *cap* is also anything that covers the top of something. The top of a bottle, tube, or pen is a *cap.* *[noun]*
•**caps.**

caps

capital · care

Cc

capital (KAP uh tuhl)

1. The *capital* of a nation or state is the city where laws are made. Washington, D.C., is the *capital* of the United States. Every state has a *capital*. [noun]

capital

2. A, B, C, D, or any other large letter is also called a *capital*. Your name starts with a *capital*. [noun]
• **capitals.**

capsule (KAP suhl)

1. A *capsule* is a tiny bit of medicine. [noun]
2. A *capsule* is also the front section of a rocket made to carry tools or astronauts into space. [noun]
• **capsules.**

car (KAR)

1. A *car* is a machine that people ride in. A *car* has an engine and four wheels. Another word for *car* is *automobile*. [noun]
2. A *car* is also part of a train. A train *car* can have places to sit, sleep, and eat, or it can carry things. [noun]
• **cars.**

car

card (KARD) A *card* is a flat piece of stiff paper or plastic. You can take out books with a library *card*. You might receive a funny *card* on your birthday. Some games are played with *cards*. [noun] • **cards.**

cardinal (KARD uh nuhl) A *cardinal* is a small, bright red bird with a thick bill. [noun] • **cardinals.**

care (KAIR)

1. If you *care* for something or someone, you watch out for or are in charge of that person or thing: *Will you care for my cat while I am away?* [verb]

2. If you *care* about something, you like it or are interested in it: *I only care about playing baseball.* [verb]

3. *Care* is great thought or attention: *Please take care to do the job right.* [noun]
•**cares, cared, caring.** •**cares.**

careful (KAIR fuhl)

1. Being *careful* means thinking about what you do and paying attention to it: *Be careful when you cross the street.* [adjective]

2. If you do something in a *careful* way, you do it with thought and attention: *She does careful work.* [adjective]

careful

carefully (KAIR fuhl ee) If you do something *carefully*, you do it in a careful way: *Pick up that box carefully.* [adverb]

careless (KAIR luhss) If you are *careless*, you are not thinking about what you are doing: *She was careless and broke the cup.* [adjective]

carpenter (KAR puhn ter) A *carpenter* is a person who builds and repairs things made of wood. [noun] •**carpenters.**

carrot (KA ruht) A *carrot* is a long, orange vegetable that grows underground. *Carrots* are eaten cooked or raw. [noun] •**carrots.**

carry (KA ree) When you *carry* something, you take it from one place to another: *We carried the groceries into the house.* [verb] •**carries, carried, carrying.**

carry

I can carry my toy to my room.

car seat • cassette

car seat (KAR SEET) A *car seat* is a special chair for babies or young children. It attaches to the seat of a car with a seat belt. *Car seats* should always be put in the back seat of a car if possible. •**car seats.**

cart (KART) A *cart* is a kind of wagon used for carrying things from place to place. A grocery *cart* is a metal basket on four wheels. Other *carts* are wooden and can be pulled by animals. *[noun]* •**carts.**

cart

carton (KART uhn) A *carton* is a small paper box: *I bought a carton of milk. [noun]* •**cartons.**

cartoon (kar TOON)
1. A *cartoon* is a short, funny movie made of several pictures put together. *[noun]*
2. A *cartoon* is also a funny drawing, often found in newspapers or magazines. *[noun]*
•**cartoons.**

cashier

cash (KASH) *Cash* is money in the form of coins and paper money: *This store accepts only cash, no checks. [noun]*

cashier (ka SHEER) A *cashier* is a person in charge of taking customers' money and making change in a store or a bank. *[noun]* •**cashiers.**

cash machine (KASH muh SHEEN) A *cash machine* is a bank machine that gives out cash. People use a *cash machine* instead of a bank. •**cash machines.**

cassette (kuh SET) A *cassette* is a container holding special tape for recording and playing back pictures, sound, or computer information. *[noun]* •**cassettes.**

cast (KAST) A *cast* is a hard covering used to shape or hold something: *The doctor put a cast on my broken leg.* [noun] •**casts.**

castle (KASS uhl) A *castle* is a large stone building with thick walls and a tower. Long ago, kings and queens lived in *castles.* [noun] •**castles.**

castles

cat (KAT) A *cat* is a small, furry animal often kept as a pet. Many *cats* like to chase mice. [noun] •**cats.**

catch (KACH) To *catch* means to take and hold something that is moving: *I caught the ball with one hand.* [verb] •**catches, caught, catching.**

catcher

catcher (KACH er) A *catcher* is a baseball player who stands behind the batter and catches the balls thrown by the pitcher. [noun] •**catchers.**

caterpillar (KAT er pil er) A *caterpillar* is an insect that looks like a furry worm. *Caterpillars* turn into moths or butterflies. [noun] •**caterpillars.**

cattle (KAT uhl) *Cattle* are animals raised for their meat, milk, or skins. Cows and bulls are *cattle.* [noun plural]

caught (KAWT) *My uncle caught a fish. I caught the ball. My sister has caught a bad cold.* [verb]

cause (KAWZ)

1. A *cause* is something that makes something else happen: *Lightning was the cause of the fire.* [noun]
2. When you *cause* something, you make it happen: *The storm caused the accident.* [verb]
•**causes.** •**causes, caused, causing.**

67

cave · cellar

cave (KAYV) A *cave* is a hollow space in the side of a hill or mountain. *Caves* are usually underground. *[noun]* •**caves**.

CD (SEE DEE) *CD* is a short form of the words *compact disc. [noun]*

CD-ROM (SEE DEE ROM) A *CD-ROM* is a compact disc you use with a computer. It can show words, pictures, movies, and play sounds. *[noun]*

ceiling (SEE ling) The *ceiling* is the part of a room opposite the floor. Lights can hang from the *ceiling.* *[noun]* •**ceilings**.

celebrate (SEL uh brayt) When you *celebrate,* you do something special in honor of a special person or day: *We celebrate our birthdays with big parties.* *[verb]* •**celebrates, celebrated, celebrating.** celebrate

celebration (sel uh BRAY shuhn) A *celebration* is a special activity for a special person or day: *We had a birthday celebration. [noun]* •**celebrations**.

celery (SEL uh ree) *Celery* is a long, greenish-white vegetable. *Celery* grows in stalks and can be eaten cooked or raw. *[noun]*

cell (SEL) A *cell* is a very small piece of living matter. All living things are made up of *cells. [noun]* •**cells**.

cellar (SEL er) A *cellar* is a space under a building. *Cellars* can be used to store food, tools, or other things. *[noun]* •**cellars**.

celery

We love celery!

cello (CHEL oh) A *cello* is a musical instrument with strings. It is like a violin but much larger, and it has a lower sound. *[noun]* •**cellos.**

cello

cement (suh MENT) *Cement* is a fine, gray powder. *Cement* is mixed with water to make concrete. *[noun]*

cent (SENT) A *cent* is the smallest amount of money in the United States and Canada. One hundred *cents* make one dollar. *[noun]* •**cents.**

center (SEN ter)
1. The *center* is the middle part of something: *The vase was in the center of the table.* *[noun]*
2. A *center* is also a place people go for a certain purpose: *We skate at the sports center.* *[noun]*
•**centers.**

central (SEN truhl) If something is *central,* it is at the center or near the center of something else. *[adjective]*

centimeter (SEN tuh mee ter) A *centimeter* is a unit of length about this long: ——— . There are 100 *centimeters* in a meter. *[noun]* •**centimeters.**

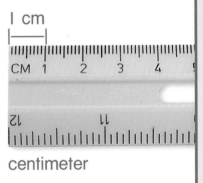
centimeter

cereal (SEER ee uhl) *Cereal* is a food made from wheat, corn, rice, or other grains. Many people eat *cereal* with milk for breakfast. *[noun]* •**cereals.**

certain (SERT uhn)
1. If you are *certain* about something, you are very sure: *I am certain I am right.* *[adjective]*
2. *Certain* can also mean some but not all: *Certain plants grow in dry soil.* *[adjective]*

certainly · change

chalk

certainly (SERT uhn lee) If you say that you will *certainly* do something, you are very sure that you will do that thing: *I will certainly be there.* [adverb]

chair (CHAIR) A *chair* is a seat with a back and four legs and, sometimes, arms. [noun] •**chairs.**

chalk (CHAWK) *Chalk* is a soft, white rock used for writing or drawing. *Chalk* is often used on a chalkboard. [noun]

chalkboard (CHAWK bord) A *chalkboard* is a smooth, hard surface on which you can write or draw with chalk. Another word for *chalkboard* is *blackboard.* [noun] •**chalkboards.**

chameleon (kuh MEE lee uhn) A *chameleon* is a small lizard. *Chameleons* change the color of their skin depending on their environment. [noun] •**chameleons.**

chance (CHANSS)

1. A *chance* is a good time to do something: *I had a chance to visit Washington, D.C.* [noun]
2. A *chance* is also an event that is possible: *There is a chance that it may snow.* [noun]
•**chances.**

change (CHAYNJ)

1. To *change* means to make or become different: *We will change the color of our house from white to yellow.* [verb]

change

2. A *change* is something different that happens: *Since it rained, we had to make a change in our picnic plans.* [noun]

3. To *change* also means to put different clothes on: *Please change that dirty shirt.* [verb]

4. *Change* is also the money you get back when you pay too much: *I gave the cashier ten dollars and got fifty cents change.* [noun]

•**changes, changed, changing.** •**changes** *for definition 2.*

chapter (CHAP ter) A *chapter* is one of the main parts of a book. [noun] •**chapters.**

character (KA rik ter) A *character* is a person or animal in a story. [noun] •**characters.**

charge (CHARJ)

1. To *charge* means to ask as a price: *My friend charged me ten dollars to fix my computer.* [verb]

2. To *charge* also means to buy something now and pay for it later: *We can charge my new shoes today and pay the bill at the end of the month.* [verb]

•**charges, charged, charging.**

chart (CHART) A *chart* is a list or drawing that shows facts: *This chart shows the amount of snow we had last winter.* [noun] •**charts.**

chase (CHAYSS) When you *chase* someone, you run after them: *Some cats chase mice. The children chased the ball down the hill.* [verb] •**chases, chased, chasing.**

chat (CHAT) A *chat* is an easy, friendly talk: *The grandparents had a chat about old times.* [noun] •**chats.**

chart

Snowfall

cheap (CHEEP) If something is *cheap,* it has a low price: *Fresh carrots are cheap in the summer.* [adjective] •**cheaper, cheapest.**

check (CHEK)

1. When you *check* something, you prove it is true or right by comparing it with something else that you know is right: *I always check my answers against those at the back of the book.* [verb]

check

2. To *check* can also mean to look for information and advice from something: *Check the dictionary if you don't know how to spell a word.* [verb]

3. A *check* is a mark (✓) to show that something has been looked at or compared: *Put a check next to the answers that are correct.* [noun]

4. A *check* is also a written order for money from a bank: *We wrote a check to pay the bill.* [noun]
•**checks, checked, checking.** •**checks.**

checker

checker (CHEK er)

1. A *checker* is a piece used in the game of checkers. [noun]

2. A *checker* is also the person you pay for the things you buy at a supermarket or store. Another word for *checker* is *cashier.* [noun] •**checkers.**

checkerboard

checkerboard (CHEK er bord) A *checkerboard* is a board marked with 64 squares. 32 of the squares are one color, and 32 are another color. A *checkerboard* is used to play checkers or chess. [noun]
•**checkerboards.**

I am checking my answers.

checkers (CHEK erz) *Checkers* is a game played by two people, each with 12 flat, round pieces to move on a checkerboard. Each piece is called a *checker*. [noun]

cheek (CHEEK) Your *cheek* is the part of your face just below your eye. [noun] •**cheeks.**

cheek

cheer (CHEER) When you *cheer,* you call out or yell loudly to show you like something: *Let's cheer for our team.* [verb] •**cheers, cheered, cheering.**

cheerful (CHEER fuhl) If you are *cheerful,* you are full of good feelings and very glad: *She is a smiling, cheerful girl.* [adjective]

cheese (CHEEZ) *Cheese* is a solid food made from milk: *I like cheese and crackers.* [noun]

chef (SHEF) A *chef* is a cook, especially the cook in charge of a big restaurant. [noun] •**chefs.**

cherry (CHAIR ee) A *cherry* is a small, round, red fruit that grows on trees. *Cherries* have hard seeds. [noun] •**cherries.**

chess (CHESS) *Chess* is a game played by two people. Each player has 16 pieces. The pieces can be moved in different ways on a checkerboard. [noun]

chest (CHEST)
1. Your *chest* is the front part of your body between your neck and your stomach. [noun]

chef

chew · child

2. A *chest* is also a large box with a heavy top: *The pirates buried a chest filled with jewels and coins.* [noun] •**chests.**

chew (CHOO) When you *chew* something, you crush it with your teeth: *Chew your food well before swallowing.* [verb] •**chews, chewed, chewing.**

chew

Chiapas (chee AH pahss) *Chiapas is a state in the east part of Mexico.* [noun]

chick (CHIK) A *chick* is a young chicken. [noun] •**chicks.**

chicken (CHIK uhn)

1. A *chicken* is a bird raised for food. Hens and roosters are *chickens.* [noun]
2. *Chicken* is the meat of this bird used for food: *I like fried chicken.* [noun] •**chickens** *for definition 1.*

chief (CHEEF) A *chief* is the leader or head of a group: *She is the chief of police. Red Cloud was an American Indian chief.* [noun] •**chiefs.**

Chihuahua (chee WAH wah) *Chihuahua is a state in the north part of Mexico.* [noun]

child (CHYLD)

1. A *child* is a young girl or boy: *That child is only two years old.* [noun]

child

This is my child Pete.

2. A *child* is also a son or daughter: *My mother is my grandfather's only child.* [noun]
•**children.**

children (CHILD ruhn)

1. *Children* are young boys and girls: *There are a lot of new children in our school this year.* [noun plural]

2. *Children* can also mean sons and daughters: *Their children are still in school.* [noun plural]

chimney (CHIM nee) A *chimney* is a tall, hollow tower built to carry away smoke from a fireplace or furnace. [noun] •**chimneys.**

chimpanzee (chim pan ZEE) A *chimpanzee* is an animal with long arms and no tail. *Chimpanzees* are small apes. [noun] •**chimpanzees.**

chimpanzee

chin (CHIN) Your *chin* is the part of your face below your mouth. [noun] •**chins.**

chip (CHIP)

1. A *chip* is a small, thin piece of something: *We used chips of wood to start the fire.* [noun]

2. When you *chip* something, you break a small, thin piece from it: *I saw him chip the cup when he knocked it against the table.* [verb]
•**chips.** •**chips, chipped, chipping.**

chipmunk

chipmunk (CHIP muhnk) A *chipmunk* is a small, striped animal like a squirrel. *Chipmunks* live underground. [noun] •**chipmunks.**

chirpy · choose

Cc

chirpy (CHERP ee) If something is *chirpy,* it makes short, sharp sounds like those some small birds and insects make: *She has a chirpy watch that makes a noise every hour.* [adjective] •**chirpier, chirpiest.**

chocolate (CHOK luht)

1. *Chocolate* is a powder or syrup made from the seeds of a certain tree. It has a rich, sweet taste. [noun]

2. *Chocolate* is also candy made with chocolate: *They gave us a box of chocolates.* [noun]
•**chocolates** *for definition 2.*

chocolate

choice (CHOISS)

1. When you make a *choice,* you pick something out from a group: *I had to make a choice as to which book to read.* [noun]

2. Your *choice* is the person or thing you picked or chose: *He is my choice for president.* [noun]
•**choices.**

choke (CHOHK) If you *choke,* you cannot breathe because something is blocking your throat: *I started to choke on a piece of meat.* [verb] •**chokes, choked, choking.**

If you choke, you you should raise your arms.

choke

choose (CHOOZ) When you *choose* something, you pick it out from a group: *Will you help me choose a new hat?* [verb] •**chooses, chose, chosen, choosing.**

Cc

chop (CHOP) To *chop* means to cut by hitting with something sharp: *He used an ax to chop the tree down. [verb]* •**chops, chopped, chopping.**

chore (CHOR)
1. A *chore* is a small or easy job that you have to do often: *Feeding our pets is my daily chore. [noun]*
2. A *chore* is also a difficult or disagreeable thing to do: *Painting the house is a real chore. [noun]*
•**chores.**

chose (CHOHZ) *We chose to see the movie about robots. [verb]*

chosen (CHOH zuhn) *He was chosen to be the leader. [verb]*

chow (CHOW) *Chow is another word for food: I would rather eat at the place where we get the best chow. [noun]*

Christmas (KRISS muhss) *Christmas* is December 25, a day when some people give gifts and go to church. *[noun]* •**Christmases.**

church (CHERCH) A *church* is a building where some people go to worship. *[noun]*
•**churches.**

circle (SER kuhl)
1. A *circle* is a round line. A ring is a *circle. [noun]*
2. A *circle* is also anything round like a circle: *Sit in a circle on the rug. [noun]*
3. When you *circle* something, you draw a circle around it: *Circle the correct answer. [verb]*
•**circles.** •**circles, circled, circling.**

circles

Cc

circus • classmate

circus (SER kuhss) A *circus* is a show that travels from place to place. A *circus* has clowns, horses, acrobats, and wild animals. *[noun]* •**circuses.**

city (SIT ee) A *city* is a large, important town with many people living in it. Washington, D.C., and New York are *cities. [noun]* •**cities.**

clam (KLAM) A *clam* is a sea animal with a soft body inside a hard shell. Its shell has two halves. *[noun]* •**clams.**

clap (KLAP)

1. When you *clap,* you hit your hands together to make a sound: *We clap to the music. We clapped for the actors. [verb]*

clap

2. A *clap* is a sudden loud noise: *We heard a clap of thunder. [noun]*
•**claps, clapped, clapping.** •**claps.**

clarinet (kla ruh NET) A *clarinet* is a plastic or wooden musical instrument that is played by blowing into it and pressing keys. *[noun]* •**clarinets.**

class (KLASS) A *class* is a group of students learning together: *Our class is working on a project. [noun]* •**classes.**

classmate (KLASS mayt) Your *classmate* is a person in your class in school. *[noun]* •**classmates.**

classmates

78

classroom (KLASS room) A *classroom* is a room in a school in which classes are held. *[noun]* •**classrooms.**

claw (KLAW)

1. A *claw* is one of the sharp, curved nails on the foot of an animal or bird. *[noun]*
2. A *claw* is also part of a lobster or crab's body. *[noun]*
•**claws.**

clay (KLAY) *Clay* is a soft rock that comes from the earth. Wet *clay* can be shaped easily. It becomes hard when it dries. *[noun]*

clean (KLEEN)

1. When something is *clean,* there is no dirt on it: *Please put on clean clothes.* *[adjective]*
2. When you *clean* something, you take away any dirt that is on it: *We clean the kitchen floor every week.* *[verb]*
•**cleaner, cleanest.** •**cleans, cleaned, cleaning.**

clear (KLEER)

1. Something that is *clear* is bright: *A clear sky is free of clouds.* *[adjective]*
2. If something is *clear,* it is easy to see through: *I poured the milk into a clear glass.* *[adjective]*
3. When something is *clear,* it is easy to hear, see, or understand: *Everyone understood her clear directions.* *[adjective]*
4. If you *clear* something, you make it clean or open: *Please clear the table. I cleared my throat.* *[verb]*
•**clearer, clearest.** •**clears, cleared, clearing.**

clean

clear

clerk · clock

Cc

clerk (KLERK) A *clerk* is a person who sells things in a store or shop. *[noun]* •**clerks.**

clever (KLEV er) A *clever* person is quick at learning and understanding: *My clever friend won a math contest.* Another word for *clever* is *smart.* *[adjective]* •**cleverer, cleverest.**

click (KLIK)

1. A *click* is a short, sharp sound: *I heard a click as the key turned in the lock.* *[noun]*
2. To *click* is to make a short, sharp sound: *Wait for the key to click in the lock.* *[verb]* •**clicks.** •**clicks, clicked, clicking.**

cliff (KLIF) A *cliff* is the steep, rocky side of a hill. *[noun]* •**cliffs.**

cliff

climb (KLYM) When you *climb,* you go up something, usually by using your hands and feet: *We climb hills. The children climbed into the bus.* *[verb]* •**climbs, climbed, climbing.**

clip¹ (KLIP) If you *clip* something, you cut it, trim it, or cut it off: *Barbers clip people's hair. Mom clipped the bushes in our yard.* *[verb]* •**clips, clipped, clipping.**

clip² (KLIP) If you *clip* something, you attach it to something else so the two things hold together: *Clip the note to the paper.* *[verb]* •**clips, clipped, clipping.**

clock (KLOK) A *clock* is a thing that shows what time it is. Some *clocks* have hands that point to the hour and the minute. Other *clocks* show the time only with numbers. *[noun]* •**clocks.**

clock

80

close[1] (KLOHZ)

1. To *close* something means to shut it: *Please close the door. Close your eyes.* [verb]

2. If something *closes,* it shuts, finishes, or ends: *The store closes every day at five o'clock. That museum exhibit closes next week.* [verb]
•**closes, closed, closing.**

close[2] (KLOHSS) If you are *close* to something, there is not much space between you and it. Something that is *close* is near: *The houses were built close together.* [adjective] •**closer, closest.**

closely (KLOHSS lee)

closely

1. If you follow someone *closely,* you do not leave much space between you and the other person: *The puppy followed closely behind the boy.* [adverb]

2. If you do something *closely,* you do it in a careful way or completely: *Watch closely while I do this trick.* [adverb]

clothes

closet (KLOZ uht) A *closet* is a small room used to store clothes, shoes, or other things: *Please put your coat in the closet.* [noun] •**closets.**

cloth (KLAWTH) *Cloth* is wool, cotton, silk, or any other material. *Cloth* is used to make clothes, curtains, and other things. [noun]

clothes (KLOHZ) *Clothes* are things you wear on your body. Dresses, pants, shirts, sweaters, and jeans are *clothes.* [noun plural]

clothing · coach

Cc

clothing (KLOH thing) *Clothing* is another word for *clothes: People need food and clothing.* [noun]

cloud (KLOWD) A *cloud* is a white or gray shape floating high in the sky. *Clouds* are made up of tiny drops of water or ice. [noun] •**clouds.**

clown (KLOWN) A *clown* is a person who dresses in funny clothes and tries to make people laugh: *The clown tripped over a bucket and slid into a row of pies.* [noun] •**clowns.**

club (KLUHB)
1. A *club* is a group of people joined together for some special reason: *My sister belongs to the science club.* [noun]
2. A *club* is also a large stick, thicker at one end than the other. A *club* can be used as a weapon. [noun] •**clubs.**

clue (KLOO) A *clue* is something that helps you find an answer to a question or puzzle: *Give me a clue so I can answer the riddle.* [noun] •**clues.**

clue

clumsy (KLUM zee) A *clumsy* person does not move easily: *The cast on my broken leg made me clumsy.* [adjective] •**clumsier, clumsiest.**

coaches

coach (KOHCH)
1. A *coach* is a person who teaches or trains others: *My swimming coach says I'm doing well.* [noun]
2. When you *coach* someone, you train or teach them: *My brother and I coach the baseball team together.* [verb]
•**coaches.** •**coaches, coached, coaching.**

Coahuila (kwah WEE lah) *Coahuila* is a state in the north part of Mexico. [*noun*]

coal (KOHL) *Coal* is a black rock that gives off heat when it is burned. *Coal* comes from plants that died millions of years ago. [*noun*]

coast (KOHST)

1. The *coast* is the land along the sea: *We sailed along the coast.* Another word for *coast* is shore. [*noun*]

2. When you *coast*, you slide down a hill on a sled or ride a bike without pedaling: *I like to coast down the hill on my bike.* [*verb*]

•**coasts.** •**coasts, coasted, coasting.**

coast

coat (KOHT)

1. A *coat* is a piece of clothing worn over other clothes: *My new winter coat is very warm.* [*noun*]

2. A *coat* is also an animal's hair, fur, or wool: *Collies have a thick coat.* [*noun*]

3. A *coat* is also a thin layer of something: *This wall needs another coat of paint.* [*noun*]

•**coats.**

cocoa (KOH koh)

1. *Cocoa* is a powder made from the seeds of a certain tree. It tastes like chocolate. [*noun*]

2. *Cocoa* is also a drink made from cocoa: *We drank hot cocoa after playing in the snow.* [*noun*]

cocoa

coconut · Colima

Cc

coconut (KOH kuh nuht) A *coconut* is a large, round fruit with a very hard, brown shell. The inside of a *coconut* is white and sweet. *Coconuts* grow on a certain kind of palm tree. *[noun]* •**coconuts.**

cocoon (kuh KOON) A *cocoon* is the covering made by caterpillars to live in while they are turning into moths or butterflies. *[noun]* •**cocoons.**

cocoons

code (KOHD) A *code* is letters, numbers, or words used instead of ordinary writing to write a secret message: *My friends and I write to each other in code.* *[noun]* •**codes.**

cold

coffee (KAW fee) *Coffee* is a hot drink made from special seeds. *[noun]* •**coffees.**

coin (KOIN) A *coin* is a piece of metal used as money. Pennies, nickels, dimes, and quarters are *coins.* *[noun]* •**coins.**

cold (KOHLD)

1. Something that is *cold* is not hot, or not as warm as your body: *Snow and ice are cold.* *[adjective]*
2. *Cold* is a cold temperature or cold weather outside: *Come in out of the cold.* *[noun]*
3. A *cold* is a sickness that makes you cough and sneeze: *Did you catch a cold last winter?* *[noun]*
•**colder, coldest.** •**colds** *for definition 3.*

Colima (koh LEE mah) *Colima* is a state in the southwest part of Mexico. *[noun]*

Cc

collar (KOL er)

1. A *collar* is the part of a coat, dress, or shirt that goes around the neck. *[noun]*
2. A *collar* is also a band that is put around the neck of a dog or other pet. *Collars* can be made of leather or plastic. *[noun]*
•**collars.**

collect (kuh LEKT) If you *collect* things, you bring them together or gather them together: *The student collected the crayons. The teacher collected money for the field trip. [verb]* •**collects, collected, collecting.**

collect

collection (kuh LEK shuhn) A *collection* is a group of things that are from many places but are brought together: *The stamps in his collection are from fifty different countries. [noun]* •**collections.**

collie (KOL ee) A *collie* is a large dog that makes a good pet. *Collies* are used to protect sheep and other farm animals. *[noun]* •**collies.**

color (KUHL er)

1. A *color* is either red, yellow, blue, or any of these colors mixed together: *I have eight colors of crayons. [noun]*
2. If you *color* something, you paint or mark it with color, or you put color on it: *She likes to color during free time. [verb]*
•**colors.** •**colors, colored, coloring.**

Colorado (kol uh RAD oh *or* kol uh RAH doh) *Colorado* is one of the fifty states of the United States. *[noun]*

color

colt · command

Cc

combs

colt (KOHLT) A *colt* is a young horse, donkey, or zebra. A horse is called a *colt* until it is four or five years old. *[noun]* •**colts.**

comb (KOHM)

1. A *comb* is a piece of plastic or metal that has teeth. It is used to keep your hair neat. *[noun]*
2. When you *comb* your hair, you fix it and make it neat: *Comb your hair every morning before school.* *[verb]*
3. The thick red part of the top of a rooster's head is called a *comb: The bright red comb on a rooster makes him easy to see.* *[noun]*
•**combs.** •**combs, combed, combing.**

come (KUHM) *You can come over anytime. My mom comes home at six o'clock.* *[verb]* •**comes, came, come, coming.**

comfortable (KUHMF ter buhl *or* KUM fer tuh buhl) When you are *comfortable* you feel nice, warm, and snug: *The blanket helped the cold boy feel comfortable.* *[adjective]*

comics (KOM iks) *Comics* are a group of pictures that tell a funny or exciting story. *[noun plural]*

comma (KOM uh) A *comma* is a mark (,) of punctuation. A *comma* is used where you would wait if you were saying a sentence out loud. *[noun]* •**commas.**

command (kuh MAND)

1. A *command* is an order: *The dog won't move until a command is given.* *[noun]*

Roll over!

command

2. When you *command* someone, you give them an order: *The police officers commanded the driver to stop the car.* [verb]
•**commands.** •**commands, commanded, commanding.**

common (KOM uhn) If something is *common,* it is often seen or found. *Common* can also mean *usual: Yellow is a common color for school buses.* [adjective] •**commoner, commonest.**

community (kuh MYOO nuh tee) A *community* is a place where people live, work, and play. *Communities* are different sizes. Stores, houses, and libraries are all part of a *community.* [noun] •**communities.**

communities

compact disc (KOM pakt DISK) A *compact disc* is a small, thin plastic disk that contains music, computer programs, and other kinds of information. The abbreviation for *compact disc* is *CD.* •**compact discs.**

compass

compare (kuhm PAIR) When you *compare* people or things, you find out or point out how people or things are alike and how they are different: *The boys compared their lunches.* [verb] •**compares, compared, comparing.**

compass (KUHM puhss) A *compass* is something that shows directions. A *compass* has a needle that always points to the north. [noun] •**compasses.**

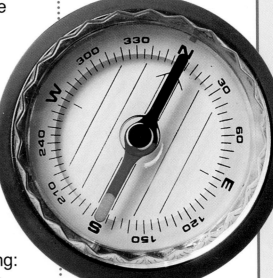

complain (kuhm PLAYN) If you *complain,* you say that something is wrong or are upset about something: *The children complained about too much homework.* [verb] •**complains, complained, complaining.**

complete · concrete

complete (kuhm PLEET)

1. If something is *complete,* it has all the parts and is whole: *We have a complete set of pieces for the puzzle.* [adjective]

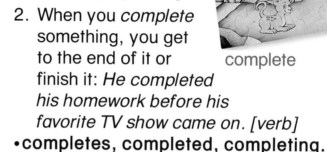

complete

2. When you *complete* something, you get to the end of it or finish it: *He completed his homework before his favorite TV show came on.* [verb]
•**completes, completed, completing.**

completely (kuhm PLEET lee) If you do something *completely,* you do it until it is all done or finished: *She completely finished her dinner so that she could have some dessert.* [adverb]

compound (KOM pownd) A *compound* is two words that are put together to make up one new word. *Outside* and *playground* are two *compound* words. [noun] •**compounds.**

computer (kuhm PYOO ter) A *computer* is a machine that can store and give back information. A *computer* can do many kinds of work. It can play games and give answers to problems. [noun] •**computers.**

concerts

concert (KON sert) A *concert* is a show where people play musical instruments or sing. [noun] •**concerts.**

concrete (KON kreet *or* kon KREET) *Concrete* is cement, sand, small stones, and water mixed together. When *concrete* dries, it is very hard. It is used to make buildings, sidewalks, roads, dams, and bridges. [noun]

conductor (kuhn DUHK ter)

1. A *conductor* is a person who helps the people who ride trains: *The conductor collects tickets and fares.* [noun]

2. A *conductor* is also someone who leads a group of musicians: *The conductor started the concert.* [noun]
•**conductors.**

conductor

cone (KOHN)

1. A *cone* is something that has a flat, round base and is pointed at the top. [noun]

2. A *cone* is also anything shaped like a cone: *The ice cream cone began to melt.* [noun]

3. A *cone* is also the part that holds the seeds of trees that have needles. Pine trees have *cones.* [noun]
•**cones.**

confuse (kuhn FYOOZ)

1. If something *confuses* you, you are not sure about it: *Her directions confused me, and I got lost.* [verb]

2. If you *confuse* things or people, you are not able to tell them apart: *People often confuse this girl with her twin sister.* [verb]
•**confuses, confused, confusing.**

confuse

People always confuse me with my sister.

connect (kuh NEKT) If you
connect something to something else, you join the things together: *The firefighters connected the hoses.* [verb]
•**connects, connected, connecting.**

Connecticut (kuh NET uh kuht) *Connecticut* is one of the fifty states of the United States. [noun]

conservation · content

Cc

conservation (kon ser VAY shuhn) *Conservation* is the saving of things in nature from being used up or wasted: *The class is interested in the conservation of our forest land.* [noun]

consonant (KON suh nuhnt) *Consonants* are all the letters in the alphabet except *a, e, i, o,* and *u*. Any letter that is not a *consonant* is a vowel. [noun] •**consonants.**

constellation (kon stuh LAY shuhn) A *constellation* is a group of stars that form a picture. [noun] •**constellations.**

construction (kuhn STRUHK shuhn) *Construction* is the work of building something or putting something together: *The construction took a year.* [noun]

consumer (kuhn SOO mer) A *consumer* is a person who buys and uses food, clothing, or anything that is made or done by someone else. People who buy groceries are *consumers.* People who get haircuts are also *consumers.* [noun] •**consumers.**

contain (kuhn TAYN) If something *contains* something else, it holds it inside: *This box contains cereal.* [verb] •**contains, contained, containing.**

container (kuhn TAY ner) A *container* is a box, can, jar, or anything that can contain or hold something. [noun] •**containers.**

My school box is a container.

content (kuhn TENT)

1. If something *contents* you, it makes you happy or pleases you: *His favorite books content him when he is sick.* [verb]

constellations

container

2. If something makes you *content,* it makes you happy or pleased: *Will you be content to wait till tomorrow? [adjective]*
•**contents, contented, contenting.**

contented (kuhn TEN tid) If you are *contented,* you are feeling happy. A *contented* person is happy with the way things are. *[adjective]*

contents (KON tentss)

1. The *contents* of a box or a house are all the things inside it: *An old chair and a bed were the only contents of the room. [noun plural]*

2. The *contents* can also be the chapters or sections in a book. A *table of contents* gives a list of these. *[noun plural]*

contents

contest (KON test) A *contest* is something you enter to win a prize. A *contest* can be between two people or many people. *[noun]* •**contests.**

continent (KON tuh nuhnt) A *continent* is a very large area of land. There are seven *continents* on the earth. We live on the *continent* of North America. *[noun]* •**continents.**

continent

continue (kuhn TIN yoo)

1. If you *continue* doing something, you keep on going and do not stop: *These roads continue for miles. [verb]*

2. To *continue* also means to go on with something after stopping for a while: *The teacher said that she would continue the story tomorrow. [verb]*
•**continues, continued, continuing.**

contraction · coop

Cc

contraction (kuhn TRAK shuhn) A *contraction* is a short form of a word. *Don't* is a *contraction* for *do not.* [*noun*] •**contractions.**

control (kuhn TROHL)

1. *Control* is power over something or someone: *The boy did not lose control of his bike.* [*noun*]

2. When you *control* something, you hold it back: *I couldn't control the barking dog.* [*verb*]

3. A *control* is a switch on a machine. A *control* can start or stop a machine or move it in different directions. [*noun*]
•**controls, controlled, controlling.** •**controls** *for definition 3.*

control

cook (KUK)

1. When you *cook,* you make food ready to eat by using heat. Boiling, frying, roasting, and baking are ways to *cook.* [*verb*]

2. A *cook* is a person who cooks: *My dad is the cook at our house.* [*noun*]
•**cooks, cooked, cooking.** •**cooks.**

cookie (KUK ee) A *cookie* is a small, flat, sweet cake. [*noun*] •**cookies.**

cool (KOOL) When it is *cool,* the weather is more cold than hot. On a *cool* day, a person should wear a sweater or a light jacket but not a heavy coat. [*adjective*] •**cooler, coolest.**

coop (KOOP) A *coop* is a small cage or pen for chickens, rabbits, or other small animals. [*noun*] •**coops.**

cookies

cooperate (koh OP uh rayt) When people *cooperate*, they work together: *We should all cooperate and clean up after the class party.* [verb] •**cooperates, cooperated, cooperating.**

copper (KOP er) *Copper* is a soft, red metal. *Copper* is used to make pots, pans, pennies, wire, and many other things. [noun]

copper

copy (KOP ee)

1. When you *copy* something, you make it like something else: *Copy your spelling list from the chalkboard.* [verb]

2. A *copy* is a thing made to look just like something else: *This copy looks like the famous painting. He made six copies of that page.* [noun]
•**copies, copied, copying.** •**copies.**

coral (KOR uhl) *Coral* is a hard red, pink, or white material. *Coral* is made up of the skeletons of tiny sea animals. It is often used for jewelry. [noun]

coral

cord (KORD)

1. A *cord* is a thick, strong string or a very thin rope. [noun]

2. A *cord* is also a pair of wires covered with plastic or rubber. A *cord* has a plug at one end. It is used to connect an appliance or a lamp to electric current. [noun]
•**cords.**

cork (KORK) *Cork* is the light, thick, outer bark of a kind of oak tree. *Cork* is used to close the tops of bottles. [noun] •**corks.**

Cc

corn · cottage

corn (KORN) *Corn* is a yellow or white vegetable that grows on a tall, green plant. Farm animals and people eat *corn*. [noun]

corner (KOR ner)
1. A *corner* is the place where two lines or two sides meet: *He put his wet boots in the corner.* [noun]
2. A *corner* is also the place where two streets meet: *There is a traffic light at the corner.* [noun]
•**corners.**

corner

costumes

corral (kuh RAL) A *corral* is a pen for horses, cattle, and other animals. [noun] •**corrals.**

correct (kuh REKT)
1. If something is *correct,* it is right and has no mistakes: *The girl gave the correct answer to the math problem.* [adjective]
2. If you *correct* something, you mark the mistakes or take them away: *I always correct the misspelled words in my paper.* [verb]
•**corrects, corrected, correcting.**

cost (KAWST) The *cost* of something is the amount of money you need to buy it: *The cost of this book is five dollars.* [noun] •**costs.**

costume (KOSS toom) *Costumes* are clothes that a person can put on to look like someone else. A *costume* may be worn in a play. It may also be worn just for fun. [noun] •**costumes.**

cottage (KOT ij) A *cottage* is a small house. [noun] •**cottages.**

cotton (KOT uhn) *Cotton* is a kind of cloth that people wear in warm weather. *Cotton* comes from a plant that grows near the ground. *[noun]*

cough (KAWF) When you *cough*, you blow air out from your lungs with a loud noise: *I heard her cough all night. [verb]* •**coughs, coughed, coughing.**

could (KUD) *She could ski very well. Perhaps I could go with you tomorrow. [verb]*

couldn't *Couldn't* is a shorter form of *could not: He couldn't hear us. [contraction]*

count (KOWNT)

I am seven years old.

1. To *count* is to name numbers in order: *He can count to one hundred. [verb]*
2. To *count* also means to add up or find the amount of something: *She broke her bank so she could count the pennies. [verb]*

count

3. When something *counts*, it is very important: *The teacher said that spelling would count. [verb]*
4. If you *count* on someone, you depend on that person to do something: *Can I count on you to clean your room after school today? [verb]*
•**counts, counted, counting.**

countdown (KOWNT down) A *countdown* is the calling out of the minutes or seconds left before a rocket flies away. This is done by counting backward from a certain time to zero: *We started the countdown at fifteen. [noun]* •**countdowns.**

counter • court

Cc

counter (KOWN ter)

1. A *counter* is a long table, or some shelves covered with glass. A clerk stands behind a *counter* to sell things. Food can be prepared and eaten at a *counter*. [noun]

2. A *counter* is also something used for counting: *Use your counters to find the answer to 5 plus 2*. [noun]
•**counters.**

country

country (KUHN tree)

1. The *country* is the land outside a city: *There were many farms in the country*. [noun]

2. A *country* is also the land and a group of people with the same leader. People from the same *country* usually speak the same language. Our *country* is the United States. [noun]
•**countries** *for definition 2*.

county (KOWN tee) A *county* is a part of a state. A state is made up of a number of *counties*. Each *county* has its own government. [noun] •**counties.**

courage (KER ij)
Courage is being able to meet danger instead of running away from it: *It takes courage to rescue someone from a burning house*. [noun]

courage

course (KORSS) A *course* is the direction you take: *After reading the compass, the Cub Scout troop decided to take a course straight north*. [noun]
•**courses.**

court (KORT)

1. A *court* is a place where a judge decides questions of law. [noun]

2. A *court* is also a place where games such as tennis and basketball are played. *[noun]*
•**courts**.

cousin (KUHZ in) Your *cousin* is the son or daughter of your uncle or aunt. *[noun]* •**cousins**.

cover (KUH ver)

1. When you *cover* something, you put something else over it: *I like to cover my feet with a blanket. [verb]*

2. A *cover* is anything that protects or hides: *I made the cover for my math book from a paper bag. [noun]*
•**covers, covered, covering**. •**covers**.

covers

covering (KUH ver ing) A *covering* is anything that covers: *Hair is covering for the head. Feathers, fur, and fish scales are coverings for different kinds of animals. [noun]* •**coverings**.

cow (KOW) A *cow* is a large farm animal that gives milk. A female elephant or buffalo is also called a *cow.* *[noun]* •**cows**.

coward (KOW erd) A *coward* is a person who is easily scared and runs from danger. *[noun]* •**cowards**.

cowboy (KOW boi) A *cowboy* is a person who works on a cattle ranch. *Cowboys* also take part in rodeos. *[noun]* •**cowboys**.

cowboy

cowgirl (KOW gerl) A *cowgirl* is a woman who works on a cattle ranch. *Cowgirls* also take part in rodeos. *[noun]* •**cowgirls**.

coyote · crane

Cc

coyote (ky OH tee *or* KY oht) A *coyote* is a small animal that looks something like a wolf. *Coyotes* have light yellow fur and bushy tails. *[noun]* •**coyotes.**

cozy (KOH zee) If you are *cozy,* you are warm, comfortable, and snug: *The cat lay in a cozy corner near the fireplace. [adjective]* •**cozier, coziest.**

crab (KRAB) A *crab* is a water animal that has a broad, flat shell. *Crabs* have eight legs and two claws. Some *crabs* are good to eat. *[noun]* •**crabs.**

crab

crack (KRAK)

1. A *crack* is a long, narrow break: *The old window had a crack in it. [noun]*
2. When you *crack* something, you break it without separating it into parts: *The baseball didn't make a hole in the window, but it did crack it. [verb]*
3. A *crack* is also a sudden, sharp noise like the noise made by thunder. *[noun]*
•**cracks.** •**cracks, cracked, cracking.**

cracker (KRAK er) A *cracker* is a thin, crisp piece of bread. *[noun]* •**crackers.**

crackers

crane (KRAYN)

1. A *crane* is a machine with a long, swinging arm. A *crane* is used for lifting and moving heavy things. *[noun]*
2. A *crane* is also a large bird with long legs, a long neck, and a long bill. *Cranes* live near water. *[noun]*
•**cranes.**

cranky (KRANG kee) If you are feeling *cranky,* you are very easily annoyed and upset: *Being sick made him cranky.* [adjective] •**crankier, crankiest.**

crash (KRASH)

1. A *crash* is a sudden, loud noise: *We heard the crash of thunder.* [noun]

2. When something *crashes,* it makes a loud, sudden noise: *The glass crashed to the floor.* [verb] •**crashes.** •**crashes, crashed, crashing.**

crash

crater (KRAY tuhr)

1. A *crater* is a hole in the ground shaped like a bowl: *This crater was made by a meteor.* [noun]

2. A *crater* is also the opening at the top of a volcano. [noun] •**craters.**

crawl (KRAWL) When you *crawl* you move on your hands and knees or with your body close to the ground: *Babies crawl before they begin to walk. Worms, snakes, and lizards crawl.* [verb] •**crawls, crawled, crawling.**

crayon (KRAY on *or* KRAY uhn) A *crayon* is a stick or pencil of colored wax. *Crayons* are used for drawing and coloring pictures. They come in many colors. [noun] •**crayons.**

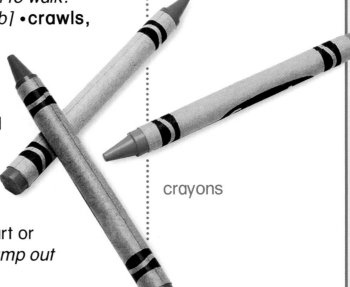
crayons

crazy (KRAY zee)

1. If something is *crazy,* it is not a smart or clever thing to do: *It was crazy to jump out of such a high tree.* [adjective]

creak · creep

2. If people are *crazy,* their minds are sick and they need a doctor. *Crazy* is not a polite word to use to describe a person that is sick in this way. *[adjective]*
•**crazier, craziest.**

creak (KREEK) When something *creaks,* it squeaks loudly: *I heard the old door creak when it opened. [verb]* •**creaks, creaked, creaking.**

cream (KREEM) *Cream* is a part of milk. Butter is made from *cream. [noun]*

create (kree AYT)

create

1. When you *create* something, you make something which has not been made before: *She wants to create music. [verb]*
2. To *create* something is also to cause it to happen: *The noise will create a problem. [verb]*
•**creates, created, creating.**

creature (KREE cher) A *creature* is any living person or animal: *We fed the lost dog because the poor creature was hungry. [noun]* •**creatures.**

creek (KREEK) A *creek* is a small stream of running water. Another word for *creek* is *brook. [noun]* •**creeks.**

creeks

creep (KREEP) When you *creep,* you move with your body close to the floor: *I saw the cat creep toward the mouse. [verb]* •**creeps, crept, creeping.**

crept (KREPT) *The tiger crept through the jungle.* [verb]

crew (KROO) A *crew* is a group of people working together: *It takes a crew of ten people to sail that ship. A group of people who make movies is called a film crew.* [noun] •**crews.**

crib (KRIB) A *crib* is a small bed with high sides to keep a baby from falling out. [noun] •**cribs.**

cricket (KRIK uht) A *cricket* is a black or brown insect that makes a loud noise. *Crickets* have four wings. They eat plants. The male *cricket* makes a noise by rubbing its front wings together. [noun] •**crickets.**

cricket

crisp (KRISP) Something that is *crisp* is hard, thin, and easy to break: *Dry toast is crisp. Crackers are crisp.* [adjective] •**crisper, crispest.**

croak (KROHK)

1. A *croak* is a deep, rough sound made by a frog or a crow. [noun]
2. To *croak* means to make that deep, rough sound: *They heard frogs croak.* [verb]
•**croaks.** •**croaks, croaked, croaking.**

crocodile (KROK uh dyl) A *crocodile* is a large animal with thick skin, four short legs, and a pointed nose. *Crocodiles* look a lot like alligators. [noun] •**crocodiles.**

crocodile

crooked (KRUK uhd) When something is *crooked,* it is not straight. Other words that mean *crooked* are *bent, curved,* and *twisted: The crooked road was hard to follow.* [adjective]

crop • crowded

crop (KROP) *Crops* are plants grown by farmers for food. Corn and wheat are important *crops* in the United States. *[noun]* •**crops.**

cross (KRAWSS)

1. A *cross* is a straight line with another across it to form a T, a †, or an ✕. *[noun]*
2. To *cross* means to mark with an ✕ or draw a line through something: *He tried to cross out his mistake. [verb]*
3. When you *cross* the street, you move from one side to another: *The children were not allowed to cross the street alone. [verb]*

•**crosses.** •**crosses, crossed, crossing.**

crosswalk (KRAWSS wawk) A *crosswalk* is a place for people to cross the street. The *crosswalk* is marked with white lines. *[noun]* •**crosswalks.**

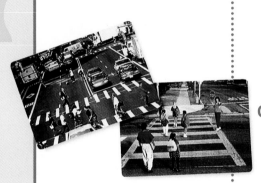

crosswalks

crow (KROH) A *crow* is a large, shiny black bird with a loud cry. *[noun]* •**crows.**

crowd (KROWD)

1. A *crowd* is a large number of people together: *A crowd waited for the actor. [noun]*
2. To *crowd* means to collect or gather in large numbers: *Don't crowd around the door. [verb]*

•**crowds.** •**crowds, crowded, crowding.**

crowd

crowded (KROW did) If a place is *crowded,* there are too many people or things there: *The store was crowded with people shopping. Our garage is crowded with junk. [adjective]*

crown (KROWN)
A *crown* is a head covering for a king or queen. A *crown* is made out of gold or silver and jewels. *[noun]* •**crowns.**

crown

crumb (KRUHM) A *crumb* is a very small piece of something that has broken off from a larger piece: *The boy quickly ate his piece of cake and left crumbs all over. [noun]* •**crumbs.**

crush (KRUHSH)
1. When you *crush* something, you squeeze it very hard in order to break it: *If you stand on that box, you will crush it. [verb]*
2. To *crush* also means to break something into very small pieces by hitting it or pressing it: *The workers had to crush the stones before they could be used in concrete. [verb]*
•**crushes, crushed, crushing.**

crust (KRUHST)
1. The *crust* is the hard outside part of bread. *[noun]*
2. The *crust* is also the bottom and top coverings of pies. *[noun]*
•**crusts.**

crutch (KRUHCH) A *crutch* is something that helps a person walk. It is a stick with a soft bar at the top that fits under the person's arm and holds part of his or her weight in walking. *[verb]* •**crutches.**

cry (KRY)
1. If you *cry*, you sob with tears falling down your cheeks: *I heard the boy cry with pain after he fell down. [verb]*

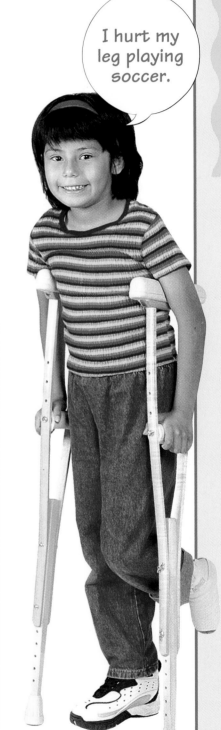
I hurt my leg playing soccer.

crutches

103

cub · cup

Cc

cubs

2. A *cry* is a loud call: *The parents heard the boy's cry for help.* [*noun*]

3. To *cry* also means to call loudly: *We had to wave and cry "Stop!"* [*verb*]

4. A *cry* is also the call of an animal: *The cry of the injured dog made us all feel sorry for it.* [*noun*]
•**cries, cried, crying.** •**cries.**

cub (KUHB) A *cub* is a baby bear, fox, lion, or other large animal. [*noun*] •**cubs.**

cubby (KUB ee) A *cubby* is a small space like a closet without a door, used for storing things: *The children leave their boots and gloves in their cubbies.* [*noun*] •**cubbies.**

cube (KYOOB) A *cube* is a block with six square sides that are all equal in size. [*noun*] •**cubes.**

cub scout (KUHB SKOWT) A *cub scout* is someone who belongs to the Boy Scouts of America. *Cub scouts* are between eight and eleven years old. •**cub scouts.**

cucumber (KYOO kuhm ber) A *cucumber* is a long, green vegetable that grows on a vine. *Cucumbers* are eaten in slices and used to make pickles. [*noun*] •**cucumbers.**

cup (KUHP)

1. A *cup* is a dish you use to drink from. A *cup* is usually round and has a handle. [*noun*]

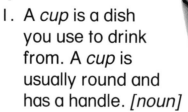

cups

2. A *cup* is also an amount of liquid. You also use a *cup* to measure sugar and flour in recipes. [*noun*]
•**cups.**

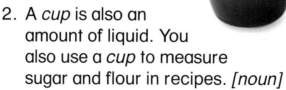

cupboard (KUHB erd) A *cupboard* is a set of shelves that are sometimes closed in by a door. Clothes, dishes, and food can be stored in *cupboards*. *[noun]* •**cupboards.**

cupcake (KUHP kayk) A *cupcake* is a small cake about the size and shape of a cup. *[noun]* •**cupcakes.**

cupcakes

curb (KERB) A *curb* is the raised edge of cement on a sidewalk or street: *The back wheel hit the curb as he parked the car. [noun]* •**curbs.**

curious (KYOOR ee uhss) When people are *curious*, they want to know things: *Small children are very curious, and they ask many questions. [adjective]*

curl (KERL)

1. When you *curl* something, you twist it into rings: *She wants to curl her hair for the party. [verb]*
2. A *curl* is a lock of hair that is twisted and curved: *The hat covered the curl on her forehead. [noun]*
3. If a person or animal *curls* up, they make themselves take up less space: *He likes to curl up in a chair and read. [verb]*
•**curls, curled, curling.** •**curls.**

curly

curly (KER lee) Something that is *curly* is bent or curling: *He was born with curly hair. [adjective]* •**curlier, curliest.**

current (KER uhnt)

1. A *current* is a flow or stream of something. Running water or moving air makes a *current.* *[noun]*

curtain · cut

2. A *current* is also a flow of electricity through a wire: *When the current went off, all of his clocks and lights stopped working.* [noun]
•**currents** *for definition 1.*

curtain (KERT uhn)

1. A *curtain* is a cloth or other material hung across a window or other space. *Curtains* are often used to keep out light and to keep a room private. *[noun]*

2. A *curtain* is also a cloth or screen that hangs between the stage and the audience in a theater. *[noun]*
•**curtains** *for definition 1.*

curve (KERV)

1. A *curve* is a line that has no straight part. A circle is a closed *curve.* [noun]

2. A *curve* is also a bend in the road: *Mountain roads have many curves.* [noun]
•**curves.**

curved (KURVD) If something is *curved*, it is not straight. *[adjective]*

custom (KUHSS tuhm)

1. A *custom* is an old or usual way of doing things: *Other countries often have different customs.* [noun]

2. A *custom* is any usual action or habit: *It was her custom to get up early.* [noun]
•**customs.**

customer (KUHSS tuh mer) A *customer* is a person who buys things in a store: *There was one customer in line ahead of me.* [noun] •**customers.**

cut (KUHT)

1. When you *cut* something you divide it into pieces with something sharp: *Mom cut the orange into two pieces. He cut the paper with scissors.* [verb]

curtain

cut

2. A *cut* is an opening made by something sharp: *She covered the cut with a bandage.* [noun]

3. To *cut* also means to hurt something with something sharp: *She cut her finger on broken glass.* [verb]
•**cuts, cut, cutting.** •**cuts.**

cute (KYOOT) If something is *cute,* it is nice to look at or pretty: *He is a cute baby. The girls thought the new boy was cute. That's a cute sweater.* [adjective] •**cuter, cutest.**

cute

cyclone (SY klohn) A *cyclone* is a storm with very strong winds. During a *cyclone,* the winds move in a circle. Another word for *cyclone* is *tornado.* [noun] •**cyclones.**

cymbal (SIM buhl) A *cymbal* is a round metal plate used as a musical instrument. *Cymbals* are used in pairs. They make a loud, ringing sound when hit against each other. [noun] •**cymbals.**

cymbal

That's loud!

dad · dam

Dd

daisies

dad (DAD) A *dad* is a father. [*noun*] •**dads**.

daddy (DAD ee) *Daddy* is another word for *father*. [*noun*] •**daddies**.

daily (DAY lee) If something is done or happens *daily*, it is done or happens every day: *She exercises daily.* [*adverb*]

dairy (DAIR ee) A *dairy* is a place where milk and cream are kept and made into butter and cheese. [*noun*] •**dairies**.

daisy (DAY zee) A *daisy* is a flower with white or colored petals around a yellow center. [*noun*] •**daisies**.

dam (DAM) A *dam* is a wall built to hold back the water of a creek or river. [*noun*] •**dams**.

Dd

damp (DAMP) If something is *damp*, it is a little wet: *Use a damp cloth to wipe the table.* [*adjective*]
•**damper, dampest.**

dance (DANSS)
1. When you *dance*, you move in rhythm to music: *She loves to dance.* [*verb*]
2. A *dance* is a special way of moving in rhythm with music: *We learned a new dance.* [*noun*]
•**dances, danced, dancing.**
•**dances.**

dancer (DAN ser) A *dancer* is a person who dances. [*noun*]
•**dancers.**

dancer

dandelion (DAN duh ly uhn) A *dandelion* is a weed with yellow flowers. [*noun*]
•**dandelions.**

danger (DAYN jer)
1. If something is in *danger*, there is a chance that it could be hurt: *The big waves put the small boat in danger of sinking.* [*noun*]
2. A *danger* is also something that may hurt you: *This wet road is a danger to drivers.* [*noun*]
•**dangers** for definition 2.

dangerous (DAYN jer uhss) Something that is *dangerous* is not safe: *Skating on thin ice is dangerous.* [*adjective*]

dark

dark (DARK)
1. When it is *dark*, there is no light: *Don't go into that dark cave.* [*adjective*]
2. *Dark* means not light colored: *He wore a dark green shirt.* [*adjective*]
•**darker, darkest.**

dash · day

Dd

dash (DASH)

1. To *dash* means to rush: *We dashed to catch the bus.* [verb]
2. A *dash* is a rush: *We made a dash for the bus.* [noun]
•**dashes, dashed, dashing.** •**dashes.**

dash

date¹ (DAYT)

1. A *date* is the time when something happens or happened: *August 21, 1959, is the date that Hawaii became a state.* [noun]
2. To *date* something means to put a date on it: *I dated my letter March 5.* [verb]
•**dates.** •**dates, dated, dating.**

date² (DAYT) A *date* is the sweet fruit of a kind of palm tree. [noun] •**dates.**

daughter (DAW ter) A *daughter* is a female child. A girl or woman is the *daughter* of her mother and father. [noun] •**daughters.**

dawn (DAWN) *Dawn* is the beginning of the day. At *dawn*, the first light shows in the east: *In summer, dawn comes early.* [noun] •**dawns.**

day (DAY)

1. A *day* is the time of light between sunrise and sunset: *A summer day is longer than a winter day.* [noun]
2. A *day* is the 24 hours from one midnight to the next: *It it hard to stay awake a whole day.* [noun]
3. A *day* is also the hours for work and activities: *Our school day is from nine to three.* [noun]
•**days.**

This is my daughter, Kara.

daughter

day care (DAY kair) *Day care* is the care given to small children during the day while their parents are at work.

daylight (DAY lyt)
1. *Daylight* is the light of day: *Bats do not often fly around in daylight.* [noun]
2. *Daylight* is also the dawn: *We were up at daylight.* [noun]

dead (DED) When something is *dead*, it is no longer alive or living: *The plant is dead because no one watered it.* [adjective]

deaf (DEF) If someone is *deaf,* that person is not able to hear or not able to hear well: *Many deaf people know sign language.* [adjective] •**deafer, deafest.**

dear (DEER) If someone is *dear* to you, you love them very much. You can also use the word *dear* to start a letter: *Her aunt was very dear to her. "Dear Grandmother" is a polite way to begin a letter.* [adjective] •**dearer, dearest.**

December (di SEM ber) *December* is the twelfth month of the year. It has 31 days. It comes after November and before January. [noun]

decide (di SYD) When you *decide,* you choose something: *We usually decide to stay home.* [verb] •**decides, decided, deciding.**

day care

December

deck · deliver

Dd

deer

deck (DEK) A *deck* is one of the floors of a ship. A *deck* divides a ship into different parts. *[noun]* •**decks.**

deep (DEEP) If something is *deep,* it goes a long way down from the top or surface: *The snow was deep in our backyard. [adjective]* •**deeper, deepest.**

deer (DEER) A *deer* is a very fast animal with hoofs. The male *deer* has antlers. *[noun]* •The plural of *deer* is *deer.*

define (di FYN) When you *define* a word, you explain what it means: *She was asked to define three words. [verb]* •**defines, defined, defining.**

definition (def uh NISH uhn) A *definition* is a sentence or group of words that explains what another word means. One *definition* of *school* is "a place for teaching and learning." *[noun]* •**definitions.**

Delaware (DEL uh wair) *Delaware* is one of the fifty states of the United States. *[noun]*

delicious (di LISH uhss) When something is *delicious,* it tastes or smells very good: *The cookies were delicious. [adjective]*

deliver (di LIV er) When you *deliver* something, you carry it and give it out: *He will deliver the invitations on his bicycle. [verb]* •**delivers, delivered, delivering.**

deliver

Dd

dent (DENT)

1. A *dent* is a bent place in the surface of something: *Bumping the garage door put a dent in the car.* [noun]
2. When you *dent* something, you hurt it by making a bent place in it: *We saw him dent the chair when he moved it.* [verb]
•**dents.** •**dents, dented, denting.**

dentist (DEN tist) A

dentist is a doctor who takes care of people's teeth. A *dentist* fixes tooth problems and cleans, repairs, straightens, or pulls teeth. [noun]
•**dentists.**

dentist

depend (di PEND)

1. When something *depends* on another thing, the first thing is a result of the second thing: *The success of his garden will depend on the weather.* [verb]
2. When you *depend* on something, you believe that thing will do what it is supposed to: *I depend on the alarm clock to wake me.* [verb]
•**depends, depended, depending.**

describe (di SKRYB) When you *describe*

someone or something, you tell in words how that person or thing looks, feels, or acts: *Please describe the giant in the story.* [verb]
•**describes, described, describing.**

description (di SKRIP shuhn) A

description is words that tell how someone or something looks, feels, or acts: *They gave a description of the stolen car.* [noun]
•**descriptions.**

description

The bunny is bright yellow. It has a smooth, pink nose. It looks very friendly.

desert · dial

Dd

desert (DEZ ert) A *desert* is a place without water or trees but with a lot of sand. It is usually hot. *[noun]* •**deserts.**

desert

desire (di ZYUR)

1. Another word for *desire* is wish: *Her desire was to be a doctor.* *[noun]*

2. If you *desire* something, you want it very much: *Hungry people desire food.* *[verb]* •**desires.** •**desires, desired, desiring.**

desk (DESK) A *desk* is a piece of furniture with a flat or slanting top. People write, read, and use computers at *desks.* *[noun]* •**desks.**

desk

dessert (di ZURT) A *dessert* is a sweet food such as pie, cake, ice cream, or fruit. *Desserts* are served at the end of a meal. *[noun]* •**desserts.**

detail (di TAYL *or* DEE tayl) A *detail* is a small part or a part that is not important: *She left out one detail in her report.* *[noun]* •**details.**

detective (di TEK tiv) A *detective* is a police officer or other person whose work is getting information and solving mysteries. *[noun]* •**detectives.**

develop (di VEL uhp) To *develop* means to grow or become bigger: *Will a leaf develop from this bud? Red spots can develop on your skin if you touch this plant.* *[verb]* •**develops, developed, developing.**

dial (DY uhl)

1. A *dial* is a part of a radio or television that lets you choose a station. It has numbers, letters, or marks and something that points to those marks. The face of a clock has a *dial.* *[noun]*

2. When you *dial* a number, you use a telephone to reach the person who has that number. *[verb]*
•**dials.** •**dials, dialed, dialing.**

diamond (DY muhnd)

diamond

1. A *diamond* is a kind of stone that is worth a lot of money. *Diamonds* are put in rings and other jewelry. *Diamonds* can be clear or different colors. *[noun]*
2. A *diamond* is also a figure shaped like this ◊. *[noun]*
•**diamonds.**

diaper (DY per) A *diaper* is a piece of cloth or paper folded and used as underwear for a baby. *[noun]*
•**diapers.**

diary (DY uhr ee) A *diary* is a book for writing about your thoughts or your activities: *I kept a diary while I was on vacation. [noun]* •**diaries.**

dictionary (DIK shuh nair ee) A *dictionary* is a book that tells what words mean and how they are spelled. The words are listed in alphabetical order. *[noun]*
•**dictionaries.**

did (DID) *Did she see them yesterday? Yes, she did. You did not clean your room. I did clean my room. [verb]*

didn't *Didn't* is a shorter form of *did not*: *He didn't go to the park with them. [contraction]*

die (DY) When someone or something *dies,* they stop living or become dead: *The plant died because no one watered it. [verb]* •**dies, died, dying.**

difference · dining room

different

Dd

difference (DIF er uhnss)

1. A *difference* is a way things are not alike: *One difference between an ape and a monkey is that monkeys have tails.* [noun]

2. A *difference* is also what is left after you subtract one number from another: *The difference between 8 and 14 is 6.* [noun]
•**differences.**

different (DIF er uhnt) When two things are *different*, they are not alike: *Leaves have different shapes. Basketball is different from baseball.* [adjective]

difficult (DIF uh kuhlt) If something is *difficult*, it is hard to do or understand: *Learning to juggle is difficult for some people. This is a difficult problem.* [adjective]

dig (DIG) When you *dig*, you use a shovel, hands, or claws to make a hole: *Many animals dig holes to bury food.* [verb]
•**digs, dug, digging.**

digit (DIJ it) A *digit* is any of the numbers *0, 1, 2, 3, 4, 5, 6, 7, 8, 9.* Sometimes 0 is not called a *digit.* [noun]
•**digits.**

dig

dime (DYM) A *dime* is a coin in the United States and Canada worth 10 cents. Ten *dimes* make one dollar. [noun] •**dimes.**

dining room (DY ning ROOM) A *dining room* is a room in which dinner and other meals are served.
•**dining rooms.**

Dd

dinner (DIN er) *Dinner* is the main meal of the day: *We eat dinner at six o'clock.* [noun] •**dinners.**

dinosaur (DY nuh sor) A *dinosaur* is an animal that lived many millions of years ago. Some *dinosaurs* were bigger than elephants. Some were smaller than cats. No *dinosaurs* are alive today. [noun] •**dinosaurs.**

dinosaur

dip (DIP)

1. When you *dip* something, you put it under water or any liquid and lift it out again quickly: *Dip your hand in the bath to see if it is warm.* [verb]

2. To *dip* means to drop down: *I watched the eagle fly from the branch and dip to the ground.* [verb]

•**dips, dipped, dipping.**

direction (duh REK shuhn) A *direction* is the way something is moving or pointing. North, south, east, and west are *directions: In what direction does this path lead?* [noun] •**directions.**

directions (duh REK shuhnz) *Directions* are something that tells you what to do or how to do something: *She listened carefully as the policeman gave her directions to the museum.* [noun plural]

dirt (DURT)

1. *Dirt* is anything that is not clean. Mud and dust are *dirt. Dirt* soils skin, clothing, houses, or furniture. [noun]

2. *Dirt* is the earth. Flowers and vegetables are planted in *dirt.* [noun]

dirty · dish

Dd

dirty

dirty (DUR tee) If something is *dirty*, it is soiled by mud or dust: *I got dirty planting my garden.* The opposite of *dirty* is clean. *[adjective]* •**dirtier, dirtiest.**

disappear (diss uh PEER)

1. To *disappear* means to go out of sight: *He watched them disappear down the stairs to the subway.* [verb]
2. To *disappear* also means to stop being: *Because of pollution, some animals have disappeared.* [verb]
•**disappears, disappeared, disappearing.**

disappoint (diss uh POINT)

1. If you *disappoint* someone, you do not do what that person wished or hoped you would do: *Our poor baseball team may disappoint you.* [verb]
2. If you *disappoint* someone, you do not keep a promise to that person: *I don't want to disappoint you by forgetting to call you.* [verb]
•**disappoints, disappointed, disappointing.**

discover (diss KUHV er) To *discover* means to find out. When you *discover* something, you see or learn about it for the first time: *He discovered tiny insects living under the stone.* [verb]
•**discovers, discovered, discovering.**

discover

disease (di ZEEZ) A *disease* is a sickness. People, animals, and plants can have *diseases.* [noun]
•**diseases.**

dish (DISH) A *dish* is anything to serve food in. Plates, bowls, cups, and saucers are all *dishes.* [noun] •**dishes.**

disk (DISK)

1. A *disk* is a flat, thin, round thing shaped like a coin. [noun]
2. A *disk* is also something that is used to store music, movies, or other information. Computers read some kinds of *disks*. [noun]
•**disks.**

dismay (diss MAY)

1. If you feel *dismay,* you have a sudden, helpless fear: *I was filled with dismay when the basement began to flood.* [noun]
2. If something *dismays* you, it troubles you very much or makes you afraid: *The thought that she might fail the test dismayed her.* [verb]
•**dismays, dismayed, dismaying.**

distance (DISS tuhnss) *Distance* is the space in between two places: *The distance between these dots is an inch •*   *•.* [noun] •**distances.**

distance

2 miles

District of Columbia (DISS trikt uhv kuh LUHM bee uh)
The *District of Columbia* is the land covered by the city of Washington, the capital of the United States. [noun]

disturb (diss TURB) When you *disturb* someone, you bother that person by talking or by being noisy: *Don't disturb the sleeping baby.* [verb] •**disturbs, disturbed, disturbing.**

dive (DYV)

1. When you *dive,* you jump into water. People usually *dive* with their heads and hands going first: *Can you dive into the pool?* [verb]
2. A *dive* is a jump into water: *He made a perfect dive and won first place.* [noun]
•**dives, dived** or **dove, diving.** •**dives.**

divide · dog

Dd

divide

divide (duh VYD) When you *divide* something, you break it into smaller parts: *Divide the class into four groups.* [verb] •**divides, divided, dividing.**

dizzy (DIZ ee) If you are *dizzy,* you feel that you are going to fall or spin around. You do not feel steady: *When some people look down from a very high place, they feel dizzy.* [adjective] •**dizzier, dizziest.**

do (DOO) *Do your homework carefully. We will do the dishes. Do you like rain? What would you do? We do believe you.* [verb] •**does, did, done, doing.**

dock (DOK) A *dock* is a concrete or wooden surface built at the edge of the water. Ships load at a *dock.* [noun] •**docks.**

doctor (DOK ter) A *doctor* is a person who treats diseases and helps keep people healthy. [noun] •**doctors.**

doctor

does (DUHZ) *He does his work quickly. Does she skate well?* [verb]

doesn't *Doesn't* is a shorter form of *does not: She doesn't own a pet.* [contraction]

dog (DAWG) A *dog* is an animal with four legs and fur. People keep *dogs* as pets. *Dogs* are also used to help in hunting or for guarding property. [noun] •**dogs.**

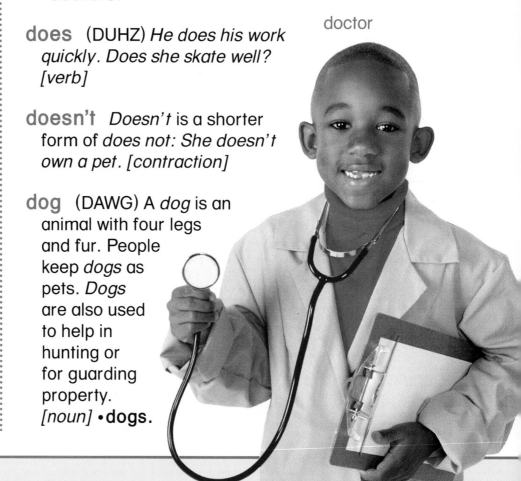

Dd

doghouse (DAWG howss) A *doghouse* is a small house for a dog. *[noun]* •**doghouses.**

doll (DOL) A *doll* is a toy that looks like a baby, a child, or a grown person. *[noun]* •**dolls.**

doll

dollar (DOL er) A *dollar* is an amount of money in the United States and Canada. A *dollar* is equal to 100 cents. $1.00 means one *dollar*. A *dollar bill* is a *dollar* made of paper. *[noun]* •**dollars.**

dollhouse (DOL howss) A *dollhouse* is a toy house. Children use *dollhouses* when playing with dolls. *[noun]* •**dollhouses.**

dolphin (DOL fin) A *dolphin* is a sea animal. *Dolphins* look like small whales. *[noun]* •**dolphins.**

done (DUHN) *She has done her homework. What has he done? [verb]*

donkey (DONG kee) A *donkey* is an animal that is like a small horse but with longer ears. *[noun]* •**donkeys.**

don't *Don't* is a shorter form of *do not: Don't be late for dinner. They don't want to come with us. [contraction]*

door (DOR) A *door* is a piece of wood, metal, or glass that you open or close to get in or out of a building, room, or closet. Cars also have *doors. [noun]* •**doors.**

donkey

dot (DOT)
  1. A *dot* is a tiny, round mark: *Put a dot on your map to show where a city is. [noun]*
  2. A *dot* is also a small spot: *I wore a green shirt with white dots. [noun]*

doubt · dragon

Dd

doughnuts

3. If you *dot* something, you mark it with a dot: *Dot the letter "i."* [verb]
•**dots.** •**dots, dotted, dotting.**

doubt (DOWT) If you *doubt* something, you do not believe it or are not sure about it: *I doubt that the team will win.* [verb] •**doubts, doubted, doubting.**

doughnut (DOH nuht) A *doughnut* is a small, sweet cake. *Doughnuts* usually have a hole in the middle. [noun] •**doughnuts.**

down (DOWN) When you go *down,* you go to a lower place. When you are *down,* you are in a lower place: *They ran down the stairs. The dog was down in the basement.* [preposition or adverb]

dozen (DUHZ uhn) A *dozen* is 12 or a group of 12 things: *I baked a dozen cookies for the bake sale. I sold three dozen cookies.* [noun] •**dozens** or *(after a number)* **dozen.**

Dr. (DOK ter) *Dr.* is an abbreviation of *Doctor*: *Her doctor's name is Dr. J. T. Jones.* •**Drs.**

drag (DRAG) When you *drag* something, you pull or move it along the ground: *She had to drag the big box to the car.* [verb] •**drags, dragged, dragging.**

drag

dragon (DRAG uhn) In stories, a *dragon* is a huge, fierce animal that looks like a lizard with wings, scales, and claws. *Dragons* are supposed to breathe out fire and smoke. [noun] •**dragons.**

Dd

dragonfly (DRAG uhn fly) A *dragonfly* is a large insect with a long, thin body and two pairs of wings. It flies very fast to catch flies, mosquitoes, and other insects. *[noun]* •**dragonflies.**

drank (DRANGK) *We drank all the lemonade in a few minutes. [verb]*

draw (DRAW)

1. When you *draw* something, you make a picture of it with pen, pencil, or crayon: *Draw a picture of your favorite animal. [verb]*

2. To *draw* something also means to pull it out of something else: *Each player should draw one card from the pile. [verb]*
•**draws, drew, drawn, drawing.**

drawbridge (DRAW brij) A *drawbridge* is a bridge that can be lifted or moved to one side. In castles, *drawbridges* were lifted to keep out enemies. A *drawbridge* over a river is raised to let boats pass underneath. *[noun]* •**drawbridges.**

drawer (DROR) A *drawer* is a box with handles in a table, desk, or other piece of furniture. *Drawers* are made to slide in and out easily. *[noun]* •**drawers.**

drawing (DRAW ing)

1. A *drawing* is a picture done with pen, pencil, or crayon. *[noun]*

2. *Drawing* is making a picture: *She is good at drawing and painting. [noun]*
•**drawings** for definition 1.

drawn (DRAWN) *The pony has drawn the cart before. Has he drawn a card yet? She had drawn a picture of her cat. [verb]*

dragonfly

drawing

Dd

dream · drink

dream (DREEM)

1. A *dream* is something you think, feel, or see when you are asleep: *He had a nice dream.* [noun]
2. When you *dream,* you think, feel, hear, or see things while you are asleep: *I often dream about school.* [verb]

•**dreams.** •**dreams, dreamed, dreaming.**

dream

dress (DRESS)

1. A *dress* is a piece of clothing worn by women and girls: *She has a new dress for the party.* [noun]
2. When you *dress,* you put clothes on: *My little brother can dress himself.* [verb]

•**dresses.** •**dresses, dressed, dressing.**

drew (DROO) *She drew a picture. The pony drew the cart.* [verb]

drill (DRIL)

1. A *drill* is a tool or machine for making holes: *Always wear safety goggles when using a drill.* [noun]
2. When you *drill,* you make a hole in something: *I had to drill a hole in the wall.* [verb]
3. To *drill* also means to teach people to do something by having them do a thing over and over: *The teacher often drills the class in subtraction.* [verb]

•**drills.** •**drills, drilled, drilling.**

drink

drink (DRINGK)

1. When you *drink,* you swallow a liquid, such as water or milk: *I drink a glass of milk with every meal.* [verb]
2. A *drink* is a liquid that people can swallow: *Lemonade is a good drink on a hot day.* [noun]

•**drinks, drank, drunk, drinking.** •**drinks.**

Dd

drip (DRIP) When something *drips,* it falls in drops: *She could hear rain drip on the roof. She dripped syrup over her pancakes.* [verb] •**drips, dripped, dripping.**

drip

drive (DRYV)

1. When you *drive* a car, bus, or truck, you make it go: *My sister is learning to drive a car.* [verb]

2. To *drive* also means to go somewhere or carry people in a car or bus: *Please drive us to school. I drove to the hospital.* [verb]
•**drives, drove, driven, driving.**

driven (DRIV uhn) *She has driven us to school every day.* [verb]

driver (DRY ver) A *driver* is a person who drives a car, bus, or truck. [noun] •**drivers.**

driveway (DRYV way) A *driveway* is a road leading from a house or garage to the street. [noun] •**driveways.**

drivers

drop (DROP)

1. A *drop* is a small amount of liquid in a round shape. [noun]

2. When you *drop* something, you let it fall. If you *drop,* you fall: *Don't drop the box on the floor! We dropped to the floor during the fire drill.* [verb]

3. To *drop* something can also mean to leave it out: *Drop the "e" in* hope *before adding* "ing." [verb]
•**drops.** •**drops, dropped, dropping.**

125

drove • dry

Dd

drove (DROHV) *He drove us to the party.* [verb]

drug (DRUHG)
1. A *drug* is a kind of medicine used to treat sickness. [noun]
2. A *drug* is also something that can make bad changes in a person's body. [noun]
•**drugs.**

drugstore (DRUHG stor) A *drugstore* is a store that sells drugs, medicines, and other things such as film and magazines. [noun] •**drugstores.**

drum (DRUHM) A *drum* is a musical instrument that makes a sound when it is beaten. A *drum* is hollow with a cover stretched tight over each end. [noun] •**drums.**

drummer (DRUHM er) A *drummer* is a person who plays a drum. [noun] •**drummers.**

drunk (DRUHNGK) *The dog has drunk all the water in her bowl.* [verb]

dry (DRY)
1. When something is *dry,* it is not wet or damp: *Be sure the paint is dry before you sit down.* [adjective]
2. When you *dry* something, you take the water or other liquid from it: *Dry your hands on a clean towel.* [verb]

drum

dry

3. If a place is *dry,* it does not have enough rain: *A desert is a hot, dry place.* [adjective] •**drier, driest.** •**dries, dried, drying.**

dryer (DRY er) A *dryer* is a machine that takes water from things by heat or air. [noun] •**dryers.**

duck (DUHK) A *duck* is a bird with a flat bill, short neck, and short legs. [noun] •**ducks.**

duck

ducklings

duckling (DUHK ling) A *duckling* is a young duck: *We read a story about ducklings.* [noun] •**ducklings.**

dug (DUHG) *The dog dug a hole in the lawn. We have dug a hole for the new tree.* [verb]

dull (DUHL)
1. If something is *dull,* it is not sharp or pointed: *Her dull scissors will not cut the heavy paper.* [adjective]
2. If something is *dull,* it is not interesting: *The book was dull because none of the characters did anything.* Another word for *dull* is *boring.* [adjective]
•**duller, dullest.**

dumb (DUHM) Something that is *dumb* is silly or not smart: *Leaving your coat at the park was a dumb thing to do.* [adjective]
•**dumber, dumbest.**

dump

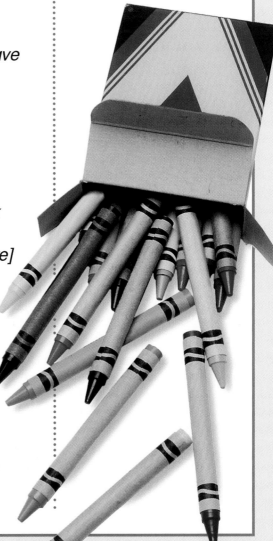

dump (DUHMP) When you *dump* something, you empty it out or throw it down: *The boys dump the trash in the garbage can every week.* [verb] •**dumps, dumped, dumping.**

dune • dwarf

Dd

dune (DOON) A *dune* is a large pile of sand. Beaches and deserts have *dunes*. [noun] •**dunes.**

Durango (du RANG goh) *Durango* is a state in the northwest part of Mexico. [noun]

during (DER ing) *They talked all during the movie. Call at any time during the morning.* [preposition]

dusk (DUSK) *Dusk is the time just before dark: We saw the first star come out at dusk.* [noun]

dust (DUHST)

1. *Dust is light, dry dirt: The wind covered the sidewalk with dust.* [noun]

2. When you *dust* something, you brush or wipe the dust from it: *We dust furniture and wash dishes.* [verb]
•**dusts, dusted, dusting.**

dwarf (DWORF)

1. A *dwarf* is a person, animal, or plant that is much smaller than usual size. [noun]

2. In fairy tales, a *dwarf* is an ugly little man who is able to do magic. [noun]
•**dwarfs** or **dwarves.**

dune

dusk

Ee

each (EECH) *Each child was invited to the party. Each of them brought a gift. The prizes were fifty cents each. [adjective* or *pronoun* or *adverb]*

eagle (EE guhl) An *eagle* is a large bird that can see far and fly far. The *eagle* is the symbol of the United States. *[noun]* •**eagles.**

ear (EER) Your *ear* is the part of your body that you use to hear with. *[noun]* •**ears.**

early (ER lee)

1. If something happens *early,* it happens near the beginning: *Early in the school year, the children didn't know each other very well. [adjective* or *adverb]*

2. *Early* can also mean before the usual time: *She got up early yesterday morning. [adverb]*
•**earlier, earliest.**

ears

earn • easy

earrings

Ee

earn (URN) When you *earn* something, you get it by working for it: *She will earn ten dollars a week for delivering newspapers. His project earned him a lot of respect.* [verb] •**earns, earned, earning.**

earring (EER ing) An *earring* is a piece of jewelry you wear on your ear: *She lost an earring when she took off her hat.* [noun] •**earrings.**

Earth or **earth** (URTH)

1. *Earth* is the planet we live on. The *Earth* moves around the sun. [noun]

2. The *earth* is also the ground: *The earth in the garden was soft enough for planting flowers.* [noun]

earthquake (URTH kwayk) An *earthquake* happens when rocks beneath the Earth's surface move suddenly. During an *earthquake,* buildings, bridges, and roads can crack or fall apart. [noun] •**earthquakes.**

easel (EE zul) An *easel* is a stand that can hold a picture. People use *easels* when they paint. [noun] •**easels.**

easily (EE zuh lee) If you can do something *easily,* you can do it without trying hard: *The boy was strong enough to lift the table easily.* [adverb]

east (EEST) *East* is the direction that the sun rises. *East* is the opposite of west. [noun]

easel

easy (EE zee) If something is *easy,* it is not hard to do or understand: *The directions were easy to follow. The question was easy to answer.* [adjective] •**easier, easiest.**

eat (EET) When you *eat,* you chew and swallow food: *Babies do not eat the same foods as their parents.* [verb] •**eats, ate, eaten, eating.**

eaten (EET uhn) *Have you eaten lunch yet?* [verb]

eat

echo (EK oh) An *echo* is a sound that comes back to you so that you hear it again. You hear an *echo* when a sound bounces back from a hill or a wall. [noun] •**echoes.**

edge (EJ)

1. An *edge* is the line or place where something ends: *He parked at the edge of the road.* [noun]

2. An *edge* is also the thin side of something that cuts: *The knife has a sharp edge.* [noun]

•**edges.**

effect (uh FEKT) An *effect* is something that happens because of something else: *One effect of the heavy snow was the great number of people riding on sleds.* [noun] •**effects.**

eggs

egg (EG) An *egg* is something that is laid by female birds, fish, and reptiles. Baby birds, fish, and reptiles are hatched from *eggs.* People eat chicken *eggs* as food. [noun] •**eggs.**

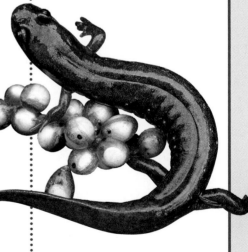

eight (AYT) *Eight* is one more than seven. It is also written 8: *Four and four equals eight. I have eight books.* [noun or adjective] •**eights.**

eighteen (AY teen) *Eighteen* is eight more than ten. It is also written 18: *Five and thirteen equals eighteen. We have eighteen students in our class.* [noun or adjective] •**eighteens.**

Ee

eighteenth · electricity

Ee

eighth

eighteenth (AY teenth) *Eighteenth* is the next after the seventeenth. It is also written 18th: *We met on the eighteenth day of last month.* [*adjective*]

eighth (AYTTH) *Eighth* is the next after the seventh. It is also written 8th: *She was eighth in line.* [*adjective*]

eighty (AY tee) *Eighty* is ten more than seventy. It is also written 80: *I saw eighty birds on the lake.* [*noun or adjective*]

either (EE <u>ther</u>) *Choose either of these toys to give to the baby. Either come in or go out. There are lights on either side of the driveway. If you don't go, she won't go either.* [*pronoun or conjunction or adjective or adverb*]

elbow (EL boh) Your *elbow* is the part of your arm that bends. It is the joint in the middle of your arm. [*noun*]
•**elbows.**

electric (i LEK trik) If something is *electric*, it is run by electricity: *He turned on the electric fan.* [*adjective*]

electrician (i lek TRISH uhn) An *electrician* is a person who fixes electric wires, lights, motors, and anything run by electricity. [*noun*]
•**electricians.**

electricity (i lek TRISS uh tee) *Electricity* is a kind of energy that makes light and heat. *Electricity* also runs motors. *Electricity* makes light bulbs shine, radios and televisions play, and cars start. [*noun*]

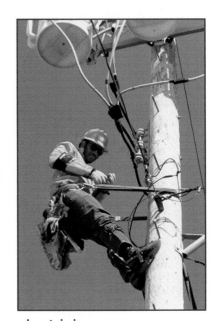

electrician

elephant (EL uh fuhnt) An *elephant* is a very large mammal. *Elephants* have large ears and long trunks. *[noun]* •**elephants.**

elevator (EL uh vay ter) An *elevator* is a machine that carries people or things up or down in a building. It is like a small room with a door in front. *[noun]* •**elevators.**

eleven (i LEV uhn) *Eleven* is one more than ten. It is also written 11: *I ate eleven apples last week. [noun* or *adjective]* •**elevens.**

eleventh (i LEV uhnth) *Eleventh* is the next after the tenth. It is also written 11th: *He was the eleventh person to ask that question. [adjective]*

elf (ELF) In stories, an *elf* is a tiny person. *Elves* like to play tricks on people. *[noun]* •**elves.**

elf

else (ELSS) *What else do you want to eat? Do you expect anyone else? What else could he do? [adjective* or *adverb]*

embarrassed (em BAIR uhst) When you feel *embarrassed,* you feel that people are thinking of you badly because of something you have said or done: *When I realized that I had given the wrong answer, I was embarrassed. [adjective]*

emerald (EM er uhld) An *emerald* is a kind of stone that is worth a lot of money. An *emerald* is usually bright green. *Emeralds* are put in rings and other jewelry. *[noun]* •**emeralds.**

emergency • enemy

Ee

empty

emergency (i MUR juhn see) An *emergency* is a time when you need to do something right away. Fires, hurricanes, and floods are *emergencies. In an emergency, dial 911. [noun]* •**emergencies.**

empty (EMP tee)

1. When something is *empty,* there's nothing inside it: *She finished her cereal and left the empty bowl in the sink. [adjective]*

2. When you *empty* something, you pour out or take out all that is in it: *I asked him to empty the trash into the truck. [verb]*
•**emptier, emptiest. •empties, emptied, emptying.**

encyclopedia (en sy kluh PEE dee uh) An *encyclopedia* is a book or set of books giving information about many things. Information in an *encyclopedia* is in alphabetical order. *[noun]*
•**encyclopedias.**

end (END)

1. The *end* of something is the last part of it. The *end* is also the part where a thing begins or stops: *A rope has two ends. We read to the end of the story. [noun]*

end

2. When you *end* something, you finish or stop it: *The girls' mother asked them to end their argument. [verb]*
•**ends. •ends, ended, ending.**

enemy (EN uh mee)

1. An *enemy* is a person or a group of people that is against you or wants to hurt you: *When two countries fight each other, they are enemies. [noun]*

2. An *enemy* is also anything that will hurt something else: *Pollution is our enemy.* [noun]
•**enemies.**

energy (EN er jee)

1. *Energy* is the power to work, move, or play: *Children have so much energy they can't sit still.* [noun]

2. *Energy* is also the power to do work, such as lifting or moving an object. Light, heat, and electricity are different forms of *energy.* [noun]

energy

engine (EN juhn)

1. An *engine* is a machine that does work or makes something move. Many *engines* are run by gas or electricity. [noun]

2. An *engine* is the machine that pulls a railroad train. [noun]
•**engines.**

engineer (en juh NEER)

1. An *engineer* is the person who runs a railroad engine. [noun]

2. An *engineer* is also a person who plans and builds machines, roads, bridges, and buildings. [noun]
•**engineers.**

enjoy (en JOY) When you *enjoy* something, it makes you happy: *The children enjoy their visits to the park.* [verb] •**enjoys, enjoyed, enjoying.**

enough (i NUHF) If you have *enough* of something, you have as much or as many as you need: *Are there enough sandwiches for all of us? He has had enough to eat. They have been gone long enough.* [adjective or *noun* or *adverb*]

enter • erase

enter

enter (EN ter) When you *enter* a place, you go into or come into it: *He likes to enter the school by the front door.* [verb] •**enters, entered, entering.**

entry word (EN tree WURD) An *entry word* is written or printed in a book or a list. Each word listed in alphabetical order in this dictionary is an *entry word.* •**entry words.**

envelope (EN vuh lohp) An *envelope* is a folded paper cover. An *envelope* is used to mail a letter or something else that is flat. [noun] •**envelopes.**

environment (en VY ruhn muhnt) The *environment* is everything in the world that surrounds a living thing: *Plants grow better in an environment where there is enough light and water.* [noun] •**environments.**

equal (EE kwuhl)

1. If two things are *equal,* they are the same in size, number, or amount: *Five pennies are equal to one nickel. The two dogs are equal in size.* [adjective]

2. To *equal* means to be the same as something else: *Five plus four equals nine.* [verb] •**equals, equaled, equaling.**

equator

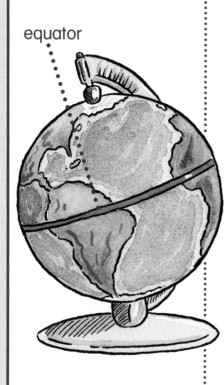

equator (i KWAY ter) The *equator* is a line on a map or globe that shows where the middle of the Earth is. The weather at the *equator* is the warmest weather in the world. [noun]

erase (i RAYSS) When you *erase* something, you rub it out or wipe it away: *He erased his wrong answer and wrote in the right one.* [verb] •**erases, erased, erasing.**

eraser (i RAY ser) An *eraser* is something used to rub out marks made with pencil, ink, or chalk: *The teacher bought a new eraser for the chalkboard.* [noun] •**erasers.**

escalator (ESS kuh lay ter) An *escalator* is a set of moving stairs. You can go from one floor to another by standing on one step and riding up or down. [noun] •**escalators.**

escape (uh SKAYP)

1. To *escape* means to get free or to get out and away: *Did you see the hamster escape from its cage?* [verb]

2. An *escape* is a way to get away: *His escape was made at night.* [noun]

•**escapes, escaped, escaping.** •**escapes.**

especially (uh SPESH uh lee)

1. *Especially* means more than any other thing: *This book was made especially for students.* [adverb]

2. You can use the word *especially* to mean very: *The weather is especially nice today.* [adverb]

estimate (ESS tuh mit *or* ESS tuh mayt *for definition 2*)

1. An *estimate* is a guess about how much or how many. An *estimate* is made from what you already know: *The painter gave an estimate of how much it would cost to paint the house.* [noun]

2. To *estimate* is to guess about how much or how many, using what you already know: *He asked her to estimate the answer to the addition problem.* [verb]

•**estimates.** •**estimates, estimated, estimating.**

erasers

estimate

I estimate that there are 50 jellybeans in the jar.

Ee

even · everything

Ee

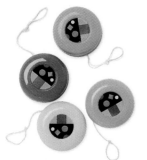

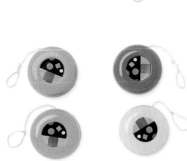

even

even (EE vuhn)

1. When something is *even,* it is flat and smooth: *The edges of the paper are even.* [adjective]

2. *Even* also means exactly as high as: *The roof is even with the tops of the trees.* [adjective]

3. *Even* numbers are able to be divided by two with none left over: *Two and eight are even numbers.* [adjective]

evening (EEV ning) The *evening* is the part of the day between afternoon and night: *Last evening we stayed up late.* [noun] •**evenings.**

event (i VENT) An *event* is something important that happens: *The visit from the President was an exciting event.* [noun] •**events.**

events

ever (EV er) *Is he ever at home? When will she ever get here?* [adverb]

every (EV ree) *Every child needs to bring his or her books to class. Every morning we fix our own breakfast.* [adjective]

everybody (EV ree buhd ee) *Everybody likes the new principal. Ask everybody to be quiet.* [pronoun]

everyone (EV ree wuhn) *Everyone got to school on time yesterday. She wanted everyone she knew to come to the party.* [pronoun]

everything (EV ree thing) *She did everything she could to help. He got everything he wanted for his birthday.* [pronoun]

everywhere (EV ree wair) *I looked everywhere for my gloves. Everywhere we went, we met people we knew.* [adverb]

evil (EE vuhl) When something is *evil*, it hurts people and is bad or wrong: *The monster in the story made an evil plan.* [adjective]

exact (eg ZAKT) *Exact* means without any mistake. If something is *exact*, there is no more and no less than there is supposed to be: *Mom gave the waiter the exact amount for our bill.* [adjective]

exactly (eg ZAKT lee) If you do something *exactly*, you do it without any mistake. You do it just the right way: *He followed my directions exactly.* [adverb]

example (eg ZAM puhl)
1. An *example* is something that shows what other things should be like: *She is an example of a good student.* [noun]
2. An *example* is also a problem in math: *He wrote the example on the board.* [noun]
•**examples.**

excellent (EK suh luhnt) When something is *excellent*, it is very, very good. It is better than other things: *An excellent story was printed in this month's magazine.* [adjective]

except (ek SEPT) *The store is open every day except Sunday. Except for one question, I had all the answers correct.* [preposition]

example

excited · exercise

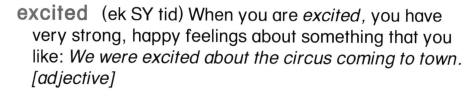

Ee

excited

excited (ek SY tid) When you are *excited,* you have very strong, happy feelings about something that you like: *We were excited about the circus coming to town.* [*adjective*]

exciting (ek SY ting) If something is *exciting,* it causes strong, happy feelings: *It was an exciting game because the score was so close.* [*adjective*]

exclaim (ek SKLAYM) When you *exclaim,* you cry out with strong feeling: *I heard her exclaim "Oh, no!" as she dropped her ice cream cone on the sidewalk.* [*verb*] •**exclaims, exclaimed, exclaiming.**

excuse (ek SKYOOZ *for definitions 1 and 3 or* ek SKYOOSS *for definition 2*)

1. To *excuse* something is to give a reason for it: *He tried to excuse his mistake by saying he was tired.* [*verb*]

2. An *excuse* is a reason you give to explain something you said or did: *He had a good excuse for coming home late.* [*noun*]

3. To *excuse* is to forgive: *Please excuse me for saying that.* [*verb*]
•**excuses, excused, excusing.** •**excuses.**

exercise (EK ser syz)

1. When you *exercise,* you move your body to make it strong and to stay healthy: *If you exercise often, you can work and play longer.* [*verb*]

2. An *exercise* is something that helps develop a skill: *The athlete does this*

exercise

exercise every day. After I study, I do the exercises at the end of the chapter. [noun]
•**exercises, exercised, exercising.** •**exercises.**

exit (EG zit)

1. An *exit* is a way out: *The exit is at the end of the hall.* [noun]

2. To *exit* means to go out or leave: *Please exit by the doors at the back of the room.* [verb]
•**exits.** •**exits, exited, exiting.**

expand (ek SPAND) When something *expands,* it grows larger or swells up: *A balloon expands when it is blown up. Metal expands when it is heated.* [verb]
•**expands, expanded, expanding.**

expect (ek SPEKT) To *expect* something is to think that it will probably come or happen: *We expect it to rain tomorrow.* [verb] •**expects, expected, expecting.**

expensive (ek SPEN siv) When something is *expensive,* it costs a lot of money: *His mother bought him an expensive sweater for his birthday.* [adjective]

experiment (ek SPAIR uh ment *for definition 1 or* ek SPAIR uh muhnt *for definition 2)*

1. When you *experiment,* you test or try something out: *The cook experiments with new recipes.* [verb]

2. An *experiment* is a test to find out something: *We do experiments in science class.* [noun]
•**experiments, experimented, experimenting.** •**experiments.**

explain (ek SPLAYN) When you *explain* something, you tell about it so that people are able to understand

expand

experiment

Ee

explode · eye

Ee

it: *The teacher began to explain what to do on the test. He explained why he couldn't make it to the meeting.* [*verb*] •**explains, explained, explaining.**

explode (ek SPLOHD) When something *explodes,* it bursts with a loud noise: *The building burned when the gas furnace exploded.* [*verb*] •**explodes, exploded, exploding.**

explore (ek SPLOR)

1. When you *explore,* you travel to discover new areas: *Astronauts want to explore outer space.* [*verb*]

2. When you *explore* something, you go over it carefully and look at it: *The children couldn't wait to explore the new playground.* [*verb*]
•**explores, explored, exploring.**

explore

extra (ek STRUH) Something that is *extra* is more than what is usual, expected, or needed: *We asked for extra milk for our cereal.* [*adjective*]

eye (EYE) Your *eye* is the part of your body you use to see. [*noun*] •**eyes.**

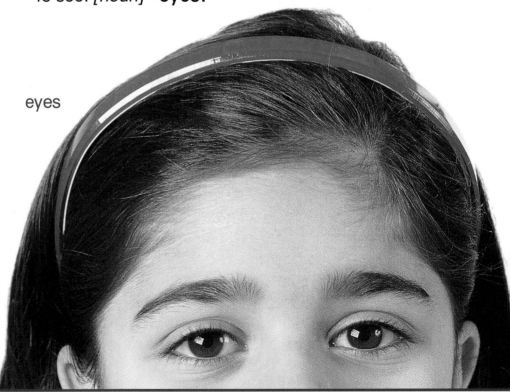

eyes

Ff

fable (FAY buhl) A *fable* is a story that teaches a lesson. Many *fables* are about animals that talk. *[noun]* •**fables.**

fabric (FAB rik) *Fabric* is woven or knitted cloth. Clothes are made from *fabric. [noun]* •**fabrics.**

face (FAYSS)

1. Your *face* is the front part of your head. Your eyes, nose, and mouth are parts of your *face. [noun]*

2. When you *face* something, you turn your face toward it. When things *face* each other, they have their front parts toward each other: *The houses face each other. The teacher asked us to face the board. [verb]*
•**faces.** •**faces, faced, facing.**

face

fact · fairy

Ff

fact (FAKT) A *fact* is a thing that is known to be true: *It is a fact that the Earth orbits the Sun.* [noun] •**facts.**

factory (FAK ter ee) A *factory* is a building or group of buildings where people make things. A *factory* usually has machines in it: *We visited a broom factory.* [noun] •**factories.**

factory

fail (FAYL)

1. If you *fail*, you are not able to do something: *If you think you will fail, you just might.* [verb]

2. To *fail* also means not to do what should be done: *Never fail to follow the directions.* [verb]

•**fails, failed, failing.**

fair¹ (FAIR) If you are *fair*, you go by the rules. People who are *fair* treat everyone the same: *Try to be fair in everything you do.* [adjective] •**fairer, fairest.**

fair² (FAIR)

1. A *fair* is an outdoor show of farm animals and other things: *We enjoyed ourselves at the county fair.* [noun]

2. A *fair* is also a sale of some kind: *Our school held a fair to raise money for new library books.* [noun]

•**fairs.**

fair²

fairy (FAIR ee) In stories, a *fairy* is a tiny person who can help or hurt people. *Fairies* often have wings. [noun] •**fairies.**

fall (FAWL)
1. If you *fall,* you drop or come down from a higher place: *Leaves fall from the trees. Did you see him fall off the chair?* [verb]
2. A *fall* is a dropping from a higher place: *She had a bad fall down the stairs.* [noun]
3. *Fall* is the season of the year between summer and winter. *Fall* is the season when the harvest takes place. Another word for *fall* is *autumn.* [noun]
•**falls, fell, fallen, falling.** •**falls** *for definition 2.*

fallen (FAWL uhn) *She has fallen off the swing.* [verb]

false (FAWLSS) If something is *false,* it is not true. Something that is *false* is wrong or not correct: *What he said is false.* [adjective]

family (FAM lee *or* FAM uh lee)
1. A *family* is parents and children. The people you live with and who take care of you are your *family.* [noun]
2. Your *family* is also all of your relatives: *Grandmother invited the family for Thanksgiving dinner.* [noun]
•**families.**

famous (FAY muhss) When you are *famous,* many people know who you are and think you are important: *The famous singer was met by a large crowd at the airport.* [adjective]

fan (FAN)
1. A *fan* is a machine that blows air around. [noun]
2. A *fan* is also a thing you can hold in your hand and use to move air around. *Fans* are often made of paper and can be very pretty. [noun]
•**fans.**

fan

fancy · farthest

fang

fang

fancy (FAN see) If something is *fancy,* it is not plain. *Fancy* things have a lot of extra things or parts: *She will wear a fancy dress with ribbons. [adjective]* •**fancier, fanciest.**

fang (fang) A *fang* is a long, pointed tooth. Dogs and snakes have *fangs. [noun]* •**fangs.**

far (FAR) If something is *far,* it is a long way away: *The moon is far from the earth. [adjective]* •**farther, farthest.**

fare (FAIR) Your *fare* is the money you pay to ride in a bus, taxi, plane, or subway. *[noun]* •**fares.**

farm (FARM)

1. A *farm* is the land on which a person grows food and raises animals. *[noun]*
2. When you *farm,* you raise crops or animals to eat or to sell: *Both of my aunts farm. [verb]*

•**farms.** •**farms, farmed, farming.**

farmer (FAR mer) A *farmer* is a person who raises crops or animals on a farm. *[noun]* •**farmers.**

farmer

farther (FAR ther) *My house is farther from school than your house is. [adjective]*

farthest (FAR thuhst) *In the race, my sister ran farthest of all. [adverb* or *adjective]*

fast (FAST) If something is *fast,* it moves quickly. Something that is *fast* takes very little time to get from one place to another: *He is a fast runner. Airplanes go fast. [adjective]* •**faster, fastest.**

fat (FAT)

1. If a person or animal is *fat,* that person or animal weighs more than usual: *That dog is too fat. [adjective]*

2. *Fat* is a white or yellow material formed in the body of animals. *Fat* is also found in plants, especially in some seeds. *[noun]*
•**fatter, fattest.** •**fats.**

father (FAH <u>ther</u>) A *father* is a man who has a child or children. *[noun]* •**fathers.**

favorite (FAY ver it)

1. Your *favorite* thing is the one you like better than all the others: *What is your favorite flower? [adjective]*

2. A *favorite* is a person or thing that you like very much: *Pizza is a favorite with me. [noun]*
•**favorites.**

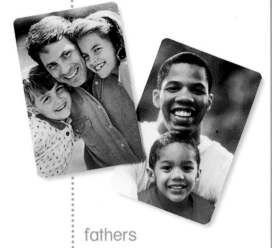

fathers

fear (FEER)

1. *Fear* is a feeling that danger or something bad is near: *I have a fear of high places. [noun]*

2. If you *fear* something, you are afraid of it: *We fear storms. [verb]*
•**fears.** •**fears, feared, fearing.**

feather (FE<u>TH</u> er) A *feather* is one of the light, soft things that cover a bird's body. *[noun]*
•**feathers.**

feathers

Ff

females

February (FEB roo air ee *or* FEB yoo air ee) *February* is the second month of the year. It has 28 days, except in some years when it has 29 days. It comes after January and before March. *[noun]*

fed (FED) *I fed the dogs. Dad has fed them too. [verb]*

feed (FEED) When you *feed* something, you give food to it: *I helped feed the baby. [verb]* •**feeds, fed, feeding.**

feel (FEEL)

1. To *feel* is to touch something: *Feel this smooth stone. [verb]*
2. When you *feel* a certain way, you have a certain state of mind: *She feels sad. They feel angry. [verb]*

•**feels, felt, feeling.** feel

feeling (FEE ling) A *feeling* is how you feel about something. A *feeling* is a state of mind. Joy, fear, and love are *feelings. [noun]* •**feelings.**

feet (FEET) *Feet* is the plural of the word *foot: I have two feet. Bill is four feet tall. [noun plural]*

fell (FEL) *She fell on her knees. [verb]*

felt (FELT) *The baby felt the cat's soft fur. Mom felt better today. [verb]*

female (FEE mayl) A *female* is the kind of person or animal that can give birth or that can lay eggs. Women and girls are *females.* A hen is a *female* chicken. *[noun]* •**females.**

fence (FENSS) A *fence* is something you put around a yard, garden, or field to keep people or animals out or in. A *fence* also shows where the end of a yard is. Most *fences* are made of wood, wire, or metal. *[noun]* •**fences.**

fern (FERN) A *fern* is a kind of plant that has only roots, stems, and leaves. *Ferns* have no flowers or seeds. *[noun]* •**ferns.**

fern

ferret (FAIR it) A *ferret* is a small animal with a long body and short legs. *Ferrets* are sometimes kept as pets. *[noun]* •**ferrets.**

ferry (FAIR ee) A *ferry* is a boat that carries people and things across water. *[noun]* •**ferries.**

few (FYOO) If you have *few* of something, you do not have many. If you have *few* of something, you have a small number: *Few people came to the meeting. Pick the ripe apples and take a few to your grandparents.* *[adjective* or *noun]* •**fewer, fewest.**

fiction (FIK shuhn) *Fiction* is a story that is not true: *Our library has many books of fiction. [noun]*

fierce

field (FEE uhld) A *field* is a piece of land without trees used to grow crops or for some other special purpose: *The corn field lay behind the barn. The baseball field is only two blocks away. [noun]* •**fields.**

fierce (FEERSS) If something is *fierce,* it is dangerous. *Fierce* animals are often very big or strong: *A fierce lion roared in the jungle.* *[adjective]* •**fiercer, fiercest.**

fifteen · fill

Ff

fifteen (fif TEEN) *Fifteen* is five more than ten. It is also written 15. *[noun* or *adjective]* •**fifteens.**

fifteenth (fif TEENTH) *Fifteenth* is the next after the 14th. It is also written 15th. *[adjective]*

fifth (FIFTH)
1. *Fifth* is the next after the fourth. It is also written 5th: *I was fifth in the race. [adjective]*
2. A *fifth* is one of five equal parts: *A fifth of twenty cookies is four cookies. [noun]*
•**fifths.**

fifty (FIF tee) *Fifty* is ten more than forty. It is also written 50. *[noun* or *adjective]* •**fifties.**

fight (FYT)
1. A *fight* is an angry argument between people. Sometimes people in a *fight* try to hurt each other: *Without rules, the game turned into a fight. [noun]*
2. To *fight* is to have an argument: *The kids fought over who was going to take the garbage out. [verb]*
•**fights.** •**fights, fought, fighting.**

figure (FIG yer)
1. A *figure* is the form or shape of a human body: *In the dark I thought I saw a figure of someone outside the window. [noun]*
2. To *figure* means to use numbers to find out the answer to some problem: *Can you figure out the cost of building a doghouse? [verb]*
•**figures.** •**figures, figured, figuring.**

fill (FIL) When you *fill* something, you make it so full that there is no more room for anything more: *Fill this glass with milk. All the rooms in the hospital were filled. [verb]* •**fills, filled, filling.**

fill

film (FILM)

1. *Film* is something used in a camera to take photographs. *[noun]*
2. A *film* is a movie: *We saw a film about dogs.* *[noun]*
•**films** *for definition 2.*

fin (FIN) A *fin* is one of the parts of a fish's body. A fish can swim by moving its *fins.* *[noun]* •**fins.**

fin

finally (FY nuh lee) If something *finally* happens, it happens after a long time of waiting: *Our team finally won a game.* *[adverb]*

find (FYND)

1. When you *find* something, you look for it and get it: *He finds friends everywhere. Did you find your hat?* *[verb]*
2. To *find* also means to learn about something or discover something: *Find the answer to the first problem.* *[verb]*
•**finds, found, finding.**

fine (FYN) When something is *fine,* it is very good or excellent: *He cooked a fine meal. She was sick last week, but now she feels fine.* *[adjective]* •**finer, finest.**

finger (FING ger) Your *finger* is one of the five end parts of your hand. *[noun]* •**fingers.**

fingerprint (FING ger print) Your *fingerprint* is the mark of lines and circles that your finger or thumb makes when you press it against something. Every person's *fingerprints* are different. *[noun]* •**fingerprints.**

fingers

finish • first

Ff

firefighter

finish (FIN ish) When you *finish* something, you get to the end of it or complete it: *Finish your dinner before you go.* [verb] •**finishes, finished, finishing.**

fire (FYR) *Fire* is the flame, heat, and light caused by something burning: *We built a fire to keep warm.* [noun] •**fires.**

fire engine (FYR EN jin) A *fire engine* is a special truck that can pump water to put out fires. *Fire engines* are also called *fire trucks*. •**fire engines.**

firefighter (FYR fy ter) A *firefighter* is a person whose work is putting out fires. [noun] •**firefighters.**

firefly (FYR fly) A *firefly* is a small insect that gives off flashes of light when it flies at night. [noun] •**fireflies.**

firehouse (FYR howss) A *firehouse* is a building where fire engines are kept. [noun] •**firehouses.**

fireplace (FYR playss) A *fireplace* is a place built to hold a fire. [noun] •**fireplaces.**

fire truck (FYR TRUHK) A *fire truck* is a special truck that can pump water to put out fires. *Fire trucks* are also called *fire engines*. •**fire trucks.**

fireworks (FYR wurks) *Fireworks* are things that make a loud noise or go up high in the air and make a shower of sparks. [noun plural]

fire truck

first (FERST)

1. If something or someone is *first*, that person or thing comes before all the others: *I am in the first row.* [adjective]

Ff

2. The word *first* is also used to describe a person, thing, or place that is first: *We were the first to get here. [noun]*

first aid (FERST AYD) *First aid* is emergency care that you give to a hurt or sick person before a doctor sees the person.

fish (FISH)

1. A *fish* is an animal that lives in water. *Fish* are usually covered with scales and have fins for swimming. Many people like to eat certain kinds of *fish. [noun]*

fish

2. When you *fish,* you catch or try to catch fish: *We fish every summer. [verb]*
   •**fish** or **fishes.** •**fishes, fished, fishing.**

fisherman (FISH er muhn) A *fisherman* is a person whose job is catching fish. *[noun]*
•**fishermen.**

fist (FIST) Your *fist* is your closed hand: *He held a coin in his fist. [noun]* •**fists.**

fit (FIT)

1. If you are *fit,* you are healthy and strong: *Exercise helps keep us fit. [adjective]*
2. If things *fit,* they are the right shape or size: *My new shoes fit well. [verb]*
   •**fitter, fittest.** •**fits, fitted, fitting.**

five (FYV) *Five* is one more than four. It is also written 5. *[noun* or *adjective]* •**fives.**

five

fix (FIKS)

1. When you *fix* something, you make it work right again or repair it: *Can he fix a watch?* [verb]

2. To *fix* something also means to make or prepare it: *We fixed our own breakfast today.* [verb]
•**fixes, fixed, fixing.**

flag (FLAG) A *flag* is a piece of colored cloth with stars or other symbols on it. Every country and state has its own *flag.* [noun] •**flags.**

flags

flagpole (FLAG pohl) A *flagpole* is a pole that a flag flies from. [noun] •**flagpoles.**

flame (FLAYM) A *flame* is the part of a fire that you can see shoot up into the air: *We could see the flames above the roof of the burning building.* [noun] •**flames.**

flash (FLASH)

1. A *flash* is a light or flame that lasts only a short time: *I just saw a flash of lightning.* [noun]

2. To *flash* is to give out a light or flame: *The light flashed on and off.* [verb]
•**flashes.** •**flashes, flashed, flashing.**

flashlight (FLASH lyt) A *flashlight* is a small light that can be carried. A *flashlight* runs on batteries. *[noun]* •**flashlights.**

flashlights

flat (FLAT)
1. Something that is *flat* is smooth and even: *The land around the edge of the lake is flat.* *[adjective]*
2. When something is *flat,* it does not have enough air inside it: *Mom drove over some broken glass and got a flat tire.* *[adjective]*
•**flatter, flattest.**

flavor (FLAY ver) A *flavor* is the special taste a food has: *Chocolate is her favorite flavor.* *[noun]* •**flavors.**

flea (FLEE) A *flea* is a small, jumping insect without wings. *Fleas* live on the bodies of dogs, cats, and other animals and feed on their blood. *[noun]* •**fleas.**

flew (FLOO) *The bird flew away. We flew to New York on our vacation.* *[verb]*

float (FLOHT) To *float* means to move in a slow way on top of the water or in the air. Corks and balloons will *float.* *[verb]* •**floats, floated, floating.**

flock (FLOK) A *flock* is a group of animals of the same kind: *A flock of geese landed near the pond.* *[noun]* •**flocks.**

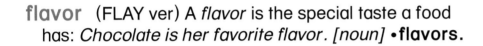

flocks

flood (FLUHD)
1. A *flood* is a large amount of water over what is usually dry land: *We had a flood in the backyard.* *[noun]*
2. To *flood* is to cover or fill something with water: *Will the water flood the streets?* *[verb]*
•**floods.** •**floods, flooded, flooding.**

floor · flour

floor (FLOR)

1. The *floor* is the part of a room that you walk on: *She picked her pencil up off the floor.* [noun]

2. A *floor* is also one of the stories of a building: *We live on the tenth floor.* [noun]
•**floors.**

I am tired!

flop

flop (FLOP) To *flop* is to drop or fall down in a heavy way: *Mother was so tired she just wanted to flop into a chair.* [verb] •**flops, flopped, flopping.**

Florida (FLOR uh duh) *Florida* is one of the fifty states of the United States. [noun]

floss (FLOSS)

1. *Floss* is a special thread you use to clean between your teeth. [noun]

2. To *floss* means to use this special thread: *I flossed my teeth this morning.* [verb]
•**flosses, flossed, flossing.**

floss

flour (FLOW er) *Flour* is a fine powder made of wheat or other grain. *Flour* is used to make bread, cakes, and pies. [noun]

flow (FLOH) To *flow* means to move like water: *Most rivers flow toward the ocean.* [verb] •**flows, flowed, flowing.**

flower (FLOW er) A *flower* is a part of a plant or tree that produces the seed. *Flowers* often have beautiful colors and shapes. [noun] •**flowers.**

flown (FLOHN) *She has flown in an airplane many times.* [verb]

flute (FLOOT) A *flute* is a metal musical instrument that is played by blowing into it and pressing keys. [noun] •**flutes.**

fly[1] (FLY) A *fly* is an insect with two wings. [noun] •**flies.**

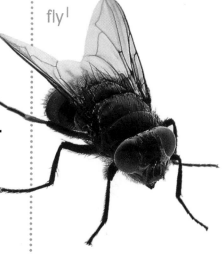

fly[1]

fly[2] (FLY)

1. To *fly* is to move through the air with wings: *Some birds fly south for the winter.* [verb]
2. To *fly* is also to float or make something float in the air: *The boys are flying kites.* [verb]
3. To *fly* also means to travel by airplane: *We flew to Hawaii.* [verb]
•**flies, flew, flown, flying.**

fog (FOG) *Fog* is a cloud of fine drops of water that floats in the air just above the ground. *Fog* makes it hard to see. [noun]

fold (FOHLD)

1. When you *fold* something, you turn or bend part of it down over another part: *Fold the letter before you mail it.* [verb]
2. A *fold* is a mark or line made when you fold something: *Cut the paper along the fold.* [noun]
•**folds, folded, folding.** •**folds.**

fold

Ff

folks (FOHKS) *Folks* is another word for *people:* *Most folks enjoy eating.* [noun plural]

follow (FOL oh)

1. When you *follow* someone or something, you go or come after that person or thing: *Let's follow him. Tuesday follows Monday.* [verb]

2. When you *follow* something, you pay attention to it and do what it says or go along it: *Follow the directions. Follow the signs. Follow the path to the lake.* [verb]
•**follows, followed, following.**

food (FOOD) *Food* is anything that living things eat or drink. *Food* makes them live and grow and gives them energy. [noun] •**foods.**

fool (FOOL) When you *fool* someone, you joke with them or pretend to do something: *I was only fooling. Don't try to fool me.* [verb] •**fools, fooled, fooling.**

foot (FUT)

1. Your *foot* is the part of your body at the end of your leg. [noun]

2. A *foot* is also a unit of length equal to 12 inches. A ruler is one *foot* long. [noun]
•**feet.**

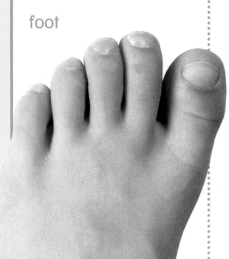

foot

football (FUT bawl)

1. *Football* is a game played on a field by two teams. Each team tries to kick, throw, or carry a ball past the other team's goal. [noun]

2. A *football* is the ball used in this game. [noun]
•**footballs** *for definition 2.*

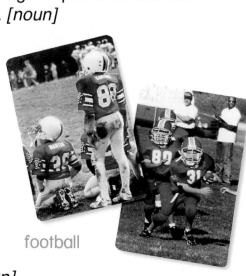

football

footprint (FUT print) A *footprint* is a mark made by a foot: *He saw a footprint in the soft sand.* [noun] •**footprints.**

for (FOR) *He gave me a dime for two nickels. Here is a pot for the soup. We talked for a minute.* [preposition]

forehead (FOR id *or* FOR hed) Your *forehead* is the part of your face above your eyes. [noun] •**foreheads.**

forehead

forest (FOR ist) A *forest* is a large area with many tall trees: *Many animals live in the forest.* [noun] •**forests.**

forever (fer EV er) *Forever* means always or all the time: *He's forever asking questions.* [adverb]

forget (fer GET) When you *forget* something, you can't remember it: *Don't forget to wear your gloves.* [verb] •**forgets, forgot, forgotten, forgetting.**

forgive (fer GIV) When you *forgive* someone, you do not have any angry feelings toward them anymore: *She forgave me for losing her scarf.* [verb] •**forgives, forgave, forgiven, forgiving.**

forgot (fer GOT) *I forgot to thank her.* [verb]

forgotten (fer GOT uhn) *She has never forgotten to thank me.* [verb]

fork (FORK) A *fork* is something to eat with. A *fork* has two or more sharp points. A *fork* is used to lift solid food from a plate or dish to your mouth. [noun] •**forks.**

forks

form (FORM)

I. A *form* is a shape. Circles and squares are *forms.* [noun]

forty · four

Ff

2. A *form* is also a kind or sort of something. Ice is a *form* of water. [noun]

3. When something *forms,* it starts to have a certain shape. When you *form* something, you give it a certain shape: *Clouds form in the sky. I can form a vase with the clay.* [verb]
•**forms.** •**forms, formed, forming.**

forty (FOR tee) *Forty* is ten more than thirty. It is also written 40. [noun or adjective] •**forties.**

forward (FOR werd) When something moves *forward,* it moves to the front: *The cafeteria line moved forward.* [adverb]

fossil (FOS uhl) A *fossil* is a part or print of a plant or animal that lived a long time ago. *Fossils* are found in rock or ice. *Fossils* of the bones of dinosaurs that lived many millions of years ago have been dug up in North America. [noun] •**fossils.**

fossils

fought (FAWT) *The puppies fought over the bones.* [verb]

found (FOWND) *I found a dime. The cat has found her way home.* [verb]

four

fountain (FOWN tuhn) A *fountain* is water that rises into the air in a stream: *People stopped to admire the beautiful fountain. The drinking fountain is over there.* [noun]
•**fountains.**

four (FOR) *Four* is one more than three. It is also written 4. [noun or adjective] •**fours.**

fourteen (FOR TEEN) *Fourteen* is four more than ten. It is also written 14. *[noun* or *adjective]* •**fourteens.**

fourteenth (FOR TEENTH) *Fourteenth* is next after 13th. It also written 14th. *[adjective* or *noun]*

fourth (FORTH)
1. Something that is *fourth* is next after the third. It is also written 4th. *[adjective]*
2. A *fourth* is one of four equal parts. *[noun]* •**fourths.**

Fourth of July (FORTH uhv ju LY) The *Fourth of July* is a holiday in the United States. It is also called *Independence Day.*

Fourth of July

fox (FOKS) A *fox* is a wild animal that looks something like a dog. A *fox* has a pointed nose, thick fur, and a bushy tail. *[noun]* •**foxes.**

fraction (FRAK shuhn) A *fraction* is a part of a whole thing. Each of two halves of something is equal to the *fraction* $\frac{1}{2}$. Two of five equal parts of something is equal to the *fraction* $\frac{2}{5}$. *[noun]* •**fractions.**

freckle (FREK uhl) A *freckle* is a small, light brown spot that some people have on their skin: *She has freckles on her nose. [noun]* •**freckles.**

freckles

free (FREE)
1. If you are *free,* you are not under someone else's control or rule: *We live in a free country. [adjective]*
2. If something is *free,* it does not cost any money: *We got free tickets to the play. [adjective* or *adverb]*

freeze · friend

Ff

3. When you *free* something, you let it loose or let it go: *We freed the bear cub.* [verb]
•**freer, freest** *for definition 1.* •**frees, freed, freeing.**

freeze (FREEZ) To *freeze* is to make or become very cold and hard. Water turns into ice when it *freezes.* [verb]
•**freezes, froze, frozen, freezing.**

freeze

French horn (FRENCH HORN) The *French horn* is an instrument that is made of a long, narrow tube bent in a circle.
•**French horns.**

fresh (FRESH)

1. When something is *fresh,* it is just made, grown, or gathered. When something is *fresh,* it is new: *The bread is fresh. Please make a fresh copy.* [adjective]
2. *Fresh* also means pure and not spoiled: *Is this milk fresh? Smell the fresh air.* [adjective]
•**fresher, freshest.**

Friday (FRY day) *Friday* is the day after Thursday. *Friday* is the sixth day of the week. [noun] •**Fridays.**

fried (FRYD) If something is *fried,* it is cooked in hot fat: *We enjoy eating fried chicken.* [adjective]

friend (FREND) A *friend* is someone you like and who likes you. [noun] •**friends.**

friend

friendly (FREND lee) When someone is *friendly*, that person is kind and acts like a friend to you: *She is a friendly teacher*. *[adjective]* •**friendlier, friendliest.**

frighten (FRYT uhn) If you *frighten* people, you scare them or make them afraid: *The storm frightened the puppy*. *[verb]* •**frightens, frightened, frightening.**

Frisbee (FRIZ bee) *Frisbee* is the name of a round, flat toy. You can play with a *Frisbee* by throwing it in the air. *[noun]* •**Frisbees.**

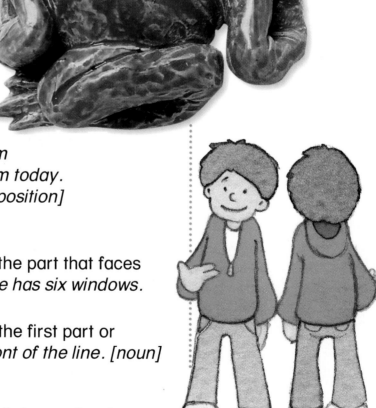
frog

frog (FROG) A *frog* is a small animal that lives part of the time in water and part of the time on land. Young *frogs* hatch from eggs and are called *tadpoles*. They live in the water until they grow legs. *[noun]* •**frogs.**

from (FRUHM) *Steel is made from iron. I start school two weeks from today. She is suffering from a cold.* *[preposition]*

front (FRUHNT)
1. The *front* part of something is the part that faces forward: *The front of our house has six windows.* *[noun]*
2. The *front* of something is also the first part or beginning of it: *Move to the front of the line.* *[noun]*
•**fronts** for definition 1.

frost (FRAWST) *Frost* is very small drops of water frozen on the surface of something: *There is frost on the windows today.* *[noun]*

front

frown · full

Ff

frown (FROWN)

1. A *frown* is a forehead with wrinkles and a sad mouth: *We could see a frown on her face.* [noun]
2. When you *frown,* you wrinkle your forehead to show you are angry or do not like something: *She frowned as she asked us not to make so much noise.* [verb]

•**frowns.** •**frowns, frowned, frowning.**

froze (FROHZ) *The pond froze early this year.* [verb]

frozen (FROH zuhn)

1. If something is *frozen,* it is turned into ice or it is very cold: *The frozen river made travel by boat impossible.* [adjective]
2. *Frozen* is also a form of the verb *freeze*: *The pond has frozen solid. His hands are frozen.* [verb]

frozen

fruit (FROOT) *Fruit* is the part of a tree, bush, or vine that has seeds in it and is good to eat. Apples, oranges, strawberries, and bananas are *fruit.* [noun]

•**fruit** or **fruits.**

fruit

fry (FRY) When you *fry* something, you cook it in hot fat: *Should I fry the potatoes or boil them?* [verb]

•**fries, fried, frying.**

full (FUL) If something is *full,* it is not able to hold any more: *His glass is full.* [adjective] •**fuller, fullest.**

fun (FUHN) When you have *fun,* you have a good time: *He had fun at the party.* [noun]

funny

funny (FUHN ee) If something is *funny,* it makes you laugh: *All the kids laughed at the clown's funny faces.* [adjective] •**funnier, funniest.**

fur (FER) *Fur* is the soft, thick hair that covers the skin of many animals. [noun]

furnace (FER niss) A *furnace* is something that you can make a very hot fire in. *Furnaces* are used to heat buildings. [noun] •**furnaces.**

furniture (FER ni chur) *Furniture* is the things you need in a room or house. Beds and desks are *furniture.* [noun]

furry (FER ee) If something is *furry,* it is covered with fur. [adjective] •**furrier, furriest.**

future (FYOO cher) The *future* is the time to come. The *future* is all the days, months, and years that will come. [noun]

Ff

galaxy · garage

Gg

game

galaxy (GAL uhk see) A *galaxy* is a very large group of stars. Earth and the sun are in the Milky Way *galaxy*. [noun] •**galaxies.**

gallon (GAL uhn) A *gallon* is an amount of liquid. Large amounts of liquid are often measured by the *gallon*. A *gallon* is equal to four quarts. [noun] •**gallons.**

gallop (GAL uhp) To *gallop* is to run very fast: *The horse galloped down the road.* [verb] •**gallops, galloped, galloping.**

game (GAYM) A *game* is something you play or have fun doing: *The children play games at recess.* [noun] •**games.**

garage (guh RAHZH *or* guh RAHJ) A *garage* is a place where cars are parked or fixed. Mechanics fix cars in *garages*: *My father parks his car in the garage.* [*noun*] •**garages.**

garbage (GAR bij) *Garbage* is bits and pieces of food and paper to be thrown away. *Garbage* is often put in a *garbage can.* Another word for *garbage* is *trash.* [*noun*]

garbage collector (GAR bij kuh LEK ter) A *garbage collector* is a person whose job is picking up garbage and taking it away. •**garbage collectors.**

garbage truck (GAR bij TRUHK) A *garbage truck* is a special truck that picks up people's garbage. •**garbage trucks.**

garden (GARD uhn) Your *garden* is the part of your yard where you grow vegetables or flowers. [*noun*] •**gardens.**

gardens

gas (GASS)

1. A *gas* is something that is not solid or liquid. A *gas* has no special size or shape. Most *gases* have no color and cannot be seen. The air we breathe is made of several *gases.* Another kind of *gas* is put into some stoves to make fire for cooking. [*noun*]

2. *Gas* is also a short word meaning *gasoline.*
•**gases** *for definition* 1.

gasoline (GASS uh leen *or* gass uh LEEN) *Gasoline* is the liquid that is put into cars and other machines to make them go. [*noun*]

gas station (GASS STAY shuhn) A *gas station* is a place to buy gasoline and oil. •**gas stations.**

gas station

167

gate • geometry

Gg

gate (GAYT) A *gate* is a door in a fence or wall. [noun] •**gates.**

gather (GA<u>TH</u> er) When you *gather* things, you bring them together in one place. When people *gather*, they come to the same place: *Please gather your toys and put them away. The crowd gathered to hear the governor.* [verb] •**gathers, gathered, gathering.**

gather

gave (GAYV) *She gave her mother a flower.* [verb]

geese (GEESS) *Geese* is the plural of the word *goose.* [noun plural]

gentle (JEN tuhl)
1. If something is *gentle,* it is soft, not rough: *The gentle moving of the boat made us sleepy.* [adjective]
2. If you are *gentle,* you are kind and friendly: *We have a gentle dog.* [adjective]
•**gentler, gentlest.**

gently (JENT lee) When you do something *gently,* you do it in a gentle or soft way: *The rain fell gently. She spoke gently to the baby.* [adverb]

geography (je OG ruh fee) *Geography* is the study of where people and places can be found on the earth. [noun]

geometry (je OM uh tree) In mathematics, *geometry* is the study of shapes such as triangles and circles. [noun]

geometry

Georgia (JOR juh)
Georgia is one of the fifty states of the United States. [noun]

gerbil

gerbil (JER bul) A *gerbil* is a small animal that looks like a mouse. Many people keep *gerbils* as pets. [noun] •**gerbils.**

get (GET) *I hope to get a bike for my birthday. It gets hot in the summer. When I get home, I usually have a snack. Get the windows open. Please get me a drink of water. Try to get them to come, too. The teacher explained the math problem again, but I still didn't get it.* [verb] •**gets, got, gotten, getting.**

ghost (GOHST) In stories, a *ghost* is a white shape that scares people. *Ghosts* are not real. [noun] •**ghosts.**

giant (JY uhnt)
1. In stories, a *giant* is a person who is very large. [noun]
2. If something is *giant,* it is much bigger than usual: *We made a giant sandwich for lunch.* [adjective]
•**giants.**

giant

gift (GIFT) A *gift* is a present. A *gift* is something that people give you because they want to: *My uncle brought me a gift when I was sick.* [noun] •**gifts.**

gigantic (jy GAN tik) Something that is *gigantic* is like a giant. *Gigantic* things are very large and strong: *Some dinosaurs were gigantic.* [adjective]

giggle (GIG uhl)
1. When you *giggle,* you laugh in a silly way: *The children giggled when the clowns came in.* [verb]

ginger · glad

Gg

gingerbread

2. A *giggle* is a silly laugh: *We heard a loud giggle from the back of the room.* [noun]
•**giggles, giggled, giggling.** •**giggles.**

ginger (JIN jer) *Ginger* is a spice made from the root of a plant. *Ginger* has a sharp, hot taste. [noun]

gingerbread (JIN jer bred) *Gingerbread* is a kind of spicy cake or cookie. [noun]

giraffe (juh RAF) A *giraffe* is a large animal with a very long neck and spots on its skin. *Giraffes* are the tallest living animals. [noun] •**giraffes.**

girl (GERL) A *girl* is a female child. A *girl* grows up to be a woman. [noun] •**girls.**

girl scout (GERL SKOWT) A *girl scout* is a person who belongs to the Girl Scouts of America. This group helps girls grow into healthy, strong young women.
•**girl scouts.**

give (GIV)
1. When you *give* someone something, you let that person have it. You do not want anything back from the person: *I'll give her my sweater to keep.* [verb]
2. To *give* also means to pay: *I will give you three dollars for the necklace.* [verb]
•**gives, gave, given, giving.**

give

given (GIV uhn) *He has given his bike to me.* [verb]

glad (GLAD) When you are *glad,* you are happy and pleased: *She is glad to be home after a long trip.* [adjective] •**gladder, gladdest.**

glass (GLASS)

1. *Glass* is something that you can see through. *Glass* is easy to break. Windows are made of *glass*. [noun]

2. A *glass* is something to drink from: *Would you like a glass of water?* [noun]
•**glasses** *for definition 2*.

glasses (GLASS iz)

Glasses are what people who need help seeing wear. *Glasses* are made of glass or plastic and sit on your nose. [noun plural]

glasses

globe (GLOHB)

A *globe* is a round copy of the earth. A *globe* has a map of the earth drawn on it: *Can you find Canada on the globe?* [noun] •**globes.**

glove (GLUHV)

1. A *glove* is a covering for your hand, with a place for each finger and for the thumb. *Gloves* keep your hands warm and are made of cloth or leather. [noun]

2. A *glove* is also used when you play baseball. A baseball *glove* has extra layers of material to protect your hand. [noun]
•**gloves.**

glue (GLOO)

1. *Glue* is something used to stick things together. *Glue* can come in a bottle or as a stick: *Mom fixed the broken chair with glue.* [noun]

2. When you *glue* things, you stick them together with glue: *We glued the parts of the model plane.* [verb]
•**glues, glued, gluing.**

gloves

glum · gobble

Gg

glum (GLUHM) When you feel *glum,* you feel sad and tired: *I felt very glum when my friend moved away.* *[adjective]* •**glummer, glummest.**

gnat (NAT) A *gnat* is a small fly with two wings. Most *gnats* bite, and their bites itch. *[noun]* •**gnats.**

go (GOH)

1. To *go* is to move from one place to another: *We wanted to go to the store yesterday. Are you ready to go? [verb]*
2. To *go* also means to act or work: *The car won't go because the battery is dead. [verb]*
3. To *go* is also to have a place to be or belong: *These dishes go on the first shelf. [verb]*
•**goes, went, gone, going.**

goal (GOHL)

1. A *goal* is the place that players try to put the ball in some games. *[noun]*
2. A *goal* is also something you want very much: *His goal was to become a lawyer. [noun]*
•**goals.**

goal

goalposts (GOHL pohsts) *Goalposts* show where the ball should go to score points in football, soccer, and hockey. *[noun plural]*

goat (GOHT) A *goat* is an animal with horns. *Goats* have hair under their chins. People raise *goats* for their milk and their skins. *[noun]* •**goats.**

gobble (GOB uhl) When you *gobble,* you eat quickly with a lot of noise: *The hungry dogs gobble their dinner. [verb]* •**gobbles, gobbled, gobbling.**

goat

goblin (GOB luhn) In stories, a *goblin* is a mean dwarf. *[noun]* •**goblins.**

goes (GOHZ) *Everywhere I go, my little sister goes.* *[verb]*

goggles (GOG uhlz) *Goggles* are glasses that fit against your forehead. People wear *goggles* to protect their eyes from light, water, and dust. *[noun plural]*

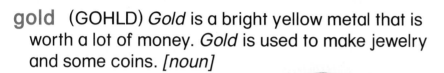

goggles

gold (GOHLD) *Gold* is a bright yellow metal that is worth a lot of money. *Gold* is used to make jewelry and some coins. *[noun]*

goldfish (GOHLD fish) A *goldfish* is a small orange fish. Many people keep *goldfish* in glass bowls as pets. *[noun]* •**goldfish** or **goldfishes.**

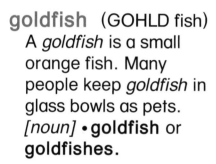

goldfish

golf (GOLF) *Golf* is a game you play outdoors with a small, hard ball and a set of clubs with metal or wooden heads. The *golf ball* has little dents on it. *Golf clubs* have long handles. Players try to hit the ball into a hole. The player who hits the ball the fewest times before it goes into the hole wins. *[noun]*

gone (GON) *He has gone to a movie.* *[verb]*

good (GUD)
1. Something that is *good* is right or done well. Things that are *good* are as they should be: *He does good work.* *[adjective]*
2. A person or animal who is *good* is friendly, kind, and behaves well: *That's a good dog.* *[adjective]*

Gg

3. Something that is *good* is fun, and you enjoy it: *I hope you have a good time at the ball game.* *[adjective]*
•**better, best.**

good-bye (gud BY) *Good-bye* is what people say when they are going away. People also use this word when they finish talking on the telephone. *[interjection or noun]*
•**good-byes.**

good-bye

gooey (GOO ee) Something that is *gooey* is soft and sticky: *I like gooey candy.* *[adjective]* •**gooier, gooiest.**

goose (GOOSS) A *goose* is a large bird with a long neck. A *goose* looks like a duck but is larger. *[noun]* •**geese.**

gorilla

gorilla (guh RIL uh) A *gorilla* is a large animal with long arms, no tail, and a lot of hair. A *gorilla* is the biggest and strongest of the apes. *[noun]* •**gorillas.**

got (GOT) *It got cold last night. He got a sweater.* *[verb]*

gotten (GOT uhn) *She has gotten many presents this year. Has Mom gotten up yet?* *[verb]*

grab (GRAB) When you *grab* something, you take it suddenly: *I saw the dog grab the bone and run.* *[verb]* •**grabs, grabbed, grabbing.**

grade (GRAYD)

1. A *grade* is a year of study in school: *He is in second grade.* *[noun]*

2. A *grade* is also a number or letter that shows how well you have done: *Did you get a good grade on the test?* [noun]

3. When you *grade* something, you give a grade to it: *Please grade each other's papers.* [verb]
•**grades.** •**grades, graded, grading.**

grain (GRAYN)

1. *Grain* is the seed of wheat, rice, corn, and other plants. [noun]

2. A *grain* of something is a tiny bit. Sand, salt, and sugar have *grains.* [noun]
•**grains.**

gram (GRAM) A *gram* is a unit of weight. A paper clip weighs about one *gram.* [noun] •**grams.**

grandchild (GRAND chyld) A *grandchild* is a child of your son or daughter. [noun] •**grandchildren.**

grandfather (GRAND fah ther) Your *grandfather* is the father of your mother or father. [noun] •**grandfathers.**

grandma (GRAND mah) *Grandma* is another word for *grandmother.* [noun] •**grandmas.**

grandmother (GRAND muh ther) Your *grandmother* is the mother of your mother or father. [noun] •**grandmothers.**

grandpa (GRAND pah) *Grandpa* is another word for *grandfather.* [noun] •**grandpas.**

grain

grandma

Gg

175

Gg

grandparent (GRAND pair uhnt) Your *grandparent* is a parent of your mother or father. A *grandparent* is a grandfather or grandmother. *[noun]* •**grandparents.**

grape (GRAYP) A *grape* is a small, round fruit that grows on a vine. *Grapes* are red, purple, or green. *[noun]* •**grapes.**

grapes

grapefruit (GRAYP froot) A *grapefruit* is a yellow fruit that looks like a large orange but is not as sweet. *Grapefruit* grow on trees. *[noun]* •**grapefruit** *or* **grapefruits.**

graph (GRAF) A *graph* is a line or drawing showing information. A *graph* can show how your height has changed over the last four years. *[noun]* •**graphs.**

grass (GRASS) *Grass* is a plant with thin leaves. *Grass* is green and grows in fields, parks, and yards. Horses, cows, and sheep eat *grass. [noun]*

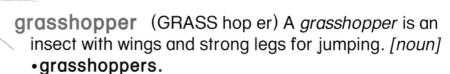

grasshopper

grasshopper (GRASS hop er) A *grasshopper* is an insect with wings and strong legs for jumping. *[noun]* •**grasshoppers.**

gravel (GRAV uhl) *Gravel* is pieces of rock that are larger than sand. *Gravel* is used for roads and paths. *[noun]*

gray (GRAY)

1. *Gray* is a color made by mixing black and white. *[noun]*

2. If something is *gray,* it has this color: *We saw the gray clouds in the sky. [adjective]*
•**grays.** •**grayer, grayest.**

great (GRAYT)

1. If something is *great*, it is very good or important: *This painting was done by a great artist.* [adjective]
2. If something is *great*, it is also very big or large: *A great cloud of smoke rose over the fire.* [adjective]
•**greater, greatest.**

great-grandfather (grayt GRAND fah <u>ther</u>) Your *great-grandfather* is the father of your grandparent. [noun] •**great-grandfathers.**

great-grandmother (grayt GRAND muh <u>ther</u>) Your *great-grandmother* is the mother of your grandparent. [noun] •**great-grandmothers.**

great-grandparent (grayt GRAND pair uhnt) A *great-grandparent* is a great-grandfather or a great-grandmother. [noun] •**great-grandparents.**

greedy (GREE dee) If you are *greedy*, you want more than your share: *Help yourself to some candy, but don't be greedy.* [adjective] •**greedier, greediest.**

green (GREEN)

1. *Green* is the color of most growing plants. [noun]
2. If something is *green*, it has this color: *She wore a green sweater.* [adjective]
•**greens.** •**greener, greenest.**

green

greenhouse (GREEN howss) A *greenhouse* is a building with a glass or plastic roof and sides. A *greenhouse* is kept warm and full of light for growing plants. [noun] •**greenhouses.**

grew (GROO) *The grass grew very fast from all the rain.* [verb]

grin • group

Gg grin

grin (GRIN)

1. When you *grin,* you smile with your teeth showing: *Grin at the camera!* [verb]
2. A *grin* is a wide smile that shows your teeth: *He had a friendly grin on his face.* [noun]

•**grins, grinned, grinning.** •**grins.**

grip (grip)

1. When you *grip* something, you hold it in a tight way: *She gripped the handle.* [verb]
2. When you have a *grip* on something, it is in your hand or under your control, and it won't slip: *The dog had a tight grip on the bone.* [noun]

•**grips, gripped, gripping.** •**grips.**

grocery (GROH suh ree) A *grocery* is a store that sells food. *Groceries* are the foods and things for the house that you buy at a *grocery* store. [noun]

•**groceries.**

ground (GROWND) The *ground* is the soil or dirt on the surface of the earth: *The ground was rocky.* [noun]

groundhog (GROWND hog) A *groundhog* is a small animal with a bushy tail. [noun] •**groundhogs.**

group (GROOP)

1. A *group* is a number of persons or things together: *We saw a group of children laughing.* [noun]
2. When you *group* things, you gather them together: *Can you group all the pictures of cats on the page?* [verb]

•**groups.** •**groups, grouped, grouping.**

group

grow (GROH) When you *grow,* you get bigger: *A cactus will grow in sand. She wants to be a doctor when she grows up.* [verb] •**grows, grew, grown, growing.**

grow

growl (GROWL)
To *growl* is to make a deep, angry sound in the throat: *I heard the dog growl at the squirrels.* [verb] •**growls, growled, growling.**

grown (GROHN) *Our sunflowers have grown very tall.* [verb]

grown-up (GROHN uhp) A *grown-up* is a person who has finished growing: *A grown-up coaches the soccer team.* Another word for *grown-up* is *adult.* [noun] •**grown-ups.**

grown-up

grumble (GRUHM buhl) If you *grumble,* you complain about things and other people: *Don't grumble about the weather all day.* [verb] •**grumbles, grumbled, grumbling.**

grumpy (GRUHM pee) If you are *grumpy,* you are rude to others and grumble about things: *My brother is grumpy when he gets up in the morning.* [adjective] •**grumpier, grumpiest.**

Guanajuato (gwah nah HWAH toh) *Guanajuato is a state in central Mexico.* [noun]

guard (GARD)
1. When you *guard* something, you take care of it and keep it safe: *The dogs guard the house at night.* [verb]

Gg

Guerrero • guinea pig

Gg

2. A *guard* is a person who takes care of something: *The crossing guard helped them cross the street.* [noun] •**guards, guarded, guarding.** •**guards.**

guard

Guerrero (guh RAIR oh) *Guerrero* is a state in the south of Mexico. [noun]

guess (GESS)

1. When you *guess,* you try to give the answer to something when you are not sure you are right: *She tried to guess before she looked up the answer. I guess it will rain tomorrow.* [verb]

2. A *guess* is an idea you have when you are not sure of something: *My guess is that the tree is ten feet high.* [noun] •**guesses, guessed, guessing.** •**guesses.**

guest (GEST) A *guest* is a person who is visiting someone else's house: *She was our guest for dinner.* [noun] •**guests.**

guide (GYD) When you *guide* people, you show them the way or lead them: *The compass will guide us back to camp.* [verb] •**guides, guided, guiding.**

guide word (GYD WERD) A *guide word* is a word put at the top of a page as a guide. *Guide words* tell what the first and last words on the page are. The *guide words* for this page are *Guerrero* and *guinea pig.* •**guide words.**

guinea pig

guinea pig (GIN ee PIG) A *guinea pig* is a small, fat animal with short ears and a short tail or no tail. People often keep *guinea pigs* as pets. •**guinea pigs.**

guitar (guh TAR) A *guitar* is a musical instrument that usually has six strings. You play a *guitar* with your fingers. *[noun]* •**guitars.**

gull (GUHL) A *gull* is a bird that lives near lakes and oceans. A *gull* has long wings and a strong beak. *[noun]* •**gulls.**

gully (GUHL ee) A *gully* is a long, deep hole made by heavy rains or running water. *[noun]* •**gullies.**

gum[1] (GUHM) *Gum* is something sweet that you chew but don't swallow: *We are not allowed to chew gum in school.* *[noun]*

gum[2] (GUHM) Your *gums* are the soft pink part of your mouth that your teeth grow out of. *[noun]* •**gums.**

gun (GUHN) A *gun* is a weapon with a metal tube for shooting bullets. *[noun]* •**guns.**

gym (JIM) A *gym* is a room or building where you can exercise and play games. *[noun]* •**gyms.**

gymnastics (jim NASS tikss) *Gymnastics* is a sport in which very difficult exercises are done very carefully. *[noun]*

gum[1]

Gg

gymnastics

habit · hadrosaur

Hh

habit (HAB it) A *habit* is something you do over and over again, sometimes without thinking: *Brushing your teeth is a good habit. Biting your nails is a bad habit.* [noun] •**habits.**

habitat (HAB uh tat) A *habitat* is a place where a plant or an animal lives. The jungle is the *habitat* of monkeys. [noun] •**habitats.**

had (HAD) *I had a pet cat. We had to leave early for school. You had enough time.* [verb]

hadn't *Hadn't* is a shorter form of *had not*: *She hadn't seen him in a long time.* [contraction]

hadrosaur (HAD ruh sor) The *hadrosaur* was a dinosaur with a bill that looked like a duck's bill. The *hadrosaur* lived on both water and land. It had feet like a duck's feet. [noun] •**hadrosaurs.**

hadrosaur

hail (HAYL)
1. *Hail* is small, round pieces of ice that come down like rain: *The noise of hail on the roof woke us.* *[noun]*
2. When it *hails,* small pieces of ice fall like rain: *Sometimes it will hail during a summer storm.* *[verb]*
•**hails, hailed, hailing.**

hair (HAIR) *Hair* is the thin pieces that look like threads and grow from your head and your skin. *Hair* may be straight or curly. People and animals both have *hair*. *[noun]* •**hair** or **hairs.**

hair

hairbrush (HAIR brush) A *hairbrush* is a stiff brush you use to make your hair smooth and neat. *[noun]* •**hairbrushes.**

haircut (HAIR kuht) When you get a *haircut,* someone cuts your hair shorter. *[noun]* •**haircuts.**

half (HAF) A *half* is one of two equal parts: *He ate half of an orange for lunch. He had the other half after school. Both halves tasted good. [noun]* •**halves.**

hall (HAWL) A *hall* is a long, narrow space that leads to other rooms in a building: *The hall leads to the auditorium. [noun]* •**halls.**

Halloween (hal oh EEN) *Halloween* is October 31, when children dress up in costumes and ask for treats at other people's houses. *[noun]* •**Halloweens.**

halves (HAVZ) *Halves* is the plural of the word *half*. *[noun plural]*

half

ham · hand

Hh

ham (HAM) *Ham* is a kind of meat. *Ham* comes from the top part of a pig's leg. *[noun]*
•**hams.**

hamburger (HAM ber ger) *Hamburger* is a kind of meat. *Hamburger* is made out of ground beef. *Hamburgers* are also a kind of sandwich made of hamburger meat cooked in a round, flat shape and served on a bun. *[noun]*
•**hamburgers.**

hamburger

hammer (HAM er)

1. A *hammer* is a tool you use to hit nails. A *hammer* has a long handle with a heavy piece of metal at one end. *[noun]*

2. When you *hammer* something, you hit it with a hammer: *She hammered a nail into the wall to hold up a picture. [verb]*
•**hammers.** •**hammers, hammered, hammering.**

hamster (HAM ster) A *hamster* is an animal that looks a little like a large mouse. Some people have *hamsters* as pets. *[noun]* •**hamsters.**

hand (HAND)

1. Your *hand* is the part of your body at the end of your arm. Each *hand* has four fingers and a thumb. *[noun]*

2. When you *hand* a person something, you pass it with your hands: *Please hand me the salt. [verb]*
•**hands.** •**hands, handed, handing.**

handkerchief (HANG ker chif) A *handkerchief* is a square piece of soft cloth you use to wipe your nose, face, and hands: *My dad carries a handkerchief in his pocket.* *[noun]* •**handkerchiefs.**

handle (HAN duhl) A *handle* is the part of something that you hold on to. Pans, suitcases, and rakes have *handles.* *[noun]* •**handles.**

hang (HANG) When you *hang* something, you put it up on a hook so that it won't touch the ground. When something *hangs,* it is held up so that it doesn't touch the ground: *Hang up your coat. Monkeys hang by their tails.* *[verb]* •**hangs, hung, hanging.**

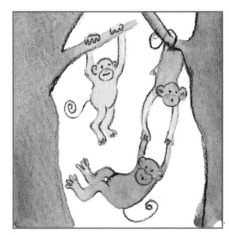
hang

Hanukkah (HAH nuh kuh) *Hanukkah* is a holiday celebrated by some people once a year. *Hanukkah* usually comes in December and lasts for eight days: *At Hanukkah we give each other presents and light Hanukkah candles.* *[noun]*

happen (HAP uhn) When something *happens,* it takes place: *What do you think will happen?* *[verb]* •**happens, happened, happening.**

happy (HAP ee) When you are *happy,* you feel as you do when you have a good time. When you are *happy,* you are glad and pleased: *He is happy that you came to visit.* *[adjective]* •**happier, happiest.**

harbor (HAR ber) A *harbor* is an area of water where ships are safe: *The boat sailed for the harbor when the storm began.* *[noun]* •**harbors.**

Hanukkah

hard • hatch

Hh

hard (HARD)

1. Something that is *hard* is not soft. Something that is *hard* does not move when someone touches it: *The turtle has a hard shell.* [adjective]

2. Something that is *hard* takes a lot of work or energy to do. Something that is *hard* is difficult: *Cleaning out the garage is a hard job; it is not easy.* [adjective]

•**harder, hardest.**

hardly (HARD lee) *Hardly* means only just or not quite: *We had hardly finished eating when the telephone rang.* [adverb]

harmonica (har MON uh kuh) A *harmonica* is a small musical instrument shaped like a thick candy bar. It is played by breathing in and out through it. [noun] •**harmonicas.**

harmonica

harvest (HAR vist)

1. The *harvest* is the ripe crops that are picked after the growing season is over: *The corn harvest was poor after the hot, dry summer.* [noun]

2. When you *harvest*, you gather in the crops and store them: *We harvested the apples in late fall.* [verb]

•**harvests.** •**harvests, harvested, harvesting.**

has (HAZ) *The teacher has my paper. He has to go to sleep. She has been on vacation.* [verb]

hat (HAT) A *hat* is a kind of clothing you wear on your head: *She wore a hat outside in the cold.* [noun] •**hats.**

hatch (HACH) When something *hatches,* it comes out from an egg to be born. Birds and some snakes *hatch*: *Two chickens hatched today.* [verb] •**hatches, hatched, hatching.**

hats

hate (HAYT) If you *hate* someone or something, you do not like them at all: *Cats and dogs often hate each other. He hated to go to the barber.* [verb] •**hates, hated, hating.**

haul (HAWL) To *haul* means to pull or drag something heavy: *The truck hauled her car away.* [verb] •**hauls, hauled, hauling.**

haul

haunted (HAWN tid) If a place is *haunted,* people think that it is visited by ghosts or that it is a scary place: *They were afraid to go into the haunted house.* [adjective]

have (HAV) *I have a nickel in my pocket. We have to go now. We always have breakfast in the kitchen. They have asked for their mail.* [verb] •**has, had, having.**

haven't *Haven't* is a shorter form of *have not: We haven't eaten yet. They haven't any eggs.* [contraction]

Hawaii (huh WY ee) *Hawaii* is one of the fifty states of the United States. [noun]

hawk (HAWK) A *hawk* is a bird with a strong beak and large claws. *Hawks* eat birds and other small animals. [noun] •**hawks.**

hawk

hay (HAY) *Hay* is grass and other plants that are cut and dried. *Hay* is used as food for cows and horses. [noun]

haystack (HAY stak) A *haystack* is a large pile of hay stored outside. [noun] •**haystacks.**

he (HEE) *He is my friend. My dog is so old he can't see.* [pronoun]

Hh

head · heart

Hh

head (HED)

1. Your *head* is the top part of your body or the front part of most animal bodies. Your *head* is where your eyes, ears, nose, mouth, and brain are. *[noun]*

2. The *head* of something is its top or front part: *We put the pillow at the head of the bed. She went to the head of the line. [noun]*

•**heads.**

headphones (HED fohnz)

You put *headphones* on your ears to listen to music. Some *headphones* protect your ears from loud noises. *[noun plural]*

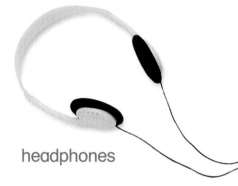

headphones

heal (HEEL)

If you *heal,* you become well. If someone is *healed,* that person is made well: *The cut healed quickly. The medicine healed my sore throat quickly.* *[verb]* •**heals, healed, healing.**

healthy (HEL thee)

If you are *healthy,* you feel well and strong: *We got a lot of exercise because we wanted to stay healthy. [adjective]* •**healthier, healthiest.**

hear (HEER)

When you *hear,* you take in sounds through your ears: *She could hear the bell ringing.* *[verb]* •**hears, heard, hearing.**

heard (HERD)

I heard the noise. The siren could be heard a mile away. [verb]

heart (HART)

1. Your *heart* is the part of your body inside your chest that pumps blood through your body. *[noun]*

2. Your *heart* is also the part of you that has feelings: *She knew in her heart that she had done a good job. [noun]*

hear

I can hear my watch ticking.

3. A *heart* is also a figure shaped like this ♥: *The card was covered with hearts.* [noun]
   •**hearts.**

heat (HEET)

1. *Heat* means being hot or very warm: *We enjoy the heat of a fire on a cold day.* [noun]
2. When you *heat* something, you make it warm or hot: *She heated the soup on the stove.* [verb]
   •**heats, heated, heating.**

heat

heavy (HEV ee)
When something is *heavy,* it is hard to lift or carry. Something that is *heavy* weighs a lot: *The piano was very heavy.* [adjective] •**heavier, heaviest.**

heel (HEEL)

1. Your *heel* is the back part of your foot, below your ankle. [noun]
2. A *heel* is the part of a sock or shoe that covers your heel. [noun]
3. A *heel* is also the back part of a shoe or boot that is under your heel. [noun]
   •**heels.**

height (HYT)
Height is how tall a person is. *Height* is also how high something is: *The school nurse measured my height. We measured the height of the door to see if the table would fit through it.* [noun] •**heights.**

held (HELD)
He held the kitten gently. The swing is held by strong ropes. [verb]

helicopter

helicopter (HEL uh kop ter)
A *helicopter* is a machine that flies without wings. A *helicopter* has large, flat,

hello • here

Hh

turning parts that keep it in the air and make it go. *[noun]* •**helicopters.**

hello (huh LOH *or* he LOH) *Hello* is what people say when they meet someone. We usually say *hello* when we answer the telephone. *[interjection]*

helmet (HEL mit) A *helmet* is a covering that protects your head. *Helmets* can be made out of metal, plastic, leather, and other materials. *[noun]* •**helmets.**

helmet

help (HELP)

1. When you *help,* you do something useful for someone: *He promised to help me with my homework.* *[verb]*

2. To *help* can also mean to make something better: *The medicine should help my cold.* *[verb]* •**helps, helped, helping.**

hen (HEN) A *hen* is a female chicken or other female bird. *Hens* lay eggs. *[noun]* •**hens.**

her (HER) *We have her book. We want her to come.* *[adjective* or *pronoun]*

herd (HERD) A *herd* is a group of the same kind of animal that is kept or fed together: *We saw a herd of cows when we went driving in the country.* *[noun]* •**herds.**

here (HEER) *Here* means at this place or to this place: *We will stop here. Bring the children here for their lessons.* *[adverb]*

herds

hermit crab (HER mit krab) A *hermit crab* is a crab with a soft body that does not have a shell of its own. It must live in the empty shells of snails and other sea animals to protect itself. •**hermit crabs.**

hero (HEER oh) A *hero* is someone people admire. *Heroes* do very brave or good things. [noun] •**heroes.**

heroine (HAIR oh uhn) A *heroine* is a girl or woman people admire. *Heroines* do very brave or good things. Some people use the word *hero* instead of *heroine* to describe a brave girl or woman. [noun] •**heroines.**

hers (HERZ) *This book is hers. His coat is blue; hers is red.* [pronoun]

herself (her SELF) *She hurt herself when she fell. She did it by herself.* [pronoun]

he's
1. *He's* is a shorter form of *he is: He's a big boy.* [contraction]
2. *He's* is also a shorter form of *he has: He's gone for the day.* [contraction]

hid (HID) *The dog hid his bone. She hid the presents where the children wouldn't find them.* [verb]

Hidalgo (EE THAHL goh *or* hi DAL goh) *Hidalgo* is a state in central Mexico. [noun]

hidden (HID uhn)
1. *Hidden* means kept out of sight. Something that is *hidden* is secret: *The story is about hidden treasure.* [adjective]
2. *Hidden* is a form of the verb *hide: The boy had hidden behind a big old tree.* [verb]

he's

He's my friend.

Hh

hide · hippopotamus

Hh

hide (HYD)

1. When you *hide* something, you put it where no one can see it. When you *hide,* you go where no one can see you: *Hide the package where no one else can find it.* [verb]

2. When you *hide* something, you also keep it a secret: *She tried to hide her fear.* [verb]
•**hides, hid, hidden, hiding.**

high (HY) If something is *high,* it is up above the ground: *We walked up the high hill. The airplane flew high in the sky.* [adjective] •**higher, highest.**

high

highchair (HY chair)

A *highchair* is a chair with a high seat and a tray. A *highchair* is used for feeding babies. [noun]
•**highchairs.**

hill (HIL) A *hill* is a high piece of ground, not as big or as high as a mountain. *Hills* are usually rounder than mountains. [noun] •**hills.**

him (HIM) *Take him home. We want him to come.* [pronoun]

himself (him SELF) *He cut himself. He bought the toy for himself.* [pronoun]

hip (HIP) Your *hip* is the part of your body where your leg joins your body. [noun] •**hips.**

hippopotamus (hip uh POT uh muhss) A *hippopotamus* is a very large animal with thick skin and no hair. *Hippopotamuses* live near rivers. [noun]
•**hippopotamuses.**

hippopotamus

his (HIZ) *His bicycle is lost. My car is red and his is green.* [*adjective* or *pronoun*]

history (HISS ter ee) *History is the story of what has happened in the past to a person or a nation: We study the history of the United States in school.* [*noun*]

hit (HIT) *When you hit something, you move your hand or something you are holding against something else hard or quickly: I hit the ball with the bat.* [*verb*] •**hits, hit, hitting.**

hive (HYV) A *hive* is a house or box for bees to live in. [*noun*] •**hives.**

hive

hobby (HOB ee) A *hobby* is something people like to do in their free time: *My mother's hobby is sewing. My hobby is collecting stamps.* [*noun*] •**hobbies.**

hockey

hockey (HOK ee) *Hockey is a game played by two teams on ice or on a field. The players use curved sticks to hit a ball or a hard piece of rubber, called a puck, into the other team's goal.* [*noun*]

hog (HAWG) A *hog* is a pig. Farmers raise *hogs* for meat. [*noun*] •**hogs.**

hold (HOHLD)

1. When you *hold* something, you pick it up and keep it in your hands or arms: *Will you hold my hat? His mother held his watch while he swam.* [*verb*]

2. To *hold* something is to keep it in one place or position: *Magnets hold the maps on the walls. The walls in the room hold up the ceiling.* [*verb*]

Hh

hole · honey

Hh

3. To *hold* is also to have space inside for something: *That pitcher can hold a lot of water.* [verb] •**holds, held, holding.**

hole (HOHL) A *hole* is an open or empty space in something: *There is a big hole in this sock. Rabbits dig holes in the ground.* [noun] •**holes.**

hole

holiday (HOL uh day) A *holiday* is a day when you do not work or go to school. A *holiday* is a day for having fun or celebrating: *The Fourth of July is a holiday for people in the United States.* [noun] •**holidays.**

hollow (HOL oh) If something is *hollow,* it has nothing inside. Things that are *hollow* are empty. A tube or a pipe is *hollow.* [adjective]

home (HOHM)
1. Your *home* is the place where you and your family live: *Her home is on Maple Street.* [noun]
2. Your *home* is also the town or country where you were born or brought up: *Indiana is her home.* [noun]
•**homes.**

homework (HOHM werk) *Homework* is a lesson to be studied or worked on outside of class: *After dinner, we did our homework for school.* [noun]

honest (ON ist) If you are *honest,* you tell the truth. An *honest* person does not steal or lie: *Parents teach their children to be honest.* [adjective]

honey (HUHN ee) *Honey* is a thick, sweet, yellow liquid that is good to eat. Bees make *honey* out of the drops of juice they collect from flowers. [noun]

honey

hoof (HUF) A *hoof* is the hard part of the foot of some animals. Horses, cattle, sheep, and pigs have *hoofs.* [noun] •**hoofs** *or* **hooves.**

hook (HUK)

1. A *hook* is a curved piece of metal, wood, or plastic to hang things on: *Hang your hat on the hook in the hall.* [noun]

2. A *hook* is also a bent piece of wire for catching fish. [noun]
•**hooks.**

hoop (HOOP) The *hoop* is the part of a basketball goal that the ball goes through: *We put the ball through the hoop for two more points.* [noun] •**hoops.**

hoop

hooray (hoo RAY) When you shout *hooray,* you are happy about something that was done: *"Hooray!" they shouted as the team scored again. Give a hooray for the team!* [interjection]

hooves (HOOVZ) *Hooves* is a plural of the word *hoof.* [noun plural]

hop (HOP)

1. When you *hop,* you jump on one foot: *He hopped on his left foot and then on his right.* [verb]

2. A *hop* is a jump: *Take two hops forward and one hop back.* [noun]
•**hops, hopped, hopping.** •**hops.**

hope (HOHP)

1. *Hope* is a feeling that what you want to happen will happen: *Her words gave me hope that we could really be friends.* [noun]

hop

horn · hot

horn

Hh

2. When you *hope,* you wish for something and expect it to happen: *I hope I win the race next week. [verb]*
•**hopes.** •**hopes, hoped, hoping.**

horn (HORN)

1. A *horn* is something hard that grows on the heads of some animals. *Horns* are usually curved and pointed. Cattle and goats have *horns. [noun]*

2. A *horn* is also a musical instrument that you blow into. *[noun]*

3. A *horn* is also something that makes a signal of danger: *He blew his horn to tell that the soldiers were coming. [noun]*
•**horns.**

horse (HORSS) A *horse* is a large animal with four legs, hoofs, and a mane. *Horses* pull loads and carry people: *Horses can run very fast. [noun]* •**horses.**

horseshoe (HORSS shoo) A *horseshoe* is a flat piece of metal shaped like a U. *Horseshoes* are put on the bottom of horses' hoofs to protect them. *[noun]* •**horseshoes.**

hose (HOHZ) A *hose* is a long, hollow tube for carrying a liquid or a gas. *Hoses* are used to water lawns and to fill tires with air. *[noun]* •**hoses.**

hose

hospital (HOSS pi tuhl) A *hospital* is a place where sick people are cared for. Doctors and nurses work in *hospitals. [noun]* •**hospitals.**

hot (HOT)

1. When something is *hot,* it is not cold. Something that is *hot* is much warmer than your body: *Fire is hot. [adjective]*

2. Something that is *hot* has a sharp, burning taste: *These peppers are too hot for her to eat.* [adjective]
•**hotter, hottest.**

hot dog (HOT dawg) A *hot dog* is made of ground beef or of beef and pork shaped into a tube: *Hot dogs* are eaten on a bun. •**hot dogs.**

hot dog

hotel (hoh TEL) A *hotel* is a building where people can rent a room to sleep in. People who are traveling away from home often stay at a *hotel.* [noun] •**hotels.**

hour (OWR) An *hour* is a unit of time. There are 60 minutes in one *hour.* Twenty-four *hours* make one day. [noun] •**hours.**

house (HOWSS) A *house* is a building where people live: *She moved into a new house last month.* [noun] •**houses.**

how (HOW) *Tell me how it happened. How long will it take? How much does it weigh?* [conjunction or adverb]

huddle (HUD uhl) If you *huddle,* you move very close to something or someone else: *The sheep huddled together in a corner. We huddled under the covers.* [verb] •**huddles, huddled, huddling.**

hug (HUHG)

1. When you give a *hug,* you put your arms around something or someone and hold tight: *The little boy hugged his toy bear.* [verb]

2. A *hug* is a tight squeeze with your arms: *I like a hug when I am sad.* [noun]
•**hugs, hugged, hugging. •hugs.**

hug

huge · hung

Hh

huge (HYOOJ) If something is *huge,* it is very large or there is a lot of it: *An elephant is a huge animal. He won a huge sum of money in the contest.* [adjective]

huge

hum (HUHM) When you *hum,* you sing with your lips closed, not saying any words: *We hum along with the radio.* [verb] •**hums, hummed, humming.**

human (HYOO muhn) Something that is *human* is like people: *Men, women, and children are human. We treat our pet as though he were human.* [adjective]

humble (HUHM buhl) If you are *humble,* you are not proud. *Humble* people do not talk very much about themselves: *She is very humble, even though she is good at sports.* [adjective] •**humbler, humblest.**

hummingbird (HUHM ing berd) A *hummingbird* is a very small bird with a long bill and bright feathers. A *hummingbird* moves its wings so fast that they make a humming sound. [noun] •**hummingbirds.**

hump (HUHMP) A *hump* is a round bump that sticks up: *Some camels have two humps on their backs.* [noun] •**humps.**

hundred (HUHN druhd) *Hundred* is the number after 99. A *hundred* is ten more than 90. It is also written 100: *There are a hundred cents in a dollar.* [noun or adjective] •**hundreds.**

hung (HUHNG) *She hung the picture on the wall. He hung up his coat.* [verb]

hummingbird

hungry (HUHNG gree) When you are *hungry,* you feel a strong need to eat: *She didn't eat breakfast and was hungry all morning.* [adjective] •**hungrier, hungriest.**

hunt (HUHNT)

1. To *hunt* is to kill wild birds or animals for food or for sport: *They went to the woods to hunt deer.* [verb]
2. To *hunt* also means to look for something or try to find it: *Mom helped me hunt for my missing book.* [verb]
•**hunts, hunted, hunting.**

hunter (HUHN ter) A *hunter* is a person who hunts. [noun] •**hunters.**

hurl (HERL) If you *hurl* something, you throw it as hard as you can: *Can you hurl this stone into the river?* [verb] •**hurls, hurled, hurling.**

hurricane (HER uh kayn) A *hurricane* is a fierce storm with strong winds and very heavy rain. [noun] •**hurricanes.**

hurry (HER ee) When you *hurry,* you go very quickly or rush: *He hurried to get to work on time.* [verb] •**hurries, hurried, hurrying.**

hurt (HERT) To *hurt* means to cause pain. If you *hurt,* you feel pain: *The stone in my shoe hurt my foot. My hand hurts.* [verb] •**hurts, hurt, hurting.**

husband (HUHZ buhnd) A *husband* is a man who is married. [noun] •**husbands.**

hut (HUHT) A *hut* is a small wooden cabin or house: *The kids built a hut out of old boards and pieces of cloth.* [noun] •**huts.**

Hh

hurt

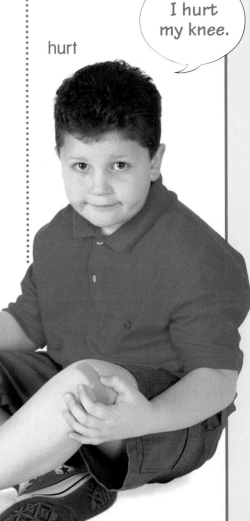

I hurt my knee.

I · ice-skate

Ii

ice skates

I (EYE) *I like dogs. I am going to get one.* [pronoun]

ice (EYESS) *Ice* is frozen water. Water turns into *ice* when it is very cold: *The pond turns to ice in winter. I put some ice in my glass of water.* [noun]

iceberg (EYESS berg) An *iceberg* is a large piece of ice floating in the sea. *Icebergs* can be bigger than houses. *[noun]* •**icebergs.**

ice cream (EYESS kreem) *Ice cream* is a sweet, frozen food made with milk and sugar. *Ice cream* comes in many different flavors.

ice skate (EYESS skayt) An *ice skate* is a shoe with a piece of metal on the bottom for skating on ice. •**ice skates.**

ice-skate (EYESS skayt) When you *ice-skate,* you

skate on ice using ice skates: *We want to ice-skate as soon as the pond freezes.* [verb] •**ice-skates, ice-skated, ice-skating.**

icicle (EYE sik uhl) An *icicle* is a hanging, pointed stick of ice. An *icicle* forms when water freezes as it drips. [noun] •**icicles.**

icicles

Idaho (EYE duh hoh) *Idaho* is one of the fifty states of the United States. [noun]

idea (eye DEE uh) An *idea* is a thought or plan: *It was my idea to go to the zoo.* [noun] •**ideas.**

if (IF) *We'll have a picnic if it doesn't rain. I wonder if it will be a sunny day.* [conjunction]

igloo (IG loo) An *igloo* is a house made of hard blocks of snow. Some people in cold parts of the world live in *igloos.* [noun] •**igloos.**

iguana (i GWAH nuh) An *iguana* is a large lizard that lives in Mexico and other warm places. [noun] •**iguanas.**

iguana

iguanodon (i GWAH nuh don) The *iguanodon* was a large dinosaur with teeth like an iguana's teeth. The *iguanodon* ate plants. [noun] •**iguanodons.**

ill (IL) Another word for *ill* is *sick.* If you are *ill,* you are not well: *She is not here today because she is ill.* [adjective] •**worse, worst.**

I'll *I'll* is a shorter form of *I will*: *I'll help you do that.* [contraction]

Illinois • important

Ii

important

Reading is important.

Illinois (il uh NOI) *Illinois* is one of the fifty states of the United States. [noun]

I'm *I'm* is a shorter form of *I am*: *I'm going to the zoo today. I'm seven years old.* [contraction]

imagination (i maj uh NAY shuhn) Your *imagination* is the power you have to make pictures or ideas in your mind. Someone with a good *imagination* can think of new or interesting things easily: *This exciting story was written by someone with a good imagination.* [noun]
•**imaginations.**

imagine (i MAJ uhn) When you *imagine* something, you make a picture or idea of it in your mind: *I can imagine myself living in outer space.* [verb]
•**imagines, imagined, imagining.**

imagine

immediately (i MEE dee it lee) If you do something *immediately*, you do it at once or right away: *I answered his letter immediately.* [adverb]

impatient (im PAY shuhnt) If you are *impatient*, you are not patient. An *impatient* person becomes angry when things are late, annoying, or not comfortable: *He is impatient with his little brother's complaining.* [adjective]

important (im PORT uhnt)
1. Something that is *important* has a lot of meaning or worth: *It is important to learn to read.* [adjective]
2. An *important* person has a lot of power or is famous: *The President is a very important person in the United States.* [adjective]

impossible (im POSS uh buhl)
If something is *impossible*,
it cannot happen.
Something that is
impossible is not
possible: *It is
impossible for a
turtle to fly.*
[adjective]

impossible

improve (im PROOV) If you *improve* something, you
make it better. If you *improve,* you become better: *If
I study the spelling words, I'm sure my spelling will
improve.* [verb] •**improves, improved, improving.**

in (IN) *It rained in the morning. I am leaving in an
hour.* [preposition]

inch (INCH) An *inch* is a unit of length. There are
12 *inches* in one foot. [noun] •**inches.**

independence (in di PEN duhnss) *Independence* is
being able to make your own choices: *The American
colonies won their independence.* [noun]

Independence Day (in di PEN duhnss DAY)
Independence Day is July 4th, a holiday we celebrate
in the United States. It celebrates the day our country
became free.

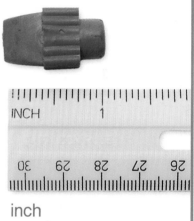

inch

index (IN deks) An *index* is a list of people, places,
and things in a book. An *index* gives the page numbers
where each of these can be found. It is arranged in
alphabetical order at the end of the book. [noun]
•**indexes.**

Indian (IN dee uhn) An *Indian* is a person from any
of the groups of people who first lived in America.
Indians lived here long before the coming of white
people. Some people of this group want to be called

Indiana · ink

American Indians. Other people want to be called *Native Americans.* The best answer is to use the special name of the group when you can. *[noun]* •**Indians.**

Indiana (in dee AN uh) *Indiana* is one of the fifty states of the United States. *[noun]*

indoors (in DORZ) If you are *indoors*, you are in or going into a house or other building: *Let's go indoors now. We stay indoors when it rains. [adverb]*

information (in fer MAY shuhn) *Information* is facts that people know about something: *She looked in the library for information about sea turtles. [noun]*

ingredient (in GREE dee uhnt) An *ingredient* is one part of something that is mixed together: *The ingredients of a cake usually are eggs, sugar, and flour. [noun]* •**ingredients.**

injure (IN jer) If you *injure* a person or animal, you hurt them: *He was injured in a car accident. [verb]* •**injures, injured, injuring.**

ink (INGK) *Ink* is a liquid used for writing or printing. This sentence is printed in black *ink.* *[noun]* •**inks.**

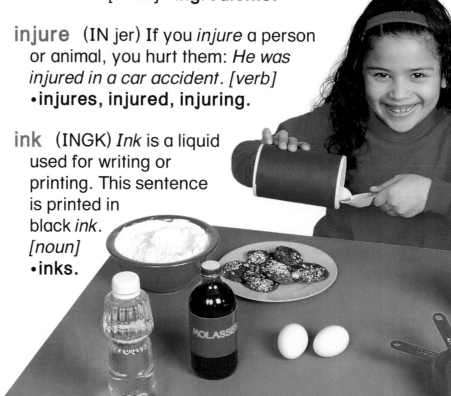

ingredients

in-line skates (IN lyn SKAYTS) *In-line skates* are special boots with wheels attached in a single line, instead of in pairs side by side. People use *in-line skates* for fun, exercise, and to play games like hockey. •**in-line skates.**

insect (IN sekt) An *insect* is a small animal with six legs and a body that has three parts. Most *insects* have four wings. Flies, bees, butterflies, and mosquitoes are *insects.* [noun] •**insects.**

insect

inside (in SYD *or* IN syd) *We stayed inside during the rain. There is a cricket inside this box. The inside of my coat is soft.* [adverb *or* preposition *or* noun]

instant (IN stuhnt) An *instant* is a very short time: *She was gone in an instant.* [noun]

instead (in STED) *Instead* means in place of something else: *I don't like beets, so I ate carrots instead.* [adverb]

instrument (IN struh muhnt)

instrument

1. An *instrument* is something that makes music: *He can play the piano and two other instruments.* [noun]
2. An *instrument* is also a tool that helps you do or make another thing: *A telescope is an instrument that makes the stars look bigger.* [noun]

•**instruments.**

insult (in SULT *for verb or* IN sult *for noun*)

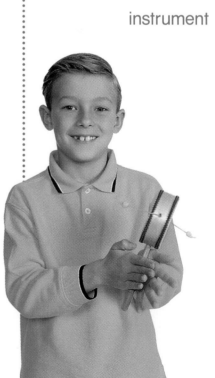

1. If you *insult* someone, you say or do something very rude to that person: *She insulted me by calling me stupid.* [verb]
2. An *insult* is something you say or do that is very rude: *It is an insult to call someone ugly or stupid.* [noun]

•**insults, insulted, insulting.** •**insults.**

interest · invention

Ii

interest (IN ter ist)
1. If you have an *interest* in something, you want to know about it or share it: *The teacher has an interest in art.* [noun]
2. If something *interests* you, it holds your attention: *That kind of music does not interest me.* [verb]
•**interests.** •**interests, interested, interesting.**

interested (IN ter uh stid) If you are *interested,* you feel or show interest in something or pay attention to something: *She was interested in seeing the play.* [adjective]

interesting (IN ter uh sting) If something is *interesting,* you want to pay attention to it or learn more about it: *The book was so interesting that I did not want it to end. What an interesting name!* [adjective]

Internet (IN ter net) The *Internet* is a large group of computers connected by telephone lines. People all over the world use the *Internet* to send and receive information. [noun]

into (IN too) *The cows walked into the barn. Heat turns ice into water. They ran into the room.* [preposition]

introduction (in truh DUHK shuhn) An *introduction* is the beginning part of a speech, a piece of music, or a book: *In his introduction, the speaker told us what his speech would be about.* [noun] •**introductions.**

invent (in VENT) If you *invent* something, you make or think of something new: *I want to invent a new kind of car.* [verb] •**invents, invented, inventing.**

invention (in VEN shuhn) An *invention* is a new thing that someone makes or thinks of: *The light bulb was a wonderful invention.* [noun] •**inventions.**

invention

This is my invention.

inventor (in VEN ter) An *inventor* is a person who makes or thinks of new things: *Thomas A. Edison was a great American inventor.* [noun] •**inventors.**

invisible (in VIZ uh buhl) If something is *invisible,* you cannot see it: *Germs are invisible without a microscope.* [adjective]

invitation (in vuh TAY shuhn) An *invitation* is a message you send asking someone to come somewhere or do something: *I got an invitation to my friend's birthday party.* [noun] •**invitations.**

invitation

invite (in VYT) If you *invite* someone, you ask them to come somewhere or do something: *Did you invite her to the party?* [verb] •**invites, invited, inviting.**

Iowa

Iowa (EYE uh wuh) *Iowa* is one of the fifty states of the United States. [noun]

iron (EYE ern)
1. *Iron* is a very common and useful metal. *Iron* is made into steel. *Iron* is used to make tools, machines, and many other things. [noun]
2. An *iron* is something used to make clothes smooth and neat. An *iron* has a flat bottom, which becomes hot, and a handle. [noun]
3. When you *iron,* you use a hot iron to make clothes smooth and neat: *My sister ironed my shirt.* [verb]
•**irons** *for definition 2.* •**irons, ironed, ironing.**

is (IZ) *Is he coming to your party? It is hot outside. She is going now. The house is on the next block.* [verb]

island · I've

Ii

island (EYE luhnd) An *island* is land with water all around it. *Islands* are found in oceans, lakes, or rivers: *The state of Hawaii is made up of a group of islands.* [noun] •**islands.**

isn't *Isn't* is a shorter form of *is not: She isn't home right now.* [contraction]

it (IT) *It is a nice day today. Your cap is where you left it. It is my turn now.* [pronoun]

itch (ICH) When you *itch,* you have an annoying feeling on your skin that makes you want to scratch: *My back itches.* [verb] •**itches, itched, itching.**

its (ITSS) *The cat licked its paw. The tree lost its leaves.* [adjective]

it's *It's* is a shorter form of *it is.* Many people confuse *it's* and *its.* Because *it's* is a contraction, you can remember to use it when you want to say "it is." *It's a beautiful day today. It's not going to rain.* [contraction]

itself (it SELF) *The bird is washing itself in a puddle.* [pronoun]

I've *I've* is a shorter form of *I have.* [contraction]

I've got a new toy.

I've

jacket · Jalisco

Jj

jacket (JAK uht) A *jacket* is a short coat: *I wore my new jacket to go skating.* [noun] •**jackets.**

jack-o'-lantern (JAK uh lan tern) A *jack-o'-lantern* is a pumpkin that has been made hollow and cut to look like a face: *We burned a candle in our Halloween jack-o'-lantern.* [noun] •**jack-o'-lanterns.**

jacks (JAKS) *Jacks* is a game you play with a small ball and little pieces of metal. As you bounce the ball, you pick up the pieces one at a time, then two at a time, then three at a time, until you are trying to pick them all up on one bounce. [noun]

jail (JAYL) A *jail* is a place where people are put when they break the law. [noun] •**jails.**

Jalisco (hah LEESS koh *or* huh LIS koh) *Jalisco* is a state in central Mexico. [noun]

jack-o'-lantern

jam • jellyfish

Jj

jam (JAM) *Jam* is a sweet fruit mixture. *Jam* is put on bread and toast. *[noun]* •**jams.**

jam

January (JAN yoo air ee) *January* is the first month of the year. It has 31 days. It comes after the December of the past year and before February. *[noun]*

jar (JAR) A *jar* is a short, wide bottle used to hold things. Many *jars* are made of glass. Cookies are often kept in a large *jar. [noun]* •**jars.**

jaw (JAW) Your *jaws* are the lower part of your face. Your teeth grow from the gums in your *jaws. [noun]* •**jaws.**

jealous (JEL uhss) If you are *jealous,* you are unhappy because someone has something that you want to have: *Seeing his friend's new bike made him jealous. [adjective]*

jeans (JEENZ) *Jeans* are pants made of strong cotton cloth. *Jeans* are often blue but can be black, white, or other colors. *[noun plural]*

jeep (JEEP) A *jeep* is a small car often used where roads are rough. *Jeeps* were first used by the United States Army. *[noun]* •**jeeps.**

jelly (JEL ee) *Jelly* is a sweet food made from fruit juice and sugar. *Jelly* is put on bread and toast. *[noun]* •**jellies.**

jellyfish

jellyfish (JEL ee fish) A *jellyfish* is a sea animal that looks like jelly. Most *jellyfish* have long, hanging tentacles that can sometimes sting. *[noun]* •**jellyfish** or **jellyfishes.**

jersey (JER zee) A *jersey* is a soft shirt that you pull on over your head. A *jersey* is often part of a team uniform: *Our soccer team wears red jerseys. [noun]*
•**jerseys.**

jersey

jester (JESS ter) A *jester* is a person who plays tricks and makes jokes for others. Long ago, kings and queens often had a *jester* to make them laugh. *[noun]*
•**jesters.**

jet (JET)
1. A *jet* is a stream of gas, steam, or liquid pushed from a small hole: *A jet of water shot up from the hose. [noun]*
2. A *jet* is also a kind of airplane. The engines of a *jet* do not have propellers. Hot gases that shoot from the back of the engines push the airplane forward. *[noun]*
•**jets.**

jewel (JOOL) A *jewel* is a stone that is worth a lot of money. Diamonds are *jewels. [noun]* •**jewels.**

jewelry (JOO uhl ree *or* JOOL ree) *Jewelry* is rings, bracelets, necklaces, and other things like these. *Jewelry* is often made of silver or gold and sometimes with jewels. *[noun]*

jiggly (JIG lee) Something that is *jiggly* shakes or moves easily: *It is hard to write at a jiggly desk. [adjective]* •**jigglier, jiggliest.**

jigsaw puzzle (JIG saw PUZ uhl) A *jigsaw puzzle* is a picture glued onto stiff paper or wood and cut into small pieces that can be fitted together again. The pieces of a *jigsaw puzzle* have all different shapes to make it

jigsaw puzzle

Jj

211

job · joy

difficult to find where they belong in the picture.
•**jigsaw puzzles.**

job (JOB)
1. Your *job* is the work that you have to do: *It is my job to take out the garbage.* [noun]
2. A *job* is also the work you do for pay: *My mom has a job in a bank.* [noun]
•**jobs.**

jog (JOG) When you *jog,* you run in a slow and steady way: *My parents jog three miles every morning.* [verb] •**jogs, jogged, jogging.**

jog

join (JOIN)
1. When you *join* things, you put them together or keep them together: *Join hands in a circle.* [verb]
2. If you *join* a group, you become a part of that group: *He wants to join the Boy Scouts.* [verb]
•**joins, joined, joining.**

joint (JOINT) A *joint* is a place in the body where two bones are joined. Your knee is a *joint* in your leg. [noun] •**joints.**

joke (JOHK) A *joke* is a short, funny story you tell to make people laugh: *She told a joke about a talking dog.* [noun] •**jokes.**

jolly (JOL ee) Another word for *jolly* is *happy. Jolly* people are cheerful and like to have fun: *The jolly group sang and laughed all evening.* [adjective] •**jollier, jolliest.**

joy (JOI) *Joy* is a very happy feeling: *Her new puppy filled the little girl with joy.* [noun] •**joys.**

judge (JUHJ)

  1. A *judge* is a person who decides questions of right and wrong under the law. A *judge* can send someone to jail. *[noun]*

  2. A *judge* is also a person who decides who or what wins a contest: *She was a judge at the art show.* *[noun]*

  3. If you *judge* something, you decide what is the best or what is right: *She judged the art show last summer.* *[verb]*

  •**judges.** •**judges, judged, judging.**

juggle (JUHG uhl) When you *juggle,* you throw things into the air, catch them, and keep them moving without letting them fall to the ground: *We watched the clown juggle five balls and two sticks.* *[verb]* •**juggles, juggled, juggling.**

juggle

juice (JOOSS) *Juice* is the liquid part of fruits and vegetables: *I drink a glass of orange juice every morning.* *[noun]* •**juices.**

July (ju LY) *July* is the seventh month of the year. It has 31 days. It comes after June and before August. *[noun]*

jump (JUHMP) When you *jump,* you throw yourself up into the air or across something: *He jumped over the puddle.* *[verb]* •**jumps, jumped, jumping.**

jump rope (JUHMP rohp) A *jump rope* is a piece of rope with handles at both ends. You hold each end, swing the *jump rope* over your head, and jump over it as it sweeps the ground. •**jump ropes.**

jump rope

Jj

June • just

Jj

June (JOON) *June* is the sixth month of the year. It has 30 days. It comes after May and before July. *[noun]*

jungle (JUHNG guhl) A *jungle* is a kind of forest with thick bushes, vines, and many trees. *Jungles* have many kinds of animals living in them. *Jungles* are found in hot countries. *[noun]* •**jungles.**

Many animals live in the *jungle.*

junk (JUHNGK) *Junk* is old, worn-out things that nobody wants anymore: *Let's throw out all the junk in the garage. [noun]*

just (JUHST) *We just got home from our trip. This coat is just my size. I just missed the bus. He is just four days old. [adverb]*

Kk

kangaroo (kang guh ROO) A *kangaroo* is an animal with small front legs and very strong back legs. *Kangaroos* move very fast by jumping. A female *kangaroo* carries her baby in a pouch in the front of her stomach. *[noun]* •**kangaroos.**

Kansas (KAN zuhss) *Kansas* is one of the fifty states of the United States. *[noun]*

kazoo (kuh ZOO) A *kazoo* is a toy musical instrument that makes a buzzing sound when you hum into it. *[noun]* •**kazoos.**

keep (KEEP) To *keep* is to have for a long time or forever: *She told me to keep the ring. Please keep his secret. [verb]* •**keeps, kept, keeping.**

Kentucky (kuhn TUHK ee) *Kentucky* is one of the fifty states of the United States. *[noun]*

kazoos

215

kept • kick

kept (KEPT) *She kept my secret. He has kept all their letters. [verb]*

kernel (KER nuhl) A *kernel* is a grain or seed like that of wheat or corn. *[noun]* •**kernels.**

kernels

ketchup (KECH uhp) *Ketchup* is a sauce people put on many different foods. Tomato *ketchup* is made of tomatoes, onions, salt, sugar, and spices. *[noun]*

kettle (KET uhl) A *kettle* is a metal pot for boiling liquids or cooking fruit and vegetables. *[noun]* •**kettles.**

key (KEE)
1. A *key* is a small piece of metal for opening and closing a lock. *[noun]*
2. A *key* is also a list that explains the abbreviations or symbols used on a map or graph. *[noun]*
3. A *key* is also a part you press to play a piano or make a computer work. *[noun]*
•**keys.**

keyboard (KEE bord) A *keyboard* is the set of keys you press to make a piano or computer work. *[noun]* •**keyboards.**

keychain (KEE chayn) A *keychain* is a ring that holds your keys. *[noun]* •**keychains.**

keyhole (KEE hohl) A *keyhole* is an opening in a lock into which you put a key. *[noun]* •**keyholes.**

kick (KIK)
1. When you *kick* something, you hit it with your foot: *Kick the ball to me. [verb]*
2. A *kick* is a hard hit with a foot: *She gave the door a kick to close it. [noun]*
•**kicks, kicked, kicking.** •**kicks.**

Kk

keychain

key

kid (KID)
1. A *kid* is a child: *There is a new kid in our class.* [noun]
2. A *kid* is also a young goat. [noun]
•**kids.**

kill (KIL) To *kill* something is to cause it to die: *A fire killed the trees.* [verb] •**kills, killed, killing.**

kilogram (KIL uh gram) A *kilogram* is a unit of weight equal to 1000 grams. This book weighs about one *kilogram.* [noun] •**kilograms.**

kilometer (kuh LOM uh ter *or* KIL uh mee ter) A *kilometer* is a unit of great length equal to 1000 meters. A *kilometer* is a little more than half a mile. Distances between cities are sometimes measured in *kilometers.* [noun] •**kilometers.**

kid

kind¹ (KYND)
Someone who is *kind* is nice, friendly, and does good things for others: *A kind woman opened the heavy door for me.* [adjective]
•**kinder, kindest.**   kind¹

kind² (KYND) A *kind* is a group of things that are alike in some way: *Dogs are a kind of animal. I like all kinds of fruit.* [noun] •**kinds.**

kindergarten (KIN der gart uhn) *Kindergarten* is a school for very young children. *Kindergarten* is the year of school before first grade. [noun] •**kindergartens.**

king (KING) A *king* is a man who rules a country. Many countries do not have *kings.* [noun] •**kings.**

Kk

kingdom · knee

Kk

kingdom (KING duhm) A *kingdom* is a country that is ruled by a king or queen. *[noun]* •**kingdoms.**

kiss (KISS)

1. When you *kiss* people, you touch them with your lips as a sign of love: *I want my mom to kiss me when I get hurt.* *[verb]*

2. A *kiss* is a touch with the lips as a sign of love: *I gave Grandmother a kiss.* *[noun]*
•**kisses, kissed, kissing.** •**kisses.**

kit (KIT) A *kit* is a package of parts that someone puts together to make something: *He bought a model airplane kit.* *[noun]* •**kits.**

kitchen (KICH uhn) Your *kitchen* is the room where you cook and store food. *[noun]* •**kitchens.**

kite (KYT)
A *kite* is a light wooden shape that is covered with paper, cloth, or plastic. *Kites* are flown in the air on the end of a long string. *[noun]*
•**kites.**

kite

kitten (KIT uhn)
A *kitten* is a young cat. *[noun]* •**kittens.**

knee (NEE) Your *knee* is the part of your leg that bends. Your *knee* is the joint between your thigh and your lower leg. *[noun]*
•**knees.**

kneel (NEEL) If you *kneel,* you go down on your knees: *He will kneel to clean up the mess.* [verb] •**kneels, knelt, kneeling.**

knelt (NELT) *I knelt to tie my little sister's shoelaces. He had knelt on the ground to pull weeds.* [verb]

kneel

knew (NOO) *I knew the answer. He knew just what to do.* [verb]

knife (NYF) A *knife* is a flat piece of metal with a handle, used to cut or spread something. You use a *knife* to spread butter. A sharper *knife* can cut wood. [noun] •**knives.**

knight (NYT) A *knight* is a soldier who rode a horse and fought for a king long ago. *Knights* often wore metal suits called *armor.* [noun] •**knights.**

knit (NIT) When you *knit,* you make clothing from yarn using long needles: *My mom and my grandma taught me how to knit.* [verb] •**knits, knitted, knitting.**

knives (NYVZ) *Knives* is the plural of the word *knife.* [noun plural]

knock (NOK)

1. When you *knock* something, you hit it or bump into it: *Knock before opening the door. You knocked my glasses off.* [verb]
2. A *knock* is a hit or bump: *They didn't hear his knock at the door.* [noun]

•**knocks, knocked, knocking.** •**knocks.**

knights

knot · Kwanzaa or Kwanza

knot (NOT) A *knot* is a place where rope or cloth has been tied together: *His shoelaces were tied in a knot.* [noun]
•**knots.**

I have a knot in my shoelace.

knot

know (NOH)

1. When you *know* something, you have the facts about it or can do it. You have the information in your mind: *I know how to swim. I know the answer to that question.* [verb]

2. When you *know* people, you have met them and talked to them. You are often friendly with people you *know*: *I know him, but I don't know his sister.* [verb]

•**knows, knew, known, knowing.**

known (NOHN) *I have known her for a long time.* [verb]

koala (koh AH luh) A *koala* is a small gray animal that looks like a bear. It has no tail. [noun] •**koalas.**

koalas

Kwanzaa or **Kwanza** (KWAN zuh) *Kwanzaa* is a holiday some people celebrate once a year. It lasts from December 26 to January 1: *During Kwanzaa, we light candles and think about our families.* [noun]

Kk

Ll

label (LAY buhl)

1. A *label* is a piece of paper or cloth that is sewed or glued onto something. A *label* tells what something is, who it belongs to, or who made it. *[noun]*

2. When you *label* something, you put or write a label on something: *The teacher asked them to label one group of pictures with the word "plants."* *[verb]*
•labels. •labels, labeled, labeling.

ladder (LAD er) A *ladder* is a set of steps between two long pieces of wood, metal, or rope. *Ladders* are used for climbing up and down. *[noun]*
•ladders.

ladle (LAY duhl) A *ladle* is a large spoon with a long handle. People use *ladles* to move hot or cold liquids from big pots to bowls or cups. *[noun]*
•ladles.

ladder

ladybug · language

ladybug

Ll

ladybug (LAY dee buhg) A *ladybug* is a small, red beetle with black spots. *Ladybugs* eat some insects that hurt crops. *[noun]* •**ladybugs.**

lagoon (luh GOON) A *lagoon* is a pond or small lake. A *lagoon* is usually connected to a bigger lake or to the ocean. *[noun]* •**lagoons.**

laid (LAYD) *He laid down the heavy bundle. The chickens have laid fewer eggs this morning than yesterday. [verb]*

lain (LAYN) *She has lain down to take a nap. [verb]*

lake (LAYK) A *lake* is water with land all around it. A *lake* is larger than a pond. It usually has fresh water in it. *[noun]* •**lakes.**

lamb (LAM) A *lamb* is a young sheep. *[noun]* •**lambs.**

lambs

lamp (LAMP) A *lamp* is a thing that gives light. Some *lamps* burn oil to give off light. Most *lamps* use electricity. *[noun]* •**lamps.**

land (LAND)

1. *Land* is the solid part of the Earth's surface: *After many weeks at sea, the sailors saw dry land. [noun]*
2. Other words for *land* are *ground* or *soil: The farmer planted wheat on his land. [noun]*
3. To *land* is to come down from the air: *The airplane will land in the field. [verb]*
•**lands** *for definition 1.* •**lands, landed, landing.**

language (LANG gwij) A *language* is all the words that people write or speak. People who speak the same *language* can understand each other: *People in different countries may not speak the same language you do.* [noun] •**languages.**

lap (LAP) Your *lap* is the top of your legs between your hips and your knees when you are sitting down: *The baby sat on her mom's lap.* [noun] •**laps.**

lap

large (LARJ) Something that is *large* is big. Something that is *large* may be made up of a lot of things or parts: *The United States is a large country. Large crowds come to see the team play.* [adjective] •**larger, largest.**

last[1] (LAST) Something that is *last* comes after all the rest: *The last letter in the alphabet is Z.* [adjective]

last[2] (LAST) If something *lasts,* it goes on or keeps on doing something: *How long do you think the snow will last?* [verb] •**lasts, lasted, lasting.**

late (LAYT)
1. *Late* means after the usual time that something happens: *He had a late breakfast because he got up late.* [adjective or adverb]
2. *Late* also means near the end of something: *The movie came on late that night.* [adjective or adverb]
•**later, latest.**

laugh (LAF)
1. When you *laugh,* you make sounds that show you are happy: *We all laughed at the clown's tricks.* [verb]

laugh

2. Your *laugh* is the sounds you make when you laugh: *The tiny girl had a loud laugh.* [noun]
•**laughs, laughed, laughing.** •**laughs.**

laughter (LAF ter) *Laughter* is the sounds of laughing: *When the boy told the joke, laughter filled the room.* [noun]

laundry (LAWN dree)

1. *Laundry* is clothes that are washed or need to be washed: *Mom asked us to put our dirty laundry in the basket.* [noun]

2. A *laundry* is a room or building where clothes are washed and ironed: *He stopped by the laundry to pick up his shirts.* [noun]
•**laundries** *for definition 2.*

laundry

law (LAW) A *law* is a rule made by the government of a country or state for all the people who live there. *Laws* are rules that everyone must follow. [noun] •**laws.**

lawn (LAWN) A *lawn* is a piece of land that is covered with grass and near a house or building. The grass of a *lawn* is usually kept short. [noun] •**lawns.**

lawnmower (LAWN moh er) A *lawnmower* is a machine people use to cut grass. [noun] •**lawnmowers.**

lawyer (LOI yer *or* LO yer) A *lawyer* is someone who has studied law and gives advice about the law. *Lawyers* can help people in court. [noun] •**lawyers.**

lay¹ (LAY)

1. When you *lay* something on something else, you put it down on a flat place: *Please lay the book on the table.* [verb]

lawnmower

2. To *lay* an egg is to be able to make an egg: *Birds, fish, and snakes lay eggs.* [verb]
•**lays, laid, laying.**

lay² (LAY) *At about nine o'clock, she lay down and fell asleep.* [verb]

layer (LAY er) A *layer* is one thin or thick sheet of something. A *layer* is also one piece of clothing you wear over another: *There are about six layers of paint on this wall. The runner wore a warm layer of clothing next to her skin.* [noun] •**layers.**

lazy (LAY zee) If a person is *lazy,* he or she does not want to work hard or to move fast: *The lazy cat lay on the rug all day.* [adjective] •**lazier, laziest.**

lead¹ (LEED)

1. When you *lead,* you show the way by going along with someone or by being in front of someone: *The teacher will lead the children across the street.* [verb]

2. If something *leads* to a place, it is a way to get to that place: *Both roads lead to the lake.* [verb]

3. If you *lead,* you are first or ahead of everyone else: *Did your team lead halfway through the game?* [verb]
•**leads, led, leading.**

lead² (LED)

1. *Lead* is a heavy, gray metal. *Lead* is used to make pipes. [noun]

2. *Lead* is also the gray material in the middle of a pencil that you write with. [noun]

leader (LEE der) A *leader* is a person who shows the way or who goes first: *He was the leader on our walk.* [noun] •**leaders.**

leader

225

leaf · leash

leaf

4

leaf (LEEF) A *leaf* is one of the thin, flat, green parts of a tree or plant. [noun] •**leaves.**

leak (LEEK)
1. A *leak* is a hole or crack that should not be there. A *leak* lets something in or out. [noun]
2. When something *leaks,* it lets something in or out in a bad way: *My feet are wet because my boots leak.* [verb]
•**leaks.** •**leaks, leaked, leaking.**

lean (LEEN)
1. To *lean* is to bend or stand in a slanted position: *The small trees lean over in the wind.* [verb]
2. If you *lean* something against something else, you put it in a slanted position: *Lean your bike against the garage door.* [verb]
•**leans, leaned, leaning.**

learn (LERN) If you *learn* something, you find out about it or come to know about it: *We learn a lot of things at school. He learned about insects.* [verb] •**learns, learned, learning.**

We learned about insects.

lease (LEESS) If you *lease* something, you rent it: *We leased an apartment for a year.* [verb] •**leases, leased, leasing.**

leash (LEESH) A *leash* is a strap made of leather, rope, or metal. *Leashes* are used to hold or keep animals where they should be: *He led the dog on a leash.* [noun] •**leashes.**

learn

least (LEEST) If something is *least,* it is less than any other: *He is the least friendly of the puppies.* [*adjective*]

leather (LE<u>TH</u> er) *Leather* is the skin of an animal that has been treated in a special way. *Leather* is used to make shoes, gloves, jackets, leashes, and other things. [*noun*]

leave (LEEV)

1. When you *leave,* you go away: *They are going to leave the room.* [*verb*]

2. To *leave* also means to go without taking something away or putting something away: *Don't leave your roller skates in the hall.* [*verb*]

• **leaves, left, leaving.**

leaves

leaves (LEEVZ) *Leaves* is the plural of the word *leaf.* [*noun plural*]

led (LED) *She led her younger brother across the street. We were led through the cave by a guide.* [*verb*]

left[1] (LEFT) *Left* is toward the direction of the first word on this line. *Left* is the opposite of right. Words are read from *left* to right: *Turn left at the next light.* [*adverb* or *adjective*]

left[2] (LEFT) *She left at noon. She had left the book at home.* [*verb*]

leg (LEG)

1. Your *leg* is the part of your body between your hip and your foot. People and animals stand and move around on their *legs.* [*noun*]

leg

lemon · less

Ll

leopard

2. A *leg* can also be anything that is shaped or used like a leg: *The leg on that chair is broken.* [noun] •**legs.**

lemon (LEM uhn) A *lemon* is a sour, yellow fruit. *Lemons* grow on trees. [noun] •**lemons.**

lemonade (LEM uhn ayd) *Lemonade* is a drink made of lemon juice, sugar, and water. [noun]

lemonade

lend (LEND) If you *lend* something to someone, you let that person use it for a while until you need it back: *Will you lend me your bike for an hour?* [verb] •**lends, lent, lending.**

length (LENGKTH)

1. *Length* is how long something is. The *length* of something is the distance from one end to the other: *The length of the rug is ten feet and the width is eight feet.* [noun]

2. *Length* is also how long something lasts in time: *The length of the movie was two hours.* [noun] •**lengths.**

lent (LENT) *She lent the boy her book. I have lent her my pencil.* [verb]

leopard (LEP erd) A *leopard* is a large animal like a cat that has yellow fur with black spots. *Leopards* can grow to be up to eight feet long. [noun] •**leopards.**

less (LESS) *We are eating less meat these days. The book report is less important than the test. My brother weighs ten pounds less than I weigh.* [adjective or adverb]

lesson (LESS uhn) A *lesson* is something that you learn. A *lesson* is also something that you are taught: *We had a spelling lesson today. My sister takes piano lessons.* [noun] •**lessons.**

lesson

let (LET) If you *let* someone do something, you do not stop that person from doing it: *I let her ride my bike. She let the door slam.* [verb] •**lets, let, letting.**

let's *Let's* is a shorter form of *let us: Let's plan the party together.* [contraction]

letter (LET er)

1. A *letter* is a part of the alphabet. A *letter* is a mark or sign that stands for any one of the sounds that make up words. There are 26 *letters* in the alphabet. [noun]

2. A *letter* is also a written message: *I wrote a letter to Grandmother yesterday.* [noun] •**letters.**

I am writing a letter to my grandmother.

lettuce (LET iss) *Lettuce* is a vegetable with crisp green leaves. *Lettuce* is used in salads. [noun]

librarian (ly BRAIR ee uhn) A *librarian* is a person who is in charge of or helps to run a library. [noun] •**librarians.**

library (LY brair ee) A *library* is a room or building where many books are kept. [noun] •**libraries.**

lick (LIK) When you *lick* something, you move your tongue over it: *She licked all the stamps. The cat licked its fur.* [verb] •**licks, licked, licking.**

letter

Ll

lie¹ · lift-off

lie¹ (LY)

1. A *lie* is something said that is not true: *He told a lie about the broken window.* [noun]

2. To *lie* is to say something that is not true: *Please don't lie to me.* [verb]
•**lies.** •**lies, lied, lying.**

lie² (LY)

1. To *lie* is to have your body in a flat position: *My head aches and I want to lie down.* [verb]

2. To *lie* also means to be flat: *Four books lie on the table.* [verb]
•**lies, lay, lain, lying.**

lie²

life (LYF)

1. *Life* is being alive. If something has *life,* it is living, breathing, and growing. People, animals, and plants have *life.* Rocks do not have *life.* [noun]

2. Your *life* is the time that you are alive. People, animals, and plants have *lives.* A dandelion has a very short *life.* [noun]
•**lives** *for definition 2.*

lift (LIFT) If you *lift* something, you raise it higher or pick it up: *He lifted the heavy box and put it on the table.* [verb] •**lifts, lifted, lifting.**

lift-off (LIFT awf) *Lift-off* is the exact moment when a rocket leaves the ground: *Watching lift-off was very exciting!* [noun] •**lift-offs**

lift-off

3, 2, 1, lift-off!

light¹ (LYT)

1. *Light* is a form of energy that gets rid of darkness and lets us see. *Light* comes from the sun, lamps, candles, and other similar things. *[noun]*

light¹

2. A *light* is anything that gives light so that we can see. The sun and a candle are *lights. [noun]*

3. If you *light* something, you set fire to it: *Light the candles on the cake. [verb]*

4. If something is *light,* it has a color that is close to white. Something that is *light* is not bright: *She has light brown hair. [adjective]*
•**lights** *for definition 2.* •**lights, lit, lighted, lighting.**
•**lighter, lightest.**

light² (LYT)
Something that is *light* is easy to lift or carry. Something that is *light* is not heavy: *A rabbit is light, but an elephant is heavy. [adjective]*
•**lighter, lightest.**

lighthouse (LYT howss)
A *lighthouse* is a tall building like a tower that has a strong, bright light which shines far out over the water. The bright light tells ships that they are close to the shore. *[noun]* •**lighthouses.**

lighthouses

lightning (LYT ning)
Lightning is a flash of electricity in the sky. The sound that *lightning* makes is thunder. *[noun]*

like¹ (LYK)
She looks like her mom. It looks like rain. He had a dollar, and I had a like amount. *[preposition* or *adjective]*

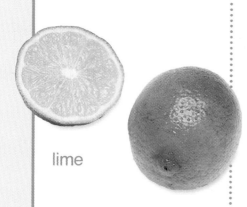

lime

like² (LYK) If you *like* someone or something, you are happy with that person or thing: *Most people like apple pie. I like all my friends.* [verb] •**likes, liked, liking.**

lime (LYM) A *lime* is a sour fruit that looks like a green lemon. *Limes* grow on trees. [noun] •**limes.**

line (LYN)

1. A *line* is a row of people or things: *We stood in a line to wait for the bus.* [noun]

2. A *line* is also a long, thin mark. Some *lines* are straight and some are curved. [noun]

3. A *line* is also a piece of string, rope, or wire: *He cut the telephone line while he was digging.* [noun]

4. If you *line* up, you form a line with other people: *The teacher asked Room 6 to line up against the wall.* [verb]
•**lines.** •**lines, lined, lining.**

link (LINGK) If you *link* two things or people, you join or connect them together: *Don't try to link me with this dumb plan.* [verb] •**links, linked, linking.**

lion (LY uhn) A *lion* is a large animal like a cat that has yellow fur. *Lions* can grow to be up to nine feet long. Male *lions* have long hair, called a *mane*, around their heads and necks. [noun] •**lions.**

lioness (LY uh nuhss) A *lioness* is a female lion. [noun]
•**lionesses.**

lioness

lip (LIP) Your *lip* is either of the two front edges of your mouth. You blow through your *lips* when you whistle. *[noun]* •**lips.**

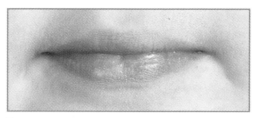

lips

liquid (LIK wuhd) A *liquid* is something that flows like water. A *liquid* is not a solid or a gas. Juice and milk are *liquids*. *[noun]* •**liquids.**

list (LIST)

1. A *list* is a group of words, names, or numbers that are written one below the other: *Don't forget your grocery list. [noun]*
2. When you *list* things, you make them into a list: *A dictionary lists words in alphabetical order. [verb]* •**lists.** •**lists, listed, listing.**

listen (LISS uhn) When you *listen,* you to try to hear something or someone: *We listened to her story. [verb]* •**listens, listened, listening.**

lit (LIT) *He lit a candle. The room was lit with many lamps. [verb]*

liter (LEE ter) A *liter* is an amount of liquid. A *liter* is a little more than a quart. *[noun]* •**liters.**

listen

literature (LIT er uh cher) *Literature* is something that has been written in a beautiful or interesting way. Stories, poems, and plays are kinds of *literature. Literature* has been written by many different people in many different places. *[noun]*

litter box (LIT uhr boks) A *litter box* is a box used to contain the waste of cats and other small animals until you throw it out. •**litter boxes.**

little · load

little (LIT uhl)

1. Another word for *little* is *small*. Something that is *little* is not big or large: *His pet is a little kitten.* [adjective]
2. If something is *little,* it is not long in time or in distance: *It will be dark in a little while.* [adjective]
3. *Little* also means not much: *A sick child eats only a little.* [noun]
•**littler, littlest.**

live (LIV)

1. If you *live,* you are alive. When you *live,* you breathe and grow. Animals *live,* but rocks do not. [verb]
2. If you *live* somewhere, that place is your home: *We live in a big city.* [verb]
•**lives, lived, living.**

lives (LYVZ) *Lives* is the plural of the word *life: Lives are saved when smoke alarms are used.* [noun plural]

living room A *living room* is a room in your house used by your whole family. People read, watch TV, or talk in their *living rooms.*
•**living rooms.**

living room

lizard (LIZ erd) A *lizard* is a long, thin animal with dry, rough skin. *Lizards* look something like snakes but do not have a dangerous bite. Most *lizards* have four legs and a long tail. [noun] •**lizards.**

lizard

load (LOHD)

1. A *load* is something that is being carried: *The truck carried a load of bricks.* [noun]
2. When you *load* things, you put what you are carrying in or on something: *Load your bags in the trunk.* [verb]
•**loads.** •**loads, loaded, loading.**

loaf (LOHF) A *loaf* is bread that is baked as one piece: *We cut the loaf of bread into slices.* [noun] •**loaves.**

loaf

loan (LOHN) If you *loan* someone something, you give it to them for a little while until you need it back: *Did you loan her your book?* [verb] •**loans, loaned, loaning.**

loaves (LOHVZ) *Loaves* is the plural of the word *loaf: A bakery bakes many loaves of bread every day.* [noun plural]

lobster (LOB ster) A *lobster* is an animal that lives in the ocean. *Lobsters* have hard shells and two large claws. People eat *lobsters.* [noun] •**lobsters.**

lock (LOK)

1. A *lock* is something that keeps doors, boxes, windows, or other things closed. Many *locks* must be opened with keys. [noun]
2. When you *lock* something, you put a lock on it so that others can't get in: *Lock the door before you leave.* [verb] •**locks.** •**locks, locked, locking.**

lock

log (LOG) A *log* is a long piece of wood cut from a tree trunk or a large branch. Some *logs* are cut into boards. [noun] •**logs.**

lonely (LOHN lee) If you are *lonely,* you feel sad because you are alone and need people to be near you: *He was lonely while his brother was away.* [adjective] •**lonelier, loneliest.**

long · lose

look

Look at the puppy!

long (LAWNG)

1. If something is *long,* there is a great distance from the beginning to the end of it: *An inch is short; a mile is long.* [adjective]

2. When something is *long,* it lasts for some time: *We went on a long trip last summer.* [adjective]
•**longer, longest.**

look (LUK)

1. When you *look* at something, you turn your eyes toward it. When you *look* at something, you see it: *Look at the elephants.* [verb]

2. When you *look* for something, you try to find it: *Did you look in the closet for your coat? Look that word up in your dictionary.* [verb]

3. If you *look* a certain way, you seem to be that way: *She looked sick this morning.* [verb]
•**looks, looked, looking.**

loom (LOOM) A *loom* is a machine for weaving cloth. [noun] •**looms.**

loose (LOOSS) If something is *loose,* it is not tight. Something that is *loose* is not connected in a strong way: *The top button on my coat is loose.* [adjective] •**looser, loosest.**

loose

lose (LOOZ)

1. If you *lose* something, you do not have it anymore: *I hope we don't lose any pieces to the puzzle.* [verb]

2. When you *lose* a game or contest, you do not win it: *We may lose the game.* [verb]
•**loses, lost, losing.**

lost (LOST) *I have lost my new pencil. She lost the race.* [verb]

lot (LOT) A *lot* is a large amount or great number of something: *There were a lot of birds on the roof.* [noun]

loud (LOWD) Something that is *loud* is not quiet. *Loud* things make a lot of noise: *The door slammed with a loud crash.* [adjective] •**louder, loudest.**

loudly (LOWD lee) If you do something *loudly,* you make a lot of noise while you do it: *He slammed the door loudly.* [adverb]

Louisiana (loo ee zee AN uh) *Louisiana* is one of the fifty states of the United States. [noun]

Louisiana

love (LUHV)
1. *Love* is a warm, good feeling you have for someone or something: *She feels love for her puppy.* [noun]
2. When you *love* someone or something, you have this warm, good feeling about that person or thing: *He loves all of his friends.* [verb] •**loves, loved, loving.**

love

low (LOH) If something is *low,* it is not far above the ground or the floor. Something that is *low* is not high or tall: *The wall was so low I climbed over it.* [adjective] •**lower, lowest.**

luck (LUHK) *Luck* is something that just seems to happen to you. A person can have good *luck* or bad *luck.* [noun]

lullaby · lying²

lullaby (LUL uh by) A *lullaby* is a soft song that makes a baby fall asleep. *[noun]* •**lullabies.**

lumber (LUHM ber) *Lumber* is wood that is cut into boards: *He bought lumber to build a doghouse. [noun]*

lunch (LUHNCH) *Lunch* is a meal eaten in the middle of the day. *Lunch* is the meal between breakfast and dinner: *We had tuna sandwiches for lunch. [noun]* •**lunches.**

lunchbox (LUHNCH boks) A *lunchbox* is a small metal or plastic box with a handle. People carry lunches to work or school in a *lunchbox. [noun]* •**lunchboxes.**

lung (LUHNG) Your *lung* is the part of your body that holds the air you breathe. People have two *lungs. [noun]* •**lungs.**

lying¹ (LY ing) *They are not telling the truth; they are lying. [verb]*

lying² (LY ing) *He is lying in the sleeping bag. [verb]*

lunchbox

lying²

We are lying in our sleeping bags.

made

I made this salad.

macaroni (mak uh ROH nee) *Macaroni* is a food made of flour and water. *Macaroni* is dried in the shape of hollow tubes. *[noun]*

machine (muh SHEEN) A *machine* is something with moving parts that does work for you. *Machines* use power to help people get things done faster and more easily. Cars, washers, and computers are *machines*. *[noun]* •**machines.**

mad (MAD) If you are *mad*, you are very angry: *He will be mad when he sees me wearing his new sweater. [adjective]* •**madder, maddest.**

made (MAYD) *My sister made the salad. She has made salads before. [verb]*

Mm

magazine · mail carrier

Mm

magazine (MAG uh zeen *or* mag uh ZEEN) A *magazine* is a collection of stories and other things written by different people and printed together. *Magazines* usually come out every week or every month. *[noun]* •**magazines.**

magic (MAJ ik) *Magic* is the power to do tricks that seem impossible: *She made rabbits appear out of the hat by magic.* *[noun]*

magician (muh JISH uhn) A *magician* is a person who can use magic or who does magic tricks. *[noun]* •**magicians.**

magician

magnet (MAG nit) A *magnet* is a piece of metal that pulls bits of iron or steel to it. *[noun]* •**magnets.**

magnifying glass (MAG nuh fy ing GLASS) A *magnifying glass* is a piece of curved glass that makes things look larger than they really are. •**magnifying glasses.**

mail (MAYL)
1. *Mail* is letters and packages sent by one person to another: *Has the mail come yet?* *[noun]*
2. When you *mail* something, you send it to someone else through the post office: *Please mail this letter for me.* *[verb]*
•**mails, mailed, mailing.**

mailbox (MAYL boks) A *mailbox* is a place where you mail letters or cards. A *mailbox* is also a place where mail is left for you. *[noun]* •**mailboxes.**

mail carrier (MAYL KA ree er) A *mail carrier* is a person whose job is bringing mail to people. •**mail carriers.**

magnifying glass

main (MAYN) *Main* means the most important: *The main road runs through the middle of town.* [adjective]

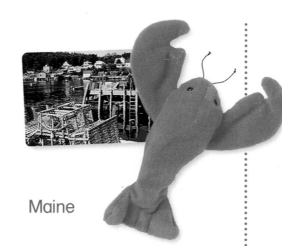

Maine

Maine (MAYN) *Maine* is one of the fifty states of the United States. [noun]

make (MAYK)
1. If you *make* something, you put it together or build it: *We will make costumes for the party.* [verb]
2. To *make* is also to cause something to happen: *Please don't make any noise. Make her sit down.* [verb]
•**makes, made, making.**

make-believe (MAYK bi leev) *Make-believe* means not real. Something that is *make-believe* is only pretend: *The story is about a make-believe monster.* [adjective]

male (MAYL) A *male* is the kind of person or animal that can be the father of children. Men and boys are *males*. A rooster is a *male* chicken. [noun or adjective] •**males.**

mall (MAWL) A *mall* is a shopping area with many stores close together. *Malls* can be inside or outside. [noun] •**malls.**

mama (MAH muh) *Mama* is another word for *mother*. [noun] •**mamas.**

mammal (MAM uhl) A *mammal* is a kind of animal that has hair or fur. A female *mammal* gives milk to her young from her own body. People, dogs, bats, and whales are all *mammals.* [noun] •**mammals.**

mammals

man (MAN) A *man* is a grown-up male person. When a boy grows up, he becomes a *man.* [noun] •**men.**

mane • march

map

Mm

mane (MAYN) A *mane* is the long, heavy hair on the back of a horse's neck. A lion also has a *mane* around its head and neck. *[noun]* •**manes.**

Manitoba (man uh TOH buh) *Manitoba* is one of the ten provinces of Canada. *[noun]*

manners (MAN erz) *Manners* are polite ways of behaving: *People with manners say "Please" and "Thank you."* *[noun plural]*

many (MEN ee) *Many* means a large number of something: *Many years ago the house was new. Do you know many people here?* *[adjective]* •**more, most.**

map (MAP) A *map* is a drawing of an area of the earth that shows many places. *Maps* often show countries, cities, rivers, seas, and lakes. *[noun]* •**maps.**

maple (MAY puhl) A *maple* is a kind of tree that is grown for shade. Some kinds of *maples* have sweet juice that is made into maple syrup. *[noun]* •**maples.**

maraca (muh RAH kuh) *Maracas* are musical instruments like large rattles. *Maracas* can be filled with little rocks or beans. *[noun]* •**maracas.**

maracas

marble (MAR buhl) A *marble* is a small glass ball used to play games. *[noun]* •**marbles.**

march (MARCH) When you *march,* you walk in a group in line with everyone else. Everyone who

is *marching* takes the same size steps: *The school band will march in the parade.* [verb] •**marches, marched, marching.**

March (MARCH) *March* is the third month of the year. It has 31 days. It comes after February and before April. [noun]

marigold (MAIR uh gohld) *Marigolds* are garden plants with yellow, orange, or red flowers. [noun] •**marigolds.**

marigolds

mark (MARK)

1. A *mark* is a line or dot made on something. [noun]
2. When you *mark* something, you put a line or dot on or around it: *Mark the cities on the map.* [verb]
•**marks.** •**marks, marked, marking.**

marker (MAR ker) A *marker* is a kind of pen used for writing or drawing. [noun] •**markers.**

marry (MA ree) If you *marry* someone, you and that person become husband and wife: *They plan to marry in June.* [verb] •**marries, married, marrying.**

marsh (MARSH) A *marsh* is low, soft land that is often wet. Grass grows in *marshes,* but trees usually do not. [noun] •**marshes.**

marshmallow (MARSH mal oh) A *marshmallow* is a soft, white, sweet food. [noun] •**marshmallows.**

Maryland (MAIR uh luhnd) *Maryland* is one of the fifty states of the United States. [noun]

mask (MASK) A *mask* is a covering that hides or protects your face: *The firefighter wore a gas mask.* [noun] •**masks.**

masks

Mm

Massachusetts · matter

Mm

Massachusetts (mas uh CHOO sits) *Massachusetts* is one of the fifty states of the United States. *[noun]*

mat (MAT) A *mat* is a small rug or a thick pad: *Wipe your feet on the mat. Put a mat under the hot dish.* *[noun]* •**mats.**

match[1] (MACH) A *match* is a short stick of wood or stiff paper. A *match* has a tip that catches fire when you rub it against something rough. *[noun]* •**matches.**

match[2] (MACH) When things *match,* they go well together. If you *match* two things, you find two things that go together: *His scarf and mittens match. Match the words with the pictures.* *[verb]* •**matches, matched, matching.**

match[2]

material (muh TEER ee uhl) *Material* is what a thing is made from or used for: *Wood is a material for building houses. Writing materials are paper, pens, and pencils.* *[noun]* •**materials.**

math (MATH) *Math* is a short word meaning *mathematics.* *[noun]*

mathematics (math uh MAT iks) *Mathematics* is the study of numbers. Addition and subtraction are a part of *mathematics.* *[noun]*

matter (MAT er) *Matter* is what things are made of. *Matter* takes up space and has weight. *Matter* can be a solid, liquid, or gas. *[noun]*

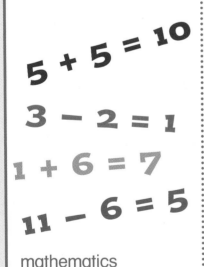

$$5 + 5 = 10$$
$$3 - 2 = 1$$
$$1 + 6 = 7$$
$$11 - 6 = 5$$

mathematics

mattress (MAT riss) A *mattress* is a covering of strong cloth stuffed with soft material. People sleep on *mattresses.* [noun] •**mattresses.**

mattress

may (MAY) *You may have an apple. It may rain tomorrow.* [verb]

May (MAY) *May* is the fifth month of the year. It has 31 days. It comes after April and before June. [noun]

maybe (MAY bee) *Maybe it will rain. Maybe she'll go to the movies.* [adverb]

me (MEE) *Please give me a piece of paper. Let me go. Come with me.* [pronoun]

meadow (MED oh) A *meadow* is a piece of land where grass grows: *There are sheep in the meadow.* [noun] •**meadows.**

meal (MEEL) A *meal* is the food you eat at one time. Breakfast, lunch, and dinner are *meals.* [noun] •**meals.**

mean¹ (MEEN)

1. If you *mean* to do something, you want to do it: *He didn't mean to break the glass.* [verb]

2. To *mean* is also to say the same thing as something else. The words *automobile* and *car mean* the same thing. [verb]

3. To *mean* is also to be a sign of or to tell something: *A red light means stop.* [verb]
•**means, meant, meaning.**

meadows

Mm

mean² · meet

Mm

mean² (MEEN) If people are *mean,* they are not kind, nice, or friendly: *Don't be mean to the puppy.* [adjective] •**meaner, meanest.**

meaning (MEE ning) The *meaning* of a word is what it means. If you do not understand a word, you can look up its *meaning* in a dictionary: *Do you know the meaning of this word?* [noun] •**meanings.**

meant (MENT) *She meant what she said. He had meant to call.* [verb]

measure (MEZH er) When you *measure* something, you find out how much or how big it is: *Measure the room to find its length.* [verb] •**measures, measured, measuring.**

meat (MEET) *Meat* is a kind of food that comes from animals. Beef and pork are kinds of *meat.* [noun] •**meats.**

mechanic (muh KAN ik) A *mechanic* is a person whose job is fixing machines: *A mechanic repaired our car.* [noun] •**mechanics.**

mechanics

medicine (MED uh suhn) *Medicine* is something used to make a sick person well: *He took some medicine for his cold.* [noun] •**medicines.**

meet (MEET)

1. When you *meet* someone, you get together with that person. To *meet* is also to be somewhere and say hello when other people get there: *I'll meet my friend at the library. They met us at the airport.* [verb]

meet

It's nice meeting you!

246

2. To *meet* also means to begin to get to know someone: *School is a good place to meet new friends.* [verb]
•**meets, met, meeting.**

melon (MEL uhn) A *melon* is a large, sweet fruit. *Melons* grow on vines. Cantaloupes and watermelons are *melons.* [noun] •**melons.**

melons

melt (MELT) When something *melts,* it turns from a solid into a liquid. Ice becomes water when it *melts.* [verb] •**melts, melted, melting.**

memory (MEM er ee) *Memory* is the power to remember things or keep things in your mind: *He should know the answer because he has a good memory.* [noun] •**memories.**

men (MEN) *Men* is the plural of the word *man: Boys grow up to be men.* [noun plural]

Mm

menu (MEN yoo) A *menu* is a list of the food served at a meal: *We looked at the menu and chose our lunch.* [noun] •**menus.**

meow (MEE ow) A *meow* is the sound made by a cat or kitten: *The cat's loud meow made us laugh.* [noun] •**meows.**

mess (MESS) A *mess* is a place or a group of things that is not clean or neat: *Please clean up the mess in your closet.* [noun] •**messes.**

mess

message (MESS ij) A *message* is the words sent by one person to another: *He got your telephone message.* [noun] •**messages.**

messy · Mèxico

Mm

messy (MESS ee) *Messy* means not neat or clean. Something that is *messy* is in a mess: *The room was so messy that it took two days to clean it.* [adjective] •**messier, messiest.**

met (MET) *They met in the park. Have you met my aunt?* [verb]

metal (MET uhl) *Metal* is a hard material such as iron, gold, silver, or steel. *Metals* are usually shiny and are found underground. *Metals* can be melted or hammered into thin sheets. [noun] •**metals.**

meteor (MEE tee er) A *meteor* is a rock that falls from space to Earth very quickly. Some people call *meteors* shooting stars. *Meteors* become so hot from falling through the air so quickly that they glow and often burn up. [noun] •**meteors.**

meteor

meter (MEE ter) A *meter* is a unit of length equal to 100 centimeters. A guitar is about one *meter* long. [noun] •**meters.**

Mexican (MEK suh kuhn)
1. A *Mexican* is a person born or living in Mexico. [noun]
2. Something that is *Mexican* belongs to or is from Mexico: *The Mexican capital is Mexico City.* [adjective]
•**Mexicans.**

Mexico (MEK suh koh) *Mexico* is the country south of the United States. [noun]

Mèxico (me HEE koh) *Mèxico* is a state in south central Mexico. [noun]

Mexican

mice (MYSS) *Mice* is the plural of the word *mouse: We saw several mice in the basement.* [*noun plural*]

Michigan (MISH uh guhn) *Michigan* is one of the fifty states of the United States. [*noun*]

Michoacán (mee choh ah KAHN) *Michoacán* is a state in southwest Mexico. [*noun*]

mice

microphone (MY kruh fohn) A *microphone* is a tool that makes your voice sound louder. Singers use *microphones.* [*noun*] •**microphones.**

microscope (MY kruh skohp) A *microscope* is something that makes small things look larger. A *microscope* helps you see things that are too small to see with your eyes. [*noun*] •**microscopes.**

microwave (MY kroh wayv) A *microwave* is a special kind of oven that cooks food very quickly. [*noun*] •**microwaves.**

microscope

middle (MID uhl) The *middle* is the center: *My cap was in the middle of the street. The middle house is ours.* [*noun* or *adjective*]

midnight (MID nyt) When it is *midnight,* it is twelve o'clock at night. *Midnight* is the middle of the night. [*noun*]

might (MYT) *Mother said we might play after dinner. He might have called yesterday while we were out.* [*verb*]

Mm

mile · mirror

Mm

mile (MYL) A *mile* is a unit of length. Distances between cities in the United States are measured in *miles*. [noun] •**miles.**

milk (MILK) *Milk* is the white liquid from cows. People drink and cook with *milk*. *Milk* helps us grow. [noun]

million (MIL yuhn) A *million* is one thousand thousand. It is also written 1,000,000. [noun or adjective] •**millions.**

milk

mind (MYND)

1. Your *mind* is the part of you that knows, thinks, feels, and remembers. You use your *mind* to learn and to imagine: *She has a good mind.* [noun]

2. When you *mind* someone or something, you look after or take care of that person or thing: *Please mind your little brother while I answer the phone.* [verb]

3. If you *mind* something, you feel bad about it: *Did you mind missing the party?* [verb]
•**minds.** •**minds, minded, minding.**

mine (MYN) *This scarf is mine.* [pronoun]

Minnesota (min uh SOH tuh) *Minnesota* is one of the fifty states of the United States. [noun]

minus (MY nuhss) Another word for *minus* is *less*: *7 minus 2 leaves 5.* [preposition]

minute (MIN it) A *minute* is one of the 60 equal parts of an hour. A *minute* is 60 seconds. [noun] •**minutes.**

mirror (MIR er) A *mirror* is a glass in which you can see yourself. [noun] •**mirrors.**

mirror

250

miss (MISS)

1. When you *miss* something, you do not find, get, or meet it: *When he throws the ball, I usually miss it. I missed his visit because I was sick.* [verb]

2. When you *miss* someone or something, you feel unhappy because that person or thing is gone: *We miss you. I did not miss my glove until I got home.* [verb]
   •**misses, missed, missing.**

Miss (MISS) *Miss* is a word you use before the name of a girl or a woman who is not married. •**Misses.**

Mississippi (miss uh SIP ee) *Mississippi* is one of the fifty states of the United States. [noun]

Missouri (muh ZUR ee) *Missouri* is one of the fifty states of the United States. [noun]

Missouri

misspell (mis SPEL) When you *misspell* a word, you write or say the wrong letters. [verb] •**misspells, misspelled, misspelling.**

mistake (muh STAYK) A *mistake* is something that is not right or not done the way it should be: *I made a mistake in adding those numbers.* [noun] •**mistakes.**

mitt (MIT) A *mitt* is a baseball glove: *He needs a catcher's mitt.* [noun] •**mitts.**

mitten (MIT uhn) A *mitten* is a kind of glove that covers the four fingers together. A *mitten* has a special place for the thumb. [noun] •**mittens.**

mittens

mix · mom

mix (MIKS)

1. When you *mix* things, you put them together and stir well: *We mixed butter, sugar, milk, flour, and eggs to make the cake.* [verb]

2. A *mix* is something that is already mixed: *We used a mix to make the pie crust.* [noun]
•**mixes, mixed, mixing.** •**mixes.**

mixture (MIKS cher) A *mixture* is something that has been mixed or put together. [noun] •**mixtures.**

mobile (MOH beel) A *mobile* is something that hangs from fine wires or threads and that moves when the air around it moves. [noun] •**mobiles.**

mobile

model (MOD uhl)

1. A *model* is a small copy of something: *A globe is a model of the earth.* [noun]

2. When you *model* something, you make it out of something soft: *Let's model an elephant out of clay.* [verb]
•**models.** •**models, modeled, modeling.**

mom (MOM) *Mom* is another word for *mother.* [noun]
•**moms.**

moment (MOH muhnt) A *moment* is a very short amount or length of time: *In a moment the bell will ring.* [noun] •**moments.**

mommy (MOM ee) *Mommy* is another word for *mother.* [noun] •**mommies.**

Monday (MUHN day) *Monday* is the day after Sunday. *Monday* is the second day of the week. [noun] •**Mondays.**

money (MUHN ee) *Money* is the coins and paper used for buying and selling things. People buy things with *money.* People who work at jobs are paid *money.* [noun]

money

monkey (MUHNG kee) A *monkey* is an animal with long arms, a long tail, and a lot of hair. There are many different kinds of *monkeys. Monkeys* eat fruits and vegetables and often live in trees. [noun] •**monkeys.**

monster (MON ster) A *monster* is a make-believe person or animal that is scary. In stories, some *monsters* are friendly, and others are not. Dragons are *monsters.* [noun] •**monsters.**

Montana (mon TAN uh) *Montana* is one of the fifty states of the United States. [noun]

month (MUHNTH) A *month* is a part of a year. There are twelve *months* in a year. They are January, February, March, April, May, June, July, August, September, October, November, and December. [noun] •**months.**

moo (MOO) A *moo* is the sound made by a cow. [noun] •**moos.**

monkey

Mm

mood · moth

Mm

mood (MOOD) Your *mood* is the way you are feeling: *A rainy day puts me in a bad mood.* [noun] •**moods.**

moon (MOON) The *moon* is the biggest and brightest light seen in the sky at night. The *moon* is round like a ball and is smaller than the Earth. It moves around the Earth. Other planets also have *moons.* [noun] •**moons.**

moon

mop (MOP)
1. A *mop* is a bundle of thick strings or a sponge on the end of a long handle. You use a *mop* to clean floors. [noun]
2. To *mop* means to wash or wipe up with a mop, sponge, or towel: *We should mop the kitchen floor.* [verb] •**mops.** •**mops, mopped, mopping.**

more (MOR) *This soup needs more salt. We need more than three players for the game. This plant needs more sun.* [adjective or adverb]

Morelos (moh RE lohss *or* muh RAY luhss) *Morelos is a state in south central Mexico.* [noun]

morning (MOR ning) *Morning* is the part of the day between night and noon: *This morning we all ate breakfast together.* [noun] •**mornings.**

mosquito (muh SKEE toh) A *mosquito* is a small insect with two wings. The female *mosquito* bites. [noun] •**mosquitoes.**

most (MOHST) *Most people like music.* [adjective]

moth (MAWTH) A *moth* is an insect with wings that looks something like a butterfly. *Moths* usually fly at night. [noun] •**moths.**

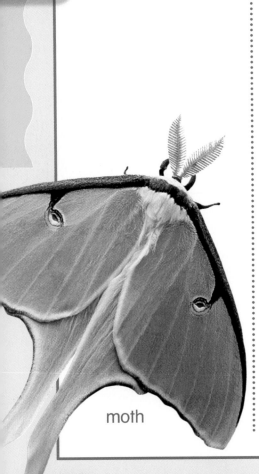

moth

mother (MUH<u>TH</u> er) A *mother* is a woman who has a child or children. *[noun]* •**mothers.**

motor (MOH ter) A *motor* is a machine that makes other machines work. *Motors* run on electricity or gas. Cars have *motors* that make them run. *[noun]* •**motors.**

motorcycle (MOH ter sy kuhl) A *motorcycle* is a thing to ride that has a motor and two wheels. A *motorcycle* looks like a bicycle but is heavier and larger. *[noun]* •**motorcycles.**

motorcycle

mountain (MOWN tuhn) A *mountain* is a very high hill. *[noun]* •**mountains.**

mouse (MOWSS)

1. A *mouse* is a small animal with soft fur and a long, thin tail. Some *mice* live in people's houses. Some *mice* live in fields and meadows. *[noun]*
2. A *mouse* is also a tool used with a computer. It helps you move around the screen. *[noun]* •**mice.**

mouth (MOWTH) Your *mouth* is the part of your body that helps you eat and talk. Your *mouth* is part of your face, and your tongue and teeth are inside your *mouth*. *[noun]* •**mouths.**

mouth

move (MOOV)

1. When you *move,* you go from one place to another. When you *move* something, you put it in a different place: *Please move to the back of the line. Please move your bicycle out of the driveway.* *[verb]*

Mm

movie · mug

2. To *move* also means to change the place where you live: *We live in the city now, but my parents want to move to the country.* [verb]
•**moves, moved, moving.**

movie (MOO vee) A *movie* is a story in pictures. The pictures are taken by a special camera and shown on a screen. [noun] •**movies.**

Mr. (MISS ter) *Mr.* is a word you use before a man's name.

Mrs. (MISS iz) *Mrs.* is a word you use before a married woman's name.

Ms. (MIZ) *Ms.* is a word you use before a woman's name.

much (MUHCH) *Much* is a large amount: *I don't have much money. I like swimming very much.* [adjective]
•**more, most.**

mud (MUHD) *Mud* is very wet dirt that is soft and sticky: *We got some mud on our boots.* [noun]

mudslide (MUHD slyd) A *mudslide* is a large amount of dirt and mud moving down a hill at once. A *mudslide* can hurt houses and cars. [noun]
•**mudslides.**

mudslides

mug

muffin (MUF uhn) A *muffin* is a small, round cake often made with fruit. *Muffins* are often served hot for breakfast. [noun] •**muffins.**

mug (MUHG) A *mug* is a heavy cup with a handle. [noun] •**mugs.**

Mm

multiply (MUHL tuh ply) When you *multiply,* you add one number a number of times: *To multiply 2 by 5 means to add 2 five times, making 10.* [verb] •**multiplies, multiplied, multiplying.**

muscle (MUHSS uhl) A *muscle* is a part of your body that helps you move. Without *muscles,* you could not lift and carry things. Your body has *muscles* of different sizes and shapes. *[noun]* •**muscles.**

muscles

museum (myoo ZEE uhm) A *museum* is a building for keeping and showing interesting things. People visit art *museums,* science *museums,* and *museums* with things from long ago. *[noun]* •**museums.**

mushroom (MUHSH room) A *mushroom* is a small living thing like a plant. A *mushroom* often has the shape of an umbrella and grows very fast. Some *mushrooms* are good to eat, but some can hurt you. *[noun]* •**mushrooms.**

music (MYOO zik) *Music* is the sounds made by a piano, a violin, a guitar, and other musical instruments. The sound of a person singing is also *music: I hear music in the next room.* [noun]

Mm

musical • mystery

Mm

musical (MYOO zuh kuhl)
If something is *musical*, it sounds beautiful like music: *We heard the musical song from a robin in the tree.* [adjective]

musical instrument
(MYOO zuh kuhl IN struh muhnt) A *musical instrument* is something that makes beautiful sounds. Guitars, violins, and pianos are *musical instruments.* •**musical instruments.**

musician

musician (myoo ZISH uhn) A *musician* is a person who sings, plays, or writes music. [noun] •**musicians.**

must (MUHST) *You must eat the right food. I must go now.* [verb]

mustache (muh STASH) A *mustache* is the hair that grows on a man's top lip. [noun] •**mustaches.**

mustard (MUHSS terd) *Mustard* is a yellow powder or paste with a sharp, hot taste. *Mustard* is made from the seeds of a plant: *I like mustard on my hot dog.* [noun]

mustard

my (MY) *I forgot my gloves. My house is around the corner.* [adjective]

myself (my SELF) *I can do it myself. I cut myself. I like to be by myself sometimes.* [pronoun]

mystery (MISS ter ee) A *mystery* is something that you cannot understand or explain: *It was a mystery why the radio started playing in the middle of the night.* [noun] •**mysteries.**

nail · name

Nn

nail (NAYL)

1. A *nail* is a thin piece of metal that has a point at one end. You hammer *nails* through pieces of wood to hold them together. *[noun]*

2. Your *nails* are also the hard parts at the ends of your fingers and toes. *[noun]*

•**nails.**

My name is Michael.

name (NAYM)

1. A *name* is the word you use to talk about or call a person, animal, place, or thing: *Our dog's name is Lightning. [noun]*

2. When you *name* someone or something, you give a name to that person or thing: *They named the baby after his father. [verb]*

•**names.** •**names, named, naming.**

259

nap • near

Nn

nature

nap (NAP)
1. A *nap* is a short sleep: *Grandma took a nap after lunch.* [noun]
2. When you *nap*, you sleep for a little while: *We must be quiet while the baby naps.* [verb]
•**naps.** •**naps, napped, napping.** nap

napkin (NAP kin) A *napkin* is a piece of cloth or paper. People use *napkins* at meals to protect their clothes and to wipe their lips and fingers. [noun] •**napkins.**

narrow (NA roh) If something is *narrow,* it is not far from one side to the other. Something that is *narrow* is not wide: *It was hard to drive down the narrow street.* [adjective] •**narrower, narrowest.**

nation (NAY shuhn) A *nation* is a group of people living in one country with the same laws and usually the same language. [noun] •**nations.**

Native American (NAY tiv uh MAIR uh kuhn) A *Native American* is a person from one of the groups of people who have lived in America since before the first white people came. •**Native Americans.**

nature (NAY cher) *Nature* is everything in the world not made by people. Plants, animals, air, water, mountains, and people are parts of *nature.* [noun]

navy (NAY vee) The *navy* is a large group of sailors and ships. A *navy* fights in a war. [noun] •**navies.**

Nayarit (ny uh REET) *Nayarit* is a state in the west part of Mexico. [noun]

near (NEER) *Near* means close to. If you are *near* something, you are not far away from it: *We live near a lake. My birthday is near his.* [adverb or adjective] •**nearer, nearest.**

nearby (NEER BY) *Nearby* means not far away. Another word for *nearby* is *near: We visited a park nearby. [adverb]*

neat (NEET)

1. If something is *neat*, it is clean and things are not lying around: *She kept her room neat. [adjective]*

2. If something is *neat*, it can also be very nice or wonderful: *My uncle gave me a neat gift. [adjective]*

•**neater, neatest.**

This is a neat toy.

neat

Nebraska (nuh BRASS kuh) *Nebraska* is one of the fifty states of the United States. *[noun]*

neck (NEK) Your *neck* is the part of your body between your head and shoulders. *[noun]* •**necks.**

necklace (NEK liss) A *necklace* is a kind of jewelry you wear around your neck. *Necklaces* may be made of gold, silver, or beads. *[noun]* •**necklaces.**

need (NEED) If you *need* something, you cannot do without it: *Plants need water to grow. People need air to breathe. [verb]* •**needs, needed, needing.**

needle (NEE duhl)

1. A *needle* is a very thin, sharp tool used in sewing. A *needle* has a small hole in one end for thread to go through. *[noun]*

2. A *needle* is also a thin tube with a sharp point. Doctors use *needles* to give shots. *[noun]*

•**needles.**

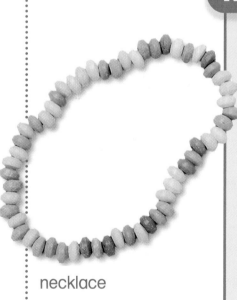

necklace

Nn

neigh · never

Nn

neigh (NAY) A *neigh* is a sound that a horse makes: *We heard a soft neigh from the stable.* [noun] •**neighs.**

neighbor (NAY ber) A *neighbor* is someone who lives near you: *Our neighbors were outside raking leaves in the yard.* [noun] •**neighbors.**

neighbor

neighborhood (NAY ber hud) Your *neighborhood* is the streets and houses around the place where you live: *We have a school and a park in our neighborhood.* [noun] •**neighborhoods.**

neither (NEE <u>th</u>er *or* NY <u>th</u>er) *Neither child wanted to go to school. Neither of us can do that.* [adjective *or* pronoun]

nephew (NEF yoo) Your *nephew* is a son of your brother or sister. [noun] •**nephews.**

nest (NEST) A *nest* is a kind of home that birds build. Birds lay their eggs in *nests. Nests* are made in the shape of a bowl from straw, twigs, and leaves. [noun] •**nests.**

nest

net (NET) A *net* is a kind of cloth with holes in it. A *net* is made of string tied together. *Nets* are used in sports like soccer and basketball. *Nets* are also used to catch fish. [noun] •**nets.**

Nevada (nuh VAD uh *or* nuh VAH duh) *Nevada* is one of the fifty states of the United States. [noun]

never (NEV er) *He has never flown on an airplane. I will never get all of this work done.* [adverb]

new (NOO)

1. If something is *new,* it has never been made or thought of before. Something that is *new* is not old: *She had a new idea for an art project.* [adjective]

2. If something is *new,* it has not been used yet. Something that is *new* is not worn out or used up: *Dad bought a new car.* [adjective]

•**newer, newest.**

new

newborn (NOO born)
A person or animal that is *newborn* was only just born: *Wash your hands before you hold the newborn baby.* [adjective]

New Brunswick (noo BRUHNZ wik)
New Brunswick is one of the ten provinces of Canada. [noun]

Newfoundland (NOO fuhnd luhnd)
Newfoundland is one of the ten provinces of Canada. [noun]

New Hampshire (noo HAMP sher)
New Hampshire is one of the fifty states of the United States. [noun]

New Jersey (noo JER zee)
New Jersey is one of the fifty states of the United States. [noun]

New Mexico (noo MEK suh koh)
New Mexico is one of the fifty states of the United States. [noun]

news (NOOZ)

1. *News* is facts about something that has just happened: *Mom told us the good news about her job.* [noun]

2. *News* is also a report in a newspaper or on TV or radio about what is happening in the world. [noun]

New Mexico

Nn

newspaper • nightmare

Nn

New York

newspaper (NOOZ pay per) A *newspaper* is sheets of paper printed every day or week telling news and advertising things for sale: *My parents read the newspaper every morning.* [*noun*] •**newspapers.**

New Year's Day (NOO YEERZ DAY) *New Year's Day* is January 1. It is a holiday.

New York (noo YORK) *New York* is one of the fifty states of the United States. [*noun*]

next (NEKST) *I borrowed some paper from the girl next to me. I missed school on Monday, but I went back the next day.* [*adverb* or *adjective*]

nice (NYSS) Someone who is *nice* is kind and friendly. Another word for *nice* is *good: I had a nice time at the party. They were nice to me.* [*adjective*] •**nicer, nicest.**

nickel (NIK uhl) A *nickel* is a coin in the United States and Canada worth five cents. Five *nickels* make one quarter. [*noun*] •**nickels.**

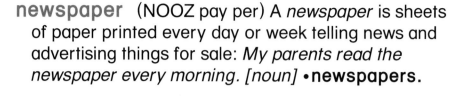

nickels

niece (NEESS) Your *niece* is a daughter of your brother or sister. [*noun*] •**nieces.**

night (NYT) *Night* is the time between evening and morning. [*noun*] •**nights.**

nightmare (NYT mair) A *nightmare* is a very frightening dream: *I had a nightmare about falling off a high building.* [*noun*] •**nightmares.**

nine (NYN) *Nine is one more than eight. It is also written 9.* [*noun* or *adjective*] •**nines.**

nineteen (NYN teen) *Nineteen is nine more than ten. It is also written 19.* [*noun* or *adjective*] •**nineteens.**

nineteenth (NYN teenth) *Nineteenth is the next after 18th. It is also written 19th.* [*adjective*]

ninety (NYN tee) *Ninety is ten more than eighty. It is also written 90.* [*noun* or *adjective*] •**nineties.**

ninth (NYNTH) *Ninth is the next after the eighth. It is also written 9th.* [*adjective*]

no (NOH) *There are no trees in our front yard. Just say "No, thank you" if you don't want any more to eat.* [*adjective* or *adverb*]

nobody (NOH buhd ee) *Nobody wanted to go home before the game ended.* [*pronoun*]

nod (NOD) *When you nod, you bow your head a little bit and raise it again: Some people nod when they see people they know.* [*verb*] •**nods, nodded, nodding.**

noise (NOIZ) *A noise is a sound that you do not want to hear: The noise of the dog barking kept me from sleeping.* [*noun*] •**noises.**

noisy (NOI zee) *If something is noisy, it makes a lot of noise. If a place is noisy, it is full of sounds you do not want to hear: The washing machine was noisy. We live on a noisy street.* [*adjective*] •**noisier, noisiest.**

nine

noise

Nn

none · not

none (NUHN) *None of the dishes were broken. None of the children wanted to play at the park.* [pronoun]

noodles (NOO duhlz) *Noodles* are a food made of flour and water and sometimes milk or eggs. *Noodles* are often served with a tomato sauce or butter or in soup. [noun plural]

noodles

noon (NOON) *Noon is the middle of the day. Noon is 12 o'clock: Many people eat lunch at noon.* [noun]

north (NORTH) *North is the direction to the right as you face the setting sun. North is the opposite of south.* [noun]

North America (NORTH uh MAIR uh kuh) *North America is a continent. North America is one of the large areas of land on the Earth.* [noun]

North Carolina (NORTH ka ruh LY nuh) *North Carolina is one of the fifty states of the United States.* [noun]

North Dakota (NORTH duh KOH tuh) *North Dakota is one of the fifty states of the United States.* [noun]

Northwest Territories (NORTH west TAIR uh tor eez) *Northwest Territories is one of the three territories of Canada.* [noun]

nose (NOHZ) Your *nose* is the part of your face that sticks out just above your mouth. Your *nose* is used for smelling and breathing. [noun] •**noses.**

not (NOT) *I am not going to school today. Two and two are not five. It is not time to leave.* [adverb]

nose

This is my nose.

266

note (NOHT)

1. A *note* is a very short letter: *I sent Grandma a note to thank her for the gift.* [noun]

2. A *note* is also a sign in music that shows what sound to make. [noun]

•**notes.**

nothing (NUHTH ing)
There was nothing in the empty closet. [pronoun]

notice (NOH tiss) If you *notice* something, you look at it or see it: *Did you notice the cat's unusual eyes?* [verb]
•**notices, noticed, noticing.**

nothing

noun (NOWN) A *noun* is a word that names a person, place, animal, or thing. In the sentence "They get balloons to take home," *balloons* and *home* are *nouns.* They name a thing and a place. [noun] •**nouns.**

Nova Scotia (NOH vuh SKOH shuh) *Nova Scotia* is one of the ten provinces of Canada. [noun]

November (noh VEM ber) *November* is the eleventh month of the year. It has 30 days. It comes after October and before December. [noun]

now (NOW) *Please take the dog out now. I used to live on Bay Street, but now I live on Lake Avenue.* [adverb]

nowhere (NOH wair) *He searched the house, but the book was nowhere to be found. This arguing is getting us nowhere.* [adverb]

Nuevo León (nway voh lay OHN) *Nuevo León* is a state in the north part of Mexico. [noun]

Nova Scotia

Nn

number · nut

number   (NUHM ber)
1. A *number* is a word that tells how many. Two is a *number*. Twelve is a *number*. *[noun]*
2. A *number* is also a symbol that stands for a number. 9 is a *number*. 481 is a *number*. *[noun]*
•**numbers.**

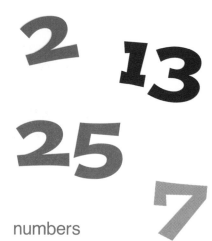

numbers

Nunavut   (NOO nuh VOOT) *Nunavut* is one of the three territories of Canada. *[noun]*

nurse   (NERSS) A *nurse* is a person who takes care of sick people. Many *nurses* work in hospitals. Others visit sick people in their homes. *[noun]*
•**nurses.**

nut   (NUHT) A *nut* is a dry fruit or seed with a hard shell. *Nuts* hold only one seed. Most *nuts* grow on trees. An acorn is a *nut*. *[noun]* •**nuts.**

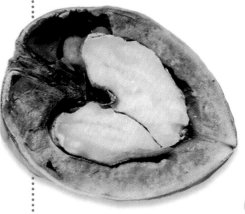

nuts

oak · object

oak (OHK) An *oak* is a kind of tree. *Oaks* have hard wood and nuts called *acorns*. [noun] •**oaks.**

oatmeal (OHT meel) *Oatmeal* is a kind of breakfast cereal that is served hot: *I cooked my own oatmeal this morning.* [noun]

Oaxaca (wah HAH kuh) *Oaxaca* is a state in the southeast part of Mexico. [noun]

obey (oh BAY) When you *obey* a law or rule, you do what it tells you to do: *The careful driver obeyed all the traffic laws. You must obey the rules in school.* [verb] •**obeys, obeyed, obeying.**

object (OB jikt) An *object* is anything solid that you can see or touch. A desk, a pen, and a book are *objects.* [noun] •**objects.**

Oaxaca

oboe · off

oboe (OH boh) An *oboe* is a musical instrument that has a thin, high sound. *[noun]* •**oboes.**

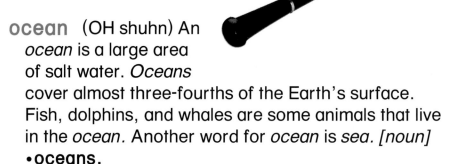

oboe

ocean (OH shuhn) An *ocean* is a large area of salt water. *Oceans* cover almost three-fourths of the Earth's surface. Fish, dolphins, and whales are some animals that live in the *ocean.* Another word for *ocean* is *sea. [noun]* •**oceans.**

o'clock *O'clock* is a word we use to say what time it is: *We eat lunch at twelve o'clock. [adverb]*

October (ok TOH ber) *October* is the tenth month of the year. It has 31 days. It comes after September and before November. *[noun]*

octopus (OK tuh puhss) An *octopus* is a sea animal. It has a soft, thick body and eight arms. *[noun]* •**octopuses.**

odd (OD)

1. *Odd* means to have one left over when something is divided by two: *Seven, nine, and eleven are odd numbers. [adjective]*
2. If someone is *odd,* that person acts in a strange way: *She has an odd habit of looking over her shoulder at people. [adjective]*
•**odder, oddest** *for definition 2.*

of (UHV *or* OV) *The leaders of the team gave a party for everyone. They built a house of bricks. The state of Alaska is very big. [preposition]*

off (AWF) *The cat jumped off the bench. The radio is off. [preposition* or *adjective]*

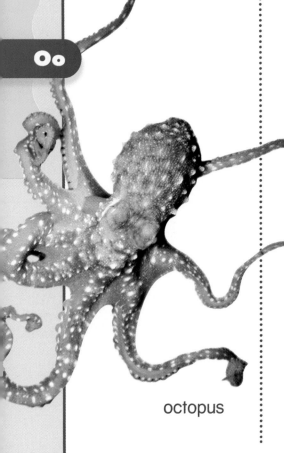

octopus

offer (AW fer *or* OF er) When you *offer* something to someone, you ask that person if he or she wants it: *Should I offer her some help?* [verb] •**offers, offered, offering.**

office (OF iss) An *office* is a place where people work: *Mom left the house and went to her office.* [noun] •**offices.**

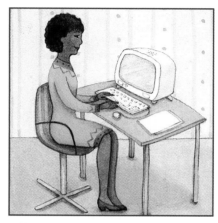
office

often (AW fuhn *or* OF tuhn) *Often* means to happen many times: *It often snows in January. We have been there often.* [adverb]

oh (OH) *Oh* is a word used to show surprise, joy, pain, and other feelings: *Oh, no! The tiger escaped from the cage!* [interjection]

Ohio (oh HY oh) *Ohio* is one of the fifty states of the United States. [noun]

oil (OIL)

oil

1. *Oil* is a thick liquid from animal fat or vegetable fat: *Mother uses vegetable oil when she cooks.* [noun]
2. *Oil* is also a liquid that comes from the earth. Gasoline is made from *oil.* [noun]
3. When you *oil* something, you put oil on or in it: *Did you oil your bicycle?* [verb]
•**oils** for definition I. •**oils, oiled, oiling.**

Oklahoma (oh kluh HOH muh) *Oklahoma* is one of the fifty states of the United States. [noun]

old (OHLD)

1. When someone is *old,* that person has lived a long time: *My grandfather is very old.* [adjective]

on · onto

2. When something is *old,* it was not made or thought of just a short time ago. Something that is *old* is not new: *My cousin has an old bike.* [*adjective*]
•**older, oldest.**

on (ON) *The lizard is on the rock. Put your left shoe on your left foot. There is a calendar on the wall. This is a book on dinosaurs.* [*preposition*]

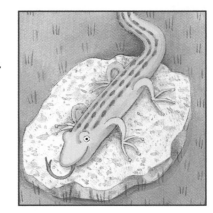

on

once (WUHNSS)
1. *Once* is one time: *Play that song once more.* [*adverb*]
2. *Once* also means at some time in the past: *The plant was once a sprout.* [*adverb*]

one (WUHN)
1. *One* is the number 1. [*noun* or *adjective*]
2. *One* is also a single thing: *Which one do you want to sit in?* [*noun* or *pronoun*]
•**ones.**

onion (UHN yuhn) An *onion* is a vegetable with a strong flavor. An *onion* grows from an underground bulb. [*noun*] •**onions.**

only (OHN lee) *This is the only road to town. He is an only child. She had three pictures but she sold only two.* [*adjective* or *adverb*]

Ontario (on TAIR ee oh) *Ontario* is one of the ten provinces of Canada. [*noun*]

onto (ON too) *He climbed onto the roof. She drove the car onto the beach.* [*preposition*]

onion

open (OH puhn)

1. When something is *open*, people and things can get in or out. Something that is *open* is not shut: *The window was open for fresh air.* [adjective]

2. When you *open* something, you make it open: *Open the window. The store doesn't open until 9 o'clock. Please open your books to page 30.* [verb]
•**opens, opened, opening.**

opossum (uh POSS uhm) An *opossum* is a small animal that often carries its babies on its back. When it is caught, it pretends to be dead. [noun] •**opossums.**

opossum

opposite (OP uh zit) If things are *opposite,* they are as different from each other as they can be. East and west are *opposite* directions. Running fast is the *opposite* of walking slow. [adjective or noun]

or (OR) *Is that apple sweet or sour? Hurry, or you will be late.* [conjunction]

orange (AR inj *or* OR inj)

1. An *orange* is a round fruit that grows on trees. *Oranges* are full of juice. [noun]

2. *Orange* is the color of an orange or a pumpkin. [adjective or noun]
•**oranges.**

orangutan (uh RANG uh tan) An *orangutan* is a large animal with long arms and a lot of hair. *Orangutans* are larger than chimpanzees. [noun] •**orangutans.**

orange

orbit (OR bit)

1. An *orbit* is the path of the Earth or other planets around the sun. The path of the moon around the Earth is also an *orbit: The orbit of the Earth around the sun takes one year.* [noun]

orchestra · Oregon

2. To *orbit* is to travel around the Earth or around the sun: *The spaceship orbits the Earth several times a day.* [verb]
•**orbits.** •**orbits, orbited, orbiting.**

orchestra
(OR kuh struh) An *orchestra* is a large group of musicians playing music together. An *orchestra* usually has many violin players. [noun]
•**orchestras.**

orchestra

order (OR der)

1. The *order* of things is the way one thing comes after or before another: *Please line up in order of size to take your class picture. The words in the dictionary are in alphabetical order.* [noun]

2. An *order* is something you say to people that tells them what to do or tells them what you want: *We had orders to come straight home after school. At the restaurant, we gave our order to the waitress.* [noun]

3. When you *order* something, you say what you want. When you *order* people to do something, you tell them what to do: *The police officer ordered the driver to stop. Mom ordered lunch for all of us.* [verb]
•**orders** *for definition 2.* •**orders, ordered, ordering.**

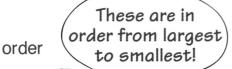

order

These are in order from largest to smallest!

ordinary (ORD uhn air ee) Something that is *ordinary* is regular and not special or unusual: *My ordinary lunch is soup, a sandwich, and milk.* [adjective]

Oregon (OR uh guhn) *Oregon* is one of the fifty states of the United States. [noun]

ornitholestes (or NITH uh LESS teez) The *ornitholestes* was a small dinosaur with a long neck and tail. The *ornitholestes* probably ate birds and lizards. *[noun]* • **ornitholestes.**

ostrich (OSS trich) An *ostrich* is a large bird with long legs. *Ostriches* can run very fast, but they cannot fly. *[noun]* • **ostriches.**

other (UHTH er) *He is better in math than the others in the class. It's raining, so we'll have to play ball some other day. I can't find my other glove. [pronoun or adjective]* • **others.**

Ottawa (OT uh wuh) *Ottawa is the capital of Canada. [noun]*

otter (OT er) An *otter* is an animal with thick brown fur and strong claws. *Otters* are good swimmers. *[noun]* • **otters.**

ounce (OWNSS)
1. An *ounce* is a unit of weight. Sixteen *ounces* equal one pound. *[noun]*
2. An *ounce* is also an amount of liquid. Sixteen *ounces* equal one pint. *[noun]*
• **ounces.**

our (AR *or* OWR) *Our team won and his team lost. [adjective]*

ours (ARZ *or* OWRZ) *This house is ours. Ours is a very large house. [pronoun]*

ourselves (ar SELVZ *or* owr SELVZ) *We helped ourselves to more cake. [plural pronoun]*

out (OWT) *The kids ran out of the yard. I called you last night, but you were out. The lights went out. [adverb]*

otter

outdoor • oven

outdoor (OWT dor) If something is *outdoor*, it is done or used outside of a house or building: *They went swimming at an outdoor pool.* [adjective]

outdoors

outdoors (owt DORZ) *Outdoors* is out of or outside a building: *Kids at our school had recess outdoors today.* [adverb]

outer (OW ter) The *outer* part of something is always on the outside. The *outer* part of a banana is the peel. [adjective]

outer space (OW ter SPAYSS) *Outer space* is the space beyond the Earth: *The moon is in outer space.*

outfit (OWT fit) An *outfit* is a set of clothes that match or go well together: *That jacket and dress make a great outfit.* [noun] •**outfits.**

outgrow (owt GROH) If you *outgrow* something, you grow too large for it: *I have outgrown my shoes twice this year.* [verb] •**outgrows, outgrew, outgrown, outgrowing.**

outside (OWT SYD) *The outside of the house needs painting. Please go outside and get the paper.* [noun or *adverb*]

oval (OH vuhl) Something that is *oval* is shaped like an egg: *Would you say a football has an oval shape?* [adjective]

oven (UHV uhn) Your *oven* is the part of your stove that you use to bake things in: *He put the turkey in the oven.* [noun] •**ovens.**

outfit

over (OH ver) *I wore a sweater over my shirt. They came over to our house after school. I have over three dollars in my bank.* [*preposition* or *adverb*]

overnight (oh vuhr NYT) Something that happens *overnight* happens during the night: *She likes to stay overnight with friends.* [*adverb*]

owe (OH) If you *owe*, you have to pay or give something to someone: *My neighbor owes me a dollar for washing her car.* [*verb*] •**owes, owed, owing.**

owl (OWL) An *owl* is a bird with a big head, big eyes, and a short, curved bill. *Owls* fly around at night. [*noun*] •**owls.**

own (OHN)

1. When you *own* something, you have or keep it because you bought it, or because someone gave it to you: *I own a bicycle and a pair of skates.* [*verb*]

2. Something that is your *own* belongs to you: *I make my own bed every morning. Eat your own candy!* [*adjective*]
•**owns, owned, owning.**

owner (OH ner) The *owner* of something is the person who owns it: *Who is the owner of this dog?* [*noun*] •**owners.**

Who's the owner of this lunch box?

I am.

owner

pachycephalosaurus · paddle

Pp

pack

pachycephalosaurus   (pak ee SEF uh loh sor uhss) The *pachycephalosaurus* was a big dinosaur with a very thick head. *[noun]* • **pachycephalosauruses.**

pack   (PAK) When you *pack,* you put things into something else so that you can carry or store them: *You can pack clothes in a suitcase. [verb]* • **packs, packed, packing.**

package   (PAK ij) A *package* is a bundle of things packed or wrapped together. A *package* is often a box of things that are mailed. *[noun]* • **packages.**

pad   (PAD) A *pad* is a flat block of writing paper: *Please hand me that pad and a pencil. [noun]* • **pads.**

paddle   (PAD uhl)

I. A *paddle* is a short piece of wood used to move a canoe. A *paddle* is also a piece of wood or plastic used to play some games. *[noun]*

2. When you *paddle* a canoe, you make it move by pulling a paddle through the water: *We watched them paddle up the river.* [verb]
•**paddles.** •**paddles, paddled, paddling.**

page (PAYJ) A *page* is one side of a sheet of paper: *Open your books to page 20.* [noun] •**pages.**

paid (PAYD) *I paid a dollar for a pair of socks. Dad is happy now that all the bills are paid.* [verb]

pail (PAYL) A *pail* is something to carry things in. You can carry water or sand in a *pail.* Another word for *pail* is *bucket.* [noun] •**pails.**

pain (PAYN) *Pain* is a feeling that hurts: *After eating too fast, she has a pain in her stomach.* [noun]
•**pains.**

paint (PAYNT)
1. *Paint* is a thin liquid that you spread on a surface to color and protect it. *Paint* comes in many colors. [noun]
2. When you *paint* something, you cover it with paint: *We painted the garage.* [verb]
•**paints.** •**paints, painted, painting.**

paintbrush (PAYNT bruhsh) A *paintbrush* is a brush you use to paint with. [noun] •**paintbrushes.**

painter (PAYN ter)
1. A *painter* is a person who paints pictures. A *painter* is usually an artist. [noun]
2. A *painter* is also a person who paints rooms, houses, or other buildings. [noun]
•**painters.**

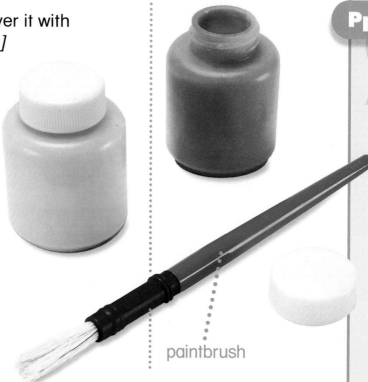

paint

paintbrush

Pp

painting · pancake

painting (PAYN ting) A *painting* is a picture made with paint. *[noun]* •**paintings.**

pair (PAIR)

pairs

1. A *pair* is a set of two things. A *pair* is two things that go together: *I can't find my brown pair of shoes.* *[noun]*
2. A *pair* is also one thing with two parts that work together: *Please hand me a pair of scissors.* *[noun]*

•**pairs.**

pajamas (puh JAH muhz *or* puh JAM uhz) *Pajamas* are clothes to sleep in. *Pajamas* have a shirt and loose pants. *[noun plural]*

palace (PAL iss) A *palace* is a very large house like a castle. Kings and queens live in *palaces.* *[noun]* •**palaces.**

palm[1] (PAHM) Your *palm* is the inside of your hand between your wrist and your fingers. *[noun]* •**palms.**

palm[2] (PAHM) A *palm* is a tree that grows in warm places. There are many kinds of *palm* trees. Most *palm* trees have tall trunks without branches. *[noun]* •**palms.**

pan (PAN) A *pan* is something you cook food in. Many *pans* are made of metal, and some have handles. *[noun]* •**pans.**

pancake (PAN kayk) A *pancake* is a thin, flat cake made of batter. *Pancakes* are fried in a pan and eaten at breakfast. *[noun]* •**pancakes.**

pancakes

Pp

panda (PAN duh) A *panda* is a large black and white animal that looks like a bear. There are very few *pandas* alive today. [noun] • **pandas.**

panda

panpipe or **panpipes** (PAN pyp) The *panpipe* is a musical instrument. You play the *panpipe* by blowing across the top. [noun]

pants (PANTS) *Pants* are clothing worn to cover the legs from the waist to the ankles. Some *pants* are short, covering only part of the legs. [noun plural]

papa (PAH puh) *Papa* is another word for *father*. [noun] • **papas.**

paper (PAY per)
1. *Paper* is what you use to write, print, or draw on. *Paper* is also used for wrapping packages and covering walls. Many bags are made of *paper*. *Paper* is made from wood. [noun]
2. A *paper* is a piece of paper with writing or printing on it: *Our teacher collected the papers we had written.* [noun]
3. *Paper* is a short word meaning *newspaper*. [noun] • **papers** *for definitions 2 and 3.*

parachute (PA ruh shoot) A *parachute* is a huge piece of cloth like a big umbrella. A *parachute* brings a person or thing down through the air in a safe way. [noun] • **parachutes.**

parachutes

parade (puh RAYD) A *parade* is a group of people marching together in rows down a street. *Parades* often have bands playing music and cars or trucks covered with paper or flowers. [noun] • **parades.**

Pp

paragraph • part

parakeet

paragraph (PA ruh graf) A *paragraph* is a group of sentences that are about one main idea. A *paragraph* begins on a new line and has a space before the first word. *[noun]* •**paragraphs.**

parakeet (PA ruh keet) A *parakeet* is a bird with bright feathers and a long tail. A *parakeet* is a kind of small parrot. *Parakeets* are often kept as pets. *[noun]* •**parakeets.**

parent (PAIR uhnt) Your *parent* is your father or mother: *All parents were invited to the class program.* *[noun]* •**parents.**

park (PARK)

1. A *park* is an area of land with grass and trees. People use many *parks* for walking and playing. Some *parks* are kept as living spaces for wild plants and animals. *[noun]*

2. When you *park* a car, truck, or bike, you leave it in one place for a time: *Dad will park the car at the curb.* *[verb]*
•**parks.** •**parks, parked, parking.**

parrot (PA ruht) A *parrot* is a bird with bright feathers and a curved bill. Some *parrots* can repeat words. *[noun]* •**parrots.**

parrots

part (PART)

1. A *part* is something less than the whole thing. A *part* is not all of something: *He ate only part of his dinner.* *[noun]*

2. A *part* is also something that helps make up a whole thing. A pedal is *part* of a bicycle. A TV has many *parts.* One of them is the screen. *[noun]*
•**parts.**

Pp

party (PART ee) A *party* is a group of people having a good time together: *The birthday party starts at noon.* [noun] •**parties.**

pass (PASS)

1. When you *pass* something, you go by it or move past it: *The truck passed two cars. Days pass quickly.* [verb]

2. When you *pass* something to someone, you hand it to them: *Please pass the carrots.* [verb]

3. When you *pass* a test, you know the right answers to the questions: *He knows he will pass his reading test.* [verb]

•**passes, passed, passing.**

pass

past (PAST)

1. The *past* is the time that has gone by: *I grew an inch in the past year. He's glad winter is past.* [adjective]

2. Other words for *past* are *by* and *beyond*: *A ball flew past my head. We rode our bikes past the park.* [adverb]

pasta (PAH stuh) *Pasta* is made of flour, water, and sometimes milk or eggs. Dry *pasta* comes in many different shapes. Macaroni and noodles are kinds of *pasta*. [noun]

paste (PAYST)

1. *Paste* is a mixture you use to stick things together: *I used paste to put the cards on the boxes.* [noun]

paste

Pp

283

patch · paw

patch

2. When you *paste* things, you stick them together with paste: *Can you paste this circle to the picture?* [verb]
• **pastes, pasted, pasting.**

patch (PACH)

1. A *patch* is a piece put on something to fix a hole or tear in it. [noun]

2. A *patch* is also a piece of ground to grow plants in: *He sat in the pumpkin patch.* [noun]

3. If you *patch* something, you fix it with a patch: *I had to patch my bicycle tire.* [verb]
• **patches.** • **patches, patched, patching.**

path (PATH) A *path* is a place to walk, made when people or animals travel over the same ground often: *We walked along a path through the woods.* [noun]
• **paths.**

patient (PAY shuhnt)

1. When you are *patient,* you are able to wait in a quiet way for something that you want: *We must be patient while we are standing in line.* [adjective]

2. A *patient* is a person who is being treated by a doctor: *The doctor had to see two more patients before going home.* [noun]
• **patients.**

paws

paw (PAW) A *paw* is one of the four feet of an animal that has claws. Dogs and cats have *paws.* [noun]
• **paws.**

Pp

pay (PAY) When you *pay,* you give money to someone for things or for work that has been done: *I can pay for the popcorn. Grandma will pay me to rake her lawn.* [verb] •**pays, paid, paying.**

pea (PEE) A *pea* is a round, green seed that people eat as a vegetable. *Peas* are small, and they grow in pods on a vine. [noun] •**peas.**

peas

peace (PEESS) When things are at *peace,* they are quiet or calm. *Peace* is a time of no wars: *Instead of arguing, let's have some peace in this house. Those two countries have lived in peace for many years.* [noun]

peach (PEECH) A *peach* is a round fruit that grows on a tree. *Peaches* have yellow and red skin. A *peach* has a lot of juice and a big seed inside. [noun] •**peaches.**

peanut (PEE nuht) A *peanut* is a seed that looks like a nut. *Peanuts* grow in shells underground and are good to eat. [noun] •**peanuts.**

peanut butter (PEE nuht BUHT er) *Peanut butter* is a food made of peanuts. *Peanut butter* is spread on bread or crackers.

pear (PAIR) A *pear* is a sweet fruit that is round at one end. *Pears* are green or yellow and grow on trees. [noun] •**pears.**

pebble (PEB uhl) A *pebble* is a small round stone. [noun] •**pebbles.**

pedal (PED uhl)
1. A *pedal* is a part of a bicycle or machine moved by your feet: *Pushing down on the pedals makes a bicycle go.* [noun]

peanut butter

Pp

2. When you *pedal,* you move something by pushing its pedals: *I can pedal my bike up the hill.* [verb]
•**pedals.** •**pedals, pedaled, pedaling.**

peel (PEEL)

1. The *peel* is the skin or the outside covering of a piece of fruit: *She never eats orange peels!* [noun]

2. When you *peel* something, you take the skin or covering off it: *He peeled the banana before he ate it.* [verb]
•**peels.** •**peels, peeled, peeling.**

peel

pelican (PEL uh kuhn) A *pelican* is a large sea bird with a pouch under its huge bill. A *pelican* picks up fish out of the water and puts them into its pouch for food. [noun] •**pelicans.**

pen[1] (PEN) A *pen* is a tool you use when you write or draw with ink. [noun] •**pens.**

pen[2] (PEN) A *pen* is a small, closed place to keep animals: *We saw pigs in a pen at the farm.* [noun] •**pens.**

penalty (PEN uhl tee) A *penalty* is something that you have to do or that happens to you when you do something you shouldn't: *The penalty for talking in class is having to clean erasers.* [noun] •**penalties.**

pencil (PEN suhl) A *pencil* is a pointed tool for writing or drawing. The part of a *pencil* you write with is called the *lead.* [noun] •**pencils.**

penguin (PEN gwin) A *penguin* is a sea bird that dives and swims but does not fly. *Penguins* live in very cold places and walk on land or ice. [noun] •**penguins.**

penguin

Pennsylvania
(pen suhl VAY nyuh) *Pennsylvania* is one of the fifty states of the United States. [*noun*]

Pennsylvania

penny (PEN ee) A *penny* is the smallest amount of money in the United States and Canada. One hundred *pennies* make one dollar. Another word for *penny* is *cent.* [*noun*] • **pennies.**

people (PEE puhl) *People* are men, women, and children: *There were only three people at the meeting.* [*noun plural*]

pepper (PEP er)
1. *Pepper* is a powder with a hot taste, used to add flavor to food. *Pepper* is a spice. [*noun*]
2. A *pepper* is also a hollow red, green, or yellow vegetable. [*noun*]

• **peppers** *for definition 2.*

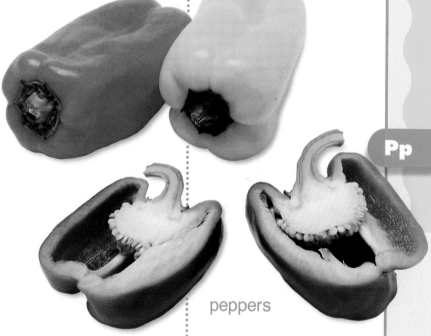

peppers

perfect (PER fikt) If something is *perfect,* there are no mistakes. Something that is *perfect* is not at all spoiled: *I had a perfect spelling paper.* [*adjective*]

perhaps (per HAPSS) *Perhaps* means something is able to happen but is not sure to happen: *Perhaps a card will come in the mail today. My aunt said that perhaps she could visit during the holidays.* [*adverb*]

period (PIR ee uhd)
1. A *period* is a length of time: *Mom asked how long my reading period in school lasts.* [*noun*]

Pp

287

2. A *period* is also a mark (.) of punctuation. A *period* is used to mark the end of a sentence or an abbreviation. *[noun]*
•**periods.**

person (PER suhn) A *person* is a girl, boy, man, or woman. A *person* is a human being. *[noun]*
•**people** *or* **persons.**

pet (PET)

1. A *pet* is a favorite animal that you take care of and treat with love: *My pet is a hamster.* *[noun]*

2. To *pet* something is to touch it gently: *When I pet the kitten, he purrs.* *[verb]*
•**pets.** •**pets, petted, petting.**

petal (PET uhl) A *petal* is one of the parts of a flower. Many *petals* have bright colors. *[noun]* •**petals.**

petal

petition (puh TISH uhn) A *petition* is a letter that many people sign to ask for something to be changed. A *petition* might ask someone in charge to make a new rule or to protect someone in some way. *[noun]* •**petitions.**

petunia (puh TOO nyuh) A *petunia* is a garden plant that has white, pink, and purple flowers. *[noun]* •**petunias.**

phone (FOHN) *Phone* is a short word meaning *telephone.* *[noun]* •**phones.**

photo (FOH toh) *Photo* is a short word meaning *photograph.* *[noun]* •**photos.**

photo album (FOH toh AL buhm) A *photo album* is a book to put photographs in. •**photo albums.**

Pp

photo album

photograph (FOH tuh graf) A *photograph* is a picture you make with a camera. *[noun]* •**photographs.**

photographer (fuh TOG ruh fer) A *photographer* is a person who takes photographs. *[noun]* •**photographers.**

piano (pee AN oh) A *piano* is a large musical instrument that you play with your fingers. *[noun]* •**pianos.**

pick (PIK)

1. When you *pick* something, you take the one you want from a group. When you *pick* something, you choose it: *I picked the red bicycle. He always picks her to be on his team. [verb]*

2. When you *pick* something, you pull it or take it away with your fingers: *We picked flowers from the garden. We picked up a lot of trash from the side yard. [verb]*
•**picks, picked, picking.**

pick

pickle (PIK uhl) A *pickle* is a cucumber or any vegetable kept in salt water or spicy liquid to keep it from spoiling. *Pickles* have a spicy taste. *[noun]* •**pickles.**

picnic (PIK nik) A *picnic* is a party with a meal outdoors: *Our class had a picnic at the park. [noun]* •**picnics.**

picture (PIK cher)

1. A *picture* is a drawing, photograph, or painting of someone or something: *We all drew pictures of our school. Dad took a picture of me and my sisters. [noun]*

picnic

pie · pillow

pie

Pp

2. When you *picture* something, you think of it or imagine it: *Picture yourself on a rocket ship!* [verb] •**pictures.** •**pictures, pictured, picturing.**

pie (PY) A *pie* is a kind of food made of fruit, meat, or some vegetables baked in a crust. There are apple *pies,* chicken *pies,* and pumpkin *pies.* [noun] •**pies.**

piece (PEESS) A *piece* is one of the parts into which something is divided or broken: *I lost one piece of the puzzle and couldn't finish it.* [noun] •**pieces.**

pig (PIG) A *pig* is an animal with a fat body, short legs, and a curly tail. Ham and pork are kinds of meat that come from *pigs.* [noun] •**pigs.**

pigeon (PIJ uhn) A *pigeon* is a bird with a round body and short legs. *Pigeons* often live in cities. [noun] •**pigeons.**

pile (PYL)

1. A *pile* is a lot of things lying on top of each other: *There was a pile of logs near the house.* [noun]

2. When you *pile* things, you make them into a pile: *Let's pile all the blankets here.* [verb] •**piles.** •**piles, piled, piling.**

pile

pill (PIL) A *pill* is medicine that is made into a tiny ball that you can swallow easily. [noun] •**pills.**

pillow (PIL oh) A *pillow* is a soft bag to put your head on when you rest or sleep. *Pillows* are usually filled with feathers or other soft things. [noun] •**pillows.**

pilot (PY luht)

1. A *pilot* is a person who flies an airplane or helicopter, or who steers a ship: *The pilot spoke to us before the plane took off.* [noun]
2. When you *pilot* something, you fly or steer it: *She will pilot the plane to the airport.* [verb]
• **pilots.** • **pilots, piloted, piloting.**

pilot

pin (PIN)

1. A *pin* is a short, thin piece of wire. A *pin* has one sharp end to stick through things and keep them together. [noun]
2. A *pin* is also a piece of wood shaped like a bottle. People try to knock over *pins* when they are bowling. [noun]
3. When you *pin* things, you keep them together with a pin: *Please pin this flower to my coat.* [verb]
• **pins.** • **pins, pinned, pinning.**

pine (PYN)
A *pine* is a tree with leaves shaped like needles. *Pine* trees have cones. [noun] • **pines.**

pineapple (PY nap uhl)
A *pineapple* is a large fruit that looks like a big pine cone. *Pineapples* grow in warm countries. [noun] • **pineapples.**

pineapple

Ping-Pong (PING pawng)
Ping-Pong is the name of a game played on a large table with small wooden paddles and a light plastic ball. [noun]

pink (PINGK)

1. *Pink* is a color that is made by mixing red and white. [noun]
2. Something that is *pink* has this color: *The clouds at sunset were pink.* [adjective]
• **pinks.** • **pinker, pinkest.**

Pp

pint · pizza

pint (PYNT) A *pint* is an amount of liquid. Two cups are equal to one *pint*. Two *pints* are equal to one quart. [*noun*] •**pints.**

pipe (PYP) A *pipe* is a tube through which liquid or gas flows. *Pipes* are made of metal or plastic. [*noun*] •**pipes.**

pirate (PY ruht) Long ago, a *pirate* was a person who robbed ships at sea. [*noun*] •**pirates.**

pitch (PICH)

1. To *pitch* means to throw something: *She pitched the ball to the catcher.* [*verb*]
2. A *pitch* is a throw: *The game started as she threw the first pitch.* [*noun*]

•**pitches, pitched, pitching.** •**pitches.**

pitch

pitcher¹ (PICH er) A *pitcher* is something that holds liquids. A *pitcher* has a handle on one side and a place for pouring on the other side. [*noun*] •**pitchers.**

pitcher² (PICH er) A *pitcher* is a player on a baseball team who throws the ball to the catcher. [*noun*] •**pitchers.**

pizza (PEE tsuh) A *pizza* is a kind of food made of flat crust covered with tomatoes, cheese, spices, and other things such as meat or vegetables. A *pizza* is baked in an oven. Most *pizzas* are round. [*noun*] •**pizzas.**

pizza

Pp

place (PLAYSS)

1. A *place* is the space where a person or thing is: *Our neighborhood is a nice place to live. Do not leave your place in line.* [noun]
2. A *place* is also a city, town, island, building, or other space: *The auditorium is a big place. We went to a place called Johnstown.* [noun]
   •**places.**

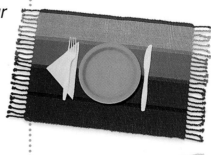

place mat (PLAYSS mat) A *place mat* is a piece of cloth or plastic you put under your plate to protect the table. •**place mats.**

plain (PLAYN) If something is *plain,* it is simple and does not have a lot of extra things. Something that is *plain* is also clear or easy to understand: *She wanted a plain shirt without a ribbon. The meaning of this sentence is plain.* [adjective] •**plainer, plainest.**

place mats

plan (PLAN)

1. A *plan* is something you have thought out and will do: *Does anyone have a plan for earning money?* [noun]
2. When you *plan,* you think out how something should be done: *We are planning a party.* [verb]
   •**plans.** •**plans, planned, planning.**

plane (PLAYN) *Plane* is a short word meaning *airplane.* [noun] •**planes.**

planets

planet (PLAN it)
A *planet* is one of the nine large objects that move around the sun. The Earth is a *planet.* [noun]
•**planets.**

plant · player

plants

plant (PLANT)

1. A *plant* is any living thing that can make its own food from sunlight, air, and water. *Plants* cannot move about. Trees, bushes, vines, grass, flowers, and vegetables are all *plants. [noun]*

2. When you *plant* something, you put it in the ground to grow: *Plant these seeds in the spring. [verb]*

•**plants.** •**plants, planted, planting.**

plastic (PLASS tik)
Plastic is a kind of material that can be shaped when it is hot. *Plastic* becomes hard when it is cool. *Plastic* can be very strong. Many dishes, toys, and combs are made of *plastic. [noun]*

•**plastics.**

plate (PLAYT)
A *plate* is a dish that is almost flat and is usually round. We eat food from *plates. [noun]*

•**plates.**

play (PLAY)

1. To *play* is to have fun. When you *play,* you take part in a game or sport: *Let's play ball. My sister plays with dolls. [verb]*

2. A *play* is a story acted out on a stage: *We saw a play about a king and queen. [noun]*

play

3. To *play* also means to make believe: *Let's play that this room is a store. [verb]*

4. To *play* is also to make sounds with a musical instrument: *Can you play the piano? [verb]*

•**plays, played, playing.** •**plays.**

player (PLAY er)
A *player* is a person who plays or a machine that plays: *The football player kicked the ball. The teacher turned on the CD player. [noun]*

•**players.**

playground (PLAY grownd) A *playground* is a place to play outdoors: *We enjoy going to the playground on Saturdays.* [noun] •**playgrounds.**

playhouse (PLAY howss) A *playhouse* is a small house a child can play in. [noun] •**playhouses.**

please (PLEEZ)

1. *Please* is a polite word you use when you ask someone for something: *Please sit down. Please may I go with you? Mom taught us to say please and thank you.* [adverb]

2. When you *please* people, you do something for them that they like: *Reading stories to children pleases them.* [verb]

•**pleases, pleased, pleasing.**

playhouse

pleasure (PLEZH er) A *pleasure* is something that you are happy to do: *Meeting your sister would be a pleasure.* [noun] •**pleasures.**

plow (PLOW)

1. A *plow* is a farm machine that cuts soil and turns it over before planting seeds. [noun]

2. When you *plow,* you turn up soil: *Grandpa plows his farm fields every year.* [verb]

3. To *plow* also means to move snow: *They plowed the street to clear a path through the snow.* [verb]

•**plows.** •**plows, plowed, plowing.**

plows

Pp

295

plug · plus

plug (PLUHG)
1. A *plug* is a thing at the end of a wire to connect it to an electric socket: *Don't use a lamp if it has a plug that is worn or bent. [noun]*
2. When you *plug* something in, you put a plug into an opening: *Please plug in the lamp. [verb]*
• **plugs.** • **plugs, plugged, plugging.**

plum (PLUHM) A *plum* is a round fruit with smooth skin. Red, green, purple, and yellow *plums* grow on trees. *Plums* are larger than grapes but smaller than peaches. *[noun]* • **plums.**

plumber

plumbing

plumber (PLUHM er) A *plumber* is a person whose work is putting in and repairing water pipes, sinks, and tubs. *[noun]* • **plumbers.**

plumbing (PLUHM ing) *Plumbing* is the pipes, sinks, and bathtubs in a building: *We need new bathroom plumbing. [noun]*

plump (PLUHMP) If something is *plump,* it is fat and round in a nice way: *The baby was plump, happy, and healthy. We saw several plump pigeons in the park. [adjective]*
• **plumper, plumpest.**

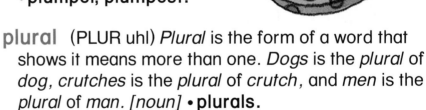
plump

plural (PLUR uhl) *Plural* is the form of a word that shows it means more than one. *Dogs* is the *plural* of *dog, crutches* is the *plural* of *crutch,* and *men* is the *plural* of *man. [noun]* • **plurals.**

plus (PLUHSS)
1. *Plus* means added to: *7 plus 2 equals 9. [preposition]*

2. *Plus* also means in addition to. Another word for *plus* is *with: This toy plus that one costs five dollars.* [preposition]

pocket (POK it) A *pocket* is a small piece of cloth sewed onto clothing for carrying things. Money and other small things are kept in *pockets.* [noun] •**pockets.**

pocket

pod (POD) A *pod* is a long, narrow part of a plant in which some seeds grow. Peas and beans grow in *pods.* [noun] •**pods.**

poem (POH uhm) A *poem* is like a song without music. *Poems* often use special words that rhyme. *Poems* show us new ways of putting words together to tell about feelings and thoughts. [noun] •**poems.**

poet (POH uht) A *poet* is a person who writes poems. [noun] •**poets.**

poetry (POH uh tree) *Poetry* is poems: *We enjoy hearing our teacher read poetry.* [noun]

point (POINT)

1. A *point* is a sharp end. Needles and pins have *points.* [noun]

2. A *point* is also a place or spot: *That mountain is the highest point in the state.* [noun]

3. When you *point,* you show the position or direction of something with your finger: *She pointed to the north.* [verb]

4. A *point* is also a unit for keeping score in a game: *The first player with ten points wins.* [noun]

•**points.** •**points, pointed, pointing.**

point

I am pointing up.

Pp

poke · polite

poke (POHK) When you *poke* something, you push against it with something sharp: *He poked me in the side with his elbow.* [verb] •**pokes, poked, poking.**

polar bear (POH ler BAIR) A *polar bear* is a large, white bear that lives in Alaska, Canada, and other cold places. •**polar bears.**

polar bears

pole (POHL) A *pole* is a long, round piece of wood or metal: *We used a fishing pole to catch fish. The flag in front of our school flies on a pole.* [noun] •**poles.**

police (puh LEESS) The *police* are a group of people who protect us and our things and make sure that laws are obeyed. The *police* also catch people who break the law. [noun plural]

police

policeman (puh LEESS muhn) A *policeman* is someone who is part of the police. A *policeman* is a police officer. [noun] •**policemen.**

police officer (puh LEESS OF uh ser) A *police officer* is someone who is part of the police. •**police officers.**

policewoman (puh LEESS wum uhn) A *policewoman* is someone who is part of the police. A *policewoman* is a police officer. [noun] •**policewomen.**

polite (puh LYT) *Polite* means behaving in a nice, friendly way. If you are *polite,* you have good manners: *A polite classmate helped me pick up my books when I dropped them in the hall.* [adjective] •**politer, politest.**

Pp

pollution (puh LOO shuhn) *Pollution* is dirty things in our air, water, or land. *Pollution* can hurt people, animals, and plants. *[noun]*

pollution

pond (POND) A *pond* is water with land all around it. A *pond* is smaller than a lake and does not have waves. *[noun]* •**ponds.**

pony (POH nee) A *pony* is a small horse. *[noun]* •**ponies.**

pool (POOL) A *pool* is a place that holds water to swim in. A *pool* can be large or small, indoors or outdoors. *[noun]* •**pools.**

poor (POR) *Poor* means having very little money: *The family was so poor that they did not have enough food.* *[adjective]* •**poorer, poorest.**

popcorn (POP korn) *Popcorn* is a kind of corn that bursts open with a lot of noise and puffs out when you heat it. *Popcorn* is often eaten with butter and salt on it. *[noun]*

porcupine

porcupine (POR kyuh pyn) A *porcupine* is a small animal that is covered with stiff, sharp hairs. *[noun]* •**porcupines.**

pork (PORK) *Pork* is the meat of a pig used for food. *[noun]*

position (puh ZISH uhn) A *position* is the place where a thing or person is: *Grandpa sat in his usual position near the fire.* *[noun]* •**positions.**

Pp

possible · potato

possible (POSS uh buhl)
1. When something is *possible,* it is able to be done: *Is it possible to get home before dark?* [adjective]
2. *Possible* also means not true for sure but perhaps true: *It is possible that he already returned the books to the library.* [adjective]

possum (POSS uhm) A *possum* is a small animal that often carries its young on its back. When it is caught, it pretends to be dead. The full name of this animal is *opossum.* [noun] • **possums.**

postcard (POHST kard) A *postcard* is a card for sending a message by mail. *Postcards* often have a picture on one side. [noun] • **postcards.**

postcards

poster (POH ster) A *poster* is a large printed piece of paper put up on a wall. [noun] • **posters.**

post office (POHST of iss) A *post office* is a place where workers take in and send out mail and sell stamps. • **post offices.**

pot (POT)
1. A *pot* is a round, deep pan used for cooking. *Pots* come in different sizes. [noun]
2. A *pot* is also a round container for a plant, usually made of plastic or clay: *The flower pot was full of daisies.* [noun]
• **pots.**

potato (puh TAY toh) A *potato* is a vegetable with a thin brown or red skin and a white inside. *Potatoes* grow underground. [noun] • **potatoes.**

potatoes

pouch (POWCH)

1. A *pouch* is a bag: *The mail carrier put the letters in her pouch.* [noun]

2. A *pouch* is also the part on the stomach of some animals that is like a bag or pocket. Kangaroos and opossums have *pouches* for carrying their young. [noun]

• **pouches.**

poultry (POHL tree) Birds that people raise for their meat or eggs are *poultry*. Chickens, turkeys, geese, and ducks are *poultry*. [noun]

pound (POWND) A *pound* is a unit of weight. A *pound* is equal to sixteen ounces. [noun] • **pounds.**

pour (POR)

1. When you *pour* something, you make it come out in a stream: *I poured milk on my cereal.* [verb]

2. When it *pours*, it rains a lot: *It poured all afternoon.* [verb]

• **pours, poured, pouring.**

pour

powder (POW der) *Powder* is very tiny bits of things ground up as fine as dust. Flour is a *powder* made from grain. [noun] • **powders.**

power (POW er) *Power* is energy that can do work: *Running water can produce electric power.* [noun]

practice (PRAK tiss) When you *practice*, you do something again and again to learn to do it well: *She practiced pitching the ball. I practice on the piano every day.* [verb] • **practices, practiced, practicing.**

Pp

prepare • pretend

prepare (pri PAIR) When you *prepare* something, you get it ready. When you *prepare,* you get yourself ready for doing something: *We all helped prepare a picnic lunch. When recess comes, we all prepare to go outside.* [verb] •**prepares, prepared, preparing.**

present¹ (PREZ uhnt) Another word for *present* is *here.* If you are *present,* you are not absent: *Every member of the class is present today.* [adjective]

present² (PREZ uhnt) A *present* is a gift. A *present* is something that someone gives you or that you give someone: *His uncle sent him a birthday present.* [noun] •**presents.**

presents²

president (PREZ uh duhnt) The *president* is the leader of a country, business, or other group. Not all countries have *presidents.* [noun] •**presidents.**

press (PRESS)

1. When you *press* something, you push it in a steady way: *Press this button to get the elevator to come.* [verb]
2. When you *press* clothes, you make them smooth with a hot iron: *I pressed my shirt to get out the wrinkles.* [verb]

•**presses, pressed, pressing.**

press

pretend (pri TEND) To *pretend* is to make believe that something is real when it is not: *Let's pretend we're camping.* [verb] •**pretends, pretended, pretending.**

pretty (PRIT ee) Something that is *pretty* is good to see or hear. Another word for *pretty* is *nice*: *She wore a pretty dress. That is a pretty song.* [adjective] •**prettier, prettiest.**

pretzel (PRET suhl) A *pretzel* is a kind of bread shaped like a knot or stick. *Pretzels* are often covered with salt. [noun] •**pretzels.**

pretzels

price (PRYSS) The *price* of something is the amount you must pay to buy it: *The price of this sweater is $10.* [noun] •**prices.**

prince (PRINSS) A *prince* is a son of a king or queen: *I read a good story about a prince.* [noun] •**princes.**

Prince Edward Island (prinss ED werd EYE luhnd) *Prince Edward Island* is one of the ten provinces of Canada. [noun]

princess (PRIN suhss *or* PRIN sess) A *princess* is a daughter of a king or queen: *I wrote a story about a princess in a castle.* [noun] •**princesses.**

principal (PRIN suh puhl) A *principal* is a person who is the head of a school. [noun] •**principals.**

principal

This is my principal.

print (PRINT)

1. When you *print,* you write words with letters that do not touch each other: *Please print your name on your paper.* [verb]

2. To *print* also means to use a machine to make copies of words and pictures on paper. This book is *printed* using different colors of ink. [verb]

•**prints, printed, printing.**

Pp

printer · product

printer (PRIN ter) A *printer* is a machine that prints. A *printer* is run by a computer. *[noun]* •**printers.**

private (PRY vuht) When something is *private,* it is not for everyone. Something that is *private* belongs to just one person or a few special people: *Only the people living on it and their visitors may use a private road. The letters a person gets are private, and others should not read them.* *[adjective]*

prize (PRYZ) A *prize* is something you win for doing something well. A *prize* is a reward: *The judges liked her story best and gave her the prize.* *[noun]* •**prizes.**

prizes

probably (PROB uh blee) *You probably know my brother. We should probably wait for them.* *[adverb]*

problem (PROB luhm) A *problem* is something you have to work out. A *problem* is a difficult question: *How did you solve that math problem? Making friends at a new school can be a problem.* *[noun]* •**problems.**

prod (PROD) When you *prod* someone, you try to get that person to do something: *My parents keep prodding me to clean my room.* *[verb]* •**prods, prodded, prodding.**

produce (pruh DOOSS)

1. To *produce* is to make or grow: *My cousin's factory produces cheese. Some farmers produce wheat and corn.* *[verb]*
2. To *produce* also means to give: *Cows produce milk. Sheep produce wool.* *[verb]*
•**produces, produced, producing.**

product (PROD uhkt)

1. A *product* is something that someone makes or

produce

Cows produce milk.

grows. Cloth is a factory *product*. Grain and milk are farm *products*. [noun]

2. The *product* is the number that you get when you multiply two or more numbers together: *10 is the product of 2 and 5*. [noun]
 • **products**.

program (PROH gram) A *program* is what you see on television or hear on the radio: *Mom and Dad watch a news program every evening*. [noun]
 • **programs**.

project (PROJ ekt) A *project* is a plan for doing something: *My project was making a poster. Our science project won a prize*. [noun]
 • **projects**.

project

promise (PROM iss)

1. A *promise* is words that you say or write that tell that you will or will not do something: *He kept his promise to walk the dog*. [noun]

2. To *promise* is to say or write that you will or will not do something: *Promise me you will help rake the yard*. [verb]
 • **promises**. • **promises, promised, promising**.

pronoun (PROH nown) A *pronoun* is a word that takes the place of a noun or nouns. The words *she, he, it, they, I, me,* and *you* are *pronouns*. "Mom and Dad stayed home because they were tired." *They* is a *pronoun* that takes the place of the nouns *Mom* and *Dad*. [noun] • **pronouns**.

prop (PROP) A *prop* is something used in a play. *Props* make what is happening on stage seem real. [noun] • **props**.

Pp

propeller • prove

propeller

propeller (pruh PEL er) A *propeller* is the part that turns and makes some boats and aircraft move. Engines make the *propellers* turn. *[noun]* •**propellers.**

proper noun (PROP er NOWN) A *proper noun* is a word that names a special person, place, or thing. "Jason and Carol left for Florida last Sunday." *Jason, Carol, Florida,* and *Sunday* are *proper nouns. Proper nouns* begin with capital letters. •**proper nouns.**

property (PROP er tee)

1. *Property* is something that someone owns: *This bike is my property. [noun]*

2. *Property* is also a piece of land: *My aunt owns property by the lake. [noun]*

3. A *property* is also a special power that something has, or something that it can do. Since wood can float, we say that wood has the *property* of floating. *[noun]*

•**properties** *for definitions 2 and 3.*

protect (pruh TEKT) To *protect* is to keep someone or something safe. An umbrella *protects* you from rain. *[verb]*
•**protects, protected, protecting.**

protect

proud (PROWD) If you are *proud,* you think well of yourself or of people or things that have something to do with you: *They were proud of their children. [adjective]* •**prouder, proudest.**

prove (PROOV) When you *prove* something, you show that it is true: *Can you prove that the dog is really yours? [verb]* •**proves, proved, proving.**

Pp

province (PROV uhnss) A *province* is one of the main parts of a country. Canada is divided into *provinces* instead of states. *[noun]* •**provinces.**

pterodactyl (tair uh DAK tuhl) A *pterodactyl* was a kind of dinosaur that could fly. *Pterodactyls* had wings like bat wings. *[noun]* •**pterodactyls.**

public (PUHB lik) Something that is *public* is for everyone. Something that is *public* belongs to the people: *Anyone can use the public library.* *[adjective]*

puck (PUHK) A *puck* is a hard, black, round piece of rubber that players use in the game of hockey. *[noun]* •**pucks.**

puddle (PUHD uhl) A *puddle* is a small amount of water: *The rain left a puddle in the yard.* *[noun]* •**puddles.**

Puebla (PWE blah) *Puebla* is a state in the southeast part of Mexico. *[noun]*

Puerto Rico (pwair tuh REE koh) *Puerto Rico* is an island off the coast of Florida. It is protected by the United States, but it makes its own laws. *[noun]*

puff (PUHF) *Puff* means to swell up: *Popcorn puffs up when you heat it.* *[verb]* •**puffs, puffed, puffing.**

pull (PUL)
1. When you *pull* something, you move it toward you: *I pulled the closet door open. We pulled the wagon up the hill.* *[verb]*

pterodactyl

puffed

Pp

pump · pupil²

2. When you *pull* something, you take hold of it with your fingers or a tool and tug it out: *I pulled weeds in the garden for an hour.* [verb]
• **pulls, pulled, pulling.**

pump (PUHMP) When you *pump* liquids or gases, you move them: *He pumped gasoline into the car. The heart pumps blood to all parts of the body.* [verb] •**pumps, pumped, pumping.**

pump

pumpkin (PUHMP kin) A *pumpkin* is a large orange fruit that grows on a vine. *Pumpkins* are used to make jack-o'-lanterns and pies. [noun] •**pumpkins.**

punctuation (puhngk choo AY shuhn) *Punctuation* is the use of periods, commas, and other marks in writing. *Punctuation* helps make the meaning of sentences clear. [noun]

punish (PUHN ish) To *punish* is to cause someone who did something wrong to be unhappy: *Pupils who don't behave in class may be punished by the teacher.* [verb] •**punishes, punished, punishing.**

punt (PUHNT) When you *punt,* you kick a ball after you drop it but before it touches the ground. [verb] •**punts, punted, punting.**

pupil¹ (PYOO puhl) A *pupil* is a person who is learning in school or being taught by someone. [noun] •**pupils.**

pupil² (PYOO puhl) The *pupil* is the center of the eye that looks like a black dot. Light enters your eyes through your *pupils.* [noun] •**pupils.**

punt

Pp

puppet (PUHP it) A *puppet* is a toy that looks like a person or an animal. You put one kind of *puppet* over your finger or hand to move it. You move another kind of *puppet* by wires or strings. *[noun]* •**puppets.**

puppet

puppy (PUHP ee) A *puppy* is a young dog or a baby dog. *[noun]* •**puppies.**

pure (PYOOR) *Pure* means not mixed with anything else: *He has a sweater made of pure wool.* *[adjective]* •**purer, purest.**

purple (PER puhl) *Purple* is a dark color that is a mixture of red and blue. *[noun or adjective]* •**purples.**

purpose (PER puhss) A *purpose* is a reason for something that someone wants to do: *Her purpose in calling was to ask us to lunch.* *[noun]* •**purposes.**

purr (PER)
1. A *purr* is a sound that a cat makes when it is pleased: *Their cat has a loud purr.* *[noun]*
2. To *purr* is to make this sound: *The cat rubbed against my leg and purred.* *[verb]*
•**purrs.** •**purrs, purred, purring.**

purse (PERSS) A *purse* is a small bag that women and girls use to carry money and other things they might need. *[noun]* •**purses.**

purses

push (PUSH) When you *push* something, you move it away from you: *She pushed the drawer shut. I pushed the chair out of my way.* *[verb]* •**pushes, pushed, pushing.**

put · python

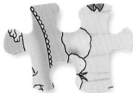

puzzle

put   (PUT)

1. When you *put* something, you set it in a place: *I put the letter in an envelope.* [*verb*]
2. To *put* means to cause something to be a certain way: *Put these words in alphabetical order. Please put the light out when you leave.* [*verb*]
• **puts, put, putting.**

puzzle   (PUHZ uhl)

1. A *puzzle* is a game that you work out for fun: *Help me put the pieces of this puzzle together.* [*noun*]
2. If you *puzzle* someone, you make it hard for someone to understand something: *Why he left so early puzzled us.* [*verb*]
• **puzzles.** • **puzzles, puzzled, puzzling.**

python   (PY thon) A *python* is a very large snake that kills other animals by squeezing them. [*noun*]
• **pythons.**

python

quality · quarrel

quality (KWAL uh tee)

1. Q*uality* is something special about a thing that makes it what it is: *One quality of sugar is its sweet taste. She has many fine qualities.* [noun]

2. *Quality* is also the measure of how good or bad something is: *This food is of poor quality.* [noun]

•**qualities** *for definition I.*

quarrel (KWOR uhl *or* KWAH ruhl)

1. A *quarrel* is a fight with words. A *quarrel* is an angry talk with someone who does not agree with you. Another word for *quarrel* is *argument: The children had a quarrel over how to divide up the candy.* [noun]

2. *Quarrel* means to fight with words. When people *quarrel,* they talk to each other in an angry way: *The two friends quarreled, and now they don't speak to each other.* [verb]

•**quarrels.** •**quarrels, quarreled, quarreling.**

Qq

311

quarry • quick

quarry (KWAR ee) A *quarry* is a place where stone is dug or cut out of the ground. *[noun]* •**quarries.**

quart (KWORT) A *quart* is an amount of liquid. Two pints are equal to one *quart*. Four *quarts* are equal to one gallon. *[noun]* •**quarts.**

quarter (KWOR ter)

1. A *quarter* is one of four equal parts: *Each of the four girls ate a quarter of the apple.* *[noun]*

2. A *quarter* is also a coin worth 25 cents. Four *quarters* make one dollar. *[noun]*

3. A *quarter* is one of four equal periods of play in games such as football, basketball, or soccer. *[noun]*
•**quarters.**

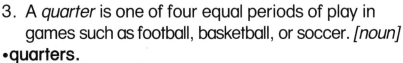

quarter

Quebec (kwi BEK) *Quebec* is one of the ten provinces of Canada. *[noun]*

queen (KWEEN) A *queen* is a woman who rules a country. She can also be a king's wife. *[noun]* •**queens.**

Querétaro (ke RE tah roh) *Querétaro* is a state in central Mexico. *[noun]*

question (KWESS chun) A *question* is a thing asked in order to find out something: *The teacher answered his questions about the story.* *[noun]* •**questions.**

question mark (KWESS chuhn MARK) A *question mark* is a mark (?) of punctuation put after a question.
•**question marks.**

quick (KWIK) *Quick* means taking very little time. Something that is *quick* is done very fast: *The cat made a quick jump onto the table. We made a quick trip to the store.* *[adjective]* •**quicker, quickest.**

question

I have a question.

Qq

quickly (KWIK lee) *Quickly* means in a short time: *When I asked him a question, he answered quickly.* [adverb]

quiet (KWY uht)

1. When something is *quiet,* it makes no sound. Something that is *quiet* is not noisy: *It was a quiet night.* [adjective]
2. *Quiet* also means not moving: *The water hardly moved on the quiet lake.* [adjective]
• **quieter, quietest.**

quilt (KWILT) A *quilt* is a soft covering for a bed. A *quilt* is usually made from two pieces of cloth sewn together with soft material between them. *[noun]* • **quilts.**

Quintana Roo (keen tah nah ROH) *Quintana Roo* is a state in the southeast part of Mexico. [noun]

quit (KWIT)

1. When you *quit,* you stop doing something: *The children quit playing when they saw the rain clouds.* [verb]
2. To *quit* also means to leave something: *He is quitting his job tomorrow and going to a new job on Monday.* [verb]
• **quits, quit, quitting.**

quite (KWYT) *There was quite a change in the weather yesterday. It is quite cold today. It is not quite five o'clock.* [adverb]

quiz (KWIZ)

1. A *quiz* is a short test: *Each week the teacher gives us a quiz in spelling.* [noun]
2. When you *quiz* someone, you find out what that person knows by asking questions: *Each week our teacher quizzes us in spelling.* [verb]
• **quizzes.** • **quizzes, quizzed, quizzing.**

quilt

Qq

rabbit · racecar

Rr

raccoon

rabbit (RAB it) A *rabbit* is a small animal with soft fur and long ears. *Rabbits* have long back legs and can hop very fast. [*noun*] •**rabbits.**

raccoon (ra KOON) A *raccoon* is a small animal with thick fur. Its tail is long and has rings of a different color. *Raccoons* look for food at night. [*noun*] •**raccoons.**

race (RAYSS)

1. A *race* is a contest to see who can do something the fastest: *Who won the bicycle race?* [*noun*]
2. When you *race,* you run or go fast with other people. The fastest person wins: *Race me to the house!* [*verb*]
•**races.** •**races, raced, racing.**

racecar (RAYSS kar) A *racecar* is a car used in races. [*noun*] •**racecars.**

racket (RAK it) A *racket* is something made of metal or wood and a tight net of strings. *Rackets* are used to hit the ball in games like tennis. [noun] •**rackets.**

racket

radio (RAY dee oh) A *radio* is a machine that brings voices and music from far away. A *radio* may be small enough to carry in your pocket. [noun] •**radios.**

radish (RAD ish) A *radish* is a small red or white vegetable with a strong flavor. *Radishes* grow underground. [noun] •**radishes.**

raft (RAFT) A *raft* is something made of wood or rubber that can carry people and things on water. A *raft* is flat and can be moved by a pole or by paddles. [noun] •**rafts.**

rag (RAG) A *rag* is a torn or worn piece of cloth: *I wiped up the spilled paint with an old rag.* [noun] •**rags.**

rail (RAYL) A *rail* is a metal bar. Railroad trains run on steel *rails.* [noun] •**rails.**

railroad (RAYL rohd) A *railroad* is a road or track of two steel rails. Trains run on *railroads.* [noun] •**railroads.**

railroad

rain (RAYN)
1. *Rain* is the water that falls in drops from the clouds: *The rain got us all wet as we walked home from school.* [noun]

Rr

rainbow • rake

2. When it *rains,* water falls in drops from clouds: *Will it rain today?* [verb]
•**rains.** •**rains, rained, raining.**

rainbow (RAYN boh)
A *rainbow* is a curved band of many colors in the sky. A *rainbow* sometimes appears when the sun shines right after it rains. [noun] •**rainbows.**

rainbow

raincoat (RAYN koht) A *raincoat* is a coat that water will not go through: *I wore a raincoat to stay dry.* [noun] •**raincoats.**

rainforest (RAYN for ist) The *rainforest* is a very thick forest in a place where rain is very heavy all year. Many different kinds of plants and animals live in *rainforests.* [noun] •**rainforests.**

rainy (RAY nee) To be *rainy* means to have a lot of rain: *This was a rainy summer.* [adjective] •**rainier, rainiest.**

raise (RAYZ)
1. When you *raise* something, you lift it up: *Raise your hand if you know the answer. We raise the flag every morning at school.* [verb]
2. When you *raise* plants and animals, you look after them so that they will grow: *My uncle raises wheat and horses on his farm.* [verb]
•**raises, raised, raising.**

raisin (RAY zuhn) A *raisin* is a small, sweet fruit. *Raisins* are dried grapes. [noun] •**raisins.**

rake (RAYK)
1. A *rake* is a tool with a long handle and a bar with

Rr

raisins

sharp points at one end: *She took the rake out of the garage. [noun]*

2. When you *rake* something, you make it clean or smooth it with a rake: *Please help me rake the leaves off the lawn. [verb]*
•**rakes.** •**rakes, raked, raking.**

ramp (RAMP) A *ramp* is a slope that connects two places that have different heights. *Ramps* are used instead of stairs: *We walked up the ramp to board the plane. [noun]* •**ramps.**

ran (RAN) *I ran all the way home. [verb]*

ranch (RANCH) A *ranch* is a very large farm and its buildings. Sheep, cattle, or horses are raised on *ranches. [noun]* •**ranches.**

ranch

rang (RANG) *When the telephone rang, I answered it. [verb]*

rare (RAIR) When something is *rare,* it is not often found. Something that is *rare* is very unusual: *Snow is rare in Louisiana. [adjective]* •**rarer, rarest.**

raspberry (RAZ bair ee) A *raspberry* is a small red or black berry. *Raspberries* grow on bushes. *[noun]* •**raspberries.**

rat (RAT) A *rat* is an animal with a long, thin tail. A *rat* looks like a large mouse. *Rats* are gray, brown, black, or white. *[noun]* •**rats.**

rather (RA<u>TH</u> er) *I would rather play soccer than basketball. He was rather annoyed by our noise. [adverb]*

raspberries

rattle · read¹

ray²

Rr

rattle (RAT uhl) If something *rattles,* it makes short, sharp sounds: *The wind rattled the loose windows on the front of the house.* [verb] •**rattles, rattled, rattling.**

raw (RAW) If something is *raw,* it is not cooked: *She will eat raw carrots but not boiled carrots.* [adjective] •**rawer, rawest.**

ray¹ (RAY) A *ray* is a line of light: *A ray of light shone through the clouds.* [noun] •**rays.**

ray² (RAY) A *ray* is a fish with a wide, flat body and very wide fins. *[noun]* •**rays.**

razor (RAY zer) A *razor* is a very sharp tool used to cut hair off your face or another part of your body. *[noun]* •**razors.**

reach (REECH)

1. When you *reach,* you stretch out your arm and hand to touch something. When you *reach* for something, you try to get it: *She reached for the milk carton.* [verb]

2. When you *reach* a place, you get or come to that place: *We will reach the campground after eight o'clock.* [verb]
•**reaches, reached, reaching.**

reach

read¹ (REED)

1. When you *read,* you look at and understand written words: *Have you learned to read?* [verb]

2. To *read* is also to speak out loud words that are written or printed: *Our teacher promised to read a story to us.* [verb] •**reads, read, reading.**

read¹

read² (RED) *He read that book last week. Have you read it yet?* [verb]

reader (REE der) A *reader* is a person who reads: *Everyone in our family is a reader.* [noun] •**readers.**

ready (RED ee) If you are *ready,* you are all set to do something: *Lunch is ready. Are they ready to leave for the movie?* [adjective] •**readier, readiest.**

real (REEL) When something is *real,* it is not make-believe. Something that is *real* is true. Pandas are *real,* but unicorns are not *real: This book is about the real adventures of an Indian girl.* [adjective]

realize (REEL lyz) When you *realize* something, you understand it very well: *Everyone realizes that she did a good job.* [verb] •**realizes, realized, realizing.**

really (REEL ee) *He was really happy to see us. Some adventure stories are fun to read, but they could not really happen.* [adverb]

rear (REER) The *rear* is the side of anything opposite the front side. The *rear* is the back part or back of something: *The rear of the house has not been painted, but the front is done.* [noun]

reason (REE zuhn) A *reason* is whatever explains why something happened or why someone did something:

receive · record

Dad couldn't figure out a reason for the car not starting this morning. He had a good reason for not playing ball yesterday, since his knee was hurting. [noun] •**reasons.**

receive (ri SEEV) When you *receive* something, you take or get something that someone gives you or sends you: *She received several gifts at her party.* [verb] •**receives, received, receiving.**

recess (REE sess *or* ri SESS) A *recess* is a short time when classroom work stops: *We'll finish the game at recess tomorrow.* [noun] •**recesses.**

recess

recipe (RESS uh pee) A *recipe* is written directions that show how to fix something to eat: *We have a good recipe for cupcakes.* [noun] •**recipes.**

recognize (REK uhg nyz) When you *recognize* something, you remember it because you knew it before: *She almost didn't recognize her friend because he had grown a mustache.* [verb] •**recognizes, recognized, recognizing.**

record (ri KOHRD *for verb or* REK erd *for noun*)

1. When you *record* something, you put it into writing or some other form for future use: *Record what the speaker says. We record history in books.* [verb]

2. A *record* is something written down and kept to look at in the future: *I kept a record of what I spent on the trip.* [noun]

3. If you *record* music, words, or pictures, you put them on a special kind of tape or CD to use in the future. *[verb]*

4. A *record* is something that gives off sounds when it is used on a record player. *Records* are round and flat and are made of plastic. *[noun]*

5. The *record* is also the highest score or speed someone has reached: *Who holds the record for running the fastest mile? [noun]*

•**records, recorded, recording.**
•**records.**

record

recorder (ri KOR der) A *recorder* is a wooden or plastic musical instrument that is like a flute. *[noun]*
•**recorders.**

record player (REK urd PLAY er) A *record player* is a machine that gives off sounds when you play records on it. •**record players.**

recover (ri KUHV er) If you *recover,* you get well: *He is recovering from his cold. [verb]* •**recovers, recovered, recovering.**

rectangle

Rr

rectangle (REK tang guhl) A *rectangle* is a shape with four sides. *[noun]* •**rectangles.**

recycle (ree SY kuhl) When you *recycle,* you prepare something like paper or glass so that it can be used again. *[verb]* •**recycles, recycled, recycling.**

red (RED)

1. *Red* is the color of blood. *[noun]*

2. Something that is *red* has a color like blood: *The band wore red uniforms. [adjective]*

•**reds.** •**redder, reddest.**

redwood · reindeer

redwood (RED wud) A *redwood* is a very large tree. *Redwoods* are the tallest trees alive today. *[noun]* •**redwoods.**

reflect (ri FLEKT) To *reflect* is to give back light, heat, or sound. The moon gives off no light of its own but *reflects* light from the sun: *A mirror reflects what is in front of it. [verb]* •**reflects, reflected, reflecting.**

reflect

reflection (ri FLEK shuhn) A *reflection* is what you see in a mirror or in still water: *I looked at my reflection in the mirror. [noun]* •**reflections.**

refrigerator (ri FRIJ er ay ter) A *refrigerator* is an electric appliance that keeps food and other things cold. *[noun]* •**refrigerators.**

refuse (ri FYUZ) If you *refuse,* you say no to someone or something: *I refused to let the stranger in the house. [verb]* •**refuses, refused, refusing.**

regular (REG yuh ler)
1. Another word for *regular* is *usual*: *He bought the regular size box of soap, not the large one. [adjective]*
2. *Regular* also means coming again and again at the same time: *She makes regular visits to the dentist. [adjective]*

reindeer (RAYN deer) A *reindeer* is a deer with large antlers. *Reindeer* live in cold places. People use *reindeer* to pull sleighs. *[noun]* •The plural of *reindeer* is *reindeer.*

reindeer

Rr

relative (REL uh tiv) Your *relative* is a person who belongs to the same family as you do. Your mother, sister, and cousin are all your *relatives.* [noun] •**relatives.**

relax (ri LAKSS) When you *relax,* you do not do work. When you *relax,* you have a good time: *We relax on vacation.* [verb] •**relaxes, relaxed, relaxing.**

release (ri LEESS) When you *release* something, you let it loose or set it free: *She released the rabbit from its cage.* [verb] •**releases, released, releasing.**

remain (ri MAYN)

1. To *remain* is to stay: *The class should remain in the room until three.* [verb]
2. *Remain* also means to be left: *A few leaves remain on the tree. If you take 10 from 20, 10 remains.* [verb]

•**remains, remained, remaining.**

remain

remember (ri MEM ber)

1. When you *remember* something, you call it back to your mind: *I can't remember their address.* [verb]
2. When you *remember* something, you keep it in your mind. You try not to forget it: *Remember to take the books back to the library.* [verb]

•**remembers, remembered, remembering.**

remind (ri MYND) When you *remind* someone, you make that person think of something: *This shell reminds me of our days at the beach.* [verb] •**reminds, reminded, reminding.**

remote control (ruh MOHT kuhn TROHL) A *remote control* is a tool you use to control a TV, VCR, or other things. •**remote controls.**

remote control

Rr

rent · reporter

rent (RENT)

1. *Rent* is the money you pay to use something: *She pays the rent on her apartment every month.* [noun]

2. When you *rent* something, you pay to use it: *We rented a car on our vacation.* [verb] •**rents.** •**rents, rented, renting.**

repair (ri PAIR) When you *repair* something, you make it good again: *Will you repair my torn coat?* [verb] •**repairs, repaired, repairing.**

repair

repeat (ri PEET) When you *repeat* something, you do, say, or make it again: *Don't repeat your mistakes. Please repeat that word.* [verb] •**repeats, repeated, repeating.**

reply (ri PLY)

1. When you *reply,* you answer: *Did you reply to her question?* [verb]

2. A *reply* is something said as an answer: *He did not make a reply to my question.* [noun] •**replies, replied, replying.** •**replies.**

report (ri PORT)

1. A *report* is words that are said or written to tell about something: *He gives the weather report on the radio.* [noun]

2. When you *report,* you make a report about something: *Dad called and reported the fire.* [verb] •**reports.** •**reports, reported, reporting.**

reporter (ri POR ter) A *reporter* is a person who gathers and reports news for a newspaper, a magazine, or a radio or television station. [noun] •**reporters.**

reporter

Rr

reptile (REP tyl) A *reptile* is an animal with dry, rough skin. Snakes, lizards, turtles, alligators, and crocodiles are *reptiles.* [noun] •**reptiles.**

rescue (RES kyoo) When you *rescue* people, you save them from danger: *Firefighters often rescue people.* [verb] •**rescues, rescued, rescuing.**

reptiles

respect (ri SPEKT) When you *respect* something or someone, you feel or show special thought for them: *We respect an honest person.* [verb] •**respects, respected, respecting.**

rest¹ (REST)

1. When you *rest,* you are still or quiet or even asleep: *She rests for an hour every afternoon.* [verb]

2. A *rest* is a short stop after working or playing hard: *Take a rest after you finish washing the windows.* [noun]

•**rests, rested, resting. •rests.**

rest² (REST) The *rest* of something is what is left: *He ate most of the apple and threw the rest away.* [noun]

rest¹

restaurant (RESS tuh ruhnt) A *restaurant* is a place to buy and eat a meal. [noun] •**restaurants.**

restroom (REST ROOM) A *restroom* is a bathroom in a building. Schools and offices have *restrooms.* [noun] •**restrooms.**

result (ri ZUHLT) A *result* is what happens because of something: *The result of her fall was a broken arm.* [noun] •**results.**

retrace · rhinoceros

retrace (ri TRAYSS) When you *retrace* something, you go back over it again: *We retraced our steps to where we started.* [verb] •**retraces, retraced, retracing.**

return (ri TERN)

1. When you *return,* you come back: *He will return soon.* [verb]
2. When you *return* something, you give it back: *Did you return the library books?* [verb]

•**returns, returned, returning.**

revise (ri VYZ) When you *revise* something you have written, you read it in a careful way so that you can correct or improve it: *She revised her story to make the ending more exciting.* [verb] •**revises, revised, revising.**

revolve (ri VOLV) To *revolve* is to move in a circle around something: *The Earth revolves around the sun. A record revolves on a record player.* [verb] •**revolves, revolved, revolving.**

revolve

reward (ri WOHRD) A *reward* is something you get in return for something you have done: *A trip to the zoo was our reward for raking all the leaves.* [noun] •**rewards.**

rewrite (re RYT) When you *rewrite* something, you write it again: *I rewrote my story to correct the spelling mistakes.* [verb] •**rewrites, rewrote, rewritten, rewriting.**

rhinoceros (ry NOSS er uhss) A *rhinoceros* is a large wild animal. A *rhinoceros* has thick skin and one or two horns above its nose. *[noun]* •**rhinoceroses.**

Rr

rhinoceros

Rhode Island (rohd EYE luhnd) *Rhode Island is one of the fifty states of the United States. [noun]*

rhyme (RYM)
1. To *rhyme* is to have words or lines that end in the same sound: *"Kitten" rhymes with "mitten." "Go to bed" and "sleepyhead" also rhyme. [verb]*
2. A *rhyme* is a word or line having the same last sound: *"Blue" is a rhyme for "true." "Five, six" and "Pick up sticks" are rhymes. [noun]*
•**rhymes, rhymed, rhyming.** •**rhymes.**

rhythm (RITH uhm) *Rhythm is the strong beat that some music or poetry has. Rhythm makes you want to clap your hands to keep time: We moved our feet to the rhythm of the music. [noun]* •**rhythms.**

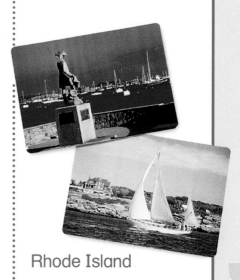

Rhode Island

rib (RIB) *Your rib is one of the bones that curve from back to front around your chest. Your ribs protect your heart and lungs. [noun]* •**ribs.**

ribbon (RIB uhn) *A ribbon is a strip or band of cloth or paper used to tie something. A person who wins a contest sometimes gets a blue ribbon. [noun]* •**ribbons.**

ribbons

rice (RYSS) *Rice is a kind of grain. Rice is often white, but it may be brown. Rice is grown in warm parts of the world. [noun]*

rich (RICH) *When someone is rich, that person has a lot of money or property: They can spend a lot because they are rich. [adjective]* •**richer, richest.**

ridden (RID uhn) *I had ridden my bicycle all day. [verb]*

Rr

riddle · rim

riddle (RID uhl) A *riddle* is a puzzle that asks a question. Here is a *riddle:* "What part of a fish weighs the most?" Answer: "The scales." [*noun*] •**riddles.**

ride (RYD)

ride

1. When you *ride,* you sit on or in something as you go somewhere: *We will ride our bikes to the park. Sunday we all rode in our new car.* [*verb*]
2. A *ride* is a trip on or in something: *We took a ride on our bikes.* [*noun*]
3. A *ride* is also a machine that people ride on for fun: *Would you be scared to go on a ride that went upside down?* [*noun*]
•**rides, rode, ridden, riding.** •**rides.**

ridiculous (ri DIK yuh luhss) Something that is *ridiculous* is very silly. People laugh at *ridiculous* things: *It would be ridiculous to walk backward all the time.* [*adjective*]

This is my right hand.

right

right (RYT)

1. Something that is *right* is the way it should be. Something that is *right* is correct or good: *The right thing to do is tell the truth.* [*adjective*]
2. *Right* is the direction toward the last word on this line. *Right* is the opposite of left: *When you get to the corner, turn right. Put up your right hand.* [*adverb* or *adjective*]

rim (RIM) A *rim* is the edge or border around anything: *The rim of the cup is chipped.* [*noun*] •**rims.**

ring¹ (RING)

rings¹

1. A *ring* is a thin circle of metal or other material you wear on your finger: *She bought a gold ring.* [noun]

2. A *ring* is also something that has a circle shape: *The dancers joined hands and formed a ring.* [noun]

•**rings.**

ring² (RING)

1. To *ring* is to make a sound like that of a bell: *I heard the phone ring.* [verb]

2. A *ring* is the sound of a bell: *There were three rings and then the person hung up.* [noun]

•**rings, rang, rung, ringing.** •**rings.**

rip (RIP)

1. When you *rip* something, you cut or pull it apart in a careless way: *They ripped the wrapping off the presents.* [verb]

2. A *rip* is a torn place: *She sewed up the rip in my sleeve.* [noun]

•**rips, ripped, ripping.** •**rips.**

ripe (RYP)

When something is *ripe,* it is grown and ready to be picked and eaten: *We bought ripe apples at the store.* [adjective] •**riper, ripest.**

rise (RYZ)

1. When you *rise,* you get up from a lying, sitting or kneeling position. When you *rise,* you stand up: *Please rise when your name is called.* [verb]

2. To *rise* also means to go up: *What time will the sun rise tomorrow? Did the price of fruit rise?* [verb]

•**rises, rose, risen, rising.**

ripe

Rr

risen · roast

roaches

risen (RIZ uhn) *The sun had already risen by the time we woke up. [verb]*

river (RIV er) A *river* is a wide stream of running water. Most *rivers* flow into a lake or ocean. *[noun]* •**rivers.**

roach (ROHCH) A *roach* is a small brown insect. *Roaches* live in kitchens and around water pipes. *Roaches* look for food at night. *[noun]* •**roaches.**

road (ROHD) A *road* is a way to go between places. A *road* is a way for a car, truck, or bus to go from one place to another: *This road goes to the city. [noun]* •**roads.**

roam (ROHM) When you *roam,* you walk around with no special plan: *On Saturday, we like to roam through the woods. [verb]* •**roams, roamed, roaming.**

roar (ROR)

1. To *roar* is to make a loud, deep sound: *The crowd roared when he caught the ball. [verb]*
2. A *roar* is a loud, deep sound: *The roar of the lion frightened some people at the zoo. [noun]*
•**roars, roared, roaring.**
•**roars.**

roar

roast (ROHST)

1. When you *roast* something, you cook it by the heat in an oven: *Grandma roasted a chicken and potatoes for dinner. [verb]*
2. A *roast* is a piece of meat cooked by roasting: *Dad cooked a roast. [noun]*
•**roasts, roasted, roasting.** •**roasts.**

rob (ROB) To *rob* is to take something that does not belong to you: *Three men robbed the bank.* [verb] •**robs, robbed, robbing.**

robber (ROB er) A *robber* is a person who robs: *The police chased him, but the robber got away.* [noun] •**robbers.**

robe (ROHB) A *robe* is a long piece of clothing like a loose coat: *I put a robe on over my pajamas.* [noun] •**robes.**

robin (ROB uhn) A *robin* is a bird with a red or orange front. *Robins* are found in most places in the United States. [noun] •**robins.**

robin

robot (ROH bot *or* ROH buht) A *robot* is a machine that is run by a computer. *Robots* help people do work. *Robots* can look like people. [noun] •**robots.**

rock (ROK)
1. *Rock* is the hard, solid part of the earth that is not soil or metal. You can find *rock* in small or large pieces. Mountains are made of *rock.* [noun]
2. A *rock* is a small piece of this hard material: *She threw a rock into the pond.* [noun]
•**rocks** *for definition 2.*

rocks

rocket (ROK it) A *rocket* is a long metal tube open at one end. A *rocket* can move forward or straight up. *Rockets* are used to send spacecraft into space very quickly. [noun] •**rockets.**

rocky (ROK ee) If something is *rocky,* it is full of rocks: *The road was very rocky and hard to drive on.* [adjective] •**rockier, rockiest.**

Rr

rode · room

rode (ROHD) *I rode my bicycle to school. [verb]*

rodeo (ROH dee oh *or* roh DAY oh) A *rodeo* is a contest or show in which cowboys and cowgirls show their skills. People ride wild horses and bulls in a *rodeo. [noun]*
•**rodeos.**

rodeo

roll (ROHL)

1. To *roll* is to move along by turning over and over: *The marbles rolled across the floor. [verb]*
2. A *roll* is something rolled up: *I bought a roll of film. [noun]*
3. A *roll* is also a kind of bread or cake: *She spread butter on the roll. [noun]*
•**rolls, rolled, rolling.** •**rolls.**

roller skate (ROH ler SKAYT) A *roller skate* is a shoe or something you wear on a shoe that has wheels. *Roller skates* are used to skate on a floor, a sidewalk, or any other flat, smooth surface.
•**roller skates.**

roller skates

roof (ROOF) A *roof* is the top covering of a building: *From our apartment we can see the roofs of many houses. [noun]* •**roofs.**

room (ROOM)

1. A *room* is a part of the inside of a building. Each *room* has walls of its own: *Please clean up your room. [noun]*
2. *Room* is also the amount of space that something takes: *There isn't enough room in the kitchen for everyone to sit down. [noun]*
•**rooms** *for definition 1.*

rooster (ROO ster) A *rooster* is an adult male chicken. *Roosters* make noise when the sun comes up each morning. *[noun]* •**roosters.**

rooster

root (ROOT)

1. The *root* is the part of a plant that grows underground. Plants get food and water through their *roots. [noun]*

2. A *root* is also a word from which other words are made. In the words *rounder* and *roundest*, the *root* word is *round. [noun]*
•**roots.**

rope (ROHP) A *rope* is a very thick string twisted together: *She tied the boat to the dock with a rope. [noun]* •**ropes.**

rose[1] (ROHZ) A *rose* is a flower that grows on a bush. *Roses* can be red, pink, white, or yellow. Some *roses* have sharp points on their stems. *[noun]* •**roses.**

rose[2] (ROHZ) *The pupils rose from their desks when the principal entered the room. [verb]*

rotten (ROT uhn) When something is *rotten,* it is no longer good. If something is *rotten,* it is spoiled: *The banana is all black outside and rotten inside. [adjective]* •**rottener, rottenest.**

rough (RUHF) When something is *rough,* it has a surface that is not even. Something that is *rough* is not smooth: *Some trees have very rough bark. His skin became rough from the cold wind. [adjective]* •**rougher, roughest.**

roses[1]

round · rude

round (ROWND) Something that is *round* is shaped like a ball or a circle. The Earth is *round*. A wheel is *round*. [adjective] •**rounder, roundest.**

route (ROOT *or* ROWT) A *route* is a way that you choose to get somewhere: *What route do you take to get to the park? We live near the school bus route.* [noun] •**routes.**

row²

row¹ (ROH) A *row* is a straight line of people or things: *We stood in a row against the wall.* [noun] •**rows.**

row² (ROH) When you *row,* you move a boat. [verb] •**rows, rowed, rowing.**

royal (ROI uhl) Something that is *royal* is from or about a king or a queen: *The knight received a royal command to go to the queen's castle.* [adjective]

rub (RUHB) To *rub* is to move something across something else again and again: *She rubbed the kitten's back. They rubbed the floor clean with a cloth.* [verb] •**rubs, rubbed, rubbing.**

rubber (RUHB er) *Rubber* is a material made from the juice of certain trees. *Rubber* can stretch and bounce. *Rubber* will not let air or water through. Pencil erasers and car tires are made of *rubber.* [noun]

ruby (ROO bee) A *ruby* is a kind of stone that is worth a lot of money. *Rubies* are red. [noun] •**rubies.**

rude (ROOD) When someone is *rude,* that person has bad manners. Someone who is *rude* is not polite: *My*

This is made of rubber.

rubber

Rr

brother was rude and didn't say hello to my best friend. [adjective] •**ruder, rudest.**

rug (RUHG) A *rug* is something that covers the floor: *The children played on the rug in the living room.* *[noun]* •**rugs.**

ruin (ROO uhn) To *ruin* something is to break or spoil it completely: *The rain ruined our picnic. [verb]* •**ruins, ruined, ruining.**

ruin

rule (ROOL)

1. A *rule* is something that tells what we must do or what we must not do: *You must obey the school rules and not run in the halls. [noun]*

2. To *rule* is to control a country and its people: *The king ruled his kingdom well. [verb]* •**rules.** •**rules, ruled, ruling.**

ruler (ROO ler)

1. A *ruler* is a straight strip of wood, metal, or plastic used to measure how long something is. *Rulers* also help you to draw straight lines. *[noun]*

2. A *ruler* is also anyone who controls a government: *Kings and queens used to be the rulers in many countries. [noun]* •**rulers.**

run

run (RUHN)

1. When you *run,* you move your legs very fast, so that you go faster than walking: *It's hard to run a mile without stopping for breath. My friend's dog ran away. [verb]*

2. If something *runs,* it works the way it should: *The washer doesn't run until it is turned on. [verb]*

Rr

rung¹ · rust

rural

3. If you *run* something, you are in charge of it: *Mom runs a restaurant.* [verb]
•**runs, ran, run, running.**

rung¹ (RUHNG) A *rung* is a round bar used as a step of a ladder. [noun] •**rungs.**

rung² (RUHNG) *The church bell has rung several times today.* [verb]

runner (RUHN er) A *runner* is a person, animal, or thing that runs: *My sister is a fast runner.* [noun]
•**runners.**

rural (RUR uhl) *Rural* means in the country: *Rural life is not like city life.* [adjective]

rush (RUHSH)
1. When you *rush,* you move quickly: *They rushed to put out the fire.* [verb]
2. A *rush* is a big hurry: *He was in a rush to get to the bank before it closed.* [noun]
•**rushes, rushed, rushing.**

rust (RUHST)
1. *Rust* is the red-brown covering that sometimes forms on iron or steel: *There's some rust on our car.* [noun]
2. When something *rusts,* it becomes covered with rust: *Don't let your tools rust.* [verb]
•**rusts, rusted, rusting.**

rusted

Rr

sad (SAD) If you are *sad*, you feel bad about something. If you are *sad*, you are not happy: *I was sad when my best friend moved away. [adjective]* • **sadder, saddest.**

safe (SAYF) When something is *safe*, it is in no danger: *We keep our money in a safe place. He looked for a safe place to swim. [adjective]* • **safer, safest.**

safely (SAYF lee) When you do something *safely*, you do it in a safe way: *Cross the street safely! [adverb]*

safety helmet (SAYF tee HEL mit) A *safety helmet* is a covering of steel or plastic you wear on your head when doing something that might be dangerous: *Wear a safety helmet when you ride your skateboard.* • **safety helmets.**

safety pin (SAYF tee pin) A *safety pin* is a pin with a special cover for the sharp point. • **safety pins.**

Ss

said · sale

said (SED) *She had said it many times. She said she would help us.* [verb]

sail (SAYL)

1. A *sail* is a large piece of cloth used on some boats. *Sails* catch the wind and help boats move. [noun]

2. When you *sail*, you travel on water: *We like to sail on Dad's new boat.* [verb]

sailboat

• **sails.** • **sails, sailed, sailing.**

sailboat (SAYL boht) A *sailboat* is a boat that is moved by the wind that pushes against the sails: *Our sailboat went quickly because there was a lot of wind.* [noun] • **sailboats.**

sailfish (SAYL fish) A *sailfish* is a kind of fish that has a long, high fin on its back. [noun] • **sailfish** *or* **sailfishes.**

sailor (SAY ler) A *sailor* is a person who works on a boat or ship. [noun] • **sailors.**

sailors

salad (SAL uhd) A *salad* is a kind of food that is usually made with lettuce and other raw vegetables: *We put lettuce and carrots in the salad.* [noun] • **salads.**

sale (SAYL)

1. A *sale* is a time or place when something is sold: *The library held a book sale last week.* [noun]

2. When something is *on sale*, it is sold for less money than usual. When something is *for sale*, you can buy it if you want to: *My new coat was on sale. Is that car for sale?* [noun]

• **sales** *for definition 1.*

salesperson (SAYLZ per suhn) A *salesperson* is someone whose job is to sell things: *The salesperson asked the woman if she needed any help.* [noun] •**salespeople** *or* **salespersons.**

salt (SAWLT) *Salt* is a white material found in the earth or in sea water. *Salt* makes food taste better and keeps it from spoiling. [noun]

salty (SAWL tee) If something is *salty*, it tastes like salt: *This popcorn is too salty to eat.* [adjective] •**saltier, saltiest.**

same (SAYM) When two things are the *same*, they are just alike. They are not different: *We have the same first name. She has the same thing for lunch every day.* [adjective]

same

sand (SAND) *Sand* is tiny bits of broken rock: *We played in the sand at the beach.* [noun]

sandbox (SAND bokss) A *sandbox* is a box full of sand to play in. [noun] •**sandboxes.**

sand castle (SAND KASS uhl) A *sand castle* is a pile of sand shaped like a castle. *Sand castles* are made by people playing at the beach. •**sand castles.**

sand castle

Ss

sandwich • sauce

sandwich (SAND wich)
A *sandwich* is made of two slices of bread with meat, cheese, or some other food between them: *He brought a peanut butter and jelly sandwich for lunch.* [noun]
• **sandwiches.**

sandwich

sang (SANG) *The mother sang to her baby.* [verb]

sank (SANGK) *The toy boat sank to the bottom of the pond.* [verb]

San Luis Potosí (sahn lweess poh toh SEE) *San Luis Potosí is a state in central Mexico.* [noun]

Saskatchewan (sa SKACH uh wahn) *Saskatchewan is one of the ten provinces of Canada.* [noun]

sat (SAT) *My father sat in his favorite chair. We sat and listened while the teacher read the story.* [verb]

satellite (SAT uh lyt) A *satellite* is something that moves in space around the Earth or another planet. The moon is a *satellite* of Earth. *Satellites* are used to send TV shows and other information across the Earth. [noun] • **satellites.**

Saturday (SAT er day) *Saturday* is the day after Friday. *Saturday* is the seventh day of the week. [noun] • **Saturdays.**

sauce (SAWSS) A *sauce* is a liquid served with food to make the food taste better: *He likes tomato sauce on spaghetti.* [noun] • **sauces.**

Ss

satellite

saucer (SAW ser) A *saucer* is a small flat dish. You set a cup on a *saucer*. [noun] •**saucers.**

save (SAYV)
1. If you *save* someone, you keep them from danger: *The fence saved the girl from falling into the hole.* [verb]
2. When you *save* something, you keep it because you want to use it later on: *He was saving money for a new bike.* [verb]
•**saves, saved, saving.**

saw[1] (SAW) A *saw* is a tool for cutting: *The carpenter used a saw to cut boards for our new stairs.* [noun] •**saws.**

saw[2] (SAW) *She saw a robin yesterday.* [verb]

saxophone (SAK suh fohn) A *saxophone* is a musical instrument that is played by blowing into it. [noun] •**saxophones.**

say (SAY) When you *say* something, you speak it out loud: *He said he couldn't come with us. Could you say that again?* [verb] •**says, said, saying.**

scale[1] (SKAYL) A *scale* is something used to see how much something weighs: *He weighed himself on the scale in the doctor's office.* [noun] •**scales.**

scale[2] (SKAYL) A *scale* is one of the thin, hard pieces that forms the skin of some fish, snakes, and lizards. [noun] •**scales.**

scare (SKAIR) If you *scare* people, you make them afraid: *The noise scared him. He was scared when he could not see what it was.* [verb] •**scares, scared, scaring.**

scales[2]

Ss

scarecrow • scissors

scarecrow (SKAIR kroh) A *scarecrow* is a figure of a person dressed in old clothes. A *scarecrow* is set in a field to scare birds away from crops that are growing. *[noun]* •**scarecrows.**

scarf (SKARF) A *scarf* is a piece of cloth you wear around your neck or on your head. *[noun]* •**scarves.**

scarves (SKARVZ) *Scarves* is the plural of the word *scarf. [noun plural]*

scary (SKAIR ee) If something is *scary,* it makes you feel afraid: *She saw a scary movie on TV. [adjective]* •**scarier, scariest.**

school (SKOOL) A *school* is a place where you learn things: *We learn to read in school. [noun]* •**schools.**

school

science (SY uhnss) *Science* is the study of the earth, the sky, animals, and people. *Science* uses the facts that we notice to tell us why things are the way they are. *[noun]* •**sciences.**

scissors

scientist (SY uhn tist) A *scientist* is a person who studies a science. A *scientist* tries to find out why things are the way they are. *[noun]* •**scientists.**

scissors (SIZ urz) A pair of *scissors* is a tool for cutting things. A pair of *scissors* has two sharp edges that work together to cut paper or cloth. *[noun or noun plural]* •The plural of *scissors* is *scissors.*

Ss

score (SKOR)

1. The *score* is the points you make in a game or on a test: *The score of the baseball game was 4 to 2.* [noun]
2. To *score* is to make points: *Our team scored first.* [verb]
•**scores.** •**scores, scored, scoring.**

scratch (SKRACH)

1. When you *scratch* something, you rub it or you make a mark on it with something sharp: *Your shoes scratched the chair. The pin scratched my arm. It's hard not to scratch mosquito bites.* [verb]
2. A *scratch* is a mark made with something sharp: *There are deep scratches on our kitchen table.* [noun]
•**scratches, scratched, scratching.** •**scratches.**

scratch

scream (SKREEM)

1. If you *scream,* you make a loud, high cry. People *scream* when they are angry, frightened, or excited. [verb]
2. A *scream* is a loud, high cry: *We heard screams from the people on the rides at the fair.* [noun]
•**screams, screamed, screaming.** •**screams.**

scream

screen (SKREEN)

1. A *screen* is a piece of woven wire that you put over a window or door. The tiny holes in a *screen* allow air but not insects to pass through. [noun]
2. A *screen* is also a glass surface where TV pictures, computer information, or video games are seen. [noun]
•**screens.**

scrub (SKRUHB)
When you *scrub* something, you rub it hard to clean it: *We helped scrub the classroom floors after the party.* [verb]
•**scrubs, scrubbed, scrubbing.**

Ss

343

sculpture · season

sculpture (SKUHLP cher)
A *sculpture* is a piece of art made from stone, wood, clay, or other things: *I saw a sculpture of a horse at the museum.* [noun] • **sculptures.**

sculptures

sea (SEE) A *sea* is a large area of salty water. *Seas* cover almost three-fourths of the earth's surface. Fish, dolphins, and whales are some animals that live in the *sea.* Another word for *sea* is *ocean.* [noun] • **seas.**

sea gull (SEE GUHL) A *sea gull* is a kind of bird that lives near the sea. • **sea gulls.**

seal¹ (SEEL) When you *seal* something, you close it very well: *He sealed the envelope before he mailed it.* [verb] • **seals, sealed, sealing.**

seal² (SEEL) A *seal* is a sea animal that has thick fur. *Seals* usually live in cold places. [noun] • **seals.**

search (SERCH) When you *search,* you try to find something by looking for it: *We searched the house for Dad's car keys.* [verb] • **searches, searched, searching.**

seashell (SEE shel) A *seashell* is the shell of any animal that lives in or near the sea. [noun] • **seashells.**

season (SEE zuhn)
1. A *season* is one of the four parts of the year. The *seasons* are spring, summer, fall, and winter. [noun]
2. When you *season* something, you add salt or spices to make it taste better: *I season my soup with pepper and salt.* [verb]
• **seasons.** • **seasons, seasoned, seasoning.**

seasons

seat (SEET) A *seat* is a place to sit or a thing to sit on: *The woman looked for a seat on the bus. The students took their seats when the teacher walked in.* [noun] •**seats.**

seat belt (SEET belt) A *seat belt* is a belt or set of belts that holds someone in a car or airplane seat if there is a crash or bump. •**seat belts.**

seaweed (SEE weed) *Seaweed* is any plant that grows in the sea. [noun]

second¹ (SEK uhnd) Something that is *second* is next after the first. *Second* is also written 2nd: *B is the second letter of the alphabet. I came in second in the race.* [adjective]

second² (SEK uhnd) A *second* is a very short period of time. Sixty *seconds* equal one minute. [noun] •**seconds.**

secret (SEE krit)
1. If something is *secret,* it is not known to everybody: *Our club has a secret code.* [adjective]
2. A *secret* is something that you don't tell anyone: *He asked her if she could keep a secret.* [noun] •**secrets.**

secretary (SEK ruh tair ee) A *secretary* is a person who writes letters, keeps records, answers the telephone, and does other things in an office. [noun] •**secretaries.**

secretly (SEE krit lee) When you do something *secretly,* you do it without letting others know: *She secretly left flowers for her sick neighbor.* [adverb]

second¹

I am second in line.

Ss

345

section • sell

section (SEK shuhn) A *section* is a part of something: *He cut the pizza into eight equal sections. We are studying the poetry section of our reader today.* [noun] •**sections.**

sections

see (SEE) When you *see* something, you look at it with your eyes: *We woke up early to see the sunrise.* [verb] •**sees, saw, seen, seeing.**

seed (SEED) A *seed* is a part of a plant that grows into a new plant. A *seed* has a tiny plant inside it. It also has the food the tiny plant needs to grow. [noun] •**seeds.**

seem (SEEM) *Does the music seem too loud to you? The dog seemed hungry, but it wouldn't eat. I slept well, but I still seem to be tired.* [verb] •**seems, seemed, seeming.**

seen (SEEN) *I have seen that movie already.* [verb]

seesaw (SEE saw) A *seesaw* is a long board that balances on something near the middle. Children can sit at opposite ends of a *seesaw* and move up and down. Playgrounds often have *seesaws.* [noun] •**seesaws.**

selfish (SEL fish) *Selfish* means caring too much for yourself and not enough for other people: *I think he is selfish because he never shares his things with anyone.* [adjective]

sell (SEL) When you *sell* something, you trade it for money: *We plan to sell our house.* [verb] •**sells, sold, selling.**

Ss

sell

346

send (SEND) When you *send* people or things, you make them go from one place to another: *Mother sent us to the store for bread. I'm sending a package to my friend.* [verb] •**sends, sent, sending.**

sense (SENSS)

1. A *sense* is one of the five *senses*: sight, smell, taste, hearing, and touch. [noun]

2. *Sense* is another word for *meaning*. Some very short words have many different *senses*: *How many senses can you find for the word* call *in this dictionary?* [noun]
•**senses.**

sent (SENT) *She sent the package last week.* [verb]

sentence (SEN tuhnss) A *sentence* is a group of words that tells a complete idea. A written *sentence* begins with a capital letter. It ends with a period, a question mark, or an exclamation mark. Sometimes a single word can be a *sentence*, like "Listen." [noun] •**sentences.**

sentences

separate (SEP uh rayt)

1. When you *separate* two things, you keep them apart: *A fence separates our yard from our neighbor's.* [verb]

2. To *separate* also means to move things apart: *He separated his books from mine.* [verb]
•**separates, separated, separating.**

Ss

September · seventeen

September (sep TEM ber) *September* is the ninth month of the year. It has 30 days. *September* comes after August and before October. *[noun]*

serious (SEER ee uhss) When something is *serious,* it is important because of the pain or trouble it may cause. Something that is *serious* is not funny: *Pollution is a serious problem for our country. Dad had a serious look on his face when he heard about the broken window. [adjective]*

serve (SERV) To *serve* is to put something to eat in front of someone: *The waiter served us our breakfast. [verb]* •**serves, served, serving.**

serve

serving (SER ving) A *serving* is the amount of food served to a person at one time: *She ate two servings of pasta. [noun]* •**servings.**

set (SET)
1. A *set* is a group of things that go together: *We bought a new set of dishes. [noun]*
2. To *set* is to put something in a place: *Set your suitcase over in that corner. [verb]*
3. To *set* is also to go down: *We'll go home when the sun sets. [verb]*
•**sets.** •**sets, set, setting.**

seven (SEV uhn) *Seven* is one more than six. It is also written 7. *[noun or adjective]* •**sevens.**

seventeen (sev uhn TEEN) *Seventeen* is seven more than ten. It is also written 17. *[noun or adjective]*

seven

seventeenth (sev uhn TEENTH) The *seventeenth* is next after the sixteenth. It is also written 17th. [*adjective*]

seventh (SEV uhnth) The *seventh* is next after the sixth. It is also written 7th. [*adjective*]

seventy (SEV uhn tee) *Seventy* is ten more than sixty. It is also written 70. [*noun* or *adjective*] •**seventies.**

several (SEV er uhl) *Several* means more than two or three but not many: *He had several questions he wanted to ask the teacher.* [*adjective*]

sew (SOH) When you *sew*, you push a needle and thread through cloth. You can *sew* by hand or with a machine. [*verb*] •**sews, sewed, sewing.**

sewn (SOHN) *She has sewn patches on her jeans.* [*verb*]

shade (SHAYD) *Shade* is a place not in the bright sun. *Shade* is where the light is blocked by something: *We sat in the shade of the tree.* [*noun*]

shadow (SHAD oh) A *shadow* is the shade made by some person, animal, or thing. A *shadow* is a dark shape made when something blocks the light. [*noun*] •**shadows.**

shake (SHAYK) When you *shake* something, you move it up and down or from side to side quickly: *Shake your head if the answer is yes. The baby shook the rattle.* [*verb*] •**shakes, shook, shaken, shaking.**

sew

shake

Ss

349

shaken • she

shaken (SHAY kuhn) *The orange juice needs to be shaken up before you pour any.* [verb]

shallow (SHAL oh) If something is *shallow,* it is not deep: *Stay in the shallow water where I can see you.* [adjective] •**shallower, shallowest.**

shape (SHAYP)

1. A *shape* is the way something looks. Squares, rectangles, triangles, and circles are kinds of *shapes.* [noun]
2. To *shape* something is to make it into a certain shape: *She shaped the clay into a ball.* [verb]
•**shapes.** •**shapes, shaped, shaping.**

shapes

share (SHAIR) When you *share,* you let someone use something with you: *The two girls shared a room. Mom shared her sandwich with me.* [verb] •**shares, shared, sharing.**

shark (SHARK) A *shark* is a large fish that lives in the sea. Some *sharks* are dangerous to people. [noun] •**sharks.**

shark

sharp (SHARP)

1. When something is *sharp,* it has a thin edge or a point: *Be careful with that sharp knife. My dog has sharp teeth.* [adjective]
2. If you are *sharp,* you notice things quickly: *I needed a sharp eye to watch out for mistakes.* [adjective]
•**sharper, sharpest.**

she (SHEE) *My mother said she would drive me to school. She will not be late.* [pronoun]

shed (SHED) A *shed* is a building used to keep things safe and dry or for storing things: *The rake is in the tool shed.* [noun] •**sheds.**

she'd *She'd* is a shorter form of *she had* or *she would*: *She'd wanted to go to the store early in the day. She'd like to buy a new dress.* [contraction]

sheep (SHEEP) A *sheep* is an animal with long, thick hair. A *sheep* is raised for wool and for meat. [noun] • The plural of *sheep* is *sheep.*

sheep

sheet (SHEET)

1. A *sheet* is a piece of paper: *The teacher asked us to write our names on a sheet of paper.* [noun]

2. A *sheet* is also a large piece of cloth used on a bed: *We changed the sheets on the guest bed.* [noun]

3. A *sheet* is also anything that is thin and flat, like a sheet of paper: *They put a sheet of metal over the hole in the street.* [noun]

•**sheets.**

shelf (SHELF) A *shelf* is a flat piece of wood, metal, or some other material that holds things. Books and dishes are often stored on *shelves.* [noun] •**shelves.**

shell

shell (SHEL)

1. The *shell* is the hard outside covering of some animals. Snails, turtles, and clams have *shells.* [noun]

2. The *shell* is also the hard outside covering of a nut or an egg. [noun]

•**shells.**

she'll *She'll* is a shorter form of *she will*: *She'll meet us at five o'clock.* [contraction]

Ss

shelves · shirt

shelves (SHELVZ) *Shelves* is the plural of the word *shelf: Dad built new shelves for the garage.* [noun plural]

she's *She's* is a shorter form of *she is* or *she has: She's happy in her new home. She's gone to visit a friend.* [contraction]

shin (SHIN) Your *shin* is the front part of your leg from your knee to your ankle. [noun] •**shins.**

shine (SHYN)
1. To *shine* is to give off a bright light: *The sun is shining.* [verb]
2. If you *shine* something, you make it bright: *Shine your shoes with this old rag.* [verb]
•**shines, shone** *for definition 1,* **shined** *for definition 2,* **shining.**

shinguard (SHIN gard) A *shinguard* is a covering that protects your shins. Soccer players, hockey players, and baseball catchers wear *shinguards.* [noun] •**shinguards.**

shiny (SHY nee) Something that is *shiny* is bright: *Mom gave me a shiny new penny.* [adjective] •**shinier, shiniest.**

ship (SHIP) A *ship* is a very large boat that travels on oceans or large lakes. [noun] •**ships.**

shirt

shirt (SHERT) A *shirt* is a kind of clothing for your arms and chest. A *shirt* can have long or short sleeves. Most *shirts* have collars and buttons. [noun] •**shirts.**

shinguard

Ss

shoe (SHOO) A *shoe* is something you wear on your foot. *Shoes* are often made of leather. *[noun]* •**shoes.**

shoelace (SHOO layss) A *shoelace* is a string used to hold a shoe on your foot. *[noun]* •**shoelaces.**

shoelaces

shone (SHOHN) *The sun shone in the morning before it began raining.* *[verb]*

shook (SHUK) *He shook the bottle before he poured the orange juice.* *[verb]*

shoot (SHOOT)

1. To *shoot* is to try to hit something with a bullet or an arrow: *He saw his uncle shoot a rabbit.* *[verb]*

2. To *shoot* is also to try to send a ball, puck, or something else to a goal to score points: *He is very good at shooting baskets.* *[verb]*

3. *Shoot* also means to move very quickly: *Flames were shooting up from the burning building.* *[verb]*

4. To *shoot* is also to take a picture with a camera: *She shot several pictures of my dog.* *[verb]*
•**shoots, shot, shooting.**

shop (SHOP)

1. A *shop* is a place where things are sold. A *shop* is also a place where things are fixed. Another word for *shop* is *store: We stopped at the candy shop. I took my broken watch to the repair shop.* *[noun]*

2. When you *shop,* you go to stores to look at or to buy things: *We shopped for clothes this morning.* *[verb]*
•**shops.** •**shops, shopped, shopping.**

Ss

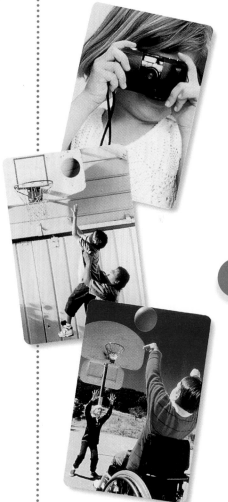

shoot

shore · shot²

shore (SHOR) The *shore* is the land at the edge of a sea or a lake: *She likes to spend time at the shore on her vacation.* [noun] •**shores.**

short (SHORT)

1. If something is *short,* there is not a large distance from the beginning to the end of it: *My friend lives on a short street.* [adjective]

2. When something is *short,* it does not last very long: *We heard a very short talk by the principal today.* [adjective]

3. Someone who is *short* is not tall: *The shortest child went to the front of the line.* [adjective]
•**shorter, shortest.**

short

shorts

shorts (SHORTS) *Shorts* are pants that stop above your knees. [noun plural]

shot¹ (SHOT)

1. A *shot* is the sound a gun makes: *We heard two shots.* [noun]

2. A *shot* is also a way to put medicine under your skin with a needle: *The doctor gave me a shot.* [noun]

3. A *shot* is also a way to score points in a game: *My sister had two shots in the basketball game, but she missed them both.* [noun]
•**shots.**

shot² (SHOT) *He shot a lot of pictures at the picnic.* [verb]

should (SHUD) *You should drink milk every day. I should have worn my boots.* [verb]

shoulder (SHOHL der) Your *shoulder* is the part of your body between your neck and the arm. [noun] •**shoulders.**

shouldn't *Shouldn't* is a shorter form of *should not*: *You shouldn't be late to school.* [contraction]

shout (SHOWT) When you *shout,* you call or yell loudly: *She shouted for help.* [verb] •**shouts, shouted, shouting.**

shovel (SHUHV uhl)

1. A *shovel* is a tool you use to dig a hole or to pick something up: *I used a snow shovel to clean off the driveway.* [noun]

2. To *shovel* is to lift and throw something with a shovel: *He shoveled the sand into the bucket.* [verb]

•**shovels.** •**shovels, shoveled, shoveling.**

shovel

show • shy

show

show (SHOH)

1. When you *show* something, you bring or put it where others can see it: *She took the bicycle out of the garage and showed it to me.* [verb]

2. To *show* also means to explain or to point out something to someone: *He showed us the way to the library. My teacher showed me how to work the problem.* [verb]

3. A *show* is something that you watch on TV or at the movies: *We watched a good show last night.* [noun]

• **shows, showed, shown, showing.** • **shows.**

shower (SHOW er)

1. A *shower* is rain that lasts only a short time: *Spring is the season of many showers.* [noun]

2. A *shower* is also a bath where you stand under running water: *He takes a shower every morning.* [noun]

• **showers.**

shrink (SHRINGK)

To *shrink* is to become smaller: *My sweater shrank in the hot water. Hot water will also shrink my wool socks.* [verb]

• **shrinks, shrank, shrunk, shrinking.**

shrink

shut (SHUHT) If you *shut* something, you close it or put a cover on it. If something *shuts*, it closes: *He shut the box of toys. Don't shut the window.* [verb] • **shuts, shut, shutting.**

shy (SHY) When someone is *shy*, that person is not comfortable around other people: *Some of the children were too shy to speak to the classroom visitor.* [adjective] • **shyer, shyest.**

Ss

sick (SIK) If you are *sick,* you do not feel well: *His mother called the school to say he was sick. She felt sick after eating too many apples.* [adjective]
• **sicker, sickest.**

sickness (SIK niss) *Sickness* means feeling sick: *There is more sickness in the winter than in the summer.* [noun] • **sicknesses.**

side (SYD)

1. A *side* is the edge of something: *A square has four sides.* [noun]

2. A *side* is also the part of something that is not the top, bottom, front, or back: *There is a door at the side of his house.* [noun]

3. A *side* is also one of two groups playing a game: *Our side won the game.* [noun]

• **sides.**

side

sidewalk (SYD wawk) A *sidewalk* is a place to walk on the side of a street. A *sidewalk* is usually made of concrete. [noun] • **sidewalks.**

sight (SYT) *Sight* is being able to see. *Sight* is one of the five senses, along with hearing, smell, taste, and touch. [noun]

sign (SYN)

1. A *sign* is a mark or words that tell you what to do or what not to do. Cars must stop at stop *signs: The sign on the door said "Open."* [noun]

2. When you *sign* something, you write your name on it: *She signed the letter and mailed it right away.* [verb]

Ss

signal • silent

3. If you can *sign,* you can use sign language: *Can you sign "I love you?"* [verb]
•**signs.** •**signs, signed, signing.**

signal   (SIG nuhl)

1. A *signal* is a sign that tells you about something: *A red light is a signal of danger.* [noun]
2. To *signal* is to tell people something with a signal: *A bell signals the end of the school day.* [verb]
•**signals.** •**signals, signaled, signaling.**

sign language   (SYN LANG gwij) *Sign language* is any language where you move your fingers, hands, and arms to show words and ideas. •**sign languages.**

sign language

silent   (SY luhnt) *Silent* means without any noise or talking: *He didn't like to come home to a silent house.* [adjective]

silk (SILK) *Silk* is a kind of soft, smooth cloth. *Silk* is made from threads spun by a certain kind of worm. The worms make the threads from their own bodies. *[noun]* •**silks.**

silly (SIL ee) If something is *silly,* it makes you laugh or smile: *She told a silly joke that made me laugh. [adjective]* •**sillier, silliest.**

silly

silo (SY loh) A *silo* is a tall, round building that stores food for farm animals. *[noun]* •**silos.**

silver (SIL ver) *Silver* is a shiny white metal. *Silver* is used to make coins, jewelry, and other things. *[noun]*

simple (SIM puhl)
1. If something is *simple,* it is easy to do or understand: *That was a simple math problem.* *[adjective]*
2. When something is *simple,* it is not fancy: *She cooked us a simple lunch of soup and sandwiches.* *[adjective]*
•**simpler, simplest.**

Sinaloa (see nah LOH ah) *Sinaloa* is a state in the west part of Mexico. *[noun]*

since (SINSS) *I have been up since dawn. He has called only once since last week. Since you are hungry, we can have dinner now. [preposition* or *conjunction]*

sing (SING)
1. When you *sing,* you make music with your voice: *He likes to sing happy songs. [verb]*
2. To *sing* is also to make pleasing sounds that are like music: *Birds were singing in the trees all morning.* *[verb]*
•**sings, sang, sung, singing.**

Ss

singer · six

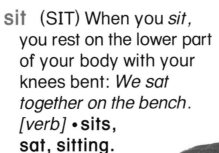

singers

singer (SING er) A *singer* is a person who sings: *The singer had a beautiful voice.* [noun] •**singers.**

single (SING guhl)

1. *Single* means only one: *This button is hanging by a single thread.* [adjective]

2. When someone is *single,* that person is not married: *My aunt is single.* [adjective]

sink (SINGK)

1. To *sink* is to go down or go under: *The ship began to sink when it hit the rock.* [verb]

2. A *sink* is a small tub that holds water: *I washed a few dishes in the kitchen sink.* [noun]
•**sinks, sank, sunk, sinking.** •**sinks.**

siren (SY ruhn) A *siren* is a thing that makes a loud sound that tells people of danger: *We could hear the ambulance siren as it came down our street.* [noun]
•**sirens.**

sister (SISS ter) A *sister* is a girl or woman that has the same parents as another person. [noun] •**sisters.**

sisters

sit (SIT) When you *sit,* you rest on the lower part of your body with your knees bent: *We sat together on the bench.* [verb] •**sits, sat, sitting.**

six (SIKS) *Six* is one more than five. It is also written 6. [noun or adjective]
•**sixes.**

sixteen (sik STEEN) *Sixteen* is six more than ten. It is also written 16. [*noun* or *adjective*] •**sixteens.**

sixteenth (sik STEENTH)
  1. The *sixteenth* is next after the fifteenth. It is also written 16th. [*adjective*]
  2. A *sixteenth* is one of 16 equal parts. [*noun*] •**sixteenths.**

sixth (SIKSTH) The *sixth* is next after the fifth. It is also written 6th. [*adjective*]

sixty (SIK stee) *Sixty* is ten more than fifty. It is also written 60. [*noun* or *adjective*] •**sixties.**

size (SYZ) Something's *size* is how big or how small it is: *What is the size of that picture? The boys are the same size.* [*noun*] •**sizes.**

size

skate (SKAYT)
  1. A *skate* is something you wear on your feet to slide or roll over a smooth surface. [*noun*]
  2. To *skate* is to move along on ice skates or roller skates: *I skated on the frozen pond.* [*verb*]
  •**skates.** •**skates, skated, skating.**

skateboard (SKAYT bord) A *skateboard* is a board with wheels attached to each end. You can move quickly over a sidewalk or street on a *skateboard.* [*noun*] •**skateboards.**

skeleton (SKEL uh tuhn) A *skeleton* is all the bones of a body. Your *skeleton* holds your body up and gives it shape. [*noun*] •**skeletons.**

skateboard

Ss

ski · skirt

ski (SKEE)

1. A *ski* is a long, narrow board that you wear on your feet to stand on and slide over snow. Some *skis* can be used on water. *[noun]*

2. When you *ski,* you go over snow or water on skis. *[verb]*

•**skis.** •**skis, skied, skiing.**

skill (SKIL) A *skill* is being able to do something well. You can develop a *skill* by practicing it. Reading and writing are important *skills. [noun]* •**skills.**

skin (SKIN) *Skin* is the outside covering of human and animal bodies, plants, fruits, and seeds: *Her skin was red from too much sun. [noun]* •**skins.**

skin

skip (SKIP)

1. When you *skip,* you hop first on one foot and then the other: *She skipped down the sidewalk. [verb]*

2. If you *skip* something, you pass over it without doing anything: *Skip the questions you can't answer and come back to them later. [verb]*

•**skips, skipped, skipping.**

skirt (SKERT) A *skirt* is a kind of clothing that hangs from the waist. *Skirts* can be long or short. *[noun]*

•**skirts.**

skirt

Ss

skull (SKUHL) Your *skull* is the part of your head and face that is bone. Your *skull* protects your brain. *[noun]* •**skulls.**

skunk (SKUHNGK) A *skunk* is a small black animal with a white stripe along its back and a large, furry tail. When a *skunk* is scared, it sprays into the air a liquid that smells bad. *[noun]* •**skunks.**

sky (SKY) The *sky* is the space high above us that seems to cover the Earth: *The sky no longer looks like it will rain. [noun]* •**skies.**

skyscraper (SKY skray per) A *skyscraper* is a very tall building. *[noun]* •**skyscrapers.**

slacks (SLAKS) *Slacks* are long pants worn especially for relaxing. *[noun plural]*

slam (SLAM) When you *slam* something, you shut it with a lot of noise: *Don't slam the door! [verb]* •**slams, slammed, slamming.**

slant (SLANT) If something *slants,* it is higher on one end than the other: *Many roofs slant. The telephone pole slants to the right because a truck ran into it. [verb]* •**slants, slanted, slanting.**

sled (SLED)
1. A *sled* is something you use to slide over ice and snow: *They rode the sled down the hill. [noun]*
2. To *sled* is to ride or coast on a sled: *They sledded down the slope. [verb]*
•**sleds.** •**sleds, sledded, sledding.**

skyscrapers

sled

Ss

363

sleep · slide

sleep (SLEEP)

1. When you *sleep,* you rest your body and mind: *It's easy to sleep when it's quiet.* [verb]

2. *Sleep* is the rest that your body and mind need each night: *I felt better after my long sleep.* [noun]

•**sleeps, slept, sleeping.**

sleep

sleepy (SLEE pee) If you are *sleepy,* you are ready to go to sleep: *He is always sleepy because he gets to bed too late.* [adjective] •**sleepier, sleepiest.**

sleeve (SLEEV) A *sleeve* is the part of a shirt, coat, dress, or sweater that covers your arm. [noun] •**sleeves.**

sleigh (SLAY) A *sleigh* is a large cart without wheels for traveling on snow or ice. *Sleighs* are often pulled by horses. [noun] •**sleighs.**

slept (SLEPT) *I slept in a big bed. I have slept in a tent.* [verb]

slice (SLYSS)

1. A *slice* is a thin, flat piece cut from something: *She cut me a slice of meat.* [noun]

2. When you *slice* something, you cut it into thin, flat pieces: *He sliced the bread.* [verb]

•**slices.** •**slices, sliced, slicing.**

slid (SLID) *Her sister slid down the hill.* [verb]

slide (SLYD)

1. To *slide* is to move in a smooth way: *Let's slide down the hill.* [verb]

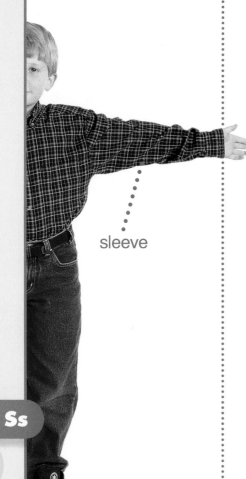

sleeve

Ss

2. A *slide* is a smooth metal surface that slants from the top of a ladder to the ground: *We used the slide on the playground.* [noun]
•**slides, slid, sliding.** •**slides.**

slimy (SLYM ee) Something that is *slimy* is sticky and wet: *The pond is too slimy to swim in.* [adjective]
•**slimier, slimiest.**

slip (SLIP)
1. If you *slip,* you slide suddenly and fall: *She will slip on the ice.* [verb]
2. To *slip* also means to move in a smooth, quiet, or quick way: *She slipped out of the room.* [verb]
•**slips, slipped, slipping.**

slipper (SLIP er) A *slipper* is a light, soft shoe you wear indoors: *Dad usually wears slippers after he comes home from work.* [noun] •**slippers.**

slither (SL<u>ITH</u> er) To *slither* is to go in a slipping or sliding way: *The snake slithered into the weeds.* [verb]
•**slithers, slithered, slithering.**

slippers

slope (SLOHP)
1. To *slope* is to be higher on one end or side: *The front yard slopes down toward the road.* [verb]
2. A *slope* is anything that is higher on one end than the other: *We could see the cattle at the bottom of the slope.* [noun]
•**slopes, sloped, sloping.** •**slopes.**

slow (SLOH) When something is *slow,* it takes a long time. Something that is *slow* is not fast or quick: *My sister is a slow reader. The slow runners could not keep up.* [adjective] •**slower, slowest.**

small (SMAWL) If something is *small,* it is not big, tall, large, or many: *We own a small house.* [adjective]
•**smaller, smallest.**

Ss

smart · smooth

smell

smart (SMART) If you are *smart*, you have a good mind: *He is very smart and learns quickly.* [adjective]
• **smarter, smartest.**

smell (SMEL)

1. When you *smell*, you use your nose to find out about something. Breathing in allows you to *smell: We could smell the flowers in the garden.* [verb]

2. *Smell* is being able to use your nose to find out something. *Smell* is one of the five senses, along with hearing, sight, taste, and touch. [noun]

3. A *smell* is also something that you breathe in and recognize: *There was a strong smell of smoke just before the fire broke out.* [noun]
• **smells, smelled, smelling.** • **smells** *for definition 3.*

smile (SMYL)

1. When you *smile*, you look happy by turning up the corners of your mouth: *The baby smiled when she saw her mother.* [verb]

2. A *smile* is when you curve up the corners of your mouth: *He has a nice smile.* [noun]
• **smiles, smiled, smiling.** • **smiles.**

smiles

smoke (SMOHK) *Smoke* is the gases that rise in a cloud from anything that is hot or burning: *Smoke rose from the burning building.* [noun]

smooth (SMOO<u>TH</u>) When something is *smooth*, it has an even surface. Something that is *smooth* is not

Ss

snail

bumpy or rough: *The road was very smooth.* [*adjective*] •**smoother, smoothest.**

snack (SNAK) A *snack* is a small amount of food you eat between meals. [*noun*] •**snacks.**

snail (SNAYL) A *snail* is a small animal with a soft body and a shell. *Snails* are very slow. [*noun*] •**snails.**

snake (SNAYK) A *snake* is a long, thin animal with dry, rough skin and no legs. *Snakes* move by sliding along the ground. Some *snakes* have a very dangerous bite. [*noun*] •**snakes.**

sneakers (SNEE kerz) *Sneakers* are light shoes with rubber bottoms. [*noun plural*]

sneeze (SNEEZ)
1. When you *sneeze,* you blow air out suddenly through your nose and mouth. A person with a cold often *sneezes: Dust in the air makes her sneeze.* [*verb*]
2. A *sneeze* is when you blow air out suddenly through your nose and mouth: *They heard a loud sneeze in the next room.* [*noun*]
•**sneezes, sneezed, sneezing.** •**sneezes.**

snorkel

snorkel (SNOR kuhl) A *snorkel* is a bent tube which lets swimmers breathe under water while swimming near the surface. [*noun*] •**snorkels.**

snow (SNOH)
1. *Snow* is water that freezes high up in the air. *Snow* falls as white snowflakes. [*noun*]
2. When it *snows,* white bits of frozen water fall from the sky: *It snowed all day.* [*verb*]
•**snows, snowed, snowing.**

Ss

snowflake · socket

snowflake (SNOH flayk) A *snowflake* is a small, light piece of snow. *[noun]* •**snowflakes.**

snowman (SNOH man) A *snowman* is snow piled into a shape that is like a person. *[noun]* •**snowmen.**

snug (SNUHG) If something is *snug,* it is warm and comfortable: *She enjoyed working in the snug corner of the living room.* *[adjective]*

snowman

so (SOH) *Don't eat so fast. The fire was so big that the firefighters couldn't put it out. The wind felt cold, so he went inside.* *[adverb* or *conjunction]*

soap (SOHP) *Soap* is something you use to wash things and get them clean. *Soap* can be in the form of a bar, powder, or liquid. *[noun]* •**soaps.**

sob (SOB) When you *sob,* you cry with short, quick breaths: *The baby sobbed until I picked her up.* *[verb]* •**sobs, sobbed, sobbing.**

soccer (SOK er) *Soccer* is a game played on a field by two teams using a round ball. Each team tries to kick or hit the ball into the goal of the other team. *Soccer* players may not use their hands or arms to hit the ball. *[noun]*

sock (SOK) A *sock* is a short knitted covering you wear on your feet. *[noun]* •**socks.**

socket (SOK it) A *socket* is a hollow part or piece which something fits into. Light bulbs and plugs are two things that are put into *sockets.* *[noun]* •**sockets.**

soccer

Ss

soft (SAWFT)

1. When something is *soft,* it moves when you press against it. Something that is *soft* is not hard: *This pillow feels very soft.* [adjective]

2. If something is *soft,* it is not loud: *Mother sang to the baby in a soft voice.* [adjective]
   • **softer, softest.**

soil¹ (SOIL) *Soil* is the top layer of the earth. *Soil* is dirt: *Our garden has such rich soil that almost anything will grow in it.* [noun] • **soils.**

soil² (SOIL) If you *soil* something, you make it dirty: *The dust soiled his white gloves.* [verb] • **soils, soiled, soiling.**

solar (SOH ler) Something that is *solar* has to do with the sun: *We learned about the solar system.* [adjective]

solar system (SOH ler SIS tuhm) Our *solar system* is our sun and all the planets, moons, and asteroids that revolve around it. • **solar systems.**

This is the sun.

solar system

sold · something

soldiers

Ss

Can you tell me something about this page?

something

sold (SOHLD) *The clerk sold me a green shirt. She could have sold me a red one too.* [verb]

soldier (SOHL jer) A *soldier* is someone in an army. [noun] •**soldiers.**

solid (SOL id)

1. A *solid* is something that takes up space and has its own shape. Wood and ice are *solids*. A *solid* is not a liquid or a gas. [noun]

2. If something is *solid,* it is not hollow: *The steel bar is solid, but the steel pipe is hollow.* [adjective]
•**solids.**

solve (SOLV) When you *solve* something, you find the answer to it: *The detective solved the mystery by using several good clues.* [verb] •**solves, solved, solving.**

some (SUHM) *Some people like to swim. Would you like to drink some more water? There must be some treats left over from the party.* [adjective]

somebody (SUHM buh dee) *Somebody left the door open.* [pronoun]

someday (SUHM day) *Someday we will take a trip to Canada.* [adverb]

someone (SUHM wuhn) *Someone is knocking at the door. Ask someone to give you a ride.* [pronoun]

somersault (SUHM er sawlt) A *somersault* is a roll or jump where you turn your heels over your head: *She turned somersaults on the rug.* [noun] •**somersaults.**

something (SUHM thing) *Something* is a word you use when you do not know exactly what you are talking about: *Something happened to my bicycle. Are we doing something after school? I lost something on the bus.* [noun]

sometime (SUHM tym) *We'll visit you sometime next summer. [adverb]*

sometimes (SUHM tymz) *Sometimes my aunt takes me to the zoo. [adverb]*

somewhere (SUHM wair) *They are hiding somewhere. [adverb]*

son (SUHN) A *son* is a male child. A boy or man is the *son* of his mother and father. *[noun]* •**sons.**

song

song (SAWNG) A *song* is music with words: *She learned a new song today. [noun]* •**songs.**

Sonora (suh NOHR uh) *Sonora is a state in the northwest part of Mexico. [noun]*

soon (SOON) *Soon* means in a short time: *I'll see you soon. [adverb]* •**sooner, soonest.**

sore (SOR) If something is *sore,* it causes pain: *I have a sore finger. [adjective]* •**sorer, sorest.**

sorry (SO ree) Someone who is *sorry* feels sad about something: *He was sorry that he broke the lamp. [adjective]* •**sorrier, sorriest.**

sort (SORT)
1. Another word for *sort* is *kind: What sort of work do you do? I like this sort of house best. [noun]*
2. When you *sort* things, you arrange them in order: *Sort these socks by color. [verb]*
•**sorts.** •**sorts, sorted, sorting.**

sort

sound · South Dakota

sound (SOWND)

1. A *sound* is something you hear: *He heard the sound of a dog barking. What is the sound of the* a *in* hat? [noun]

2. To *sound* is to make a sound or have a sound: *The wind sounds like a whistle blowing. The word* eight *sounds like the word* ate. [verb]
   •**sounds.** •**sounds, sounded, sounding.**

soup (SOOP) *Soup* is a liquid food made by cooking meat, fish, grains, or vegetables in water or milk. [noun] •**soups.**

sour (SOWR) If something is *sour,* it tastes like lemon juice. Something that is *sour* is not sweet: *Green peaches are too sour to eat.* [adjective] •**sourer, sourest.**

sour

South America

south (SOWTH) *South* is the direction to the left as you face the setting sun. *South* is the opposite of north. [noun]

South America (SOWTH uh MAIR uh kuh) *South America* is a continent. *South America* is one of the large areas of land on the Earth. [noun]

South Carolina (SOWTH ka ruh LY nuh) *South Carolina* is one of the fifty states of the United States. [noun]

South Dakota (SOWTH duh KOH tuh) *South Dakota* is one of the fifty states of the United States. [noun]

Ss

southeast (sowth EEST) *Southeast* is the direction between south and east. *[noun]*

southwest (sowth WEST) *Southwest* is the direction between south and west. *[noun]*

space (SPAYSS)
1. *Space* is room for something to fit in: *There wasn't space in the closet for everyone's clothes.* [noun]
2. *Space* is also the area around the Earth. The sun and stars are in *outer space.* [noun]
 • **spaces** *for definition I .*

space

spacecraft (SPAYSS kraft) A *spacecraft* is something used to travel through space to other planets. Another word for *spacecraft* is *spaceship.* [noun] • The plural of *spacecraft* is *spacecraft.*

spaceship (SPAYSS ship) A *spaceship* is something used to travel through space to other planets. Another word for *spaceship* is *spacecraft.* [noun] • **spaceships.**

spaceship

spaghetti (spuh GET ee) *Spaghetti* is a food made of flour and water. *Spaghetti* is rolled into long, thin sticks or strings. *[noun]*

Spanish (SPAN ish) *Spanish* is a language spoken by many people. People speak *Spanish* in parts of the United States, Mexico, and in other countries. *[noun]*

spark (SPARK) A *spark* is a small bit of something that is on fire: *Sparks flew up from the fire in the fireplace.* [noun] • **sparks.**

speak (SPEEK) When you *speak,* you say words or talk: *She spoke to her friend in the hall before school started. He spoke to our class about swimming.* [verb]
 • **speaks, spoke, spoken, speaking.**

Ss

373

speaker · spend

speaker (SPEE ker) A *speaker* is something that makes music louder. *[noun]* •**speakers.**

special (SPESH uhl) If something is *special,* it is unusual or different in some way: *Your birthday is a special day.* *[adjective]*

sped (SPED) *She sped down the hill on her sled.* *[verb]*

speech (SPEECH) A *speech* is a talk to a group of people: *We heard the governor's speech yesterday on the radio.* *[noun]* •**speeches.**

speed (SPEED)
1. *Speed* is how fast something is going: *The speed of the boat made the ride exciting.* *[noun]*
2. To *speed* is to go fast: *His car was speeding as it went around the corner.* *[verb]*
•**speeds.** •**speeds, sped, speeding.**

speed

spell (SPEL) When you *spell,* you say or write the letters of a word in order: *I showed my little sister how to spell her name.* *[verb]* •**spells, spelled, spelling.**

spelling (SPEL ing) *Spelling* is writing or saying the letters of a word in order: *She is good at spelling, and she's even better at math.* *[noun]*

spend (SPEND) When you *spend* money or time, you use it: *We will spend a lot of money on our vacation. We are going to spend a week at the lake.* *[verb]*
•**spends, spent, spending.**

I can spell cat. c - a - t

spelling

spent (SPENT) *She spent quite a bit of money on school clothes.* [verb]

spice (SPYSS) A *spice* is a seasoning used to make food taste better. Pepper is a *spice.* [noun] •**spices.**

spicy (SPY see) If something is *spicy,* it tastes or smells like spices: *The fish tasted very spicy.* [adjective] •**spicier, spiciest.**

spider (SPY der) A *spider* is a very small animal with eight legs. *Spiders* have no wings and are not insects. Many *spiders* make webs and catch insects in them. [noun] •**spiders.**

spider

spike (SPYK) A *spike* is something that has a sharp point: *Baseball players wear spikes on their shoes. Some dinosaurs had spikes on their backs.* [noun] •**spikes.**

spill (SPIL) When you *spill* something, you let it fall out or run out: *Dad spilled the syrup. All the milk spilled when the glass fell over.* [verb] •**spills, spilled, spilling.**

spin (SPIN) When you *spin,* you turn or make something turn around quickly: *Can you spin a nickel on the table?* [verb] •**spins, spun, spinning.**

splash (SPLASH) When you *splash,* you make water or another liquid fly in the air: *The children splashed in the pool. The car splashed me when it went through a puddle.* [verb] •**splashes, splashed, splashing.**

spoil (SPOIL) When something *spoils,* it becomes bad or not good to eat: *The milk spoiled because we didn't put it in the refrigerator.* [verb] •**spoils, spoiled, spoiling.**

Ss

spoke · sprang

spoke (SPOHK) *I spoke to him yesterday.* [verb]

spoken (SPOH kuhn) *My dad has already spoken to me about cutting the grass.* [verb]

sponge (SPUHNJ)
1. A *sponge* is a kind of sea animal with many small holes in it. *Sponges* live on the ocean floor. [noun]
2. A *sponge* is also a piece of sponge or material like a sponge that is used to wash things: *We washed our car with a sponge.* [noun]
• **sponges.**

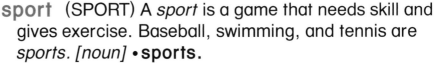

sponges

spoon (SPOON) A *spoon* is something people use to eat with. A *spoon* has a small, round bowl at the end of a handle. You can eat cereal with a *spoon.* [noun] • **spoons.**

sport (SPORT) A *sport* is a game that needs skill and gives exercise. Baseball, swimming, and tennis are *sports.* [noun] • **sports.**

sport

spot (SPOT)
1. A *spot* is a mark that you can see on the surface of something: *She has a spot of ink on her sleeve.* [noun]
2. A *spot* is also a place: *From this spot you can see the whole valley.* [noun]
• **spots.**

sprang (SPRANG) *He sprang out of bed when the phone rang.* [verb]

Ss

spray (SPRAY)

1. A *spray* is a liquid that flies through the air in small drops: *When the dog shook herself, we all got damp from the spray.* [noun]
2. To *spray* is to spread small drops of liquid on something: *He sprayed water on the plants.* [verb]
•**sprays.** •**sprays, sprayed, spraying.**

spread (SPRED)

1. To *spread* is to cover with a thin layer of something: *I like to spread peanut butter on a slice of bread.* [verb]
2. To *spread* is also to cover a large area with something: *Spread a blanket on the ground.* [verb]
•**spreads, spread, spreading.**

spring (SPRING)

1. *Spring* is the season of the year between winter and summer. *Spring* is the season when plants begin to grow. [noun]
2. To *spring* means to jump up from the ground suddenly: *I saw the deer spring over the wall.* [verb]
•**springs.** •**springs, sprang, sprung, springing.**

spring

sprout (SPROWT)

1. To *sprout* is to start growing: *The buds are sprouting on that raspberry bush.* [verb]

sprung • squawk

2. A *sprout* is a young plant or a new part of an old plant: *Sprouts were shooting up from the soil.* [noun]
•**sprouts, sprouted, sprouting.** •**sprouts.**

sprung (SPRUHNG) *The vegetables have sprung up in the garden.* [verb]

spun (SPUHN) *Her wheels spun on the wet street. Our car has spun completely around.* [verb]

spy (SPY)
1. A *spy* is a person who secretly watches what others are doing: *The spy tried to steal some secret papers.* [noun]
2. To *spy* is to watch secretly: *The other team spied on us to see if we had any secret ways to win the game.* [verb]
•**spies.** •**spies, spied, spying.**

square (SKWAIR)
1. A *square* is a shape with four sides, all of the same length: *The yard is almost a perfect square.* [noun]
2. Something that is *square* has a shape like a square: *I need a square piece of paper.* [adjective]
•**squares.**

squash[1] (SKWAWSH) If you *squash* something, you press it until it is flat: *Be careful not to squash this package.* [verb] •**squashes, squashed, squashing.**

squash[2] (SKWAWSH) A *squash* is a vegetable that grows on a vine. *Squash* have different shapes and colors. They are usually yellow, green, or white. [noun] •The plural of *squash* is *squash.*

squawk (SKWAWK) If something *squawks,* it makes a loud, annoying sound: *Hens and ducks squawk when frightened.* [verb] •**squawks, squawked, squawking.**

squash[2]

squeak (SKWEEK) To *squeak* is to make a short, high, loud sound: *This chair squeaks when you sit on it.* [verb] •**squeaks, squeaked, squeaking.**

squeal (SKWEEL) If something *squeals,* it makes a long, high noise: *A pig squeals when it is hurt.* [verb] •**squeals, squealed, squealing.**

squeeze (SKWEEZ) When you *squeeze* something, you push or press hard against it: *Will you squeeze the oranges to make juice? Squeeze these books onto the shelf.* [verb] •**squeezes, squeezed, squeezing.**

squeeze

squirrel (SKWERL) A *squirrel* is a small animal with a large, furry tail. *Squirrels* live in trees and eat nuts. [noun] •**squirrels.**

stable (STAY buhl) A *stable* is a building where horses or cattle are kept. [noun] •**stables.**

stage (STAYJ) A *stage* is the raised part of a theater where plays are given: *Several actors stood on the stage practicing their lines.* [noun] •**stages.**

stairs (STAIRZ) *Stairs* are a group of steps for going from one floor to another: *He went up the stairs.* [noun plural]

stalk (STAWK) A *stalk* is the tall stem of a plant. Corn grows on *stalks.* [noun] •**stalks.**

stalks

Ss

stamp · start

stamp (STAMP) A *stamp* is a small piece of paper with glue on the back. You put *stamps* on letters or packages before mailing them. *[noun]* •**stamps.**

stamp

stand (STAND)

1. To *stand* is to be on your feet instead of sitting or lying down: *He hates to stand in line. The umbrella always stands in the corner.* *[verb]*

2. If one thing *stands* for another, it means the same as that thing: *TV is an abbreviation that stands for television.* *[verb]*
•**stands, stood, standing.**

star (STAR)

1. A *star* is one of the very bright points of light that shines in the sky at night: *On a clear night the stars are very bright.* *[noun]*

2. A *star* is also a shape that has five or six points: *I drew a star on the paper.* *[noun]*

3. A *star* is also a very famous person: *She is a movie star.* *[noun]*
•**stars.**

stare (STAIR) If you *stare*, you look at someone with your eyes wide open for a long time: *It's rude to stare at someone.* *[verb]* •**stares, stared, staring.**

starfish (STAR fish) A *starfish* is a sea animal shaped like a star. *[noun]* •**starfish** *or* **starfishes.**

start (START) When you *start*, you begin to do something: *I started to read a book. Dad had trouble starting the car.* *[verb]* •**starts, started, starting.**

starfish

Ss

state (STAYT) A *state* is one of the parts of a country. There are fifty *states* in the United States. [noun]
• **states.**

station (STAY shuhn)
1. A *station* is a place used for a special reason or where you can get special kinds of work done. You buy gas at a gas *station.* You catch a bus at a bus *station.* [noun]
2. A *station* is also a place that sends out radio or television programs: *We receive a lot of TV stations in this city.* [noun]
• **stations.**

statues

statue (STACH oo) A *statue* is a figure made from stone, wood, or metal to look like a person or animal: *There are several statues in the park.* [noun] • **statues.**

stay (STAY) To *stay* is to be in a place for a while: *We stayed inside yesterday because it rained.* [verb]
• **stays, stayed, staying.**

steady (STED ee) When something is *steady,* it does not change very much: *Mom drove the car at a steady speed. Hold the rope steady.* [adjective] • **steadier, steadiest.**

steak (STAYK) A *steak* is a slice of meat, especially beef: *They had steak for dinner.* [noun] • **steaks.**

Ss

steal · step

steal (STEEL) To *steal* is to take something that does not belong to you: *Someone stole my bike during the night.* [verb] •**steals, stole, stolen, stealing.**

steam (STEEM) *Steam* is very hot water in the form of gas or a very fine spray. Boiling water creates *steam.* [noun]

steel (STEEL) *Steel* is a very strong metal that is made of iron mixed with other things that make it harder. *Steel* is used to make buildings, cars, tools, and many other things. [noun]

steel

steep (STEEP) If something is *steep,* it has a big slope or slant: *This hill is too steep to ride a bicycle down safely.* [adjective] •**steeper, steepest.**

steer (STEER) When you *steer* something, you make it go in the direction you want: *She steered her bike around the corner and down the street.* [verb] •**steers, steered, steering.**

stegosaurus (steg uh SAWR uhss) The *stegosaurus* was a very large dinosaur that had spikes along its back and tail. The *stegosaurus* ate plants. [noun] •**stegosauruses.**

stem (STEM) The *stem* is the main part of a plant above the ground. The trunk of a tree is a *stem.* Flowers and fruit have *stems.* [noun] •**stems.**

step (STEP)
1. A *step* is when you lift your foot and put it down in a new position: *He took a few steps across the room to the chair and sat down.* [noun]

stem

2. When you *step,* you move your legs as you do when you walk: *Please step to the front of the line.* *[verb]*

3. A *step* is also a place where you put your foot when you go up or down stairs: *She tripped just before she got to the top step.* *[noun]*
• **steps.** • **steps, stepped, stepping.**

stereo (STAIR ee oh) You use a *stereo* to listen to music or the sounds of a movie. A *stereo* can be used to play records, a radio program, or CDs. It usually has speakers. *[noun]* • **stereos.**

stick¹ (STIK)

1. A *stick* is a long, thin piece of wood: *We collected sticks to build a fire.* *[noun]*

2. A *stick* is also anything shaped like a stick: *He ate a stick of candy.* *[noun]*
• **sticks.**

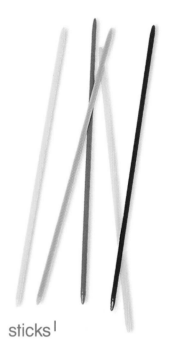

sticks¹

stick² (STIK)

1. To *stick* is to push something sharp into another thing: *Stick a fork into the potato to see if it is cooked enough.* *[verb]*

2. When you *stick* two things together, you make them stay together: *He stuck the pieces of paper together with glue.* *[verb]*
• **sticks, stuck, sticking.**

sticker (STIK er) A *sticker* is a label that has glue on the back of it. A *sticker* can be glued onto something else. *[noun]* • **stickers.**

stickers

sticky (STIK ee) If something is *sticky,* it sticks very well to something else. Tape and glue are very *sticky.* *[adjective]* • **stickier, stickiest.**

stiff · stood

stiff (STIF) When something is *stiff,* it is hard to bend or move: *New boots are always stiff. He felt stiff after the long walk.* [adjective] • **stiffer, stiffest.**

still (STIL)

1. When something is *still,* it is not moving or is not loud: *Please keep still while I am on the telephone.* [adjective]

2. *Still* also means up to now: *Is the library still open?* [adverb]

sting (STING)

1. A *sting* is a sharp pain. A *sting* is made by a bee. [noun]

2. To *sting* is to hurt with something sharp. Bees and wasps can *sting* you. [verb]
   • **stings.** • **stings, stung, stinging.**

stink bug (STINGK buhg) A *stink bug* is a kind of insect that has a wide flat body. *Stink bugs* give off a bad smell. • **stink bugs.**

stir (STER) When you *stir* something, you move it around with a spoon: *He stirred the soup to keep it from burning.* [verb] • **stirs, stirred, stirring.**

stink bug

stole (STOHL) *Someone stole my bike last week.* [verb]

stolen (STOH luhn) *Someone has stolen my bike.* [verb]

stomach (STUHM uhk) Your *stomach* is the part of your body where the food you swallow goes. [noun] • **stomachs.**

stone (STOHN) A *stone* is a small piece of rock: *We threw stones into the lake.* [noun] • **stones.**

stood (STUD) *We stood in line for an hour.* [verb]

Ss

stop (STOP)

1. When you *stop* something, you do not do it anymore: *We wished the dog would stop barking.* [verb]
2. To *stop* also means to make something stop: *You must stop your car if the traffic light is red.* [verb]

stop

3. A *stop* is a place where something stops: *She waited an hour at the bus stop.* [noun]

•**stops, stopped, stopping.** •**stops.**

store (STOR)

1. A *store* is a place to buy things: *They went to the store to buy some food.* [noun]
2. When you *store* something, you put it away to use it later: *We store a lot of winter clothes in the attic.* [verb]

•**stores.** •**stores, stored, storing.**

storm (STORM)
A *storm* is a strong wind with rain, snow, or hail. Some *storms* have lightning and thunder. [noun] •**storms.**

story (STOR ee)
A *story* tells about people and places and what happens to them. *Stories* can be true or make-believe, and they can be written or spoken: *I like adventure stories.* [noun] •**stories.**

stove (STOHV)
A *stove* is something you use to cook food. [noun] •**stoves.**

straight (STRAYT)
If something is *straight,* it does not have a bend, turn, or curve: *She drew a straight line. Try to stand up straight. Go straight to the corner and then turn left.* [adjective or adverb] •**straighter, straightest.**

Can you stand up straight?

straight

Ss

straighten · street sweeper

straighten (STRAYT uhn) If you *straighten* something, you make it straight: *He straightened the bent nail.* [verb] •**straightens, straightened, straightening.**

strange (STRAYNJ)
1. If something is *strange,* it is hard to explain or understand: *Last night I thought I heard a strange noise in the other room.* [adjective]
2. When something is *strange,* you did not know, see, or hear it before: *When I came home, a strange dog was sitting on our lawn.* [adjective]
•**stranger, strangest.**

stranger (STRAYN jer) A *stranger* is a person you have not known, seen, or heard of before: *After meeting some other kids, she didn't feel so much like a stranger.* [noun] •**strangers.**

strap (STRAP) A *strap* is a narrow strip of leather, cloth, or other material: *We used a strap to hold the skis on the roof of the car.* [noun] •**straps.**

straw (STRAW) A *straw* is a hollow tube you drink liquids through: *We drank our milk with straws.* [noun] •**straws.**

strawberry (STRAW bair ee) A *strawberry* is a red berry. *Strawberries* grow near the ground on small plants. [noun] •**strawberries.**

strawberry

stream (STREEM) A *stream* is a narrow flow of water: *We fish in the stream.* [noun] •**streams.**

street (STREET) A *street* is a road in a city or town. A *street* usually has homes or buildings along it. [noun] •**streets.**

street sweeper (STREET sweep er) A *street sweeper* is a person or machine that cleans the streets. •**street sweepers.**

Ss

stretch (STRECH) When you *stretch* something, you make it as long as it can be: *The cat yawned and stretched its legs.* [verb] •**stretches, stretched, stretching.**

string (STRING) A *string* is a very thin cord made of twisted threads: *Please tie the package with string.* [noun] •**strings.**

string bean (STRING BEEN) A *string bean* is a kind of bean. A *string bean* is long, either green or yellow, and has flat seeds. •**string beans.**

strip (STRIP) A *strip* is a long, narrow, flat piece of cloth or paper: *We tied strips of ribbon to the chairs.* [noun] •**strips.**

stripe (STRYP) A *stripe* is a long, narrow band of color: *Our flag has seven red stripes and six white stripes. Tigers have black stripes.* [noun] •**stripes.**

striped (STRYPT) When something is *striped*, it has stripes: *Dad likes striped shirts.* [adjective]

string

striped

stroll (STROHL) When you *stroll*, you take a quiet walk: *We strolled through the park after dinner.* [verb] •**strolls, strolled, strolling.**

Ss

stroller • submarine

student

stroller (STROH ler) A *stroller* is a kind of light cart in which a small child can ride. *[noun]* •**strollers.**

strong (STRAWNG) Something that is *strong* has power. A *strong* person can lift and carry things that are heavy. *Strong* means not weak: *A strong wind blew down the tree. [adjective]* •**stronger, strongest.**

struggle (STRUHG uhl) To *struggle* is to work very hard when you are facing something very difficult: *She struggled with the stuck zipper but could not open it. [verb]* •**struggles, struggled, struggling.**

stuck (STUHK) *By accident, she stuck her finger with a pin. [verb]*

student (STOOD uhnt) A *student* is someone who studies or who goes to school: *Many students at our school ride the bus. [noun]* •**students.**

study (STUHD ee) When you *study,* you try to learn by reading and thinking: *She studied math and science all afternoon. [verb]* •**studies, studied, studying.**

stuff (STUHF) *Stuff* is things you need to do something with: *Please get all your winter clothes and stuff out of the closet. [noun]*

stung (STUHNG) *The burn stung for a little while. I have been stung by a bee. [verb]*

stupid (STOO pid) A person who is *stupid* does not have a good mind or is often careless: *He made a stupid mistake, writing a 5 for a 2. [adjective]* •**stupider, stupidest.**

submarine (SUHB muh reen) A *submarine* is a ship that can go underwater. *[noun]* •**submarines.**

submarines

Ss

subtract (suhb TRAKT) When you *subtract,* you take a number away from another number: *Subtract 3 from 12 and the answer is 9.* [verb] •**subtracts, subtracted, subtracting.**

subtraction (suhb TRAK shuhn) *Subtraction* is the act of taking a number away from another number. The *subtraction* of 7 from 10 leaves a difference of 3. [noun]

$$10 - 7 = 3$$
$$6 - 4 = 2$$

subtraction

subway (SUHB way) A *subway* is an underground electric railroad. *Subways* run beneath the surface of the streets in a city. [noun] •**subways.**

success (suhk SESS) *Success* is the result that you hoped for: *The play was a great success.* [noun] •**successes.**

such (SUHCH) *Mom had such a bad cold that she stayed in bed. The cafeteria has such drinks as milk and orange juice.* [adjective]

sudden (SUHD uhn) If something is *sudden,* it happens very fast: *The sudden rain at the picnic got us all wet. If you make any sudden moves, the bird will fly away.* [adjective]

suddenly (SUHD uhn lee) *Suddenly* means very quickly: *I suddenly remembered that the door was open.* [adverb]

suds (SUHDZ) *Suds* are the bubbles that soap and water can make. [noun plural]

suffer (SUHF er) To *suffer* is to feel pain or sad feelings: *They suffered when they heard about the fire at their neighbor's house.* [verb] •**suffers, suffered, suffering.**

sugar (SHUG er) *Sugar* is something sweet to put in food and drinks: *This lemonade needs more sugar.* [noun]

Ss

suit • sunglasses

suitcase

suit (SOOT) A *suit* is a set of clothes that goes together. A man's *suit* has a jacket and pants. A woman's *suit* has a jacket and pants or a skirt. *[noun]* •**suits.**

suitcase (SOOT kayss) A *suitcase* is a flat box with a handle you use to carry clothes in when you travel: *We needed three suitcases for our trip last month.* *[noun]* •**suitcases.**

sum (SUHM)

1. A *sum* is an amount. People usually use the word *sum* for amounts of money: *She saved the sum of ten dollars last month.* *[noun]*
2. A *sum* is also a number of things added together: *The sum of 7 and 12 and 2 is 21.* *[noun]*
•**sums.**

summer (SUHM er) *Summer* is the season of the year between spring and fall. *Summer* is the warmest season of the year. *[noun]* •**summers.**

sun (SUHN) The *sun* is a hot ball of gases in the sky. It is a very great distance from the Earth. The *sun* gives us heat and light. The Earth goes around the *sun.* *[noun]* •**suns.**

Sunday (SUHN day) *Sunday* is the day before Monday. *Sunday* is the first day of the week. *[noun]* •**Sundays.**

sunflower (SUHN flow er) A *sunflower* is a large yellow flower. A *sunflower* grows on a very tall stem. *[noun]* •**sunflowers.**

sung (SUHNG) *She has sung three songs already this morning.* *[verb]*

sunglasses (SUHN glass iz) *Sunglasses* are dark glasses used to protect the eyes from the light of the

Ss

sun. *Sunglasses* are made of colored glass or plastic. *[noun plural]*

sunk (SUHNGK) *Many ships have sunk because of the storm. [verb]*

sunlight (SUHN lyt) *Sunlight is the light from the sun: Sunlight helps plants to grow. [noun]*

sunny (SUHN ee) *Sunny* means to have bright sunshine: *We enjoyed the sunny day. [adjective]* •**sunnier, sunniest.**

sunrise (SUHN ryz) *Sunrise is the time when the sun first appears in the morning. [noun]* •**sunrises.**

sunscreen (SUHN skreen) *Sunscreen* is something you put on your skin to keep it from being burned by the sun. *[noun]* •**sunscreens.**

sunscreen

sunset (SUHN set) *Sunset is the time when the sun is last seen in the evening. [noun]* •**sunsets.**

sunshine (SUHN shyn) *Sunshine is the light of the sun: After the rain, he went out into the sunshine. [noun]*

supermarket (SOO per mar kit) A *supermarket* is a large grocery store. You pick up what you want and pay on the way out. *[noun]* •**supermarkets.**

supper (SUHP er) *Supper* is a meal eaten in the evening: *We had spaghetti last night for supper. [noun]* •**suppers.**

supermarket

suppose (suh POHZ)
1. To *suppose* is to imagine that something is true: *Suppose the bus doesn't come. [verb]*
2. If you are *supposed* to do something, you have to do it: *I'm supposed to call my parents if I'm going to be late. [verb]*

•**supposes, supposed, supposing.**

sure · sweater

Ss

swamps

sure (SHER) If you are *sure,* you feel no doubt about something: *Are you sure you locked the front door?* *[adjective]* •**surer, surest.**

surface (SER fiss) A *surface* is the top part or outside of something: *The surface of the road was very wet and dangerous after the rain. A marble has a smooth, hard surface. [noun]* •**surfaces.**

surprise (ser PRYZ)

1. A *surprise* is something that happens that you did not plan: *The news about Mom's new job was a nice surprise. [noun]*

2. When you *surprise* people, you do not tell them what is going to happen: *My parents surprised me with a bike for my birthday. [verb]*
•**surprises.** •**surprises, surprised, surprising.**

surround (suh ROWND) To *surround* is to shut something in on all sides: *A fence surrounds our school playground. [verb]* •**surrounds, surrounded, surrounding.**

swallow (SWAH loh) When you *swallow,* you make something go from your mouth down your throat to your stomach: *Sometimes it's hard to swallow peanut butter. [verb]* •**swallows, swallowed, swallowing.**

swam (SWAM) *Most of us swam across the pool. [verb]*

swamp (SWAWMP) A *swamp* is land that is almost completely covered with water: *In the swamp, we saw alligators and snakes. [noun]* •**swamps.**

swan (SWAWN) A *swan* is a large white bird with a long, thin neck. *Swans* live on lakes and rivers. *[noun]* •**swans.**

sweater (SWET er) A *sweater* is a knitted piece of clothing that keeps you warm. A *sweater* is often worn over a shirt. *[noun]* • **sweaters.**

sweatshirt (SWET shert) A *sweatshirt* is a heavy shirt with long sleeves. People often wear *sweatshirts* to keep warm when they exercise. *[noun]* •**sweatshirts.**

sweep (SWEEP) When you *sweep,* you clean a floor with a broom or brush: *I need to sweep my room today.* *[verb]* •**sweeps, swept, sweeping.**

sweet (SWEET) When something is *sweet,* it tastes like sugar or honey: *These ripe grapes are very sweet.* *[adjective]* •**sweeter, sweetest.**

sweet potato (SWEET puh TAY toh) A *sweet potato* is a sweet, thick, yellow vegetable. *Sweet potatoes* grow on vines. •**sweet potatoes.**

swell (SWEL) To *swell* is to grow bigger in size: *My finger swelled up from the bee sting.* *[verb]* •**swells, swelled, swollen, swelling.**

swept (SWEPT) *He swept the dust off the stairs.* *[verb]*

swift (SWIFT) *Swift* means able to move very fast: *A deer is a swift animal.* *[adjective]* •**swifter, swiftest.**

swim (SWIM)
1. When you *swim,* you move in the water. People use their arms and legs to *swim.* Fish use their fins to *swim.* *[verb]*
2. A *swim* is a time when you swim: *Let's go for a swim this afternoon.* *[noun]*
•**swims, swam, swum, swimming.** •**swims.**

swimmer (SWIM er) A *swimmer* is a person or an animal that swims: *The swimmer rested by the side of the pool.* *[noun]* •**swimmers.**

swimsuit (SWIM soot) Another word for *swimsuit* is *bathing suit.* *[noun]* •**swimsuits.**

This is my favorite sweatshirt.

sweatshirt

Ss

393

swing • syrup

swing

swing (SWING)
1. To *swing* is to move backward and forward: *The kids were swinging from a branch of the tree.* [verb]
2. A *swing* is a seat on which you can move backward and forward: *She pushed me on the swing.* [noun]
• **swings, swung, swinging.** • **swings.**

switch (SWICH) A *switch* is a button that you can turn electricity on and off with: *The light switch is on the wall.* [noun] • **switches.**

swollen (SWOH luhn) *My arm was swollen and sore.* [adjective]

sword (SORD) A *sword* is a long, sharp weapon with a handle. A *sword* is made of metal. [noun] • **swords.**

swum (SWUHM) *We have swum every day.* [verb]

swung (SWUHNG) *I swung the bat and hit the ball.* [verb]

syllable (SIL uh buhl) A *syllable* is a word or part of a word. A word is made up of one or more *syllables*. The word *syllable* has three *syllables* in it. [noun] • **syllables.**

symbol (SIM buhl) A *symbol* is something that stands for something else: *The eagle is a symbol of the United States.* [noun] • **symbols.**

synagogue (SIN uh gog) A *synagogue* is a building where some people go to worship. [noun] • **synagogues.**

synonym (SIN uh nim) A *synonym* is a word that means almost the same thing as another word. *Car* is a *synonym* of *automobile.* [noun] • **synonyms.**

syrup

syrup (SI ruhp *or* SER uhp) *Syrup* is a sweet, thick liquid. Sugar boiled with water or fruit juice makes *syrup*. Maple *syrup* comes from maple trees. [noun] • **syrups.**

Ss

Tabasco (tah BAHS koh *or* tuh BAS koh) *Tabasco* is a state in the southeast part of Mexico. *[noun]*

table (TAY buhl) A *table* is a piece of furniture with a flat top on legs: *We ate supper sitting around the kitchen table. [noun]* •**tables.**

taco (TAH koh) A *taco* is a thin corn pancake filled with chopped meat or chicken, cheese, and other things. *[noun]* •**tacos.**

tadpole (TAD pohl) A *tadpole* is a very young frog or toad. It has a tail and lives in the water. *[noun]* •**tadpoles.**

tag¹ (TAG) A *tag* is a small card that is put on something: *There is a price tag on every dress. [noun]* •**tags.**

tag² (TAG) *Tag* is a game where one player, who is "it," tries to catch and touch the other players. *[noun]*

taco

Tt

tail · tall

tail (TAYL) The *tail* is the part of an animal's body farthest from its head: *A lion has a long tail.* [noun] •**tails.**

tail

tailor (TAY ler) A *tailor* is someone who makes or repairs clothes. [noun] •**tailors.**

take (TAYK)

1. When you *take* something, you hold it. When you *take* something, you may also carry it to another place: *Take my hand before we cross the street. I think you should take your gloves to school.* [verb]

2. *Take* can also mean to get what someone gives you: *I'll take that old baseball glove if you don't want it.* [verb]

3. *Take* also means to use: *I take a bus to get to school.* [verb]

4. To *take* a picture is to make one with a camera: *She took a picture of me.* [verb]
•**takes, took, taken, taking.**

taken (TAY kuhn) *He has always taken the bus.* [verb]

tale (TAYL) A *tale* is a story that is told or read over and over: *Let's read a fairy tale.* [noun] •**tales.**

talented (TAL uhn tid) If you are *talented*, you are born with a special gift for doing something very well: *She is a talented musician.* [adjective]

talk (TAWK) When you *talk*, you use words or you speak: *She likes to talk to her friends at lunch. We talked about a lot of things.* [verb] •**talks, talked, talking.**

tall

tall (TAWL) Something that is *tall* reaches a long way from top to bottom. Something that is *tall* is not short: *That building is very tall.* [adjective] •**taller, tallest.**

Tamaulipas (tah mow LEE pahss) *Tamaulipas* is a state in the north part of Mexico. *[noun]*

tambourine (tam buh REEN) A *tambourine* is an instrument that looks like a small drum with pairs of metal disks around its edge. You play a *tambourine* by hitting it or shaking it. *[noun]* •**tambourines.**

tame (TAYM) When something is *tame,* it is no longer wild: *My cousin in the country has a tame raccoon.* *[adjective]* •**tamer, tamest.**

tape (TAYP)

1. *Tape* is a thin strip of sticky material used to put things together: *He fixed the torn pages with tape.* *[noun]*

2. To *tape* means to make a sound or video recording on a special kind of plastic tape: *The teacher taped our class play.* *[verb]*

3. A *tape* can also be a kind of tape that has been used to record something: *The class watched tapes of the program.* *[noun]*
•**tapes, taped, taping.** •**tapes** *for definition 3.*

tape recorder (TAYP ri KOR der) A *tape recorder* is a machine that records sound on plastic tape and plays the sound back. •**tape recorders.**

taste (TAYST)

1. *Taste* is the flavor something has when you put it in your mouth: *The taste of sugar is sweet.* *[noun]*

2. When you *taste* something, you find out if something is sweet, sour, salty, or bitter by putting it in your mouth. You *taste* things with your tongue. *[verb]*

3. *Taste* is also the power to take in the flavors that things have. *Taste* is one of the five senses, along with hearing, sight, smell, and touch. *[noun]*
•**tastes** *for definition 1.* •**tastes, tasted, tasting.**

tambourine

This lemon tastes sour.

taste

Tt

tasty · tease

tasty (TAY stee) Something that is *tasty* has a good taste. *[adjective]* •**tastier, tastiest.**

taught (TAWT) *He taught me how to play basketball. [verb]*

taxi (TAK see) *Taxi* is a shorter form of *taxicab*. *[noun]* •**taxis.**

taxicab (TAK see kab) A *taxicab* is a car with a driver that you pay to take you somewhere. *[noun]* •**taxicabs.**

taxicab

tea (TEE) *Tea* is a drink made from special leaves. *[noun]* •**teas.**

teach (TEECH) When you *teach* people, you help them learn: *He teaches people how to play the piano. [verb]* •**teaches, taught, teaching.**

teacher (TEE cher) A *teacher* is a person who helps people learn. *[noun]* •**teachers.**

team (TEEM) A *team* is a group of people working or playing together: *My sister is on the basketball team. [noun]* •**teams.**

tear[1] (TEER) A *tear* is a drop of salty water that comes from your eye. *Tears* fall when you cry. *[noun]* •**tears.**

tear[2] (TAIR) If you *tear* something, you pull it into pieces or pull it apart: *Please don't tear the page out of the book. [verb]* •**tears, tore, torn, tearing.**

tease (TEEZ) If you *tease* people, you annoy or upset them with jokes, questions, or noises: *The children teased the dog until it barked at them. [verb]* •**teases, teased, teasing.**

teacher

teddy bear (TED ee BAIR)
A *teddy bear* is a soft toy bear.
•**teddy bears.**

teddy bear

teeth (TEETH) *Teeth* is the
plural of the word *tooth.*
[*noun plural*]

telephone (TEL uh fohn) A *telephone* is something
you use to talk to people far away: *Please answer the
telephone if it rings.* [*noun*] •**telephones.**

telescope (TEL uh skohp) A *telescope* is something
you look through to make things far away seem nearer
and larger: *We looked at the moon through a
telescope.* [*noun*] •**telescopes.**

television (TEL uh vizh uhn) A *television* is a machine
that brings sounds and pictures from far away. [*noun*]
•**televisions.**

tell (TEL)

1. When you *tell* something, you put it into words or
   say it: *Please tell us a story.* [*verb*]
2. To *tell* is also to know who someone is or recognize
   someone: *Can you tell who that is over there?*
   [*verb*]
•**tells, told, telling.**

temperature

temperature (TEM per uh cher) The *temperature*
is how hot or cold something is: *If her temperature
is 101, that means she is very sick. The temperature
outside today is almost ninety.* [*noun*] •**temperatures.**

ten (TEN) *Ten* is one more than nine. It is also written
10. [*noun* or *adjective*] •**tens.**

tender (TEN der) Something that is *tender* is soft:
Cooking the meat made it tender and easy to chew.
[*adjective*] •**tenderer, tenderest.**

Tt

Tennessee · test

Tennessee (ten uh SEE) *Tennessee* is one of the fifty states of the United States. *[noun]*

tennis (TEN iss) *Tennis* is a game played on a special court. Two or four players hit a ball from one side to the other across a net. *[noun]*

tennis

tent (TENT) A *tent* is a large piece of cloth held up by ropes and poles. A *tent* covers you when you camp outside: *He slept in a tent under the trees. [noun]* •**tents.**

tentacle (TEN tuh kuhl) A *tentacle* is the long, thin arm of an octopus or a jellyfish: *Jellyfish have many stinging tentacles. [noun]* •**tentacles.**

tenth (TENTH) *Tenth* is the next after the ninth. It is also written 10th. *[adjective]*

tepee (TEE pee) A *tepee* was a tent used by North American Indians. *[noun]* •**tepees.**

terrarium (tuh RAIR ee uhm) A *terrarium* is a glass container that you can keep plants or small land animals in. *[noun]* •**terrariums.**

terrible (TAIR uh buhl) Something that is *terrible* is awful or causes fear: *The terrible storm flooded our house. [adjective]*

territory (TAIR uh tor ee) A *territory* is one of the parts of a country. There are three *territories* in Canada. *[noun]* •**territories.**

test (TEST) A *test* is a way to find out what you know or what you can do. *Tests* have questions that you answer: *We had a math test today. [noun]* •**tests.**

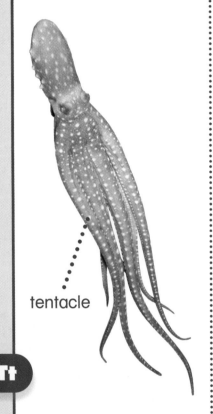
tentacle

Tt

Texas (TEK suhs) *Texas is one of the fifty states of the United States.* [noun]

than (THAN) *Your house is bigger than ours. My sister sings better than I do.* [conjunction]

Texas

thank (THANGK) You *thank* someone for something they give you or do for you. You say "Thank you" when you are pleased about something: *We thanked her for the ride.* [verb] •**thanks, thanked, thanking.**

Thanksgiving (thangks GIV ing) *Thanksgiving* is a holiday in November. [noun] •**Thanksgivings.**

that (THAT) *Should we take this ball or that one? That is my book. I know that we can have a picnic today.* [adjective or pronoun or conjunction]

that's *That's* is a shorter form of *that is: That's the one I would like to have.* [contraction]

the (thuh or THEE) *What is the name of your street? The house we live in is white.*

theater (THEE uh ter) A *theater* is a place where people go to see movies or plays: *We saw the movie at the new theater.* [noun] •**theaters.**

their (THAIR) *They raised their hands in class. They like their new friends.* [adjective]

theirs (THAIRZ) *Our car is black and theirs is white. Theirs is the red house down the street.* [pronoun]

that's

That's a funny story.

401

them · they're

thermometers

them (THEM) *Call the kids next door and ask them to play with us. The kittens were very young, so we had to be careful playing with them.* [pronoun]

themselves (them SELVZ) *They recognized themselves in the old photos. The kids themselves asked for a new coach.* [pronoun]

then (THEN) *The noise stopped and then began again. If he broke the dish, then he should clean it up.* [adverb]

there (THAIR) *There are 12 houses on our block. Is there a park near here?* [adverb]

there's *There's is a shorter form of there is: There's room for one more.* [contraction]

thermometer (ther MOM uh ter) *A thermometer is something you use to measure how hot or cold something or someone is: Let's check the thermometer to see how hot it is outside.* [noun] •**thermometers.**

thermos (THER muhss) *A thermos is a bottle or container that keeps hot foods hot and cold foods cold.* [noun] •**thermoses.**

these (THEEZ) *I've read all these books. These are his books, and those are mine.* [adjective or pronoun]

thermos

they (THAY) *They are both my friends.* [pronoun]

they're *They're is a shorter form of they are: They're going to the circus with us.* [contraction]

thick (THIK)

1. When something is *thick,* it is big from one side to the other. Something that is *thick* is not thin: *Dad got thick slices of ham for our sandwiches. This book is about an inch thick.* [adjective]

2. If something is *thick,* it is like glue. It does not flow easily: *The thick syrup was too cold to pour.* [adjective]
•**thicker, thickest.**

thigh (THY) Your *thigh* is the part of your leg between your hip and your knee. [noun] •**thighs.**

thin (THIN)

1. When something is *thin,* it is not big from one side to the other. Something that is *thin* is not thick: *A sheet of paper is very thin.* [adjective]

2. *Thin* also means not weighing very much. Someone or something that is *thin* is not fat: *He is thin.* [adjective]

3. Something that is *thin* is like water. *Thin* liquids flow easily: *The cocoa was too thin, and we didn't like it.* [adjective]
•**thinner, thinnest.**

thick and thin

thing (THING) *That was a smart thing to do. Please put these things away.* [noun] •**things.**

think (THINGK)

1. When you *think,* you use your mind or have ideas: *She will think about it before answering you.* [verb]

2. To *think* also means to believe something without knowing it: *I think it will rain.* [verb]
•**thinks, thought, thinking.**

third (THERD)

1. *Third* is the next after the second. It is also written 3rd: *They answered on the third ring.* [adjective]

thirsty · thousand

2. A *third* is one of 3 equal parts: *We gave them a third of the cake.* [*noun*]
•**thirds.**

thirsty (THER stee) If you are *thirsty,* you need a drink: *All that playing made me thirsty.* [*adjective*]
•**thirstier, thirstiest.**

thirsty

thirteen (ther TEEN) *Thirteen* is three more than ten. It is also written 13. [*noun* or *adjective*]

thirteenth (ther TEENTH) *Thirteenth* is the next after the twelfth. It is also written 13th. [*adjective*]

thirty (THER tee) *Thirty* is ten more than twenty. It is also written 30. [*noun* or *adjective*] •**thirties.**

this (THISS) *This coat is mine, and that one is hers. This is my sister.* [*adjective* or *pronoun*]

those (THOHZ) *Those books are yours, and these are mine. Those are my books.* [*adjective* or *pronoun*]

though (THOH) *Though it looked like rain, we went on our walk anyway.* [*conjunction*]

thought

thought (THAWT)

1. A *thought* is something that a person thinks. A *thought* is an idea: *She had a sudden thought about what to give her brother.* [*noun*]
2. *We thought it would snow today. He suddenly thought of the right answer.* [*verb*]
•**thoughts.**

thousand (THOW zuhnd) A *thousand* is ten times one hundred. It is also written 1000. [*noun* or *adjective*]
•**thousands.**

Tt

thread (THRED) *Thread* is very thin string that is used for sewing: *He used white thread to sew on the button.* [*noun*] •**threads.**

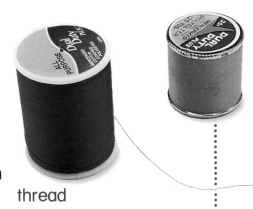

thread

three (THREE) *Three* is one more than two. It is also written 3. [*noun* or *adjective*]

threw (THROO) *She threw the ball back to him.* [*verb*]

throat (THROHT) Your *throat* is the part of your body that carries air to your lungs and food to your stomach. Your *throat* is the front part of your neck. [*noun*] •**throats.**

through (THROO) *The kitten ran through the house. We learned a new song all the way through. She won the prize through hard work.* [*preposition* or *adverb*]

throw (THROH) When you *throw* something, you send it through the air: *Let's throw the ball around for practice.* [*verb*] •**throws, threw, thrown, throwing.**

thrown (THROHN) *She has thrown the ball so much her arm is sore.* [*verb*]

thumb (THUHM)

1. Your *thumb* is the short, thick finger on each of your hands: *He hurt his thumb.* [*noun*]
2. The *thumb* is also a part of a glove or mitten that covers your thumb: *There was a hole in the thumb of her mitten.* [*noun*]
•**thumbs.**

thumb

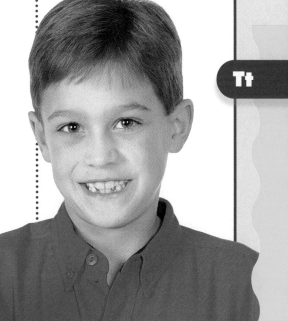

thunder (THUHN der) *Thunder* is the loud noise from the sky that comes after a flash of lightning. [*noun*]

Thursday • tiger

Thursday (THERZ day) *Thursday* is the day after Wednesday. It is the fifth day of the week. *[noun]* •**Thursdays.**

tick (TIK) A *tick* is a short, clicking sound made by a clock or watch: *We heard the tick of the clock from the hall. [noun]* •**ticks.**

ticket (TIK it) A *ticket* is a card or piece of paper that gives you the right to do something or to go somewhere: *We bought our tickets to the movie. [noun]* •**tickets.**

tickle

tickle (TIK uhl) When you *tickle* people, you touch them in a way that makes them laugh: *Mom tickled my arm. [verb]* •**tickles, tickled, tickling.**

tidy (TY dee) When something is *tidy,* it is neat and in order: *Her room is tidy. [adjective]* •**tidier, tidiest.**

tie (TY)
1. To *tie* is to hold something together by putting string or rope around it: *She tied this package very well. [verb]*
2. To *tie* also means to pull strings into a knot to hold things together: *He tied his shoes. [verb]*
3. A *tie* is a narrow strip of cloth worn around the neck. A *tie* is worn under the collar of a shirt, tied in front: *Dad likes his new tie. [noun]*
•**ties, tied, tying.** •**ties.**

tiger (TY ger) A *tiger* is a large animal like a cat that has yellow fur with black stripes. *[noun]* •**tigers.**

tiger

tight (TYT)

1. When something is *tight,* it is put together in a strong way. Something that is *tight* is not loose: *He tied a tight knot in the rope.* [adjective]

2. If something is *tight,* it fits closely or too closely: *His jacket is too tight.* [adjective]
•**tighter, tightest.**

till (TIL) *The children played outside till nine o'clock.* [preposition *or* conjunction]

time (TYM) *Time is all the days and hours there have been or ever will be. Time is always going by. Seconds, minutes, hours, days, months, and years are ways we measure time: Look at the clock, and tell me what time it is.* [noun]

times (TYMZ) *Times means multiplied by: 3 times 2 is 6.* [preposition]

tin (TIN) *Tin is a soft metal. Tin is mixed with other metals to make cans and other things.* [noun]

tiny (TY nee) *Tiny means very small: The new kitten was so tiny that he fit in the palm of my hand.* [adjective] •**tinier, tiniest.**

tiptoe (TIP toh) When you *tiptoe,* you walk on your toes in a quiet way: *She tiptoed along the hall.* [verb] •**tiptoes, tiptoed, tiptoeing.**

tire (TYR) A *tire* is the rubber part of a wheel: *Dad had to change a tire on the car.* [noun] •**tires.**

tired (TY erd) When you are *tired,* you feel worn out and ready to rest: *The long walk made me tired.* [adjective]

tissue (TISH oo) *Tissue is a thin, soft paper: Wipe your eyes with this tissue.* [noun] •**tissues.**

tiny

tired

I am really tired.

Tt

407

Tlaxcala · tomato

toaster

toast

Tlaxcala (tlah SKAH lah) *Tlaxcala* is a state in the central part of Mexico. [*noun*]

to (TOO *or* TUH) *Are you going to the park after school? You can tape the sign to the wall. She likes to read. The score of the game was six to five.* [*preposition*]

toad (TOHD) A *toad* is a small animal that looks like a frog. *Toads* usually live on land. [*noun*] •**toads.**

toast (TOHST) *Toast* is slices of bread made crisp and brown by heat: *Would you like some toast?* [*noun*]

toaster (TOH ster) A *toaster* is a machine that makes bread into toast. [*noun*] •**toasters.**

today (tuh DAY) *Today* is this day: *Today is my uncle's birthday. Are you going swimming today?* [*noun* or *adverb*]

toe (TOH) Your *toe* is one of the five end parts of your foot: *He hurt his big toe when he hit it on the chair leg.* [*noun*] •**toes.**

together (tuh GETH er) *We all drove together to the lake. Mix the sugar and butter together.* [*adverb*]

toilet (TOI lit) A *toilet* is a bowl with a seat used to take away waste. [*noun*] •**toilets.**

told (TOHLD) *She told me about the play. Has she told you about it?* [*verb*]

tomato (tuh MAY toh) A *tomato* is a round, red fruit. *Tomatoes* are eaten as vegetables. [*noun*] •**tomatoes.**

tomato

tomorrow (tuh MOR oh) *Tomorrow* is the day after today: *Tomorrow is supposed to be rainy. We'll get together tomorrow.* [*noun* or *adverb*]

tongue (TUNG) Your *tongue* is the part inside your mouth that moves. [*noun*] •**tongues.**

tonight (tuh NYT) *Tonight* is this night. *Tonight* is the night that follows today: *Tonight I'm getting my homework done early.* [*adverb*]

too (TOO) *After walking all day, the visitors were hungry and tired too. You gave me too much food.* [*adverb*]

took (TUK) *Who took my book? She took the bus to school.* [*verb*]

tool (TOOL) A *tool* is something that helps you do work. Saws and rakes are *tools.* [*noun*] •**tools.**

tooth (TOOTH) Your *tooth* is one of the hard, white parts in your mouth. You bite and chew food with your *teeth.* [*noun*] •**teeth.**

toothbrush (TOOTH bruhsh) A *toothbrush* is a small brush you use to clean your teeth. [*noun*] •**toothbrushes.**

toothpaste (TOOTH payst) *Toothpaste* is a very thick liquid like paste. You use *toothpaste* to clean your teeth. [*noun*]

top¹ (TOP)

1. The *top* is the highest part of anything: *We climbed to the top of the mountain.* [*noun*]

2. The *top* is also the cover of something: *Where is the top to this jar?* [*noun*]
•**tops.**

tool

top² · town

top² (TOP) A *top* is a toy that spins: *The kids played with the top.* [noun] •**tops.**

tore (TOR) *He tore his jeans when he fell off his bicycle.* [verb]

torn (TORN) *The high winds have torn off part of the garage roof.* [verb]

tornado (tor NAY doh) A *tornado* is a very strong spinning wind. [noun] •**tornadoes.**

top²

touch (TUHCH)
1. When you *touch* something, you feel it with your hand: *The stove is too hot to touch.* [verb]
2. *Touch* is the power by which a person knows about things by feeling or handling them. *Touch* is one of the five senses, along with hearing, sight, smell, and taste. [noun]
•**touches, touched, touching.**

tow (TOH) To *tow* something is to pull it behind you, especially attached to your boat or car: *The car is towing a big trailer.* [verb] •**tows, towed, towing.**

toward (TORD) *He walked toward the door.* [preposition]

towel (TOW uhl) A *towel* is a piece of cloth or paper you use to dry something: *He dried the dishes with a towel.* [noun] •**towels.**

tower (TOW er) A *tower* is a tall building or part of a building: *The castle had many towers.* [noun] •**towers.**

town (TOWN) A *town* is a large group of houses and other buildings. A *town* is smaller than a city. [noun] •**towns.**

tornadoes

tow truck (TOH truhk) A *tow truck* is a truck that can tow cars away. •**tow trucks.**

toy (TOI) A *toy* is something to play with. Dolls, blocks, and teddy bears are *toys*. [noun] •**toys.**

toys

trace (TRAYSS) When you *trace* something, you copy it by following its lines with a pen or pencil: *She traced the picture of the clown.* [verb] •**traces, traced, tracing.**

track (TRAK)

1. A *track* is a pair of steel rails that the wheels of a train run on: *Be careful crossing the railroad track.* [noun]
2. A *track* is also a mark left by something that passed by: *There were tire tracks in the snow.* [noun]

•**tracks.**

tractor (TRAK ter) A *tractor* is a machine used for farm work. [noun] •**tractors.**

tractor

trade (TRAYD) When you *trade,* you give one thing to get another: *Will you trade your sweater for my jacket?* [verb] •**trades, traded, trading.**

traffic (TRAF ik) *Traffic* is the cars, trucks, and buses moving along a road at the same time: *This road has a lot of traffic in the morning and evening.* [noun]

traffic light (TRAF ik LYT) A *traffic light* is a signal at a corner where streets cross. A red light means "stop," a yellow light means "get ready to stop," and a green light means "go." •**traffic lights.**

trail (TRAYL) A *trail* is a path across a field or through the woods: *We followed the trail until we came to the river.* [noun] •**trails.**

trailer · tray

trailer (TRAY ler) A *trailer* is a small two-wheeled or four-wheeled cart used for hauling something behind a car or truck: *My uncle bought a new boat trailer.* [noun] •**trailers.**

train (TRAYN)

train

1. A *train* is a line of railroad cars pulled by an engine along a track: *The train blocked traffic for twenty minutes.* [noun]
2. If you *train* a person or animal, you teach them: *She trained her dog to sit and to roll over.* [verb] •**trains.** •**trains, trained, training.**

trap (TRAP)

1. A *trap* is a thing for catching an animal: *We set several mouse traps in the closet.* [noun]
2. If you *trap* something, you catch it in a trap: *They trapped two groundhogs in the yard and set them free in the woods.* [verb] •**traps.** •**traps, trapped, trapping.**

trash (TRASH) *Trash* is anything of no use or that is worn out. *Trash* is things to be thrown away or garbage. [noun]

travel (TRAV uhl) To *travel* is to go from one place to another: *They want to travel to the mountains this summer. Sound and light travel through the air.* [verb] •**travels, traveled, traveling.**

tray (TRAY) A *tray* is a flat piece of metal or plastic. *Trays* are used in cafeterias to carry your food to your table. [noun] •**trays.**

tray

Tt

treasure (TREZH er) *Treasure* is something that is worth a lot, such as money and jewels: *The pirates buried the treasure of gold coins under the palm tree.* [*noun*] •**treasures.**

treat (TREET)

1. To *treat* means to try to heal someone: *The doctor is treating my dad's sore shoulder.* [*verb*]
2. A *treat* is a gift of food, drink, a free ticket, or the like: *She gave us treats on the last day of school.* [*noun*]

•**treats, treated, treating.** •**treats.**

tree (TREE) A *tree* is a large plant with a trunk, branches, and leaves. Oaks and maples are common *trees.* [*noun*] •**trees.**

trees

tremble (TREM buhl) If you *tremble,* you shake because you are excited, afraid, or cold: *We could see that she was afraid because her hands trembled.* [*verb*] •**trembles, trembled, trembling.**

triangle (TRY ang guhl)

1. A *triangle* is a shape with three sides. [*noun*]
2. A *triangle* is also a musical instrument. To play a *triangle,* you hit it with a piece of metal. [*noun*]

•**triangles.**

triceratops (try SAIR uh topss) The *triceratops* was a dinosaur with a large horn above each eye and a smaller horn on its nose. It had a hard plate over the back of its neck and a long tail. [*noun*] •**triceratopses.**

triceratops

trick (TRIK)

1. A *trick* is something done to make people laugh or to fool them: *The magician showed us a few tricks with cards.* [*noun*]

413

tricycle · trouble

2. When you *trick* people, you play a trick on them: *He tricked me into telling the answer to the riddle.* [verb]
•**tricks**. •**tricks, tricked, tricking**.

tricycle (TRY suh kuhl) A *tricycle* is a toy for small children to ride. It has one wheel in front and two wheels in back. [noun] •**tricycles**.

I'm *too* big for a tricycle.

tricycle

tried (TRYD) *He tried to pick up the chair. She has tried on several pairs of shoes.* [verb]

trip (TRIP)

1. When you take a *trip,* you go from one place to another: *We took a trip to the beach last fall.* [noun]

2. If you *trip,* you hit your foot against something: *She tripped over a roller skate and almost fell down the stairs.* [verb]
•**trips**. •**trips, tripped, tripping**.

troll (TROHL) In stories, a *troll* is an ugly giant or dwarf who lives in caves or underground. [noun] •**trolls**.

trombone (TROM bohn *or* trom BOHN) A *trombone* is a metal musical instrument that you play by blowing into it. [noun] •**trombones**.

troop (TROOP) A *troop* is a group of people: *We have a large Boy Scout troop at our school.* [noun] •**troops**.

trouble (TRUHB uhl)

1. *Trouble* is something that makes you upset, bothers you, or gives you pain: *Dinner was late tonight because we had trouble with the car and couldn't get home. I had a lot of trouble working those math problems.* [noun]

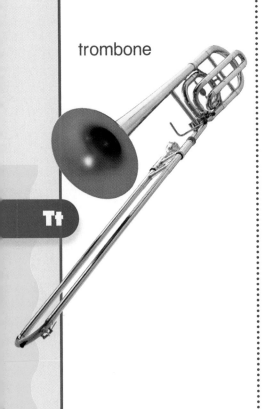

trombone

Tt

2. If you are *in trouble,* people are angry or upset with you: *You will be in trouble if you knock that can of paint over.* [noun]
•**troubles** *for definition 1.*

trousers (TROW zerz) *Trousers* are clothes you wear to cover your legs from your waist to your ankles. Another word for *trousers* is *pants.* [noun plural]

truck (TRUHK)
A *truck* is a large machine that can carry heavy loads. [noun]
•**trucks.**

truck

true (TROO) Something that is *true* is correct. Something that is *true* is not false or make-believe: *This is a true story because everything in it really happened.* [adjective] •**truer, truest.**

trumpet (TRUHM pit) A *trumpet* is a metal musical instrument that is played by blowing into it and pressing keys. [noun] •**trumpets.**

trunk (TRUHNGK)

1. A *trunk* is the main stem of a tree. Branches and roots grow from the *trunk.* [noun]

2. A *trunk* is also a part of an elephant's body that looks like a very long nose. Elephants feed themselves with their *trunks.* [noun]

3. A *trunk* is also a large box for carrying clothes. [noun]

4. A *trunk* is also a place for carrying things in a car, behind the rear seat. Not all cars have *trunks.* [noun]
•**trunks.**

trunk

An elephant has a trunk.

Tt

trust • tulip

trust (TRUHST) When you *trust* people, you believe in them or depend on them: *I don't trust him because he lies.* [verb] •**trusts, trusted, trusting.**

truth (TROOTH) The *truth* is something that is true: *The truth is that she doesn't want to go.* [noun]

try (TRY) When you *try* to do something, you want to do it if you can: *Let's try to cut the grass before noon. He tried out for the team.* [verb] •**tries, tried, trying.**

T-shirt (TEE shert) A *T-shirt* is a thin shirt. A *T-shirt* usually has short sleeves and no collar. [noun] •**T-shirts.**

tub (TUHB) A *tub* is a very large container that holds water. You take a bath in a *tub.* [noun] •**tubs.**

tuba (TOO buh) A *tuba* is a large metal musical instrument that is played by blowing into it and pressing keys. [noun] •**tubas.**

tuba

tube (TOOB) A *tube* is a small container that holds things like toothpaste or paint. [noun] •**tubes.**

Tuesday (TOOZ day) *Tuesday* is the day after Monday. It is the third day of the week. [noun] •**Tuesdays.**

tug (TUHG) When you *tug,* you pull hard on something: *He tugged on the rope, but the donkey would not move.* [verb] •**tugs, tugged, tugging.**

tugboat (TUHG boht) A *tugboat* is a small boat that can tow or push other boats. [noun] •**tugboats.**

tugboat

tulip (TOO lip) A *tulip* is a flower shaped like a

cup. *Tulips* come in many different colors. *Tulips* grow from bulbs. *[noun]* •**tulips.**

tuna (TOO nuh) A *tuna* is a large fish. People often eat *tuna*. *[noun]* •**tuna** *or* **tunas.**

tunnel (TUHN uhl)

1. A *tunnel* is a road or path under the ground: *We went through a tunnel under the mountain.* *[noun]*
2. If you *tunnel,* you make a tunnel in something: *They tunneled through the mountain to make a new road.* *[verb]*
•**tunnels.** •**tunnels, tunneled, tunneling.**

tunnel

turkey (TER kee) A *turkey* is a large bird that is raised for food. *[noun]* •**turkeys.**

turn (TERN)

1. To *turn* is to go in a new direction: *Turn here at the corner and his house is on the left.* *[verb]*
2. To *turn* is also to move around a center as a wheel does: *We watched the dancers turn around the room.* *[verb]*
3. A *turn* is a chance to do something: *It is my turn to pitch.* *[noun]*
•**turns, turned, turning.** •**turns.**

turtle

turtle (TER tuhl) A *turtle* is an animal that has a soft, round body covered by a thick, hard shell. *[noun]* •**turtles.**

TV (TEE VEE) *TV* is a short word meaning *television.* *[noun]* •**TVs.**

Tt

417

twelfth · tyrannosaurus

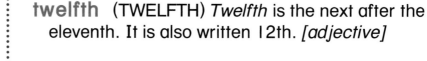

twelve

twelfth (TWELFTH) *Twelfth* is the next after the eleventh. It is also written 12th. *[adjective]*

twelve (TWELV) *Twelve* is two more than 10. It is also written 12. *[noun or adjective]*

twentieth (TWEN tee ith) *Twentieth* is the next after the nineteenth. It is also written 20th. *[adjective]*

twenty (TWEN tee) *Twenty* equals ten plus ten. It is also written 20. *[noun or adjective]* •**twenties.**

twice (TWYSS) *Twice* means two times: *She played ball twice this week. His yard is twice as big as ours. [adverb]*

twig (TWIG) A *twig* is a tiny branch that grows out of a tree or other plant. *[noun]* •**twigs.**

twin (TWIN) A *twin* is one of two children born to the same parents at the same time: *There are three sets of twins at our school. [noun]* •**twins.**

twist (TWIST) To *twist* is to turn around and around: *She twisted around, trying to get into the tight jacket. [verb]* •**twists, twisted, twisting.**

twister (TWISS ter) *Twister* is another word for *tornado. [noun]* •**twisters.**

tyrannosaurus

two (TOO) *Two* is one more than one. It is also written 2. *[noun or adjective]* •**twos.**

tyrannosaurus (ti ran uh SOR uhss) The *tyrannosaurus* was a huge dinosaur that lived in North America. It ate other dinosaurs. *[noun]* •**tyrannosauruses.**

ugly · underground

ugly   (UHG lee) If something is *ugly*, it is not nice to look at. Something that is *ugly* is not pretty: *The horse has an ugly cut on its leg.* [*adjective*] • **uglier, ugliest.**

umbrella   (uhm BREL uh) An *umbrella* is something you hold over yourself to keep yourself dry when it rains. [*noun*] • **umbrellas.**

uncle   (UHNG kuhl) Your *uncle* is your father's brother, your mother's brother, or your aunt's husband. [*noun*] • **uncles.**

under   (UHN der) *They stood under an umbrella in the rain. She had a scratch under her eye.* [*preposition* or *adverb*]

underground   (uhn der GROWND) Something that is *underground* is beneath the ground: *Some animals live underground.* [*adverb*]

umbrella

Uu

419

underneath

underline (UHN der lyn) When you *underline* something, you draw a line under it: *Underline the verb in this sentence.* [verb] • **underlines, underlined, underlining.**

underneath (uhn der NEETH) *I sat underneath the tree.* [preposition or adverb]

undershirt (UN der shert) Your *undershirt* is a shirt you wear next to your skin under a shirt. [noun] • **undershirts.**

understand (uhn der STAND) When you *understand* something, you know what it means: *I understand the directions.* [verb] • **understands, understood, understanding.**

understood (uhn der STUD) *She understood the rules of the game after I explained them to her.* [verb]

underwater (uhn der WAW ter) If something is *underwater*, it is beneath the water: *I like to swim underwater.* [adjective or adverb]

underwear (UHN der wair) Your *underwear* is the clothes you wear next to your skin. [noun]

underwear

unhappy (uhn HAP ee) Another word for *unhappy* is *sad*: *She was very unhappy when her friend moved away.* [adjective] • **unhappier, unhappiest.**

unicorn (YOO nuh korn) A *unicorn* is a make-believe animal. A *unicorn* looks like a horse but has one long horn on its forehead. [noun] • **unicorns.**

uniform (YOO nuh form) *Uniforms* are special clothes worn by people doing a certain kind of work. Police officers and nurses wear *uniforms*. [noun] • **uniforms.**

Uu

unit • upset

unit (YOO nit) A *unit* is a certain amount used as a way of measuring. An inch is a *unit* of length. A pound is a *unit* of weight. *[noun]* • **units.**

United States (yoo NY tid STAYTSS) The *United States* is a country made up of fifty states. The *United States* is part of the continent of North America. *[noun]*

universe (YOO nuh verss) The *universe* is made up of everything there is. *[noun]*

unlucky (uhn LUHK ee) If you are *unlucky*, bad things seem to happen to you often: *That unlucky boy has had many accidents.* *[adjective]* • **unluckier, unluckiest.**

until (uhn TIL) *She did not leave until the following week. We waited until the sun had set.* *[preposition or conjunction]*

unusual (uhn YOO zhoo uhl) If something is *unusual*, it does not happen very often: *It is unusual for a person to have one blue eye and one brown eye.* *[adjective]*

up (UHP) *The price of a new baseball glove has gone up. The squirrel ran up the tree. We get up for school at seven o'clock. Your time is up now.* *[adverb or preposition or adjective]*

upon (uh PON) *He sat upon the bed. Once upon a time there were three elves.* *[preposition]*

upset (uhp SET) If you are *upset*, you are very unhappy: *She was upset when her dog ran away.* *[adjective]*

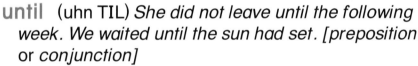

United States

up

Uu

421

upside down · Utah

upside down

upside down (UHP syd DOWN) If something is *upside down,* it has its bottom where its top should be: *You are holding the picture upside down.*

upstairs (uhp STAIRZ) Something that is *upstairs* is on the floor up the stairs: *He went upstairs to bed. Use the upstairs telephone.* [*adverb* or *adjective*]

us (UHSS) *Mom gave us a ride to school. Can you help us with this puzzle?* [*pronoun*]

use (YOOZ) When you *use* a thing, you do something with it that it was meant to do. You *use* a knife to cut. You *use* an umbrella to stay dry. [*verb*] • **uses, used, using.**

used (YOOZD) When something is *used,* it is not new: *My parents bought a used car.* [*adjective*]

useful (YOOSS fuhl) If something is *useful,* it makes work easier to do: *A hammer is a useful tool.* [*adjective*]

usual (YOO zhoo uhl) If something is *usual,* it is often seen, or it often happens. Something that is *usual* is common: *Our usual dinner time is six o'clock.* [*adjective*]

usually (YOO zhoo uh lee) If something *usually* happens, it happens very often or almost all the time: *We usually eat dinner at six o'clock.* [*adverb*]

Utah (YOO taw *or* YOO tah) *Utah* is one of the fifty states of the United States. [*noun*]

Utah

vacation   (vay KAY shuhn) A *vacation* is a time when you do not go to school or work: *Our school has a spring vacation every year.* [*noun*] •**vacations.**

vacuum cleaner   (VAK yoom KLEE ner) A *vacuum cleaner* is a machine you use to clean rugs, curtains, and floors. •**vacuum cleaners.**

Valentine's Day   (VAL uhn tynz DAY) *Valentine's Day* is February 14th, a day when people send each other cards and small presents.

valley   (VAL ee) A *valley* is a low area between mountains or hills. Rivers often run through *valleys.* [*noun*] •**valleys.**

van   (VAN) A *van* is a covered truck used for carrying people or things. [*noun*] •**vans.**

vacuum cleaner

Vv

423

vanilla · vest

vanilla (vuh NIL uh) *Vanilla* is a special flavor used to make ice cream, candy, cakes, and cookies. *[noun]*

vase (VAYSS) A *vase* is a container used to hold flowers. A *vase* is usually round and tall enough to hold flowers on stems. *[noun]* •**vases.**

vase

VCR (VEE see AR) A *VCR* is a machine that records TV programs or movies on special tape. A *VCR* can also play tapes that have already been recorded. *[noun]* •**VCRs.**

vegetable (VEJ tuh buhl) A *vegetable* is a plant that people eat. Peas, lettuce, beets, and beans are *vegetables. [noun]* •**vegetables.**

vendor (VEN der) A *vendor* is a person who sells something. *[noun]* •**vendors.**

Veracruz (vair uh KROOZ) *Veracruz* is a state in the east part of Mexico. *[noun]*

verb (VERB) A *verb* is an action word that tells what someone or something does. In the sentence "The children painted pictures today," *painted* is the *verb*. It tells what the children did. *[noun]* •**verbs.**

Vermont (ver MONT) *Vermont* is one of the fifty states of the United States. *[noun]*

very (VAIR ee) *July was very hot this year. She was very happy today.* *[adverb]*

vest (VEST) A *vest* is a a short piece of clothing without sleeves that you wear over a shirt. *[noun]* •**vests.**

vest

veterinarian (vet er uh NER ee uhn) A *veterinarian* is a doctor who helps sick animals. [noun] •**veterinarians.**

video (VID ee oh) A *video* is a tape recording of a movie, concert, TV show, or other program. A *video* can be played back on a TV screen: *He saw the video of the school play last night.* [noun] •**videos.**

veterinarian

videotape (VID ee oh tayp) When you *videotape* something, you make it into a video. [verb] •**videotapes, videotaped, videotaping.**

village (VIL ij) A *village* is a small town. There are only a few houses in a *village.* [noun] •**villages.**

vine (VYN) A *vine* is a plant that grows along the ground. Some *vines* climb up walls and fences. Pumpkins, melons, and grapes grow on *vines.* [noun] •**vines.**

violin

violin (vy uh LIN) A *violin* is a wooden musical instrument with four strings. You push and pull a stick called a bow across the strings to make sounds. [noun] •**violins.**

Virginia (ver JIN yuh) *Virginia* is one of the fifty states of the United States. [noun]

visit (VIZ it) To *visit* is to go to see places or people: *Next month we are going to visit New York. I visited my aunt for two weeks last summer.* [verb] •**visits, visited, visiting.**

Vv

visitor (VIZ uh ter) A *visitor* is a person who visits: *The two visitors from Canada asked us how to get to the hotel.* [noun] •**visitors.**

vitamin • voyage

vitamin (VY tuh min) *Vitamins* are special parts of the food you eat. *Vitamins* help keep you healthy. *Vitamins* are also given in pills. *[noun]* •**vitamins.**

voice (VOISS) Your *voice* is the sound you make with your mouth. You use your *voice* when you speak, sing, or shout. *[noun]* •**voices.**

volcano (vol KAY noh) A *volcano* is an opening on the top of a high hill or mountain. Steam, ashes, and hot, melted rock sometimes flow out of a *volcano*. *[noun]* •**volcanoes.**

volcano

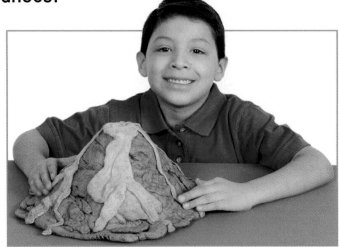

vote (VOHT)
1. A *vote* is a choice you make for or against a person or thing: *Whoever gets the most votes will win. We took a vote on where to go for vacation.* *[noun]*
2. When you *vote,* you say or write if you are for or against a person or thing: *My parents both voted for her.* *[verb]*
•**votes.** •**votes, voted, voting.**

vowel (VOW uhl) *Vowels* are the letters *a, e, i, o,* and *u*. Sometimes *y* is also called a *vowel*. All the other letters in the alphabet are consonants. *[noun]* •**vowels.**

vowels

voyage (VOI ij) A *voyage* is a trip: *We had a nice voyage across the bay.* *[noun]* •**voyages.**

Vv

waffle (WAHF uhl) A *waffle* is a flat cake with square holes on both sides. *[noun]* •**waffles.**

wagon (WAG uhn)
1. A *wagon* is a toy cart to ride in. *[noun]*
2. A *wagon* is also a large cart used to carry people or things. Horses pull *wagons.* *[noun]*
•**wagons.**

wail (WAYL) When you *wail*, you cry for a long time because of pain: *The baby wailed.* *[verb]* •**wails, wailed, wailing.**

waist (WAYST) Your *waist* is the part of your body between your ribs and your hips: *He wore a belt around his waist.* *[noun]* •**waists.**

wait (WAYT) When you *wait*, you stay where you are: *We waited at the corner for the bus.* *[verb]* •**waits, waited, waiting.**

wagon

Ww

427

waiter • walrus

waiter (WAY ter) A *waiter* is a man who brings food to people in a restaurant. *[noun]* • **waiters.**

waitress (WAY triss) A *waitress* is a woman who brings food to people in a restaurant. *[noun]* • **waitresses.**

waitress

wake (WAYK) When you *wake,* you stop sleeping or make someone else stop sleeping: *I have to wake up early to catch the bus. The noise of the train always wakes the baby. [verb]* • **wakes, woke, woken, waking.**

walk (WAWK)

1. When you *walk,* you move by putting one foot in front of the other: *Let's walk to the park today. [verb]*

2. A *walk* is a trip you make by walking: *They took a nice walk around the block with the dog. [noun]*
• **walks, walked, walking.** • **walks.**

wall (WAWL)

1. A *wall* is the side of a building or room: *We need to paint the kitchen wall. [noun]*

2. A *wall* is also something built to separate one part of a place from another. *[noun]*
• **walls.**

wallet (WAHL it) A *wallet* is a small, flat bag you use to carry money or cards. *[noun]* • **wallets.**

walrus (WAHL ruhss) A *walrus* is a large animal that lives in the sea. *Walruses* live in cold places. *[noun]* • **walruses** *or* **walrus.**

walrus

Ww

wand (WAHND) A *wand* is a thin stick: *The princess in the story waved a magic wand.* [noun] •**wands.**

want (WAHNT) When you *want* something, you wish you had it, or you wish you could do it: *My sister wants a new winter coat. We want to see the ball game.* [verb] •**wants, wanted, wanting.**

war (WOR) A *war* is a fight, sometimes with weapons, between different countries or groups of people. [noun] •**wars.**

warm (WORM) If something is *warm,* it is more hot than cold: *The water is warm enough to swim in. He sat in the warm sunshine.* [adjective] •**warmer, warmest.**

was (WUHZ *or* WAHZ) *He was very shy. I was late for dinner. The sun was shining. He was going to study.* [verb]

wash (WAHSH) When you *wash* something, you clean it with soap and water: *Be sure to wash your hands before dinner. It is my turn to wash the dishes.* [verb] •**washes, washed, washing.**

washcloth (WAHSH klawth) A *washcloth* is a small cloth for washing yourself. [noun] •**washcloths.**

washer (WAHSH er) A *washer* is a machine that washes clothes. [noun] •**washers.**

washing machine (WAHSH ing muh sheen) A *washing machine* is a washer. •**washing machines.**

Washington (WAWSH ing tuhn) *Washington* is one of the fifty states of the United States. [noun]

wand

Washington

Ww

429

Washington, D.C. · waterfall

Washington, D.C. (WAWSH ing tuhn dee cee)
Washington, D.C. is the capital of the United States.
[noun]

wasn't *Wasn't* is a shorter form of *was not: She wasn't*
home when I called. [contraction]

wasp (WAHSP) A *wasp* is an insect that has a narrow
middle and a strong sting. *[noun]* •**wasps.**

waste (WAYST)
1. If you *waste* something, you do not use it well: *She*
   didn't finish the test because she wasted time. [verb]
2. *Waste* describes anything you throw away because
   you cannot use it: *Please put all this waste paper*
   with the other trash. [adjective]
•**wastes, wasted, wasting.**

watch (WAHCH)
1. When you *watch* something, you look at it for a
   while: *We watched the kittens play. The students*
   watched the teacher do the experiment. [verb]
2. A *watch* is a small clock you wear on your wrist.
   [noun]
•**watches, watched, watching.** •**watches.**

watch

water (WAW ter)
1. *Water* is the liquid that fills oceans,
   rivers, lakes, and ponds. *Water*
   falls from the sky as rain. *[noun]*
2. If you *water* something, you give it
   water: *Mom asked me to water the*
   flowers. [verb]
•**waters, watered, watering.**

waterfall (WAW ter fawl) A *waterfall*
is the water in a stream that falls from
a high place: *The log went over the*
waterfall. [noun] •**waterfalls.**

waterfalls

watermelon (WAW ter mel uhn) A *watermelon* is a large melon that is red or pink on the inside. *Watermelons* are hard and green on the outside. *[noun]* •**watermelons.**

wave (WAYV)

1. A *wave* is the water in an ocean or lake that rises and moves forward as it comes near the shore. *[noun]*
2. When you *wave,* you move your hand up and down or side to side: *The children waved good-bye to their parents. [verb]*
•**waves.** •**waves, waved, waving.**

wax (WAKS) *Wax* is a made by bees. Bees store their honey in *wax. [noun]*

way (WAY)

1. A *way* is how something is done or can be done: *He showed us the way to work the math problem. [noun]*
2. A *way* is also the direction you follow to get to a place: *Down the hall is the way to the library. [noun]*
•**ways.**

we (WEE) *We went riding on our bikes. We are in the same class. [pronoun]*

weak (WEEK)

1. *Weak* means not having enough power: *He was too weak to lift the chair. [adjective]*
2. When something is *weak,* it can be broken easily: *The weak step broke when she stepped on it. [adjective]*
•**weaker, weakest.**

weapon (WEP uhn) A *weapon* is anything people fight with. Guns and knives are *weapons. [noun]* •**weapons.**

wear (WAIR) When you *wear* something, you have it on your body: *She needs to wear a coat today. He wears a beard with his costume. [verb]* •**wears, wore, worn, wearing.**

wave

I am wearing my favorite shirt!

wear

Ww

weather · week

weather (WE<u>TH</u> er) The *weather* is how it is outside at a certain place and time. *[noun]*

weather vane (WE<u>TH</u> er VAYN) A *weather vane* is something that shows which way the wind is blowing. You may see a *weather vane* on a roof. • **weather vanes.**

weather

weave (WEEV) To *weave* is to form threads into cloth. *[verb]* • **weaves, wove, woven, weaving.**

web (WEB) A *web* is a woven net of tiny threads made by a spider: *Tiny drops of water shone on the spider web. [noun]* • **webs.**

webbed (WEBD) *Webbed* means having toes joined by pieces of skin. Ducks have *webbed* feet. *[adjective]*

wedding (WED ing) A *wedding* is the special happy celebration when people get married: *He was invited to my cousin's wedding. [noun]* • **weddings.**

Wednesday (WENZ day) *Wednesday* is the day after Tuesday. It is the fourth day of the week. *[noun]* • **Wednesdays.**

weed (WEED) A *weed* is a plant that grows where people do not want it. *[noun]* • **weeds.**

week (WEEK) A *week* is a period of time seven days long. There are 52 *weeks* in a year. The days of the *week* are Sunday, Monday, Tuesday, Wednesday, Thursday, Friday, and Saturday. *[noun]* • **weeks.**

weddings

Ww

weigh (WAY) When you *weigh* something, you find out how heavy it is: *The nurse weighs you at the doctor's office. [verb]* •**weighs, weighed, weighing.**

weight (WAYT) The *weight* of something is how heavy it is: *My baby brother's weight is 12 pounds. [noun]* •**weights.**

welcome (WEL kuhm)

1. When you *welcome* someone, you say hello to them in a kind way: *Grandma welcomed us to her home. They welcomed the visitor with flowers. [verb]*

2. *Welcome* is a polite word. We say "You're welcome" after someone has said "Thank you." *[adjective]*
•**welcomes, welcomed, welcoming.**

well¹ (WEL)

1. When something is done *well,* it is done in a good way: *The job of painting the garage was done very well. [adverb]*

2. When you are *well,* you are healthy: *She was sick, but now she is well. [adjective]*
•**better, best.**

well² (WEL) A *well* is a hole dug in the ground to get water, gas, or oil. *[noun]* •**wells.**

We all did well in the art contest.

well¹

we'll · whale

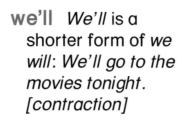

we'll *We'll* is a shorter form of *we will*: *We'll go to the movies tonight.* [contraction]

went (WENT) *He went to the library after school.* [verb]

wept

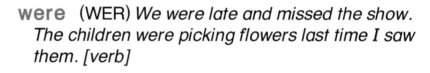

wept (WEPT) *I wept with joy when I won the race.* [verb]

were (WER) *We were late and missed the show. The children were picking flowers last time I saw them.* [verb]

we're *We're* is a shorter form of *we are*: *We're going to a picnic today.* [contraction]

weren't *Weren't* is a shorter form of *were not*: *They weren't planning on seeing the movie today.* [contraction]

west (WEST) *West is the direction of the sunset. West is the opposite of east.* [noun]

West Virginia (WEST ver JIN yuh) *West Virginia is one of the fifty states of the United States.* [noun]

wet

wet (WET) When something is *wet*, it is covered with water: *Her wet shoes made a mess of the kitchen floor.* [adjective] •**wetter, wettest.**

we've *We've* is a shorter form of *we have*: *We've seen this movie before.* [contraction]

whale (WAYL) A *whale* is a very large animal that lives in the sea. *Whales* are not fish. [noun] •**whales.**

Ww

what (WAHT *or* WUHT) *What did you say? What time does school start? I don't know what she said. What a great party! [pronoun* or *adjective* or *interjection]*

whatever (waht EV er *or* wuht EV er) *Do whatever you want to do. Take whatever books you need. [pronoun* or *adjective]*

what's *What's* is a shorter form of *what is* or *what has*: *What's that person doing over there? What's happened to your foot? [contraction]*

wheat (WEET) *Wheat* is a grain that is crushed to make flour. *[noun]*

wheat

wheel (WEEL) A *wheel* is something round that turns on its center. *Wheels* help things move and work. A car has four *wheels. [noun]* •**wheels.**

wheelbarrow (WEEL bair oh) A *wheelbarrow* is a small cart with one wheel at the front and two handles at the back. *[noun]* •**wheelbarrows.**

wheelchair (WEEL chair) A *wheelchair* is a chair on wheels, used by people who are sick or who cannot walk. *[noun]* •**wheelchairs.**

wheelbarrow

when (WEN) *When does the show begin? He laughed when the clown fell down. We had just started our picnic when it began to rain. [adverb* or *conjunction]*

Ww

where (WAIR) *Where did you put your coat? Where are you going? Where did you get those jeans? [adverb]*

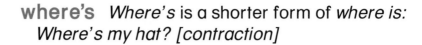

where's · who

where's *Where's* is a shorter form of *where is:*
Where's my hat? [contraction]

wherever (wair EV er) *Please sit down wherever
you like. Wherever you want to go is fine with him.*
[conjunction or adverb]

which (WICH) *Which ball is hers? This story, which
I have just finished, was a good one.* [adjective or
pronoun]

while (WYL) *We stayed at my friend's house for a little
while. The mail came a while ago. While it was raining,
he cleaned his room.* [noun or conjunction]

whisker (WISS ker) A *whisker* is a long, stiff hair near
the mouth of a cat, a rabbit, or other animal. [noun]
•**whiskers.**

whisper (WISS per) When you *whisper,* you speak in
a very quiet way: *Please don't whisper to me in class.*
[verb] •**whispers, whispered, whispering.**

whistle (WISS uhl)
1. When you *whistle,* you make a clear, high sound
   by blowing air through your teeth or lips: *The boy
   whistled and his dog ran to him.* [verb]
2. A *whistle* is a small, hollow metal thing you blow
   into to make a whistling sound. [noun]
•**whistles, whistled, whistling.** •**whistles.**

white (WYT)
1. *White* is a very light color. *White* is the opposite of
   black. [noun]
2. Something that is *white* has this color: *The pages
   of this book are white.* [adjective]
•**whites.** •**whiter, whitest.**

who (HOO) *Who is at the door? Tell me who you think
spells the best in our class.* [pronoun]

whisper

Ww

whoever (hoo EV er) *Whoever reaches the goal first wins. Whoever wants to go, get in the car.* [pronoun]

whole (HOHL) Something that is *whole* has all its parts or is in one piece: *This is not the whole set of books because one book is lost. The dog swallowed the meat whole.* [adjective]

whole

whom (HOOM) *The boy to whom I spoke is new in school.* [pronoun]

who's *Who's* is a shorter form of *who is* or *who has*: *Who's going to the park with me? Who's already paid for the ticket?* [contraction]

whose (HOOZ) *Whose sweater is this? Whose mittens are these?* [pronoun]

why (WY) *Why did she bring her cat to class? She doesn't know why the baby is crying. That is the reason why we left early.* [adverb or *conjunction*]

wide (WYD) When something is *wide*, it is big from one side to the other. Something that is *wide* is not narrow: *The road was wide enough for the truck to pass us.* [adjective] • **wider, widest.**

width (WIDTH) The *width* of something is how wide it is: *The width of that road is ten feet.* [noun] • **widths.**

wife (WYF) A *wife* is a woman who is married. [noun] • **wives.**

wild (WYLD) When something is *wild*, it is not raised or grown by people. *Wild animals live in the forest.* [adjective] • **wilder, wildest.**

Why did the chicken cross the road?

To get to the other side!

why

Ww

will · wire

will (WIL) *She will start the job soon. He will go if you go. The boat will hold four people easily.* [verb]

win (WIN) When you *win,* you are first in a race or contest: *I hope our team will win.* [verb] •**wins, won, winning.**

wind (WIND) *Wind* is air that is moving: *The wind blew the leaves off the trees.* [noun] •**winds.**

windmill (WIND mil) A *windmill* is a machine that works by using the wind for power. *Windmills* are used to pump water and make electricity. [noun] •**windmills.**

windmill

window (WIN doh) A *window* is an opening in a wall or roof. A *window* lets in light or fresh air. [noun] •**windows.**

wing (WING)

1. A *wing* is one of the parts of a bird, insect, or bat. *Wings* move and are used in flying. [noun]

2. A *wing* is also one of the parts of an airplane that helps it fly: *That plane's wing was sixty feet long.* [noun]

•**wings.**

winter (WIN ter) *Winter* is the season of the year between fall and spring. *Winter* is the coldest season of the year. [noun] •**winters.**

wipe (WYP) When you *wipe* something, you rub it until it is clean or dry: *Wipe your shoes on the mat. Please wipe up the spilled milk.* [verb] •**wipes, wiped, wiping.**

wire (WY er) A *wire* is a piece of metal that is long, strong, and thin. Electricity is carried through *wires.* [noun] •**wires.**

wing

Ww

438

Wisconsin (wiss KON suhn) *Wisconsin* is one of the fifty states of the United States. [*noun*]

wish (WISH)
1. When you *wish* for something, you hope to have it or do it. If you *wish* for something, you want it: *He wishes he had a new bike. I wish it would stop raining.* [*verb*]
2. A *wish* is something you wish for: *Her wish for a new friend came true.* [*noun*]
•**wishes, wished, wishing.** •**wishes.**

witch (WICH) In stories, a *witch* is a woman that can do magic. [*noun*] •**witches.**

with (WI<u>TH</u> or WITH) *I cut the meat with a knife. Do you want sugar with your tea?* [*preposition*]

without (wi<u>th</u> OWT or with OWT) *A cat walks without making any noise. She left without saying good-bye.* [*preposition*]

Wisconsin

wives (WYVZ) *Wives* is the plural of the word *wife.* [*noun plural*]

wizard (WIZ erd) In stories, a *wizard* is a man that can do magic. [*noun*] •**wizards.**

woke

woke (WOHK) *I woke up early today.* [*verb*]

woken (WOH kuhn) *He has woken up early every morning to go fishing.* [*verb*]

wolf (WULF) A *wolf* is a wild animal that looks like a large dog. *Wolves* live together in large groups. [*noun*] •**wolves.**

wolves · woodpile

wolves (WULVZ) *Wolves* is the plural of the word *wolf*. *[noun plural]*

woman (WUM uhn) A *woman* is a grown-up female person. When a girl grows up, she becomes a *woman*. *[noun]* •**women.**

women (WIM uhn) *Women* is the plural of the word *woman*. *[plural noun]*

won (WUHN) *Their team won the game. They have won three games. [verb]*

wonder (WUHN der) When you *wonder* about something, you want to know about it: *I wonder what will happen next. He wondered what time it was. [verb]* •**wonders, wondered, wondering.**

wonder

wonderful (WUHN der fuhl) If something is *wonderful*, you like it very much: *The ocean was a wonderful sight. She had a wonderful time at the party. [adjective]*

won't *Won't* is a shorter form of *will not*: *I won't help you clean your room. [contraction]*

wood (WUD) *Wood* is the hard part of a tree's trunk and branches. *Wood* is used to build houses and make paper. *[noun]* •**woods.**

wooden (WUD uhn) When something is *wooden*, it is made of wood: *There is an old wooden fence around the yard. [adjective]*

woodpile (WUD pyl) A *woodpile* is a pile of wood for fires. *[noun]* •**woodpiles.**

I am carrying wood.

wood

Ww

woods (WUDZ) *Woods* are land that is covered with trees and bushes all growing together: *We took a long walk through the woods to the shore of the lake.* [noun plural]

woof (WUF) *Woof* is a sound a dog makes. [noun] •**woofs.**

wool (WUL) *Wool* is the soft curly hair or fur that covers the body of a sheep. *Wool* is made into cloth. [noun]

word (WERD) A *word* is a sound or group of sounds that means something. We speak *words* when we talk. A *word* is also the written or printed letters that stand for a word. [noun] •**words.**

wore (WOR) *She wore her old sweater. I wore out my new shoes in one month.* [verb]

work (WERK)

1. *Work* is a job you do for a special purpose. Usually people do *work* to earn money: *Driving a truck is hard work. Digging in a garden is hard work.* [noun]
2. When you *work,* you do your job: *He works at an airplane factory.* [verb]
3. When things *work,* they do the jobs they are supposed to do in the right way: *This TV isn't working right.* [verb]
•**works, worked, working.**

worker (WER ker) A *worker* is a person who works: *He is a worker in an automobile factory.* [noun] •**workers.**

world (WERLD) The *world* is the Earth and everything on it. [noun] •**worlds.**

words

green out ball run

world

Ww

worm • woven

worm

worm (WERM) A *worm* is a small, thin animal with a soft body. *Worms* live in the ground. *[noun]* • **worms.**

worn (WORN) *I've worn these jeans all week.* *[verb]*

worry (WER ee) When you *worry,* you feel upset about something: *They will worry if we're late.* *[verb]* • **worries, worried, worrying.**

worse (WERSS) If something is *worse,* it is not as good as something else or as good as it was before: *He is worse than me at spelling. I played worse in the game today than I did last week.* *[adjective* or *adverb]*

worship (WER ship) When you *worship,* you show great love and respect for something: *Some people go to church or a synagogue to worship.* *[verb]* • **worships, worshiped, worshiping.**

worst (WERST) Something that is the *worst* is as bad as it can be: *This is the worst I've ever felt with a cold. That's the worst movie I've ever seen.* *[noun* or *adjective]*

worth (WERTH) The *worth* of something can be how much money will buy it: *I bought five dollars' worth of stamps.* *[noun]*

would (WUD) *Would you like an apple? They said they would wait for us at the corner. The kitten would play with the yarn for hours.* *[verb]*

wouldn't *Wouldn't* is a shorter form of *would not: He wouldn't help us. The car wouldn't start.* *[contraction]*

wove (WOHV) *My sister wove a basket for me. The spider wove a web.* *[verb]*

woven (WOH vuhn) *The scarf was woven out of wool. The spider has woven a web.* *[verb]*

Ww

wrap

wrap (RAP) When you *wrap* something, you cover it up, usually with paper: *We wrapped presents all morning. [verb]* •**wraps, wrapped, wrapping.**

wrinkle (RING kuhl) A *wrinkle* is a fold on the surface of something that is usually flat: *She used the iron to press out the wrinkles in her dress. [noun]* •**wrinkles.**

wrist (RIST) Your *wrist* is the part of your body between your hand and your arm. *[noun]* •**wrists.**

write (RYT) When you *write,* you make letters or words with pen, pencil, or chalk: *Write your name at the top of your paper. [verb]* •**writes, wrote, written, writing.**

written

written (RIT uhn) *I have written you a letter. [verb]*

wrong (RAWNG) When something is *wrong,* it is not the way it should be or not right. When something is *wrong,* it is not true or correct: *It was wrong to take her bike without asking her. He must have written down the wrong number. [adjective]*

Dear Erin,
We are having a good time
here at camp. We swim a
lot, play games, and make
things. We have seen many
new birds. It is fun to
watch them. At night we
sing around the campfire and
tell stories. I wish you were
here, too.
Your friend,
Latisha

wrote (ROHT) *She wrote out a list of things she has to do. [verb]*

Wyoming (wy OH ming) *Wyoming* is one of the fifty states of the United States. *[noun]*

Ww

X-ray • yard²

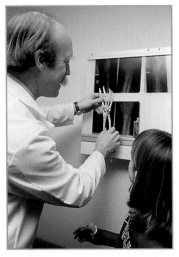

X-rays

X-ray (EKS ray) An *X-ray* is a kind of picture that shows what is inside something. An *X-ray* can tell if you have a broken bone. *[noun]* •**X-rays.**

xylophone (ZY luh fohn) A *xylophone* is a musical instrument. You play it by hitting wooden bars with two small wooden hammers. *[noun]* •**xylophones.**

yak (YAK) A *yak* is a large animal with long hair. *Yaks* live in cold places. *[noun]* •**yaks.**

yard¹ (YARD) A *yard* is a piece of ground next to a house or a school. A *yard* may have a fence around it: *He played in the front yard. [noun]* •**yards.**

yard² (YARD) A *yard* is a unit of length equal to 3 feet. Most doors are one *yard* wide. *[noun]* •**yards.**

Xx

Yy

Zz

444

yarn (YARN) *Yarn* is a kind of thread. People knit with *yarn*: *Mother bought four balls of yarn to knit me a sweater*. [noun]

yawn (YAWN) When you *yawn,* you open your mouth wide to get more air. People *yawn* when they are sleepy, tired, or bored. [verb] •**yawns, yawned, yawning.**

year (YEER) A *year* is a period of time. A *year* has twelve months. [noun] •**years.**

yell (YEL) When you *yell,* you call out with a strong, loud sound: *He yelled for help when he saw the fire.* [verb] •**yells, yelled, yelling.**

yellow (YEL oh)
1. *Yellow* is the color of lemons or butter: *Yellow is my favorite color.* [noun]
2. Something that is *yellow* has this color: *She has a yellow sweater.* [adjective]
•**yellows.** •**yellower, yellowest.**

yes (YESS) *Yes, you may go to the park. The answer to your question is yes.* [adverb]

yesterday (YESS ter day) *Yesterday* is the day before today: *Yesterday it rained all day.* [noun]

yet (YET) *We haven't given up yet. It isn't raining yet. Is she here yet?* [adverb]

yogurt (YOH gert) *Yogurt* is a soft food made from milk. Some *yogurt* is sweet and has a fruit flavor. [noun]

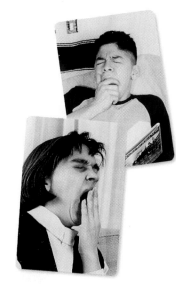

yawn

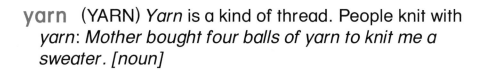

yellow

445

you • yo-yo

you (YOO) *You can use my bike if you need to. You have to be friendly to make friends.* [pronoun]

you'll *You'll is a shorter form of you will: Hurry, or you'll be late.* [contraction]

young (YUHNG) When something is *young*, it is in the early part of life. Someone who is *young* is not old: *A colt is a young horse.* [adjective]
• **younger, youngest.**

young

your (YER) *Your shoes are under the chair. Tell me about your dream.* [adjective]

you're *You're is a shorter form of you are: You're very funny.* [contraction]

yours (YERZ) *My dog is bigger than yours. Yours is the blue book and mine is the red one. Is this book yours?* [pronoun]

yourself (yer SELF) *You can see yourself in a mirror. Can you carry that heavy box yourself?* [pronoun]

yourselves (yer SELVZ) *Can you see yourselves in the mirror? Can you children do this by yourselves?* [pronoun]

you've *You've is a shorter form of you have: You've seen her before.* [contraction]

yo-yo (YOH yoh) A *yo-yo* is a toy made of two round pieces joined together. A string is tied to a *yo-yo*. The *yo-yo* goes up and down along the string. [noun]
• **yo-yos.**

yo-yos

Yucatán (yoo kuh TAN) *Yucatán* is a state in the southeast part of Mexico. *[noun]*

Yukon Territory (YOO kon TAIR uh tor ee) *Yukon Territory* is one of the three territories of Canada. *[noun]*

Zacatecas (sah kah TAY kahss) *Zacatecas* is a state in north central Mexico. *[noun]*

zebra (ZEE bruh) A *zebra* is an animal that looks like a horse. *Zebras* have black and white stripes. *[noun]* • **zebras.**

zero (ZEE roh) *Zero* is the number 0. *[noun* or *adjective]* • **zeros**.

zigzag (ZIG zag) If something is *zigzag,* it has short, sharp turns, first to one side, then to the other side: *The path through the woods goes in a zigzag direction. [adjective]*

zinnia (ZIN ee uh) A *zinnia* is a plant with large, bright flowers. *[noun]* • **zinnias.**

zip (ZIP) When you *zip* something, you close it with a zipper: *She zipped up her jacket before going outside. [verb]* • **zips, zipped, zipping.**

zipper (ZIP er) A *zipper* is something that holds two edges together. *Zippers* are used on clothes and other things. *[noun]* • **zippers.**

zoo (ZOO) A *zoo* is a place where wild animals are kept. People visit the *zoo* to see animals. *[noun]* • **zoos.**

zebra

zip

zipper

Xx

Yy

Zz

Credits

Illustrators **Lynda Calvert-Weyant:** pages 2, 7, 10, 14, 16, 19, 20, 23, 24, 110, 112, 116, 118, 122, 124, 125, 126, 128, 260, 262, 265, 267, 271, 272, 274 **Mernie Cole:** pages 167, 170, 172, 174, 178, 179, 181, 283, 289, 292, 294, 296, 302, 305, 306, 308, 316, 319, 320, 323, 324, 326, 328, 330, 335 **Steve Cox:** pages 201, 202, 203, 212, 214, 217 **Jennifer Fitchwell:** pages 1, 26, 59, 108, 129, 143, 166, 182, 200, 209, 215, 221, 239, 259, 269, 278, 311, 314, 337, 395, 419, 423, 427, 444 **Cathy Ann Johnson:** pages 185, 187, 189, 192, 194, 195, 196, 198, 240, 245, 247, 248, 255, 338, 340, 343, 344, 346, 348, 355, 356, 363, 364, 366, 371, 372, 377, 385, 387, 388, 391, 394, 396 **Darren McKee:** pages 27, 28, 31, 32, 35, 36, 39, 40, 43, 47, 48, 50, 55, 56, 58, 132, 134, 136, 136, 140, 396, 399, 404, 406, 412, 414, 417 **Kristina Stephenson:** pages 144, 146, 148, 156, 161, 163, 165 **Bari Weissman:** pages 62, 65, 66, 66, 68, 70, 72, 74, 78, 79, 81, 82, 83, 85, 86, 89, 92, 96, 99, 100, 100, 102, 107, 221, 223, 227, 229, 230, 233, 234, 236, 420, 422, 428, 433, 439, 440, 443, 446

Photographs

•**Page 2** (B) PhotoDisc; •**Page 2** (B) Bob Daemmrich/Image Works; •**Page 4** (TR) Bill Bachmann/PhotoEdit; •**Page 6** (TL) PhotoDisc; •**Page 6** (TR) PhotoDisc; •**Page 8** (T) PhotoDisc; •**Page 13** (BR) PhotoDisc; •**Page 13** (BL) Rosanne Olson/Tony Stone Images; •**Page 14** (T) Lynn M. Stone/DRK Photo; •**Page 14** (T) John Warden/Tony Stone Images; •**Page 14** (T) PhotoDisc; •**Page 20** (CL) A. J. Copley/Visuals Unlimited; •**Page 22** (B) NASA; •**Page 23** (T) Wayne Eastep/Tony Stone Images; •**Page 23** (T) Michael Newman/PhotoEdit; •**Page 26** (CL) Dale Durfee/Tony Stone Images; •**Page 26** (CL) Stephen J. Krasemann/DRK Photo; •**Page 26** (CL) Michael S. Yamashita/Corbis; •**Page 28** (CL) Dallas & John Heaton/Stock Boston; •**Page 28** (CL) Greig Cranna/©Index Stock Imagery; •**Page 29** (C) PhotoDisc; •**Page 31** (BR) Tom McCarthy/Unicorn Stock Photos; •**Page 32** (BL) Joseph Sohm/Tony Stone Images; •**Page 32** (BL) Steve Hansen/Stock Boston; •**Page 32** (BL) PhotoDisc; •**Page 33** (TR) Henry Horenstein/Stock Boston; •**Page 34** (BL) Larry Ulrich/Tony Stone Images; •**Page 34** (BL) Berenholtz/Stock Market; •**Page 36** (TL) PhotoDisc; •**Page 37** (T) Artville; •**Page 38** (CR) Jeff Greenberg/Unicorn Stock Photos; •**Page 38** (CR) Gale Zucker/Stock Boston; •**Page 40** (BL) PhotoDisc; •**Page 40** (BL) Myrleen Ferguson Cate/PhotoEdit; •**Page 42** (BL) Andy Sacks/Tony Stone Images; •**Page 42** (BL) David Sams/Stock Boston; •**Page 51** (CR) Mark Barberis; •**Page 51** (CR) PhotoDisc; •**Page 53** (BR) PhotoDisc; •**Page 54** (TR) Darrell Gulin/DRK Photo; •**Page 57** (TR) Phil Degginger/Tony Stone Images; •**Page 57** (TR) Terry Vine/Tony Stone Images; •**Page 57** (BR) Artville; •**Page 58** (TL) Paul McCormick/Image Bank; •**Page 58** (TL) Don & Pat Valenti/DRK Photo; •**Page 61** (CR) Philip Gould/Corbis; •**Page 61** (CR) Jim Stamates/Tony Stone Images; •**Page 67** (TR) SuperStock; •**Page 67** (TR) SuperStock; •**Page 69** (T) Spencer Grant/PhotoEdit; •**Page 70** (TL) SuperStock; •**Page 75** (C) PhotoDisc; •**Page 75** (B) Stephen J. Krasemann/DRK Photo; •**Page 80** (CR) Terry Donnelly/Dembinsky Photo Assoc. Inc.; •**Page 82** (BL) SuperStock; •**Page 82** (BL) Lori Adamski Peek/Tony Stone Images; •**Page 84** (TR) Michael Fogden/DRK Photo; •**Page 84** (TR) John Gerlach/DRK Photo; •**Page 87** (C) PhotoDisc; •**Page 87** (C) Peter Southwick/Stock Boston; •**Page 88** (BL) Miro Vintoniv/Stock Boston; •**Page 88** (BL) Tom Prettyman/PhotoEdit; •**Page 90** (CL) Roger Ressmeyer/Corbis; •**Page 90** (CL) Roger Ressmeyer/Corbis; •**Page 93** (BL) Hal Beral/Visuals Unlimited; •**Page 93** (BL) Mark J. Thomas/Dembinsky Photo Assoc. Inc.; •**Page 94** (TR) David Young-Wolff/PhotoEdit; •**Page 94** (TR) Howard Dratch/Image Works; •**Page 96** (CL) Tom Bean/Corbis; •**Page 96** (CL) PhotoDisc; •**Page 98** (TL) PhotoDisc; •**Page 100** (BL) George D. Lepp/NAS/Photo Researchers; •**Page 100** (BL) Darrell Gulin/DRK Photo; •**Page 101** (C) PhotoDisc; •**Page 101** (BR) Norbert Wu/DRK Photo; •**Page 102** (CL) Rafael Macia/Photo Researchers; •**Page 102** (CL) David Young-Wolff/PhotoEdit; •**Page 106** (TL) Ariel Skelley/Stock Market; •**Page 109** (C) Andrea Wells/Tony Stone Images; •**Page 111** (TR) Chip Henderson/Tony Stone Images; •**Page 111** (TR) Ellen B. Senisi/Image Works; •**Page 112** (CL) PhotoDisc; •**Page 113** (C) Tim Brown/Tony Stone Images; •**Page 114** (TR) Larry Ulrich/Tony Stone Images; •**Page 114** (TR) Arthur Gloor/Animals Animals/Earth Scenes; •**Page 121** (BR) PhotoDisc; •**Page 123** (TL) Artville; •**Page 125** (BR) Carl Purcell/Photo Researchers; •**Page 125** (BR) Amy C. Etra/PhotoEdit; •**Page 127** (C) PhotoDisc, Inc.; •**Page 128** (TR) Don & Pat Valenti/DRK Photo; •**Page 128** (TR) Sharon Gerig/TOM STACK & ASSOCIATES; •**Page 131** (TR) Dominique Braud/Dembinsky Photo Assoc. Inc.; •**Page 131** (BR) Gary Meszaros/Dembinsky Photo Assoc. Inc.; •**Page 132** (BR) Gary Conner/PhotoEdit; •**Page 134** (CR) Joe Sohm/Image Works; •**Page 138** (C) David J. Sams/Tony Stone Images; •**Page 138** (C) Lee Snider/Image Works; •**Page 140** (TL) Peter Cade/Tony Stone Images; •**Page 140** (TL) David Oliver/Tony Stone Images; •**Page 142** (TL) Bill Bachman/Photo Researchers; •**Page 142** (TL) Derke/O'Hara/Tony Stone Images; •**Page 144** (BL) William Johnson/Stock Boston; •**Page 144** (BL) Peter Beck/Stock Market; •**Page 146** (BR) PhotoDisc; •**Page 147** (C) SuperStock; •**Page 147** (C) Stephen Derr/Image Bank; •**Page 147** (BR) H. Reinhard/OKAPIA/NAS/Photo Researchers; •**Page 149** (BR) Renee Lynn/NAS/Photo Researchers; •**Page 152** (L) PhotoDisc; •**Page 153** (C) Fred Bavendam/Tony Stone Images; •**Page 153** (C) Stuart Westmorland/Tony Stone Images; •**Page 155** (BR) Art Wolfe/Tony Stone Images; •**Page 155** (BR) Richard Kettlewell/Animals Animals/Earth Scenes; •**Page 157** (CR) James Cotter/Tony Stone Images; •**Page 158** (BR) Jim Corwin/Stock Boston; •**Page 158** (BR) Tony Freeman/PhotoEdit; •**Page 161** (CR) Joe Sohm/Photo Researchers; •**Page 161** (CR) John Henley/Stock Market; •**Page 162** (T) Ron Dahlquist/Tony Stone Images; •**Page 167** (TL) G. Brad Lewis/Tony Stone Images; •**Page 167** (TL) D. Cavagnaro/Visuals Unlimited; •**Page 169** (TR) Robert Maier/Animals Animals/Earth Scenes; •**Page 172** (BR) Photo Disc, Inc.; •**Page 175** (TL) Staffan Widstrand/Corbis; •**Page 176** (BR) Artville; •**Page 180** (TR) David Young-Wolff/Tony Stone Images; •**Page 187** (BR) PhotoDisc; •**Page 190** (BL) Bruce Forster/Tony Stone Images; •**Page 190** (BL) SuperStock; •**Page 193** (C) James H. Robinson/Animals Animals/Earth Scenes; •**Page 194** (BL) Steve McAlister/Image Bank; •**Page 196** (TL) PhotoDisc; •**Page 198** (CL) SuperStock; •**Page 205** (TR) PhotoDisc; •**Page 207** (BL) SuperStock; •**Page 207** (BL) Kunio Owaki/Stock Market; •**Page 210** (BR) Eric Meola/Image Bank; •**Page 210** (BR) Nikolas Konstantinou/Tony Stone Images; •**Page 213** (CR) Lawrence Migdale/Stock Boston; •**Page 213** (CR) Gunter Marx/Corbis; •**Page 219** (BL) Aldo Brando/Tony Stone Images; •**Page 219** (BL) Rob Crandall/Stock Boston; •**Page 222** (TL) PhotoDisc; •**Page 222** (CR) Lucas Abreu/Image Bank; •**Page 222** (CR) William J. Weber/Visuals Unlimited; •**Page 223** (T) Michael Newman/PhotoEdit; •**Page 226** (TL) PhotoDisc; •**Page 227** (BR) Charles Palek/Animals Animals/Earth Scenes; •**Page 228** (BL) PhotoDisc; •**Page 231** (BR) David R. Frazier/David R. Frazier Photolibrary; •**Page 231** (BR) Chad Ehlers/Tony Stone Images; •**Page 234** (BL) PhotoDisc; •**Page 237** (C) John Elk III/Stock Boston; •**Page 237** (C) Joseph Sohm/ChromoSohm Inc./Corbis; •**Page 241** (T) SuperStock; •**Page 241** (BR) PhotoDisc; •**Page 241** (BR) PhotoDisc; •**Page 241** (BR) Digital Stock; •**Page 243** (T) Tania Midgley/Corbis; •**Page 243** (T) Galen Rowell/Corbis; •**Page 245** (BR) SuperStock; •**Page 245** (BR) Stuart Westmorland/Tony Stone Images; •**Page 246** (CR) Zigy Kaluzny/Tony Stone Images; •**Page 246** (CR) Bob Daemmrich/Stock Boston; •**Page 249** (TR) PhotoDisc; •**Page 251** (C) Dennis MacDonald/PhotoEdit; •**Page 253** (BR) PhotoDisc; •**Page 254** (T) Craig Aurness/Corbis; •**Page 254** (CL) Gary Meszaros/Visuals Unlimited; •**Page 255** (T) Marvy!-Original/Stock Market; •**Page 256** (BR) A. Ramey/PhotoEdit; •**Page 256** (BR) Tom McHugh/Photo Researchers; •**Page 262** (BL) Nick Bergkessel/ NAS/Photo Researchers; •**Page 263** (BR) SuperStock; •**Page 263** (BR) SuperStock; •**Page 264** (TL) PhotoDisc; •**Page 264** (TL) PhotoDisc; •**Page 267** (BR) SuperStock; •**Page 267** (BR) Andre Gallant/Image Bank; •**Page 269** (BR) Carolyn Brown/Image Bank; •**Page 269** (BR) SuperStock; •**Page 270** (T) Artville; •**Page 270** (BL) Stephen Frink/Corbis; •**Page 271** (BR) F. B. Grunzweig/Photo Researchers; •**Page 273** (C) PhotoDisc; •**Page 275** (BR) Tim Davis/Tony Stone Images; •**Page 276** (TR) PhotoDisc; •**Page 281** (T) Michael Dick/Animals Animals/Earth Scenes; •**Page 281** (BR) SuperStock; •**Page 281** (BR) SuperStock; •**Page 282** (T) Carolyn A. McKeone/NAS/Photo Researchers; •**Page 282** (BR) Frans Lanting/Tony Stone Images; •**Page 284** (BR) Barbara Reed/Animals Animals/Earth Scenes; •**Page 286** (BL) PhotoDisc; •**Page 287** (T) Jeff Greenberg/Photo Researchers; •**Page 287** (T) Richard Frear/Photo Researchers; •**Page 289** (BR) PhotoDisc; •**Page 291** (T) David R. Frazier/Photo Researchers; •**Page 295** (T) Rob Lewine/Stock Market; •**Page 295** (BR) Mark C. Burnett/Stock Boston; •**Page 295** (BR) Paul A. Souders/Corbis; •**Page 296** (CL) SuperStock; •**Page 296** (CL) David Young-Wolff/PhotoEdit; •**Page 298** (T) Daniel J. Cox/Tony Stone Images; •**Page 298** (BL) Michael Newman/PhotoEdit; •**Page 298** (BL) Ken Fisher/Tony Stone Images; •**Page 299** (T) Michael Collier/Stock Boston; •**Page 299** (BR) PhotoDisc; •**Page 310** (B) Gerard Lacz/Animals Animals/Earth Scenes; •**Page 314** (BL) PhotoDisc; •**Page 317** (C) SuperStock; •**Page 318** (TL) SuperStock; •**Page 318** (TL) L. Isy-Schwart/Image Bank; •**Page 322** (TR) Michael Melford/Image Bank; •**Page 322** (BL) Joe McDonald/Visuals Unlimited; •**Page 324** (BL) Jose L. Pelaez/Stock Market; •**Page 325** (TR) PhotoDisc; •**Page 325** (TR) PhotoDisc; •**Page 325** (TR) PhotoDisc; •**Page 327** (TR) Joseph Nettis/Stock Boston; •**Page 327** (TR) Kelly-Mooney Photography/Corbis; •**Page 331** (C) Leonard Lee Rue III/Visuals Unlimited; •**Page 332** (TR) SuperStock; •**Page 333** (T) Birgit Koch/Animals Animals/Earth Scenes; •**Page 334** (CR) Stephen Frisch/Stock Boston; •**Page 336** (CL) PhotoDisc; •**Page 336** (CL) PhotoDisc; •**Page 338** (BL) Magnus Rietz/Image Bank; •**Page 338** (BL) Art Stein/Photo Researchers; •**Page 339** (B) SuperStock; •**Page 340** (BL) PhotoDisc; •**Page 341** (BL) Simon D. Pollard/NAS/Photo Researchers; •**Page 341** (BR) E. R. Degginger/NAS/Photo Researchers; •**Page 342** (CR) Jeff Zaruba/Tony Stone Images; •**Page 350** (CR) Digital Stock; •**Page 351** (T) PhotoDisc; •**Page 352** (CL) Lori Adamski Peek/Tony Stone Images; •**Page 353** (BR) Bruce Ayres/Tony Stone Images; •**Page 353** (BR) SuperStock; •**Page 353** (BR) Lawrence Migdale/Tony Stone Images; •**Page 359** (TR) Zigy Kaluzny/Tony Stone Images; •**Page 359** (TR) Myrleen Ferguson Cate/PhotoEdit; •**Page 360** (TL) Jonathan Nourok/PhotoEdit; •**Page 360** (TL) Alan Becker/Image Bank; •**Page 363** (TR) PhotoDisc; •**Page 367** (T) PhotoDisc; •**Page 368** (BL) Tony Stone Images; •**Page 368** (BL) Lori Adamski Peek/Tony Stone Images; •**Page 370** (TL) Joseph Nettis/Photo Researchers; •**Page 370** (TL) PhotoDisc; •**Page 372** (BL) SuperStock; •**Page 372** (BL) PhotoDisc; •**Page 373** (TR) PhotoDisc; •**Page 374** (TL) Tom Brakefield/Corbis; •**Page 374** (TL) SuperStock; •**Page 375** (TR) PhotoDisc; •**Page 376** (BL) David Hiser/Tony Stone Images; •**Page 376** (TR) Chris McLaughlin/Animals Animals/Earth Scenes; •**Page 376** (TR) Digital Stock; •**Page 379** (BR) Paul Hutley/Eye Ubiquitous/Corbis; •**Page 379** (BR) Patrick Bennett/Corbis; •**Page 381** (CL) PhotoDisc; •**Page 381** (C) PhotoDisc; •**Page 381** (CR) PhotoDisc; •**Page 382** (L) PhotoDisc; •**Page 382** (TR) M. E. Warren/Photo Researchers; •**Page 384** (L) Leroy Simon/Visuals Unlimited; •**Page 386** (BL) PhotoDisc; •**Page 388** (TR) David Rubinger/Corbis; •**Page 388** (TR) Guido A. Rossi/Image Bank; •**Page 391** (B) PhotoDisc; •**Page 392** (C) SuperStock; •**Page 392** (B) William H. Mullins/NAS/Photo Researchers; •**Page 394** (T) PhotoDisc; •**Page 396** (T) PhotoDisc, Inc.; •**Page 398** (TR) Jonathan Nourok/PhotoEdit; •**Page 400** (CL) Lawson Wood/Corbis; •**Page 401** (T) PhotoDisc; •**Page 401** (T) Danny Lehman/Corbis; •**Page 406** (BL) PhotoDisc; •**Page 410** (CL) Alan R. Moller/Tony Stone Images; •**Page 410** (CL) SuperStock; •**Page 411** (C) Wolfgang Spunbarg/PhotoEdit; •**Page 413** (C) PhotoDisc; •**Page 414** (BL) Artville; •**Page 415** (C) Myrleen Ferguson Cate/PhotoEdit; •**Page 416** (CL) Artville; •**Page 416** (BR) PhotoDisc; •**Page 421** (TR) PhotoDisc; •**Page 421** (TR) PhotoDisc; •**Page 422** (B) John Elk III/Stock Boston; •**Page 422** (B) PhotoDisc; •**Page 425** (TR) Michael Newman/PhotoEdit; •**Page 428** (BL) Kennan Ward/Corbis; •**Page 429** (B) PhotoDisc; •**Page 429** (B) PhotoDisc; •**Page 430** (BR) PhotoDisc; •**Page 430** (BR) PhotoDisc; •**Page 431** (TR) Rick Doyle/Corbis; •**Page 432** (CL) B. & C. Alexander/Photo Researchers; •**Page 432** (CL) Kerstin Geier/Gallo Images/Corbis; •**Page 432** (CL) Bob Rowan/Progressive Images/Corbis; •**Page 434** (TR) Wally McNamee/Corbis; •**Page 434** (TR) Michael Probst/AP/Wide World; •**Page 435** (TR) PhotoDisc; •**Page 438** (CR) PhotoDisc; •**Page 438** (CL) PhotoDisc; •**Page 438** (BL) Artville; •**Page 439** (TR) SuperStock; •**Page 439** (TR) PhotoDisc; •**Page 441** (BR) PhotoDisc; •**Page 441** (BR) PhotoDisc; •**Page 442** (TL) PhotoDisc; •**Page 444** (CL) Gale Zucker/Stock Boston; •**Page 445** (TR) Mark C. Burnett/Stock Boston; •**Page 445** (TR) Bob Daemmrich/Stock Boston; •**Page 447** (TR) PhotoDisc

Table of Contents

Milk is in one of the food groups!

Fun Dictionary Activities

Anthony

Marella

Steven

There are many fun things to do with words! You and your friends can use this *First Dictionary* to help you with these activities.

Where Do You Belong?

Write your first, middle, and last name on a large piece of paper. Then form a line by standing in alphabetical order by first name. (You may have to use the second and third letters of your names to put yourselves in alphabetical order.) When you are lined up by first name, write where you are in the line under your first name. Line up again, this time in alphabetical order by middle names. Write your order in this line under your middle name on the piece of paper. Then line up again by last name. Write your order in this line under your last name on the piece of paper. If you like, you can add the three numbers. Who has the biggest number? Who has the smallest number?

Dictionary Race

Choose one person to say these words aloud: *cabin, cast, chose, come, game, get, got, quickly, rain,* and *about.* Everyone else has a dictionary and joins in a race to be the first to find an example sentence for words that were said.

Farm Animals and Zoo Animals

Divide the class or group into two teams. Team 1 should be farm animals and Team 2 should be zoo animals. Team 1 chooses a farm animal (pig, cow, and so on) and gives clues for that animal until Team 2 guesses the animal and says the first letter of the word. Both teams should use the yellow bars, guide words, and entry words to find the word in the dictionary. The first team to find the page number gets a point. Repeat, with Team 2 giving clues for a zoo animal (zebra, lion, and so on).

It Looks Like This!

Look at these adjectives in your dictionary: *sorry, blue, broad, bumpy,* and *tasty.* Did you notice the two forms of the adjective at the end of the entry? Draw a picture to illustrate all three forms. Add labels to your drawing to show the three forms of the word.

blue

Act It Out!

Look at the following action verbs in your dictionary: *relax, refuse, return, send, teach, tiptoe, paste, mix, jog,* and *invite.* Choose one and act it out for the rest of the class or group. If they guess the right verb, ask them to look it up in their dictionaries and tell the verb forms listed at the end of the entry.

Popcorn!

Word Hunt

Divide the class or group into two teams. Team 1 lines up along a wall or in front of the class. Team 2 stays seated. Have a teacher give each team a category, such as foods, animals, or toys. The first person on Team 1 says a word for something in the team's category. For example, if the category is foods, the child might say *popcorn.* Everyone on Team 2 looks up the word in the dictionary. Then one member of Team 2 spells the word while a second team member writes it on the chalkboard or a piece of paper. After Team 1 has five chances to say a word, it is Team 2's turn to say the words and Team 1's turn to look them up.

451

The United States

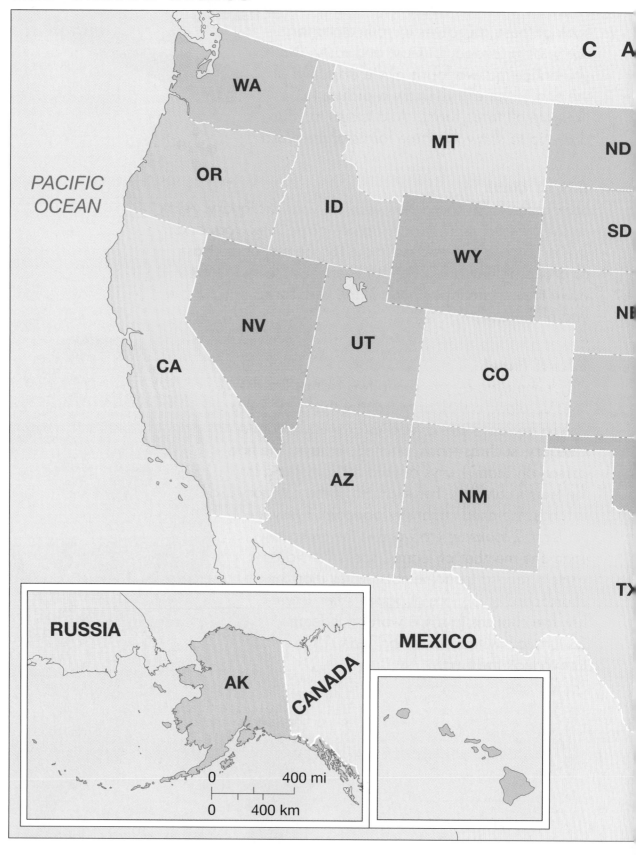

WA

OR

PACIFIC OCEAN

CA

NV

ID

UT

AZ

MT

WY

CO

NM

C A

ND

SD

NE

TX

RUSSIA

AK

CANADA

MEXICO

0   400 mi

0   400 km

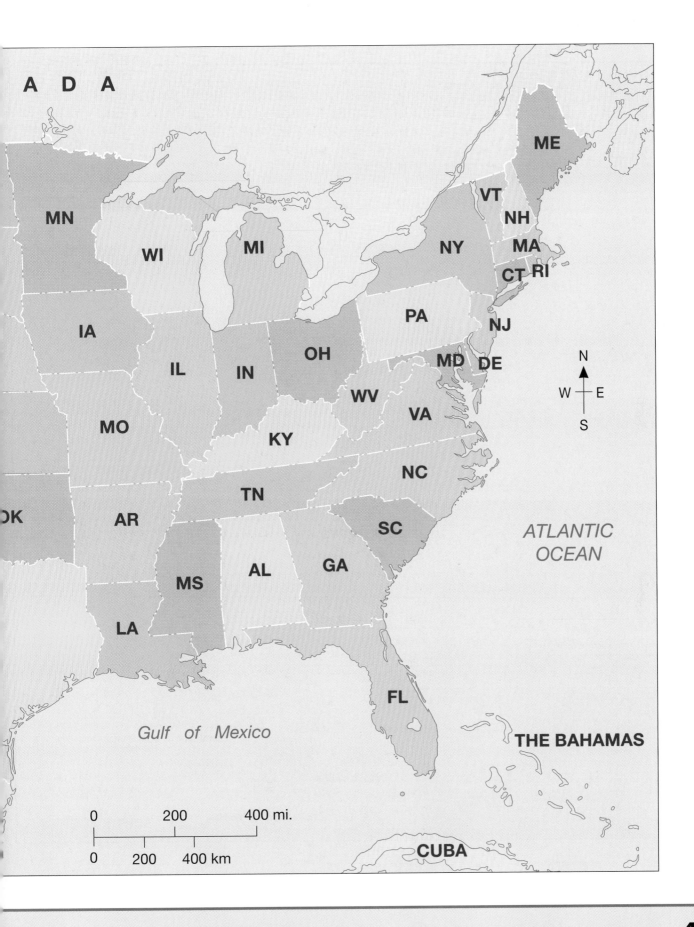

A D A

MN

WI

MI

ME

VT

NH

NY

MA

CT RI

PA

NJ

IA

IL

IN

OH

MD DE

WV

VA

MO

KY

NC

OK

AR

TN

SC

MS

AL

GA

LA

FL

ATLANTIC OCEAN

Gulf of Mexico

THE BAHAMAS

N

W   E

S

0   200   400 mi.

0   200   400 km

CUBA

Our Neighbors North and South

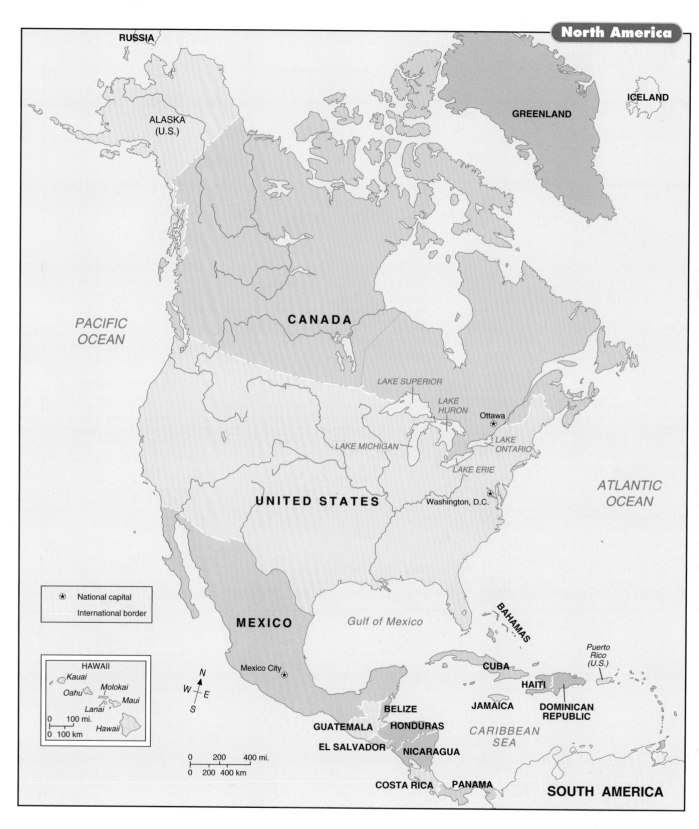

RUSSIA

ALASKA
(U.S.)

GREENLAND

ICELAND

PACIFIC
OCEAN

CANADA

LAKE SUPERIOR

LAKE
HURON

Ottawa

LAKE
ONTARIO

LAKE MICHIGAN

LAKE ERIE

ATLANTIC
OCEAN

UNITED STATES

Washington, D.C.

★ National capital

International border

MEXICO

Gulf of Mexico

BAHAMAS

Puerto
Rico
(U.S.)

CUBA

HAITI

HAWAII

Kauai

Oahu Molokai

Maui

Lanai

Hawaii

0   100 mi.

0   100 km

N

W   E

S

Mexico City ★

JAMAICA

DOMINICAN
REPUBLIC

BELIZE

GUATEMALA   HONDURAS

CARIBBEAN
SEA

EL SALVADOR   NICARAGUA

0   200   400 mi.

0   200 400 km

COSTA RICA   PANAMA

SOUTH AMERICA

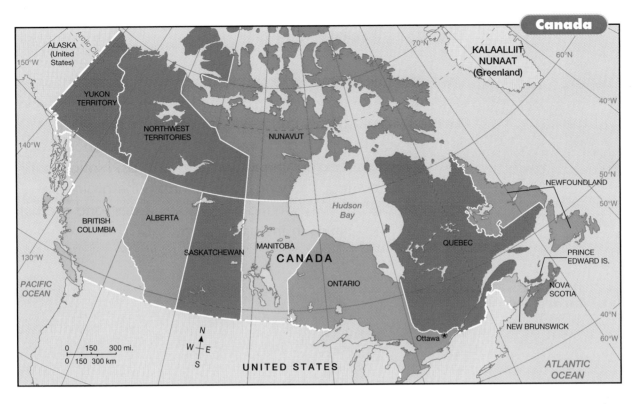

ALASKA
(United
States)

150°W

YUKON
TERRITORY

NORTHWEST
TERRITORIES

NUNAVUT

140°W

KALAALLIT
NUNAAT
(Greenland)

70°N   60°N

40°W

BRITISH
COLUMBIA

ALBERTA

SASKATCHEWAN

MANITOBA

CANADA

ONTARIO

130°W

*Hudson
Bay*

NEWFOUNDLAND

50°N

50°W

QUEBEC

PRINCE
EDWARD IS.

NOVA
SCOTIA

40°N

NEW BRUNSWICK

60°W

*PACIFIC
OCEAN*

N
W   E
S

0   150   300 mi.
0   150   300 km

Ottawa ✴

UNITED STATES

*ATLANTIC
OCEAN*

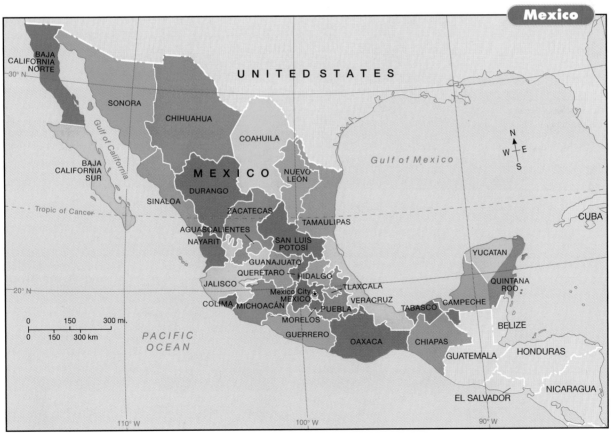

BAJA
CALIFORNIA
NORTE

30° N

UNITED STATES

SONORA

CHIHUAHUA

COAHUILA

Gulf of California

BAJA
CALIFORNIA
SUR

MEXICO

DURANGO

NUEVO
LEÓN

Gulf of Mexico

N
W   E
S

CUBA

SINALOA

ZACATECAS

TAMAULIPAS

Tropic of Cancer

AGUASCALIENTES

NAYARIT

SAN LUIS
POTOSÍ

YUCATAN

GUANAJUATO

QUERETARO   HIDALGO

20° N

JALISCO

Mexico City ✴
MEXICO

TLAXCALA

VERACRUZ

QUINTANA
ROO

CAMPECHE

COLIMA   MICHOACÁN

PUEBLA

TABASCO

BELIZE

MORELOS

0   150   300 mi.
0   150   300 km

*PACIFIC
OCEAN*

GUERRERO

OAXACA

CHIAPAS

GUATEMALA

HONDURAS

EL SALVADOR

NICARAGUA

110° W   100° W   90° W

Basic Food Groups

Your body needs many kinds of nutrients for good health. You can get these nutrients from the foods you eat. The Food Guide Pyramid below can help you choose healthy foods. It shows you the kinds and amounts of foods you should eat every day from each of the major food groups. Notice that you should eat more servings of foods from the groups in the lower part of the pyramid (vegetables, fruits, and grains) than from the groups in the upper part.

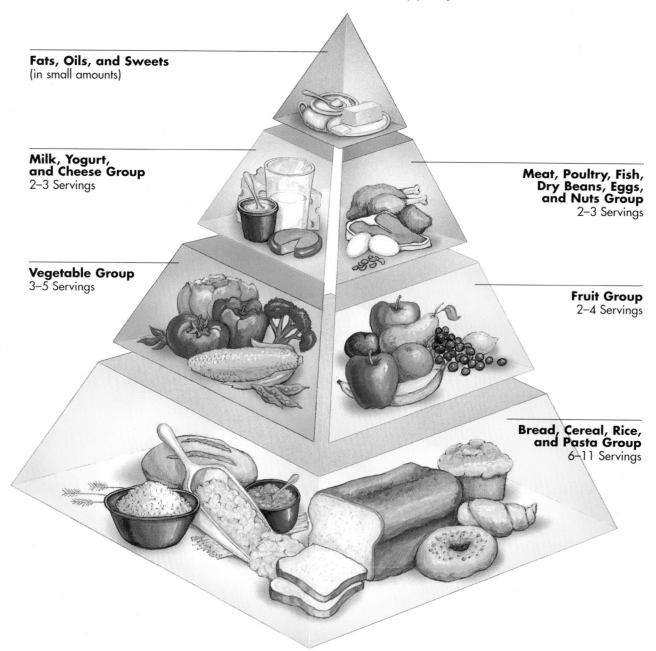

Fats, Oils, and Sweets
(in small amounts)

Milk, Yogurt, and Cheese Group
2–3 Servings

Meat, Poultry, Fish, Dry Beans, Eggs, and Nuts Group
2–3 Servings

Vegetable Group
3–5 Servings

Fruit Group
2–4 Servings

Bread, Cereal, Rice, and Pasta Group
6–11 Servings

The Human Skeleton

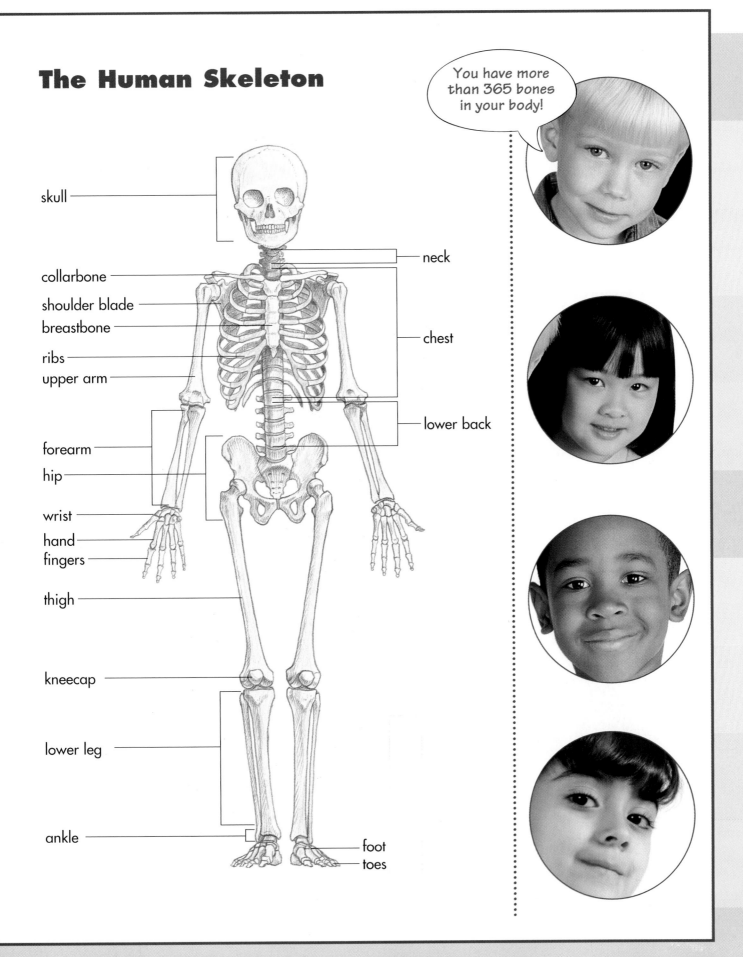

You have more than 365 bones in your body!

skull

neck

collarbone

shoulder blade

breastbone

chest

ribs

upper arm

lower back

forearm

hip

wrist

hand

fingers

thigh

kneecap

lower leg

ankle

foot

toes

Weights and Measures

◀ This bottle contains **1 liter** of water.

One brick weighs about **1 kilogram.**
▼

Metric Measurements

Length and Width

1 centimeter (cm)	= 10 millimeters (mm)
1 meter (m)	= 1000 millimeters (mm)
	100 centimeters (cm)
1 kilometer (km)	= 1000 meters (m)

Weight

1 gram (g)	= 1000 milligrams (mg)
1 kilogram (kg)	= 1000 grams (g)

Capacity

1 liter (l)	= 1000 milliliters (ml)

A teaspoon ▶ holds about **5 milliliters.**

◀ A crayon is about **8 centimeters** long.

A guitar is about **1 meter** long.
▼

One small grape ▶ weighs about **1 gram.**

Customary Measurements

Length and Width

1 foot (ft.)	=	12 inches (in.)
1 yard (yd.)	=	36 inches (in.)
		3 feet (ft.)
1 mile (mi.)	=	5,280 feet (ft.)
		1,760 yards (yd.)

Weight

1 pound (lb.)	=	16 ounces (oz.)
1 ton	=	2000 pounds (lb.)

Capacity

1 tablespoon (tbsp.)	=	3 teaspoons (tsp.)
1 fluid ounce (fl. oz.)	=	2 tablespoons (tbsp.)
1 cup (c.)	=	8 fluid ounces (oz.)
1 pint (pt.)	=	2 cups (c.)
1 quart (qt.)	=	2 pints (pt.)
1 gallon (gal.)	=	4 quarts (qt.)

1 cup

1 pint

1 quart

1 gallon

A quarter is about **1 inch** wide.

A door is about **1 yard** wide.

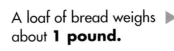

A loaf of bread weighs ▶ about **1 pound.**

A small car weighs ▶ about **1 ton.**

These are great tips!

Spelling

You can improve your spelling skills by following these rules:

Making Singular Nouns Plural

Some nouns have a special spelling in their plural form.

child—children   mouse—mice

Words Ending in a Consonant

If you have a word that 1) has one syllable, 2) ends with one consonant, and 3) has one vowel before that consonant, double the consonant before adding an ending that begins with a vowel.

step + -ed = stepped
big + -er = bigger
jog + -ing = jogging
hot + -est = hottest

Words Ending in Silent e

If a word ends with silent e, the e is usually dropped before adding an ending that begins with a vowel.

smile + -ed = smiled
large + -er = larger
skate + -ing = skating
late + -est = latest

If an ending begins with a consonant, the final e is usually kept.

safe + -ly = safely
hope + -less = hopeless
move + -ment = movement

Words Ending in y

If a word ends in a consonant + y, change the y to i before adding a suffix that begins with a consonant.

Rules for Making Singular Nouns Plural	Examples
Add -s to nouns that end in vowel + y and to most other nouns.	monkeys holidays elephants flowers
Add -s to most nouns ending in -o.	radios videos photos
Add -es to some nouns that end in o.	tomatoes potatoes heroes
Add -es to nouns that end in -sh, -ch, -s, -ss, -x, or -z.	eyelashes watches circuses glasses boxes buzzes
If a noun ends in a consonant + y, change the y to i and add -es.	baby—babies party—parties
For most nouns that end in -f or -fe, change the f to v and add -es.	leaf—leaves life—lives half—halves
Add -s to some nouns that end in -f.	cliffs hoofs roofs

beauty + -ful = beautiful
happy + -ness = happiness

The same change is made before the endings -ed, -er, -es, or -est are added.

cry + -ed = cried
funny + -er = funnier
fly + -es = flies
easy + -est = easiest

Last rule: Look it up. Always check any hard word in your dictionary.

I have a lot of toys.

Below is a list of words that boys and girls most often misspell.

Frequently Misspelled Words

absence	enough	jewelry	surprise
a lot	especially	judgment	their
again	everybody	know	there
almost	everyone	let's	thoroughly
always	everything	loose	thought
another	except	might	through
basketball	familiar	morning	tomorrow
beautiful	favorite	nickel	vacation
because	February	no one	vegetable
before	finally	outside	weather
believe	first	parallel	Wednesday
brother	foreign	people	weird
brought	found	present	we're
business	friend	pretty	were
calendar	genuine	probably	what
caught	Halloween	really	when
chocolate	handsome	receive	where
Christmas	happened	rhyme	whether
clothes	heard	rhythm	who
conscience	height	school	whole
could	hospital	scissors	with
cousin	house	something	would
defense	its	sometimes	your
desert	it's	swimming	you're

The book is under the bed.

Punctuation

Periods

Use a period after a statement, a command, or a polite request.

The book is under the bed.
Wake up.
Please pass the bread.

Use a period after most abbreviations.

Sat.   Jan.   Mr.   Ms.

Question Marks

Use a question mark after a sentence that asks something.

When is the party?

Exclamation Marks

Use an exclamation mark after a sentence or words that show strong feeling.

Look at that goldfish!   *Wow!*

Commas

Use a comma between the day and year in a date.

March 7, 1997

Use a comma between the name of a city and state.

Rapid City, South Dakota

Use a comma between a series of words in a sentence.

Rita, Jenna, and I went on a hike.

We planted carrots, turnips, and squash in our garden.

Use a comma before quotation marks or inside the end quotation marks.

The worker said, "Look at this strange glowing stone!"
"You'd better stop digging here," warned his boss.

Quotation Marks

Use quotation marks around the exact words of a speaker.

"Let's hide Mona's birthday gifts in here," Lisa said.

Apostrophes

Use an apostrophe in a contraction.

he's = he is	*don't = do not*
you're = you are	*I'm = I am*
here's = here is	*wasn't = was not*

Use an apostrophe and an *s* to form the possessive of a singular noun.

her sister's shoes	*my cousin's drawing*
Aaron's glasses	*the octopus's friend*

Look at that goldfish!

her sister's shoes

the children's clock

Use an apostrophe and an *s* to form the possessive of a plural noun that does not end in *s*.

> *the men's hats*
> *many women's jobs*
> *the children's clock*
> *the geese's wings*

Use an apostrophe to form the possessive of a plural noun ending in *s*.

> *those boys' uniforms*
> *the students' books*
> *the horses' hooves*

Colons

Use a colon between hours and minutes to indicate time.

> *10:00   8:25   12:30*

Use a colon after the greeting in a business letter.

> *Dear Ms. Falco:*
> *Dear Sir:*

Dear
Ms. Falco: